Early Christian Inscriptions of Munster
A Corpus of the Inscribed Stones

Elisabeth Okasha and Katherine Forsyth

CORK **c u p** UNIVERSITY PRESS

First published in 2001 by
Cork University Press
Cork
Ireland

British Library Cataloguing in Publication Data
A CIP catalogue record of this book is available from the British Library.

ISBN 1 85918 170 8 hardback

Library of Congress Cataloguing-in-Publication Data

Okasha, Elisabeth.
    Early Christian inscriptions of Munster : a corpus of the inscribed
stones / Elisabeth Okasha and Katherine Forsyth.

       p. cm.
    Includes bibliographical references (p. 365–74).
    ISBN 1-85918-170-8 (alk. paper)
    1. Inscriptions, Christian–Ireland–Munster. 2. Munster
(Ireland)–Antiquities. 3. Monuments–Ireland–Munster.   I. Forsyth,
Katherine. II. Title.
 CN753.173 M866 2001
 936.1'9–dc21
                            00–065879

Typeset by Phototype-Set Ltd., Dublin
Printed by MPG Books Ltd., Cornwall

CONTENTS

LIST OF ILLUSTRATIONS

All extant stones, and some lost ones, are illustrated by an interpretative scale drawing. Unless otherwise stated below, these drawings were prepared by Caitlin Evans from rubbings by KF. Ten of the drawings were prepared by Caitlin Evans from other illustrations: *Illauntannig; Monaincha 1, 5 and 6; *Shanakill; Toureen Peacaun *43, *46, *49 and *62; Tullylease *5. All extant stones are illustrated by one or more photographs. Unless otherwise stated below, these photographs were taken by Kris Lockyear. Wherever possible, lost stones are illustrated by a copy of a published drawing or photograph.

PREFACE

The material contained in the Corpus comprises carved stone monuments of various types, from simple grave-markers to ambitious, ornately decorated public monuments such as crosses. They are an important source of evidence for the history and culture of early Christian Munster, particularly in view of the paucity of contemporary historical documentation for most of the region at this period. They are also of considerable epigraphic and linguistic importance. Their texts provide examples of early Irish which are demonstrably contemporary and not modernised by later copying, as is often the case with manuscripts. The main part of the Corpus consists of a catalogue of the monuments. This is preceded by introductory material including discussion of all the monuments as a group. Wherever possible, the monuments are illustrated by both drawings and photographs.

The aim of the Corpus is the provision of primary evidence. The authors have not attempted to write a history of early Christian Munster, still less a work on early Irish language or palaeography. They have attempted instead to present the early epigraphic texts of Munster accurately, reliably and in an accessible manner. It is hoped that the Corpus may be useful to historians, palaeographers and philologists whose interests lie in the areas it covers. The authors also hope that it will be of interest to all those who appreciate the heritage of early Christian Munster.

Elisabeth Okasha
Katherine Forsyth
March, 2001

ACKNOWLEDGEMENTS

The authors acknowledge with much gratitude the assistance, guidance and support provided by many people in the course of their work.

We are grateful to the staff of several institutions in Ireland and Britain for assistance in studying material under their care. We should like to thank in particular the staff of the National Museum of Ireland, especially Raghnall Ó Floinn, the British Museum, particularly Susan Youngs, and Músaem Chorca Dhuibhne, Ballyferriter, in particular Máire Uí Shithigh and Isabel Bennett. The staff of Dúchas, Dublin, have been very helpful and we would like to thank especially Conleth Manning, Fionnbarr Moore, Grellan Rourke and Richard Stapleton. We are also grateful to the staff of the Dúchas depots at Killarney, Kilkenny and Athenry, especially Pat Herity and Eddie Geraghty.

We also wish to record our gratitude to the staff of the university libraries of Cork and Glasgow as well as to the Royal Irish Academy, University College Cork Archives and the Cork Archaeological Survey.

We are most grateful to those who provided assistance and support during the course of the field-work: Stephen Driscoll, Isabel Henderson, Kris Lockyear, Yousri Okasha and Alex Woolf. We should also like to thank the owners of sites and other local informants who were generous with their time and knowledge: Paddy Bushe, George Cunningham, Maura Flynn, Ann McLoghlin, Gerard Madden, Anne and A. J. O'Donnell and Stephen Quinn. Our thanks are also due to the boatmen who kindly arranged special trips: Bobby Goodwin (Illauntannig), Michael O'Sullivan (Lough Currane) and Denis Tiernan (Inishcaltra).

Large numbers of people have given us academic assistance and guidance. The fact that anyone is not individually thanked here should not be taken as any lack of appreciation on our part of what we owe to them. However we should like to thank the following in particular: John Carey, Máire Herbert, John Sheehan and Julian Walton of University College Cork; Isabel Bennett of Músaem Chorca Dhuibhne, Ballyferriter; John Waddell of University College Galway; Thomas Clancy and Stephen Driscoll of the University of Glasgow; Roibeard Ó Maolalaigh of the University of Edinburgh.

We are most grateful to those who supplied us with photographs and drawings, especially to those who supplied them free or at cost price only. Copyright attributions are listed in the List of Illustrations. A large number of the photographs were taken for us by Kris Lockyear of the Institute of Archaeology, University College London, and the majority of the drawings were prepared by Caitlin Evans of the University of Glasgow. We are extremely grateful to both of them.

Finally we are happy to acknowledge the financial assistance that we have been given. We received a generous award from the University

College Cork President's Research Fund; without this we could not have undertaken the essential field-work which forms the basis of this work. We are also pleased to acknowledge the award of a grant from the National University of Ireland towards the costs of publication.

ABBREVIATIONS

The following abbreviations of institutions are used:

BM: British Museum

NMI: National Museum of Ireland

OPW: Office of Public Works (now Dúchas: The Heritage Service). The nomenclature appropriate to the date of reference is used.

RIA: Royal Irish Academy.

The following also occur:

DIL: Dictionary of the Irish Language

NGR: National Grid Reference

OS: Ordnance Survey

pers. com.: personal communication

s.a.: *sub anno*

s.v.: *sub verbo*

SMR: Sites and Monuments Register.

One book has been quoted extensively: R. A. S. Macalister, *Corpus Inscriptionum Insularum Celticarum*, vol. 1 (Dublin, 1945: Stationery Office), vol. 2 (Dublin, 1949: Stationery Office). In the **Introduction**, in order to save excessive repetition, this work is abbreviated to 'CIIC' followed by the entry number. Elsewhere it appears as 'Macalister 1945' and 'Macalister 1949a', followed by the entry number, the page numbers to the entry, the plate number and the figure number.

Throughout the **Introduction**, lost stones are indicated by an asterisk, either in the form '*Inishvickillane' where only one stone was known from that location, or in the form 'Roscrea *2' where there were more than one.

The scales accompanying the drawings in the **Entries** are usually 20 cm, with the smallest unit 1cm. Some exceptionally small stones have 10 cm scales and some exceptionally large stones have 30 cm scales. Toureen Peacaun nos. 1–31 are drawn to the same scale on p. 229 and the individual drawings of these stones do not have accompanying scales.

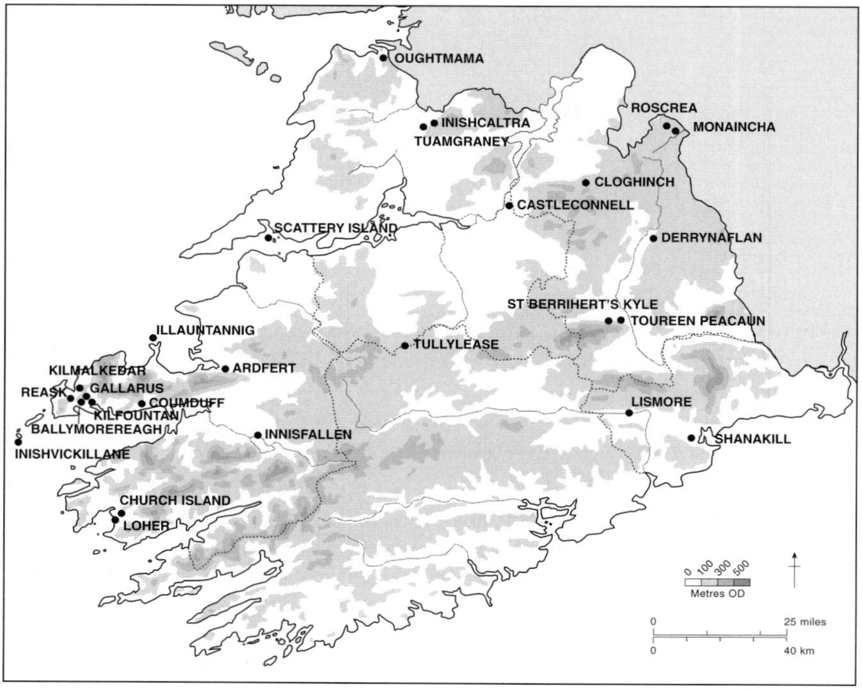
OUGHTMAMA
ROSCREA
INISHCALTRA
MONAINCHA
TUAMGRANEY
CLOGHINCH
CASTLECONNELL
SCATTERY ISLAND
DERRYNAFLAN
ST BERRIHERT'S KYLE
TOUREEN PEACAUN
ILLAUNTANNIG
TULLYLEASE
KILMALKEDAR
ARDFERT
REASK
GALLARUS
COUMDUFF
KILFOUNTAN
LISMORE
BALLYMOREREAGH
INNISFALLEN
SHANAKILL
INISHVICKILLANE
CHURCH ISLAND
LOHER
0 100 300 500
Metres OD
0
25 miles
0
40 km

Early Christian inscribed stones of Munster

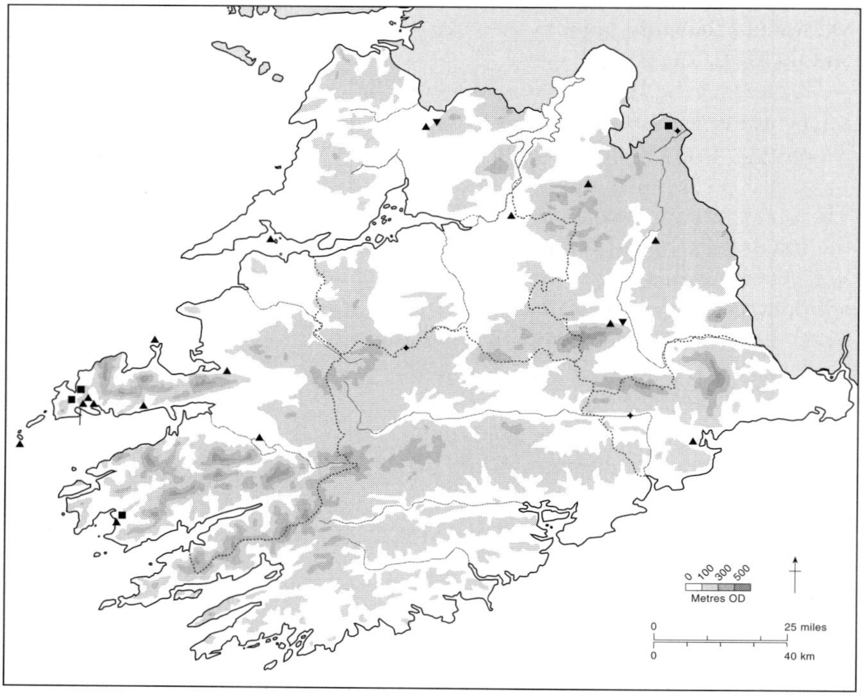
0 100 300 500
Metres OD
0
25 miles
0
40 km

Number of inscribed stones per site (Dubia excluded)

Key ▲ 1 ■ 2 ✦ 3—6 ▼ 20+

INTRODUCTION

§1 Scope of study

The Corpus catalogues the roman-alphabet inscribed stones of early Christian date from the modern counties of Munster, that is, from counties Clare, Cork, Kerry, Limerick, Tipperary and Waterford.

'Inscribed' stones are those that contain a text: stones with a cross or a *chi-rho* but with no lettering are generally excluded. An exception is, however, made in the case of the collection of stones from Toureen Peacaun, Co Tipperary: all the fragments of slabs from this site are included, even those where there is now no sign of lettering (see further under **Toureen Peacaun**).

The 'early Christian' period is taken by Irish archaeologists to be from *c.* AD 500 to *c.* AD 1200. This label has been adopted in the Corpus to avoid an unwieldly string of negatives (non-ogham, non-runic, pre-Norman etc.). While it is safe to say that all the roman-alphabet inscriptions in Munster are Christian, the use of this term is not intended to imply that inscriptions in other scripts are pagan. On the contrary, recent work on ogham (Swift 1997, Moore 1998) has underlined the explicitly Christian context of many ogham stones.

The inscribed stones in the Corpus range in date from the sixth or seventh century to the twelfth century. However twelfth-century inscribed texts using Gothic or Lombardic script are not included. The datings of individual stones and groups of stones are discussed in the individual Entries and below. There are six sets of criteria which may provide dating evidence. Three of these are discussed below: typological criteria (see §3), palaeographic criteria (see §4) and linguistic criteria (see §5). In addition, a few stones may be dated by the likely identification of an individual mentioned in the text; the known history of a site may also occasionally suggest a date-range. Finally, although there are no strict archaeological datings, one or two stones may be dated from their architectural context.

Inscribed stones containing runic texts and those containing only ogham texts are excluded from the Corpus. There are Norse runic stones from Killaloe, Co Clare (Barnes *et al.* 1997, 53-6, fig. 18 and pls XXIV-XXVI) and Beginish, Co Kerry (Barnes *et al.* 1997, 56-9 and pls XXVII-XXIX). There is also a doubtful example from the Blasket Islands, Co Kerry (Barnes *et al.* 1997, 2). On ogham stones, see Macalister 1945, McManus 1991 and Swift 1997. Two stones containing both ogham and non-ogham texts, Camp and Kilfountan, both from Co Kerry, are included in the Corpus, although the non-ogham text on the stone from Camp may not be genuine and is listed under Dubia.

Within these parameters, the present authors know of 125 stones from twenty-five sites in Munster. There are also three dubious stones (see below) and an unknown number lost from Oughtmama, giving altogether at least 129 stones from twenty-nine sites. However, two stones from Toureen Peacaun, nos 29 and 35, are included in the numbered sequence although they were probably never inscribed. Most sites contain only one or two stones but some sites have more and two sites contain a large number: there were, before some were lost, twenty-two stones from Inishcaltra and sixty-two from Toureen Peacaun.

Most of the stones are still at the locations where they were found and many are in their earliest recorded positions. Some stones are likely to be *in situ*, for example ten of the recumbent slabs from Inishcaltra (nos 5-7, 9-12, 15-16 and 18) seem to be *in situ* in the graveyard and the Inishcaltra cross-base (Inishcaltra 1) might be so also. The architectural feature Monaincha 4 is certainly *in situ*. Some stones have been moved, sometimes for safe-keeping, sometimes for other reasons. Seven are now in the National Museum of Ireland, Dublin. Three are in Dúchas, Dublin, two in the Dúchas depot in Kilkenny and two in the Dúchas depot in Athenry. One is in the British Museum in London.

All the stones still in existence have been examined by one author or by both. However, thirty-six of the 129 stones are now lost, and most regrettably some of these losses have taken place within the last few years. Details of the lost stones are given on the basis of descriptions and illustrations made while the stones were still in existence. There is no doubt that other stones have been lost without adequate descriptions having been made. Lost texts are prefixed throughout the **Introduction** with an asterisk.

There are three stones which, for various reasons, are considered doubtful and these are listed separately under the heading **Dubia**. One, from Camp, is extant and is undoubtedly inscribed with a roman alphabet text; however, the antiquity of the text is in doubt. The other two, from *Moorestown and *Dromcara, are lost and only poorly recorded: no illustration of either survives and they were not seen by Macalister.

The Catalogue is ordered by county, but for ease of reference the stones are listed here in alphabetical order of site. Unless otherwise stated there is a single stone from each site. Where no other location is given, the stones are in the locality where they were found.

Ardfert, Co Kerry
*Ballymorereagh, Co Kerry
Castleconnell, Co Limerick
Church Island (Lough Currane), Co Kerry: two stones
Cloghinch, Co Tipperary: (NMI)
*Coumduff, Co Kerry
Derrynaflan, Co Tipperary: (NMI)
Gallarus, Co Kerry
*Illauntannig (Magharee Islands), Co Kerry
Inishcaltra, Co Clare: twenty-two stones (eighteen on site; two in Dúchas, Athenry; *two lost)
*Inishvickillane (Blasket Islands), Co Kerry
Innisfallen (Lough Leane), Co Kerry
Kilfountan, Co Kerry
Kilmalkedar, Co Kerry: two stones (one on site; *one lost)
Lismore, Co Waterford: six stones
Loher, Co Kerry

Monaincha, Co Tipperary: six stones (one on site; one in NMI; two in Dúchas, Kilkenny; one in BM; *one lost)
*Oughtmama, Co Clare: at least one lost stone
Reask, Co Kerry: two stones
Roscrea, Co Tipperary: two stones (one in NMI; *one lost)
St Berrihert's Kyle, Co Tipperary
Scattery Island, Co Clare
*Shanakill, Co Waterford
*Tuamgraney, Co Clare
Toureen Peacaun, Co Tipperary: sixty-two stones (thirty-seven on site; three in Dúchas, Dublin; *twenty-two lost)
Tullylease, Co Cork: five stones (one on site; three in NMI; *one lost)

§2 Previous research

Most of the stones in the Corpus have either been previously published or, at least, have been mentioned in earlier published works. Yet scholarly interest in Irish inscribed stones began rather later than that shown in Anglo-Saxon inscribed stones or in those from Cornwall and Devon (see Okasha 1971, 1993). Before 1850, only four people published any Irish stones: Edward Ledwich, H. Pelham, Lady Chatterton and George Petrie. Ledwich, in his *Antiquities of Ireland* of 1790, illustrated Monaincha 4. In Vallancy's *Collectanea de Rebus Hibernicis* vol. 6, published in 1804, Pelham described and illustrated Kilmalkedar 1. Lady Chatterton, in her *Rambles in the South of Ireland during the year 1838* described and illustrated Gallarus and Kilmalkedar 1. These two stones were also described and illustrated by George Petrie in his *Ecclesiastical Architecture* of 1845.

Although only these three stones had been published by 1850, many more were known (see below) and there was scholarly interest in the stones. For example John Windele, 1801-65, traveled around Munster noting, *inter alia*, various objects of interest including inscribed stones. The diaries he kept of his excursions are preserved in the Royal Irish Academy; they have not been published in their entirety but some of the relevant parts have been printed (see White 1920, 1921 and (-) 1898).

From 1850 to 1880 scholarly interest in Irish antiquities increased and many new stones were recorded. Publications from this period include both short accounts of local inscribed stones (for example, Cotton 1854-55a, 1854-55b on Lismore) and longer accounts of stones from one area with a discussion of related issues (for example, Reeves 1858 on Tullylease). The most important work of this period is Petrie's *Christian Inscriptions in the Irish Language*. This was published in 1870-77 by the Kilkenny Archaeological Society as an extra volume in the series *The Annuary*. The second edition, edited by Margaret Stokes, appeared in 1878 and contains accounts of more than thirty inscribed stones from thirteen localities, including some stones which were subsequently lost.

The period from 1880 to 1918 was one of great scholarly activity and also of a growing interest in antiquities amongst a wider public. Several of the publications of this period which discuss inscribed stones are accounts of summer visits made to places of interest by local historical or archaeological societies (for example, Westropp 1897a, 1897b). Books were written both for a wide public audience, for instance Wakeman 1891, and also for a specialised scholarly one, for example Allen 1887. A notable figure from this period is Henry Crawford whose pioneering work remains valuable (Crawford 1907, 1912, 1916). Crawford knew of inscribed stones from eighteen of the thirty sites in the Corpus, although he did not know of all the stones from some sites. The early work of R. A. S. Macalister falls within this period, in particular his pioneering study of Inishcaltra (Macalister 1916-17).

The middle years of the twentieth century, up to around 1950, show similar work being published but a smaller amount of it. Notable figures from these years are Françoise Henry and Pádraig Lionard as well as Macalister. Henry and Lionard were both particularly interested in the carved decoration on stones and other objects. Macalister, however, was primarily an epigrapher and in his *Corpus Inscriptionum Insularum Celticarum* he described and discussed the inscribed stones known to him from twenty sites. He was the latest, occasionally the only, person to have examined some stones that have since been lost, for example, *Inishvickillane and *Shanakill. In this period also, the Office of Public Works became increasingly active which resulted in various finds being made and recorded, for example the large number of stones found during excavation work at Toureen Peacaun in 1944.

From the middle of the twentieth century to the present day there has again been an increase in publications. There have been detailed studies of single sites (for example, Harbison 1970, Manning 1991) and books of wide general interest, for example the third edition of the *Shell Guide to Ireland* (Killanin and Duignan 1989). A number of important descriptive catalogues have also appeared, for example Cuppage *et al.* 1986, O'Sullivan and Sheehan 1996.

The present authors fully acknowledge the contribution made by all this earlier work and, in particular, by the previous corpora, Petrie 1878 and Macalister 1949a. These works still have value but, naturally enough, do not altogether fulfil scholarly requirements of the end of the twentieth century. They are not sufficiently reliable or accurate, they do not contain high quality illustrations and insufficient attention is paid in them to the physical aspects of the monuments and their locations. Moreover, more stones have come to light in the fifty years since Macalister's corpus was compiled. He listed 74 stones from nineteen sites, compared with the 129 from twenty-nine sites included here. The present Corpus attempts to build on earlier work, in particular by using modern techniques unavailable to earlier scholars. Concordances relating the numbering of the stones used in the present Corpus with references to these earlier corpora are given at the beginning of the Catalogue.

Stones known before 1850
Co Clare: Inishcaltra 1, 13, 14, *17
Co Kerry: Gallarus; Kilfountan; Kilmalkedar 1; Reask 1, 2

Co Limerick: Castleconnell
Co Tipperary: Monaincha 2, 4; Roscrea *2
Co Waterford: Lismore 1, 2, 3, 4

Stones first recorded between 1851 and 1880
Co Clare: Inishcaltra 2, 3, 4, 5, 6, 7, 8, 9, 10, 11, 12, 15, 16, 18, *19, 20, 21;
   Scattery Island
Co Cork: *Dromcarra; Tullylease 1, ?2
Co Kerry: Camp; *Moorestown
Co Tipperary: Monaincha 1, *3; Roscrea 1; Toureen Peacaun 2, 5, 40, *58, *59,
   *60, *61
Co Waterford: Lismore 5

Stones first recorded between 1881 and 1918
Co Clare: *Oughtmama; *Tuamgraney
Co Cork: Tullylease *5
Co Kerry: Church Island 1, 2; *Inishvickillane; Kilmalkedar *2
Co Tipperary: Toureen Peacaun 14, 34, *51
Co Waterford: Lismore 6; *Shanakill

Stones first recorded between 1919 and 1950
Co Cork: Tullylease 3, 4
Co Kerry: *Ballymorereagh; *Coumduff; Loher
Co Tipperary: ?St Berrihert's Kyle; Toureen Peacaun: 1, 3, 4, 6, 7, 8, 9, 10, 11,
   ?12, 13, 15, 16, 17, 18, 19, 20, ?21, 22, 23, ?24, 25, 26, 27, ?28, 29, 30, 31, 32,
   33, 39, *41, *42, *44, *45, *47, *48, *50, *52, *53, *54, *55, *56, *57

Stones recorded from 1951 to the present
Co Clare: Inishcaltra 22
Co Kerry: Ardfert; *Illauntannig; Innisfallen
Co Tipperary: Cloghinch; Derrynaflan; Monaincha 5, 6; Toureen Peacaun 35,
   36, 37, 38, *43, *46, *49, *62

§3 Typology of the monuments

§3.1 Discussion

The Corpus covers a wide range of different kinds of monument, including
pillars, slabs of several varieties, free-standing crosses and architectural pieces.
The present authors have categorised these according to various criteria of
form, decoration and text. The resultant typology is, of course, an imposition
on the evidence by modern observers and it must be borne in mind that the
distinctions made were not necessarily meaningful to the people who originally
made and used the monuments. Nevertheless it is hoped that the typology will
facilitate the recognition of patterns in the data, and thereby help to reveal
changes in monumental practice over both time and space.

Several slabs, such as the one on Scattery Island and some on Inishcaltra, are, or appear to be, in their original, recumbent, settings. Most, however, were found or first recorded loose or in secondary locations and it is often impossible to say if they were originally upright or recumbent. Some look too thin to have stood securely in the ground (for example, Derrynaflan) although it should be noted that Church Island 1, which is currently upright, is remarkably only 8 cm thick, despite standing 161 cm tall. Sometimes the carving on the stone can provide a clue: if it extends the full length of the slab then it would have been obscured if the stone had been set in the ground. It is possible, however, that some of the smaller slabs with 'all-over' carving (for example the small slabs from Toureen Peacaun) were intended to be propped upright against a wall rather than set directly into the ground. Because of the difficulty of establishing whether a slab was upright or recumbent this characteristic, except where it can be shown to be beyond doubt, is not used in the classification.

Upright slabs
According to Macalister, the lost stone from *Ballymorereagh was carved on both sides with simple linear crosses, which presumably indicates that it was meant to stand erect. Its *or(óit) ar* N. formula distinguishes it from the other stones in the area, which are pillars, as does its small size and thinness (26 cm x 26 cm x 4 cm). It should probably therefore be classed as an upright slab. The very large cross-incised slab Church Island 1 now stands vertical. It is not known, however, if this is its original setting. Since it is carved on one face only it cannot be shown to have been intended as an upright. Other cross slabs on the site are recumbent

Small slabs with simple, or no, crosses
Toureen Peacaun has produced a large and coherent group of 'small slabs', mostly fragmentary. These are generally broader than they are tall, varying in height from 20 cm to 30 cm and in width from 30 cm to 40 cm and thus having, when complete, an average surface area of between about 700 cm^2 and 1200 cm^2. They are incised with simple linear and outline crosses and typically are inscribed only with a personal name in the nominative. The lettering is usually large relative to the size of the slab, with the single name often occupying the full width of the face. The text is generally at least as prominent as the cross. Although these small slabs could have lain recumbent over the head of grave, it has been suggested that their function was primarily liturgical rather than funerary (Moloney 1964, 105-6). They might have been engraved with the names of those to be commemorated during the Mass and arranged within the church as a frieze. The orthography and script on the small slabs from Toureen Peacaun are in accordance with an early date, perhaps seventh or eighth century. A very similar stone was found at nearby St Berrihert's Kyle. Although now incomplete, it does not appear to have borne a cross. It is possible that originally it was carved only with a personal name and that the [*orait*] *do* (if this is the correct interpretation) that is squeezed in below is a secondary addition. The lost slab from *Shanakill appears to have been of the same type as the Toureen Peacaun slabs.

Large recumbent slabs

At the opposite end of the physical scale are the large recumbent slabs from Inishcaltra which appear to date predominantly from the eleventh and twelfth centuries. These long narrow slabs range in length from about 95 cm to 160 cm, although most are in the upper half of this range and two (Inishcaltra 15 and 18) are over 175 cm. The width of the slabs is typically between about 40 cm and 60 cm; at 80 cm, Inishcaltra 6 is exceptionally wide. Most have a height-to-width ratio of about 1:2.5 but some are even slimmer: Inishcaltra 10 and 15 have a ratio of 1:3.5, and Inishcaltra 18, perhaps the latest of the group, has a ratio of 1:4. It may be that slimness increases over time since the height-to-width ratio of Church Island 2, probably dating from the thirteenth century (or possibly even later), is 1:4.6. The large recumbent slabs are very large indeed. Even the smallest (Inishcaltra 14) has a surface area of about 3600 cm², the average is closer to 8000 cm², while several are over 9000 cm² (Inishcaltra nos 4, 6, and 15, Church Island 1, Scattery Island).

These large recumbent slabs are carved with full-length Latin crosses and texts which begin *or(óit) do,* 'a prayer for'. A number are still *in situ* covering graves. They are funerary monuments in the true sense. On some of them the position of the inscription with respect to the cross suggests that individuals would kneel down at the head of a grave to pray for the deceased whose name could then be read. The prayers which the texts request were a part of individual devotion in the churchyard, rather than communal worship in the Church during Mass. The fourteen examples from Inishcaltra are very closely related. The type is also found on Scattery Island, and at Lismore (no. 4 and no. 1, although the latter contrasts with the rest in the form and layout of its carving). The slab Church Island 1, apart from currently standing upright, is otherwise very similar and Church Island 2 may be seen as a later development of this form. Both are inscribed *bendacht ar anmain N.,* 'a blessing on the soul of N.'.

Large plain (cross-less) slabs

Another distinctive group is that of the large slabs inscribed with a text only. These are on a similar scale to the large recumbent slabs and, like them, are inscribed with the *or(óit) do* formula, or variants. The text runs along the long axis of the slab in one or more lines. The examples from Monaincha (slabs 1 and 2) have very large lettering which dominates the slab. Although only small fragments, Monaincha 5 and 6 appear to have been part of similar monuments. The lost slab Roscrea *2 also appears to have been similar. The cross-less slab Inishcaltra 5 differs in having lettering on a smaller scale, as does the slab from Derrynaflan which is inscribed with a unique variant of the basic formula, *or(óit) ar anmain N.,* 'a prayer for the soul of N.'. Except for the lack of a cross, these slabs are very similar to the previous type. Indeed Inishcaltra 5 is still *in situ* in the middle of a row of large, cross-incised recumbents. The significance of the distinction between large slabs with crosses and those without remains unclear.

Miscellaneous slabs

The remaining slabs are generally smaller and squarer than those of the previous two groups, with a typical height-to-width ratio of 1:1.5 or less. The smallest are irregularly shaped, squarish slabs which are more-or-less filled by a framed cross, usually an equal-armed one. The texts, which are usually no more than a single personal name in the nominative, are often outside this frame and carved in small letters. It is the finely carved and often complex crosses which dominate visually. Three examples from Inishcaltra (nos 20-22) have crosses in rectilinear frames. These slabs measure 39 cm to 67 cm by 33 cm to 53 cm and have a surface area of approximately 2000-3000 cm². They are of a distinct type which is also found outside Munster, most notably at Clonmacnoise (Ó Floinn's 'Type A'). Ó Floinn suggested that this type of slab was current in the mid-eighth century, although it may have been in use earlier and continued later (Ó Floinn 1995, 253). The lost slab Inishcaltra *19 with its encircled cross was probably another example, as is the slab from Castleconnell with its simple encircled cross. At 34 cm x 35 cm (surface area c. 1200 cm²) it is only a little smaller than the others. It differs, however, in the length of the text which runs round the outside of the circle. Although now almost completely illegible, this text was clearly longer than a single personal name.

Encircled crosses, with text running round the outside of the circle, are also found on the stone from Cloghinch and the related fragment from Innisfallen. The Cloghinch stone is as thick as it is wide, but it seems inappropriate to class it as a pillar. Not only is it much smaller and squarer than the other pillars (35 cm x 22 cm), but it could not have stood upright without obscuring most of the carving. Instead it is very similar to a group of uninscribed monuments, identified by Kelly (1988), which comprises small, compact stones carved with encircled crosses. Although none of the others in this group appear to have been deliberately shaped, the stones selected were thinner and more obviously slab-like. Perhaps the thickness of the Cloghinch stone is due simply to what was available locally. The similarities of scale, text (single name), and layout (prominent framed cross) between the Cloghinch stone and the Castleconnell and Inishcaltra examples seem more relevant to its classification than its thickness alone.

Two stones from Lismore (nos 2 and 3) are very similar in size to the above small slabs (dimensions 54 cm x 41 cm and 41 cm x 33 cm, and surface area 2200 and 1350 cm², respectively) and have similarly square proportions (ratio 1:1.3). However, the Lismore crosses are slighter and unframed. On these stones it is the text which is dominant, with large letters filling the full width of the stone. The lower half of Lismore 1 is closely akin to these two slabs but its plain upper half makes it almost twice as long (dimensions 102 cm x 41 cm, surface area 4200 cm²). Its size and proportions are those of a large recumbent slab. This rather anomalous monument may provide a clue to the way in which Lismore 2 and 3 functioned. If Lismore 1 lay over a grave with the cross covering the head, the text would be oriented so that someone kneeling in prayer at the foot could read it. It is possible that Lismore 2 and 3 lay over the head of a grave in the same orientation. Alternatively, these two, which are remarkably unweathered, could have been propped up upright inside the church in the manner envisaged for the Toureen Peacaun slabs. The Lismore stones are like the Toureen Peacaun slabs in certain respects, in having for example a simple, unframed cross and a text occupying the full width of the slab. However Lismore 3 differs in the form of the text (*bendacht for an*(*main*) N.) and Lismore 2 differs in having a ringed cross and a patronymic in the text. The lost and somewhat doubtful Toureen Peacaun *56, supposedly incised with a ringed cross and the *or*(*óit*) *ar N.* formula, may have been more like the Lismore slabs.

The exceptionally ornate slab Tullylease 1 was designed to be viewed in an upright position. It is larger than the stones just discussed (95 cm x 63 cm, surface area 6000 cm²) but similarly broad (height to width ratio, 1:1.5). Its Latin text, an opportunistic request of a prayer from *quicumquae* ... *legerit* ('whoever will have read'), places it in a context of individual rather than communal devotion. It may well be that the fragments from Tullylease (2, 3, 4, *5) are the remains of similar slabs. The Tullylease slabs are *sui generis* not only in form and decoration, but also in the use of Latin and the unique occurrence of an Anglo-Saxon personal name.

Three other medium-sized slabs are narrower than those discussed above (Roscrea 1, *Tuamgraney, Inishcaltra *17). All are, or were, incomplete but can be reconstructed on the basis of the remaining carving to have been about 75 cm to 90 cm long and 40 cm to 50 cm wide (surface areas between 3100 and 4500 cm²). This would have given them a height-to-width ratio of about 1:1.8, broader than the large recumbents, but not as broad as Tullylease 1 and the miscellaneous small slabs. The lost slabs from *Tuamgraney and nearby Inishcaltra *17 had identical forms of cross, the former unframed, the latter framed, but only the Inishcaltra slab bore the *or*(*óit*) *do* formula, the other two having a single name only. All three were probably recumbent grave-covers. They would have been not much shorter than the smallest of the large recumbents.

There are, in addition, a few lost slabs which cannot be more closely classified due to lack of information: *Inishvickillane, possibly a large recumbent slab, *Oughtmama and *Coumduff. Finally, two slabs from Toureen Peacaun, nos 29 and 35, were probably never inscribed.

Free-standing crosses
There are three free-standing crosses, varying greatly in size, shape and date. They are Inishcaltra 2, Toureen Peacaun 40, and Lismore 5. In addition there is a cross-base which lacks its shaft (Inishcaltra 1). A lost block (Monaincha *3) which bore a tenon may also have been part of a free-standing cross.

Architectural pieces
Three twelfth-century inscriptions are architectural. Monaincha 4 is carved across the seven blocks which form a pilaster of the doorway. Ardfert is the sole surviving voussoir of an arch. The function of the anthropomorphic Lismore 6 is uncertain. It could have been a corbel (a load-bearing projection from a wall), a 'caryatid' (a column-like support for a ledge), or simply a decorative plaque.

§3.2 Typological classification

Pillars (9)

   Large, cross-incised (7)
        Gallarus
        Kilfountan
        Kilmalkedar 1, *2
        Loher
        Reask 1, 2
   Other (2)
        *Illauntannig
        Toureen Peacaun 39

Slabs (106)

   small (69)
        upright (1)
           *Ballymorereagh
        simple or no cross, prominent text (58)
           Toureen Peacaun 1-28, 30-34, 36-38, *41-*55, *57-*62
           *Shanakill
           St Berrihert's Kyle
        prominent framed cross (7)
           Inishcaltra 20-22
           Inishcaltra *19
           Castleconnell
           Cloghinch
           Innisfallen
        other (3)
           Lismore 2, 3
           ?Toureen Peacaun *56

   medium (4 + 4 possible)
        Tullylease 1 (?2, ?3, ?4, ?*5)
        Roscrea 1
        *Tuamgraney
        Inishcaltra *17

   large (26)
        plain, that is, cross-less (5 + 2 possible)
           Monaincha 1, 2 (?5, ?6)
           Roscrea *2
           Derrynaflan
           Inishcaltra 5
         recumbent, cross-incised (18)
           Lismore 1, 4
           Scattery Island
           Church Island 2

Inishcaltra 3, 4, 6-16, 18
?upright (1)
Church Island 1

unclassified (3)
*Oughtmama
*Inishvickillane
*Coumduff

Free-standing crosses (5)
Toureen Peacaun 40
Inishcaltra 2
Lismore 5
Inishcaltra 1 (base)
Monaincha *3 (?arm)

Architectural pieces (3)
Monaincha 4
Ardfert
Lismore 6

Probably never inscribed (2)
Toureen Peacaun 29, 35

§4 Texts: epigraphy

§4.1 Script

The texts on all the extant stones in the Corpus are incised, not carved in relief. In this respect the Munster stones compare with the early Christian stones of South-west Britain (Okasha 1993, 18). In other cultural milieus, however, a few texts in relief lettering are recorded. Examples include two Anglo-Saxon stones from Wensley, North Yorkshire (Okasha 1971, nos 120-1, pp. 120-1 and figs) and one Pictish stone from Tarbat, Ross and Cromarty (Okasha 1985, 61-3 and pl. VI).

Almost all the legible inscribed stones from Munster use, or used, a form of insular script described here as 'half-uncial'. There are a few exceptions. There are a few stones, for example St Berrihert's Kyle and possibly Gallarus, that use insular minuscule script. Another exception consists of those stones with at least part of their texts in insular decorative capitals, for example Toureen Peacaun 16 and 40. Both of these scripts are likely to date from earlier rather than later in the early Christian period. In particular, insular decorative capitals flourished in manuscript usage from the early eighth to the early ninth century. For a full discussion of this script, see the entry for Toureen Peacaun 40, under Interpretation and Discussion.

Insular half-uncial script is a non-capital script similar to that used in insular manuscripts of early Christian date. The letter-forms used on the stones are clearly derived from manuscript letter-forms and dated manuscripts can therefore give some indication of the date of a text on stone. Nevertheless the present authors are of the opinion that it is not justifiable to argue a direct correlation between letter-forms used in dated manuscripts and letter-forms used on stones. A different medium requires different tools, different skills and, probably, different personnel. Scribes writing manuscripts used quill pens on vellum and were literate, although not necessarily in the language they were copying. Inscribers on stone probably used a hammer and chisel and may often have been illiterate. We do not know the exact relationship between these two groups of artisans and, moreover, the conventions in which they worked could well have been different. It would seem unreasonable to expect that the same script used in such different circumstances would develop in an identical manner and at an identical rate.

Nevertheless, script can provide us with dating clues. Comparable letter-forms in a manuscript text may, for example, provide information on the period when a particular letter-form started to be used, or the time when it fell out of manuscript use. From the evidence of manuscripts, it seems likely that the use of a pointed A is late and also that two-line script is later than three-line script. Two-line script is used, for example, on the late stones from Lismore and Inishcaltra. Another indication of late date seems to be angularity of letter-form, as is found on some of the stones from Lismore and Monaincha. In general, however, the script used in the texts on the stones does not provide precise dating evidence.

The occasional capital letter-form is used in half-uncial script. Instances occur, for example, amongst the Toureen Peacaun slabs (see Toureen Peacaun: Discussion of small slabs). The majority of these texts have half-uncial forms of A and E but there are occasional instances of capital forms of these letters. The forms of A can be compared, for example, on stones 18 and 22, the forms of E on stones 25 and 26. The occasional use of these capital letter-forms does not seem to be a dating feature of the texts. Two stones, Loher and Church Island 1, text a, contain *alpha* and *omega*. The Greek letters both use (different) forms of capital A for *alpha* and use non-capital forms of ω for *omega*.

Stones containing only ogham texts are excluded from the Corpus but there are two stones that have both ogham and roman texts. These are the stones from Kilfountan and Camp, both Co. Kerry. Neither is a bi-literal stone, that is, containing the same text written twice in two different scripts. The Kilfountan stone has two different texts, both personal names, one in insular script and one in ogham. These texts are, however, unlikely to be exactly contemporary: the insular text seems to have been inscribed on a re-used ogham stone. The stone from Camp also has two different texts, one in each script, although both are in Irish and can be interpreted together. However the authenticity of the roman text on this stone is in doubt. In Ireland in general, stones with texts in more than one script are rare, and those that do exist are not bi-literal (McManus 1991, 61, §4.10). The inscribed stones of Munster fit comfortably into this pattern.

Inscribed stones containing both ogham and roman texts exist in other areas, notably in Wales and in South-west Britain. In Wales the majority of the ogham stones also contain a roman text and many are bi-literal (Nash-Williams

1950, especially pp. 2-3). In South-west Britain there are six stones with both ogham and roman texts but unfortunately only two of them have legible ogham texts. One of these, from Lewannick, Cornwall, is bi-literal, the ogham text being identical with part of the roman text (Okasha 1993, no. 24, pp. 150-3). The other, from Fardel, Devon, has two ogham and two roman texts all of which differ from each other (Okasha 1993, no. 13, pp. 103-8).

§4.2 Layout

The majority of the texts are set out in horizontal lines on the stones. In a few cases, for example Castleconnell and Cloghinch, the texts are arranged in curved lines following the line of the decoration on the stones. The rest of the stones contain texts set vertically. Most of the vertical texts read down the stone with the bottoms of the texts to the viewer's left. In a few cases, for example St Berrihert's Kyle, it is not clear which was the top of the stone and therefore which way the text read. On a small number of stones, the text read upwards, with the bottoms of the letters to the viewer's right. Such texts include Kilfountan and Reask 2, text a. No texts, however, read upwards with the bottoms of the letters to the viewer's left, or vice versa. The carvers of the texts clearly envisaged the viewers as moving their heads and reading the texts as if they were set horizontally on the stones. The carvers of the texts may indeed have cut them in this way.

It has been suggested that the vertical layout of roman texts may be derived from the vertical layout of many ogham texts (Jackson 1953, 168). The Munster stones offer some support for this suggestion, in that most of the stones with roman texts from Co. Kerry have the texts set vertically and Co. Kerry contains a large proportion of the ogham inscriptions in Ireland. Most ogham stones have vertical texts, and the majority read upwards. If the carvers of vertical roman texts were influenced by ogham in laying out their texts, then they seem to have adapted the ogham model to make it more suitable for use with roman texts. In particular they preferred to have their texts reading downwards and avoided cutting texts which might have appeared to read backwards. A similar use of vertical layout of roman texts can be observed in south-west Britain, although there there are no certain examples of texts which are set upwards (Okasha 1993, 28-9).

A few stones with horizontal texts have these texts set inverted with respect to the decoration on the stone. It is possible to be certain of this only in cases where the stone is complete or virtually complete and so it may be that such texts were more common than now appears. The use of inverted texts clearly indicates that such stones were recumbent. These stones include a group of ten slabs from Inishcaltra; such a large group suggests a deliberate practice on the island. (See the General Discussion which follows the entries for Inishcaltra). In two of these, Inishcaltra 9 and 16, the lower line has to be read before the upper, although whether by accident or design is uncertain. One stone, Lismore 4, has a text in two lines, one of which is set vertically, the other horizontally and inverted. Since all the other Lismore stones have horizontal texts that are not inverted, the layout on Lismore 4 may represent an *ad hoc* decision rather than deliberate practice. The Scattery Island stone contains two texts, one inverted and the other not.

§4.3 Abbreviations and diacritics

The inscriptions follow contemporary manuscript practice in the ready use of abbreviations of common words (for manuscript abbreviations, see Lindsay 1915 and Bischoff 1990, 86, 150-3). Within the Corpus, the most common device by which abbreviation is indicated is the horizontal bar above the first letter or letters of the syllable after which letters are omitted. Two examples occur in the final syllable of Latin words: *titulu*(m) Tullylease 1 and *episco*(po) Inishcaltra 10. The abbreviation of Latin *s*(un)t on Tullylease 2 is more properly a contraction. It is possible that the texts on Monaincha 5 and 6 originally contained similar contractions of *s*(an)c(tu)s. Macalister (1937, 224) claimed to see a contracted form *s*(an)c(t)i on Kilfountan, but this is not now visible. Various contracted forms of the Latin *dominus* are found on stones from Kilmalkedar and Reask, for example *d*(omi)n(u)s, *d*(omi)ne and *d*(omi)no, some with and some without the contractions marked (see **§5.3.3** below).

The horizontal line marking abbreviation by suspension also occurs commonly in Irish texts, most frequently in the formulaic word ōr̄ for *or*(óit). There are at least twenty-five examples of this word, from throughout Munster (see **§5.2** below). Other suspensions are ī for the definite article *i*(n) (Inishcaltra 1), AN̄ for *an*(main) (Lismore 3), F̄ for *f*(or) (Church Island 1) and M̄ for *m*(ac) (Lismore 2). In two instances the suspension mark has been preserved on a fragment but too little else to interpret the abbreviation (Toureen Peacaun 32, Tullylease 3). The horizontal line on Toureen Peacaun *51 is longer than the suspension marks found elsewhere, and apparently performs a different function, that of marking a run-on line.

Medial points are used to mark the abbreviation ·I· for Latin *id est* on Inishcaltra 2. Elsewhere medial points occasionally indicate word separation (see **§4.4** below) and, at least on Toureen Peacaun 16, apparently syllable division also. There is one instance of a suprascript point, the *punctum delens*, marking the lenition of *f* on the stone from Ardfert (see **§5.3.8** below). Further use of diacritics is restricted to two stones from Toureen Peacaun which exhibit a stroke to indicate vowel length and to mark a diphthong: Toureen Peacaun 36 *á* and Toureen Peacaun 2 *áe*. The lost stone from *Inishvickillane may have contained another example of the use of a stroke to mark vowel length (*ú*).

Lismore 5 is the sole example of an abbreviation using a tachygraphic sign, the P with a medial hook to the left for *p*(ro). This symbol is common in manuscripts from Ireland and elsewhere (Lindsay 1917, 175-6; Bischoff 1990, 151), but its use in a formal text on a public monument is unusual. This same stone has a ligature of O and R, in the personal name Co[r]mac. Other calligraphic ligatures include the A and E on Toureen Peacaun 2 and two examples on St Berrihert's Kyle, including U with tall minuscule S. The most ambitious example is the apparently densely ligatured lettering on Toureen Peacaun 40.

A few texts apparently began with an initial cross but this is not common. These include, for example, Church Island 1, text a, Inishcaltra 1 and *Inishvickillane. In this respect the Munster stones compare with the early Christian stones of South-west Britain (Okasha 1993) but differ from those of Anglo-Saxon England, where an initial cross frequently occurs (Okasha 1971).

§4.4 Word separation

Most of the inscribed texts in the Corpus do not indicate word separation. This is also the case with inscribed texts in roman script on stones from Wales, South-west Britain, Anglo-Saxon England and Pictland. It is also the case with ogham texts. The occasional indication of word separation can be marked in a variety of ways.

In modern texts, word separation is indicated by a deliberate space after each word. This was much less common in medieval texts (see Saenger 1997), and occurs even more infrequently in epigraphic than in manuscript texts. There are however a few instances in the Corpus, for example following the word *or(óit)* in several of the Inishcaltra slabs and in Scattery Island, text b.

Alternatively a new word can start a new line of text. This is of course only demonstrable in complete and legible texts that are arranged in more than one line. It can be seen, for example, in Lismore 3 which has a three-line text with each line starting with a new word. In general, it is slightly more common for words to end at line ends than for them to run over to the next line, but the numbers of texts involved are very small.

Another way of indicating a new word in a text is by placing the text around the carved decoration in such a way that the decoration separates some of the words. This can be seen, for example, in Lismore 4. A related exploitation of the carved decoration is when it is apparently used to divide personal names at their elements. This is seen, for instance, in Toureen Peacaun 2 and 4. In other cases personal names are divided in a more arbitrary manner, as in Roscrea 1.

Finally, and very occasionally, word separation is indicated by the use of a single dot in the text as occurs in Lismore 2 and 5.

In Tullylease 1, text b, several of these practices are combined. There are six deliberate spaces in the text: two of these are at word-ends, two are in the middle of the word *legerit*, and two separate the elements in the compound word which is today written *quicumque*. In this text there seems to be a clear attempt to space the text so that the ends of words come either at the cross decoration or at the ends of lines. Every word-end is indicated either by a following space, or by a line-end, or by part of the decoration. The formula of this text is more closely related to manuscript texts than are most others in the Corpus. It may be that its more consistent use of word separation is also to be related to manuscript usage.

Whereas word separation has been used consistently in written texts from the high Middle Ages, it is clear from the evidence of manuscripts that in the early Christian period it was less common (see Saenger 1997). It is interesting, therefore, that so many of the Munster epigraphic texts show an attempt to indicate the ends of words. One possible explanation is that the audience of these stones needed particular help in reading the texts. It might be that the composers of the inscribed texts considered that the people who would read them would be less literate than the readers of manuscript texts. However, we know very little about those who composed texts to be inscribed on stone and their relationship to those who composed manuscript texts. Even less is known about the audience, actual or potential, of inscribed stones. In these circumstances, discussion of levels of audience literacy in early Christian Munster can be no more than speculation.

§5 Texts: language

§5.1 List of readings (diplomatic)
System of transliteration used

The texts are given in this section, and under **Text** in each entry in the Catalogue, as they appear on the stone. The texts are transliterated into small capitals. Spaces between letters, diacritics and punctuation are only included if they appear on the stones. The following signs are used:

A indicates a legible letter A

A̲ indicates a letter A damaged but legible

[A] indicates a lost or badly damaged letter, probably A

[.] indicates one lost letter

[–] indicates lost text within defined limits

– indicates an indefinite amount of lost text

A/B indicates two ligatured letters

· indicates a deliberate dot in the text

| indicates the start of a new line of text

‖ indicates text interrupted by carving on the stone

County Clare

Inishcaltra	1	+ILAD ĪDECHENBOIR
Inishcaltra	2 R	ŌRDOARDSE[N̲]OIR HERENN ·I· DO CATHAS[A]–
	L	ŌR DO TH[–O̲.] DORIGNIĪCROI̲–
Inishcaltra	3	ŌRDOMURCHAD
Inishcaltra	4	COSCRACH | LAIGNECH
Inishcaltra	5	ŌR DOMACCU[.]–
Inishcaltra	6	ŌR DOCHELLA̲CH
Inishcaltra	7	–R̲DO̲[CA̲..]G | –[A̲]L̲
Inishcaltra	8	ŌR DOLAITH | BERTACH
Inishcaltra	9	ŌR D ‖ [O] ‖ ING̲[A̲]N | E
Inishcaltra	10	–D̲OGILLU | –EPISC̄Ō
Inishcaltra	11	ŌRDOMAE–
Inishcaltra	12	ŌRDOMNALL[–]ACART
Inishcaltra	13	ŌRDODIARMAIT | MACCDELBAID
Inishcaltra	14	ŌRDOMAEL | PATRAIC
Inishcaltra	15	ŌR̲ [–] DOMNALL
Inishcaltra	16	SE̲C ‖ H ‖ N̲AILL | [–]DOMAEL
Inishcaltra	*17	ŌRDOCHUNN
Inishcaltra	18	ŌR̲–
Inishcaltra	*19	MOE/N ‖ GAL | MAC ‖ LODGIN
Inishcaltra	20	MUIR[–] ‖ A[I̲]TH
Inishcaltra	21	DERM–
Inishcaltra	22	FLA[IT̲H̲] ‖ BERTA | CH
*Oughtmama	*text(s) not recorded*	
Scattery Island a	ŌRDOMOINACH	
b	ŌR DO | MOENACH | AITE | MOG ‖ ROIN	
*Tuamgraney	[.]ORCHIDE	

County Cork

Tullylease	1 a	XP̄S
	b	QUI CUM QUA/E ‖ HUNC T/IT/UL/Ū │ L/E G/E RIT ‖ ORAT PRO │ BERECHTUINE
Tullylease	2	[.]– │ PORA[.]– │ ESCUNT[.]– │ S̄T̄ SCR–
Tullylease	3	–DANT │ –[..][-]
Tullylease	4	[–]ES[.]– │ [–]ATISTU[–] │ [–]
Tullylease	*5	–[C]ES[…]–

County Kerry

Ardfert		‖ AḞ OGAR[.] ‖ (edge of stone)
*Ballymorereagh		O ‖ R │ AR ‖ TH
Church Island	1 a	+ │ Ā │ ω̄
	b	IH̄S XP̄S
	c	BENNACHT F̄ ANMAIN │ ANMCHADA
Church Island	2	+ BE[N]–
*Coumduff		*text uncertain*
Gallarus		COLUM │ [….]MEC
*Illauntannig	Piece a:	[–]UIN F[.]
	Piece b:	[D]A–
	Piece c:	[T]H[–] │ ..–]
*Inishvickillane		+ŌR̄ DOMACRUEDUDALAC[.]
Innisfallen		F– *or* –D
Kilfountan		[–] │ [F]INTEN
Kilmalkedar	1 a	DN̄I
	b	–BCDEFGHIKLMN │ OPQRS ‖ TUX[..]E/T
Kilmalkedar	*2	DNE–
Loher		A ‖ ω
Reask	1	DNE
Reask	2 a	DNO
	b	DNS

County Limerick

Castleconnell		[.–B.ND–L] │ A[.–]A

County Tipperary

Cloghinch		–ANLAD
Derrynaflan		ŌR̄ DOANMAIN DUBSCUL[E]
Monaincha	1	–E A │ –AENACH– │ –LUGDAC–
Monaincha	2	ŌR̄ DOBRAN [D]–
Monaincha	*3	ŌR̄ AR DO[.]–
Monaincha	4	ŌR̄DO[T]–
Monaincha	5	–[.]C̄S̄ AE[.]–
Monainach	6	–C̄[S̄.]–
Roscrea	1	R ‖ E │ CHT ‖ A[.] │ RA ‖ –

Roscrea	*2	–DOUCHERBAILL ǀ O̅R̅ [DO]RIGELE
St Berrihert's Kyle		–GU/SS/AN ǀ [–] DO
Toureen Peacaun	1	DUN ǁ –
Toureen Peacaun	2	FID ǁ LÁ/ER
Toureen Peacaun	3	–C–
Toureen Peacaun	4	DON ǁ GUS
Toureen Peacaun	5	FINDLU–
Toureen Peacaun	6	COND–
Toureen Peacaun	7	–ER ǁ LE–
Toureen Peacaun	8	–A ǁ R–
Toureen Peacaun	9	*no visible text*
Toureen Peacaun	10	FLAND
Toureen Peacaun	11	FIN–
Toureen Peacaun	12	–N–
Toureen Peacaun	13	–ALE
Toureen Peacaun	14	OU·R–
Toureen Peacaun	15	+C[.]–
Toureen Peacaun	16	CUMMENE ǀ LAD·CEN
Toureen Peacaun	17	*no visible text*
Toureen Peacaun	18	[.]AN ǁ D–
Toureen Peacaun	19	SOADBAR
Toureen Peacaun	20	*no visible text*
Toureen Peacaun	21	–CO ǁ –
Toureen Peacaun	22	–BA[.]–
Toureen Peacaun	23	*no visible text*
Toureen Peacaun	24	–[T]A–
Toureen Peacaun	25	HEL–
Toureen Peacaun	26	SOER ǁ LECH
Toureen Peacaun	27	–OTM[.]–
Toureen Peacaun	28	–[.]OSED
Toureen Peacaun	29	*no text*
Toureen Peacaun	30	*no visible text*
Toureen Peacaun	31	[D]OM NIC
Toureen Peacaun	32	–T̅–
Toureen Peacaun	33	FO[RF]–
Toureen Peacaun	34	–[.]AED CU[.]–
Toureen Peacaun	35	*no text*
Toureen Peacaun	36	FINÁNPUER
Toureen Peacaun	37	–CANI
Toureen Peacaun	38	–[E]ARASS ǀ [D.E]
Toureen Peacaun	39	– ǁ N[..]
Toureen Peacaun	40	O [..–]OR[.] ǀ A[.–] ǀ [.] O [.–R]O[..] ǀ C/ T[.]R[–] ǀ [.]/TTO[–NU̅RN̅IN̅I̅] ǀ · DERN[A]D[..G]IB
Toureen Peacaun	*41	*no visible text*
Toureen Peacaun	*42	*no visible text*
Toureen Peacaun	*43	–MNE[.]

Toureen Peacaun	*44	*no visible text*
Toureen Peacaun	*45	*no visible text*
Toureen Peacaun	*46	*no visible text*
Toureen Peacaun	*47	–[L]ETHO
Toureen Peacaun	*48	–TO–
Toureen Peacaun	*49	–[.U]–
Toureen Peacaun	*50	*no visible text*
Toureen Peacaun	*51	RAC ‖ [–.]N[D]CAEL̄
Toureen Peacaun	*52	–EC–
Toureen Peacaun	*53	*no visible text*
Toureen Peacaun	*54	*no visible text*
Toureen Peacaun	*55	*no visible text*
Toureen Peacaun	*56	OR ‖ A ‖ R ‖ AED ‖ LAC
Toureen Peacaun	*57	–DIE–
Toureen Peacaun	*58	–F[I]TS–
Toureen Peacaun	*59	*text illegible*
Toureen Peacaun	*60	FLAIT–
Toureen Peacaun	*61	*no visible text*
Toureen Peacaun	*62	–[E]

County Waterford

Lismore 1	BENDA ‖ CHT FOR ‖ ANMAIN ‖ COLGEN
Lismore 2	SUIBNE · M̄ · ‖ CONHUIDIR
Lismore 3	BEND ‖ ACHT ‖ FOR ‖ AN̄ ‖ MARTAN
Lismore 4	ŌR DO ‖ DONN ‖ CHAD
Lismore 5	[Ō]R̄ · DOCO/[R̄] ‖ MAC · P ‖ [–̄]
Lismore 6	– ‖ – ‖ [.NN..] ‖ [.RUSAU] ‖ [.....] ‖ [.UM–] ‖ [P.NN..] ‖ [.URN.]
*Shanakill	AEDUIE

Dubia

Camp	FEC[T.O]N[U]RI
*Dromcarra	*text uncertain*
*Moorestown	*text uncertain*

§5.2 List of readings (edited)

The texts here, and under **Interpretation** in each entry in the Catalogue, are given in an edited version. The texts are divided into words, the abbreviations are expanded and diacritics are added. Letters which, although lost or damaged, can reasonably be inferred from the context are added. Expanded abbreviations and *h* for lenition are given in round brackets and added letters in square brackets. Where a clear abbreviation mark appears in the text but it is not certain what it should be expanded to, the abbreviation mark is retained. Further discussion of each text, and a translation, are given in the appropriate entry in the Catalogue.

County Clare
Inishcaltra 1:   + *ilad i(n) dechenboir*
Inishcaltra 2 R: *or(óit) do ardse[n]óir hErenn i(d est) do Cathas[ach]*
             L: *or(óit) do Th[–o.] do rigni i(n) croi–*
Inishcaltra 3:   *or(óit) do Murchad*
Inishcaltra 4:   *Coscrach Laignech*
Inishcaltra 5:   *or(óit) do Maccu–*
Inishcaltra 6:   *or(óit) do Chellach*
Inishcaltra 7:   *[o]r(óit) do [Cath]g[–a]l*
Inishcaltra 8:   *or(óit) do (F)laithbertach*
Inishcaltra 9:   *or(óit) d[o] (F)ing[a]ne*
Inishcaltra 10:   *[or(óit)] do Gillu[Cristi] episco(po)*
Inishcaltra 11:   *or(óit) do Máe–*
Inishcaltra 12:   *or(óit) [do] Domnall [s]acart*
Inishcaltra 13:   *or(óit) do Diarmait macc Delbaid*
Inishcaltra 14:   *or(óit) do Máel Pátraic*
Inishcaltra 15:   *or(óit) [do] Domnall*
Inishcaltra 16:   *[or(óit)] do Máel Sechnaill*
Inishcaltra *17:   *or(óit) do Chunn*
Inishcaltra 18:   *or(óit) –*
Inishcaltra *19:   *Moengal mac Lodgin*
Inishcaltra 20:   *Muir[–]a[i]th*
Inishcaltra 21:   *Derm–*
Inishcaltra 22:   *Fla[ith]bertach*
*Oughtmama: text(s) not recorded
Scattery Island a: *or(óit) do Moínach*
            b: *or(óit) do Móenach aite Mogróin*
*Tuamgraney: *[.]orchide*

County Cork
Tullylease 1 a: *[Ihesus] Chr(istu)s*
            b: *quicumquae hunc titulu(m) legerit orat pro Berechtuine*
Tullylease 2:   *–pora [–]escunt [–] s(un)t scr–*
Tullylease 3:   *–dant –*
Tullylease 4:   *–es[–]atistu–*
Tullylease *5:   *–[c]es–*

County Kerry
Ardfert: *–[u]a F(h)ogar[t]–*
*Ballymorereagh: *or(óit) ar Th–*
Church Island 1 a: + *a(lpha) o(mega)*
            b: *Ih(esu)s Chr(istu)s*
            c: *bennacht f(or) anmain Anmchada*
Church Island 2:   + *be[nnacht] –*
*Coumduff: text uncertain
Gallarus: *Colum [–]mec*

*Illauntannig:	*–uin f[–]th [–d]a[–]*
*Inishvickillane:	*+ or(óit) do Mac Rued ú Dalac[h]*
Innisfallen:	*f– or –d*
Kilfountan:	*– [F]inten*
Kilmalkedar1 a:	*D(omi)ni*
b:	*[a]bcdefghiklmnopqrstux[–et]*
Kilmalkedar *2:	*D(omi)ne –*
Loher:	A ω
Reask 1:	*D(omi)ne*
Reask 2 a:	*D(omi)no*
b:	*D(omi)n(u)s*

County Limerick

Castleconnell:	*[–b.nd]–*

County Tipperary

Cloghinch:	*–anlad*
Derrynaflan:	*or(óit) do anmain Dubscul[e]*
Monaincha 1:	*–[or(óit) ar M]áenach [úa Máel–] Lugdac[h]*
Monaincha 2:	*or(óit) do Bran [d]–*
Monaincha *3:	*or(óit) ar Do[.]–*
Monaincha 4:	*or(óit) do [T]–*
Monaincha 5:	*–[.]c̄s̄ ae[.̄]–*
Monaincha 6:	*–c̄[s̄.]–*
Roscrea 1:	*Rechta[b]ra–*
Roscrea *2:	*– [oróit] do u Cherbaill or(óit) [do] rig Ele*
St Berrihert's Kyle:	*–gussan [–]do*
Toureen Peacaun 1:	*Dun–*
Toureen Peacaun 2:	*Fidláer*
Toureen Peacaun 3:	*–c–*
Toureen Peacaun 4:	*Dongus*
Toureen Peacaun 5:	*Findlu–*
Toureen Peacaun 6:	*Cond–*
Toureen Peacaun 7:	*–er le–*
Toureen Peacaun 8:	*–a r–*
Toureen Peacaun 9:	no visible text
Toureen Peacaun 10:	*Fland*
Toureen Peacaun 11:	*Fin–*
Toureen Peacaun 12:	*–n–*
Toureen Peacaun 13:	*–ale*
Toureen Peacaun 14:	*ou·r–*
Toureen Peacaun 15:	*+ c[.]–*
Toureen Peacaun 16:	*Cummene Lad·cen*
Toureen Peacaun 17:	no visible text
Toureen Peacaun 18:	*–[.]an d–*
Toureen Peacaun 19:	*Soadbar*

Toureen Peacaun 20: no visible text
Toureen Peacaun 21: –co–
Toureen Peacaun 22: –ba[.]–
Toureen Peacaun 23: no visible text
Toureen Peacaun 24: –[t]a–
Toureen Peacaun 25: hel–
Toureen Peacaun 26: *Soerlech*
Toureen Peacaun 27: –otm–
Toureen Peacaun 28: –osed
Toureen Peacaun 29: no text
Toureen Peacaun 30: no visible text
Toureen Peacaun 31: [D]omnic
Toureen Peacaun 32: –ī–
Toureen Peacaun 33: *Fo*[rf]–
Toureen Peacaun 34: –[b]aedcu[.]–
Toureen Peacaun 35: no text
Toureen Peacaun 36: *Finán puer*
Toureen Peacaun 37: –cani
Toureen Peacaun 38: –[e]arass [d.e]
Toureen Peacaun 39: –n–
Toureen Peacaun 40: – or(óit) [–] ·dern[a]d –
Toureen Peacaun *41: no visible text
Toureen Peacaun *42: no visible text
Toureen Peacaun *43: –mne[.]
Toureen Peacaun *44: no visible text
Toureen Peacaun *45: no visible text
Toureen Peacaun *46: no visible text
Toureen Peacaun *47: –[l]etho
Toureen Peacaun *48: –to–
Toureen Peacaun *49: –[.u]–
Toureen Peacaun *50: no visible text
Toureen Peacaun *51: –n[d] caelrac
Toureen Peacaun *52: –ec–
Toureen Peacaun *53: no visible text
Toureen Peacaun *54: no visible text
Toureen Peacaun *55: no visible text
Toureen Peacaun *56: or(óit) ar Aedlac
Toureen Peacaun *57: –die–
Toureen Peacaun *58: –f[i]ts–
Toureen Peacaun *59: text unknown
Toureen Peacaun *60: *Flait*–
Toureen Peacaun *61: no visible text
Toureen Peacaun *62: –[e]

County Waterford
Lismore 1: *bendacht for anmain Colgen*

Lismore 2:	*Suibne · m(ac) · Conhuidir*
Lismore 3:	*bendacht for an(main) Martan*
Lismore 4:	*or(óit) do Donnchad*
Lismore 5:	*[o]r(óit) · do Co[r]mac · p(ro)–*
Lismore 6:	text virtually illegible
*Shanakill:	*aeduie*

Dubia
Camp:	*fec[t.o]n[u]ri*
*Dromcarra:	text uncertain
*Moorestown:	text uncertain

§5.3 Language and formula

§5.3.1 Introduction
The total number of inscribed stones in the Corpus is 129. Of these, three are listed under Dubia, two (Toureen Peacaun 29 and 35) were probably never inscribed, two are lost with no texts recorded (*Coumduff and *Oughtmama) and two are substantially illegible (Castleconnell and Lismore 6). These are excluded from the following linguistic discussion. A further 43 stones have, or had, texts too fragmentary or too poorly preserved to be suitable for linguistic consideration. These are:

*Illauntannig
Innisfallen
Toureen Peacaun (having one or more extant letters): 3, 7, 8, 12-15, 18, 21, 22, 24, 25, 27, 28, 32, 39, *43, *47-*49, *51, *52, *57, *58, *60, *62
Toureen Peacaun (fragments of similar monuments, probably originally inscribed but having no surviving letters): 9, 17, 20, 23, 30, *41, *42, *44-*46, *50, *53-*55, *59, *61.

There remain 76 inscribed stones, approximately 60 per cent of the total, which provide sufficient evidence for linguistic discussion.

The majority of these have texts in Old or Middle Irish. The exceptions, ten in total, fall into two groups. Firstly, there are the stones from Tullylease which are, or appear to have been, inscribed with extended texts in Latin. The sole personal name recorded in this group is an Old English one, the only instance of a non-Gaelic name in the Corpus. Secondly, there is a group of five, mostly early, stones inscribed solely with *nomina sacra*. To this group may be added the Latin alphabet which occurs, along with the *nomen sacrum*, on Kilmalkedar 1. All of the stones in this latter group are from west Kerry, specifically from the Dingle and Iveragh peninsulas.

§5.3.2 Latin texts
The substantially complete slab from Tullylease (no.1) bears an extended text in Latin with no Irish. It is probable that the four recorded fragments from the site (nos 2-5) are pieces of similar monuments. Tullylease 2 is certainly in Latin

and Tullylease 4 is probably so. Too few letters remain(ed) on Tullylease 3 and
*5 to be diagnostic. The late stone Lismore 6 may, as Macalister thought, bear
the remains of an extended text in Latin, perhaps a quotation from scripture,
but the lettering is now too worn to identify the language of the text with any
certainty. No other stones bear extended Latin texts but there are two examples
of an Irish personal name followed by a Latin epithet. In both cases the Latin
expresses ecclesiastical status: Toureen Peacaun 36 (*puer*, 'boy, ?oblate') and
Inishcaltra 10 (*episcopus*, 'bishop'). If not part of a personal name, the
incomplete text on Toureen Peacaun 37 may be a further example. It appears
to contain the last few letters of a Latin noun in the genitive (*-cani*), but this is
far from certain. If correctly reconstructed, the fragments Monaincha 5 and 6
may contain an abbreviated form of the Latin *sanctus* 'saint'. Macalister (1937,
224) also read *sci* for *sancti* on Kilfountan, but this word is highly doubtful.

The Latin words which appear in the Corpus are as follows:

episco(po), 'bishop'(dat.)	Inishcaltra 10
hunc, 'this'	Tullylease 1
legerit, 'will, or might, have read'	Tullylease 1
orat, 'let him/her pray'	Tullylease 1
pro, 'for'	Tullylease 1
puer, 'boy, ?oblate' (nom.)	Toureen Peacaun 36
quicumquae, 'whoever'	Tullylease 1
titulu(m), 'inscription' (acc.)	Tullylease 1
s(un)t, 'are '	Tullylease 2
[s](*an*)*c*(*tu*)*s*, 'saint' (?)	Monaincha 5
[s](*an*)*c*(*tu*)*s*, 'saint' (?)	Monaincha 6

The symbol ·i·, originally for Latin *id est*, 'that is', was often read by Irish
scribes as *id* and rendered in Irish as *ed-ón* 'that' (Thurneysen 1946, 25 §35). It
appears on Inishcaltra 2 in the middle of a text which is otherwise entirely in
Irish and is probably functioning there more as a graphic symbol, to be
understood in Irish terms, than as an abbreviation for a fully Latin phrase.

§5.3.3 Nomina sacra

From the fourth century, Latin manuscripts of Christian texts, especially the
Bible, employed abbreviated forms of certain theological names and concepts.
These are often contractions formed from the first and last letters of the holy
names (Bischoff 1990, 152). By changing the last letter, the various oblique
cases may be expressed, a process well illustrated in the Corpus by the various
forms of *Dominus*, 'Lord'. The instances all occur on a small group of early
pillars from the western edge of the Dingle Peninsula:

dns for D(omi)n(u)s	nominative	Reask 2, text b
dne for D(omi)ne	vocative	Kilmalkedar *2, Reask 1
dn̄i for D(omi)ni	genitive	Kilmalkedar1, text a
dno for D(omi)no	dative/ablative	Reask 2, text a

The sacred monogram *ih̄s xp̄s*, based on the Greek letters for the Latin *Ihesus
Christus*, occurs on two later stones: the eighth- or ninth-century Tullylease 1

and Church Island 1 of the eleventh century. At Tullylease only the x͞p͞s has survived, the corner where one would have expected i͞h͞s having broken off. Macalister also read i͞h͞s x͞p͞s on Church Island 2 but this is no longer visible (Macalister 1949a, 98). Another reference to God, or, more usually, Christ, is the pairing of *alpha* and *omega*, the first and last letters of the Greek alphabet. This *nomen sacrum* is a reference to the Apocalpyse (for example Revelations 22:13, in the Authorised Version, 'I am Alpha and Omega, the beginning and the end, the first and the last'). In its earliest attestations *alpha* and *omega* are often associated with another sacred monogram, the *chi-rho*. In these cases the letters usually appear below, or pendant from, the arms of the cross. It is in this configuration in which *alpha* and *omega* appear on the early stone from Loher. They occur much later on the shaft of a cross incised on a stone from nearby Church Island, Church Island 1, text a. The symbolism of the Latin alphabet displayed on Kilmalkedar 1 may have a sacral quality which allows that text to be considered alongside these others.

§5.3.4 Irish texts: formulae
All the other texts are in Irish. With only a handful of exceptions these are short texts consisting simply of a personal name, or a request for a prayer or blessing for a named individual. Only one inscription, Inishcaltra 1, diverges totally from this pattern (see below).

The simplest inscriptions are those consisting of a single personal name. This group is centred on north Tipperary and east Clare and, where the stones can be dated, the majority appear to be fairly early, probably dating from the eighth and ninth centuries, with some possibly as early as the seventh century. These are Cloghinch, Inishcaltra 20, 21, 22, Roscrea 1, *Tuamgraney and almost all of the intact slabs and fragments of Toureen Peacaun. (The inscribed exceptions are Toureen Peacaun 36, 40 and *51). The outlier *Shanakill was probably also similar. Within this group Toureen Peacaun 16 is unique in bearing two unqualified names.

In two certain instances, instead of a simple name, a qualifying epithet is added. On Inishcaltra 4, this is ethnic: *Coscrach Laignech*, 'Cosgrach the Leinsterman'; on Toureen Peacaun 36, it is probably vocational, and is in Latin: *Finán puer*, 'Finán the boy, ?or oblate'). If correctly interpreted, *caelrac* 'slender' on Toureen Peacaun *51 may be a third example, in this case referring to a personal or physical quality. In the Corpus as a whole, kinship affiliations are unusual, but there are two examples of simple names with a patronymic, Inishcaltra *19 and Lismore 2. The inscription from Gallarus belongs to this general 'name only' grouping (in the sense that there is no explicit request for a prayer or blessing) but the uncertainty over the reading of the second line prevents more detailed classification.

A large group of texts contains those which ask for a prayer (*oróit*) or blessing (*bendacht*) on behalf of the person named. In Munster, as throughout Ireland, the most common formula is *oróit do N.* 'a prayer for N.' The Old Irish *oróit* (later *oráit*) is a borrowing from Latin *oratio* and means, according to *DIL* (*s.v.* *oráit*), 'probably a ritual prayer rather than an extemporare one'. In the inscriptions, *oróit* or *oráit* is all but universally abbreviated to *ōr̄*. There are at least twenty-five examples of this formula in the Corpus (see **§5.2**). The incomplete slab from St Berrihert's Kyle may also contain an example but, if so, the word [*oráit*] was probably written out in full. Where they can be dated, stones bearing this formula appear to have been carved in the ninth century or later, although the doubtful Toureen Peacaun 40 is more likely to be an eighth-century monument. The formula remained popular into the twelfth century and beyond.

In Munster, as throughout Ireland, the variant formula *or(óit) ar*, appears on only a small minority of stones. Macalister (1949a) listed about two dozen examples from elsewhere in Ireland. All four of the possible examples from Munster are on lost slabs, or the lost parts of an extant slab, and must remain doubtful to varying degrees. They are *Ballymorereagh, Monaincha 1 and *3, and Toureen Peacaun *56.

Since Macalister's examples indicate that the *or(óit) ar* formula is geographically widespread, and indeed appears at several sites along with the more usual *or(óit) do*, the variation is unlikely to be dialectal. More progress on dating inscribed slabs will be necessary before it can be judged whether or not it has chronological significance, rather than being merely a stylistic variant. No examples are firmly dated, although a bell inscribed *or(óit) ar N.* may refer to someone who died in 908 (Macalister CIIC 945).

A much smaller group of stones consists of those with texts requesting a blessing rather than a prayer. The formula found in Munster is *bendacht for anmain N.*, 'a blessing on the soul of N.'. The two examples from Lismore (nos 1 and 3) preserve the Old Irish spelling *bendacht* (from Latin *benedictum*), while Church Island 1 (and possibly also Church Island 2) reflects the Middle Irish *bennacht* (DIL *s.v. bennacht*; see also Thurneysen 1946, p. 450, §727). Castleconnell might be a further example of the formula but it is virtually illegible and must remain highly doubtful. Macalister listed only two further examples of this precise formula, the stones from Roscommon (CIIC 551, now lost) and Lemanagh, Co. Offaly (CIIC 868). There are, however, several related variants, for example *ben(dach)t die f(or) an(main) N.*, 'God's blessing on the soul of N.' (Aran Islands, CIIC 529) and *bendacht ar N.* (Kells, Co. Meath CIIC 586).

There is a small number of slabs with texts that have elements of both the above types, requesting *or(óit) ar anmain*, 'a prayer for the soul of N.' Macalister lists seven examples, three from Clonmacnoise (CIIC 679, 805, 848) and one each from Fuerty, Co. Roscommon; Kilbrecan, Aran Islands; Kilcummin, Co. Mayo and Killamery, Co. Kilkenny (respectively CIIC 550, 538, 548, 570). Within Munster there is only the slab from Derrynaflan which has what appears to be a unique variant of this formula, using the preposition *do* rather than *ar*.

The persons on whose behalf the prayers and blessings are requested are, in general, identified only by their name. A few have additional information regarding kinship ties: one is identified as the son of N. (Inishcaltra 13), three as the grandson or descendent (*úa*) of N. (*Inishvickillane, Roscrea *2, probably Monaincha 1) and one as the *aite*, 'foster-father', of N. (Scattery

Island). Five people for whom prayers are requested are identified by their name and by their social status. In two cases the status epithet immediately follows the name: Inishcaltra 12 *or(óit) do N. sacart*, and Inishcaltra 10, probably [*or(óit)*] *do N. episco(po)*. The now illegible text on Church Island 2 may have been similar. In one instance, Inishcaltra 2, a prayer is requested for someone identified first by means of their status, with their name introduced by *i(d est)*, 'that is': *or(óit) do* (status) ·i· *do* (name). On Roscrea *2 the request was probably made on behalf of the person stating their name, and then repeated indicating their status: *or(óit) do* (name), *or(óit) do* (status).

One person for whom a prayer is requested is identified as the man *do rigni i(n) croi[–]*, 'who made this cross' (Inishcaltra 2). Presumably a similar construction, such as *lasin dernad*, 'for whom was made', lies behind the *·dern[a]d* on Toureen Peacaun 40. These are the only verbal forms to appear within the Corpus, both parts of the same verb, *do-gní*, 'make, do'. Despite its length, the substantially illegible text on Toureen Peacaun 40 might simply be an extended variant of the basic *or(óit) do* formula, requesting prayers on behalf of various persons involved in the erection of the cross. A parallel may be drawn with the two- or three- part formulae found on pre-Norman reliquaries recording the commissioners, interested parties and (head) craftsmen involved (Michelli 1996, 5-6). Similar texts appear on some ninth-century stone crosses, for example from Clonmacnoise (see Toureen Peacaun 40, Interpretation). Comparison with related contemporary examples suggests that the two highly fragmentary doorway inscriptions (Monaincha 4 and Ardfert) probably followed the same basic pattern: a series of simple requests for prayers on behalf of the various people involved in the erection of the building. Thus even the more extended texts in the Corpus may well have been simple in structure and comparatively short.

As noted above, only one inscription, Inishcaltra 1, appears to diverge entirely from the 'name only' and 'request for prayer/blessing' categories. This clearly legible text is carved on the base of a cross (the cross-shaft is now missing) and labels the monument as *ilad i(n) dechenboir*, 'tomb of the ten persons'. Although there are inscriptions from other parts of Ireland referring to the monument on which they are carved, there is only one other example of an inscription labelling a cross with a specific name. This is the text carved on the base of the High Cross at Kells (CIIC 587) which labels it, significantly in Latin, as *Patricii et Columbe crux*, 'the cross of Patrick and Columba'. Other cross-bases are occasionally inscribed: the base of Muiredach's Cross at Monasterboice (CIIC 580), for example, has a prayer for its commissioner, and a cross-base from Lanhadron in Cornwall contains the word *crucem* (Okasha 1993, 129-32).

§5.3.5 Irish texts: vocabulary

Additional vocabulary, apart that is from the formulaic words already mentioned, is minimal. In two instances discussed above a text refers to the monument on which it is carved; the words used are *ilad*, 'tomb' (Inishcaltra 1) and *i(n) croi[–]*, 'this cross' (Inishcaltra 2). These two texts are also the only ones in the Corpus

to contain instances of the definite article. It seems likely that Toureen Peacaun
40 also contained a reference to the monument itself, but the text is now too
worn to read. The verb *do-gní*, 'make, do', appears twice (see above). Of the
remaining words, most are terms for people, their status and their relationships.

There follows a list of all the Irish words (excluding proper names) which
occur in the Corpus, arranged in three columns. In the first column the word is
given in normalised spelling and the nominative case, as it appears as a
headword in *DIL*, followed by an English translation. The second column
contains the name as it actually appears on the stone, with a note of the
grammatical case/form in which it is attested. In this column, unverified forms
on stones or parts of stones now lost are enclosed in single inverted commas.
The third column contains the name and number of the stone or stones on
which the word is attested.

Nouns

adbar, 'designated successor'	*'adbur'*	Church Island 2
ailad, 'tomb'	*ilad* (nom.)	Inishcaltra 1
ainim(m), 'soul'	*anmain* (dat.)	Church Island 1, Derrynaflan, Lismore 1
	'anmain' (dat.)	Church Island 2
	an(main) (dat.)	Lismore 3
aite, 'foster-father, tutor'	*aite* (dat.)	Scattery Island
ardsenóir, 'chief elder'	*ardse[n]oir* (dat.)	Inishcaltra 2
bendacht, 'blessing'	*bennacht* (nom.)	Church Island 1
	'bennacht' (nom.)	Church Island 2
	bendacht (nom.)	Lismore 1, 3
cros, 'cross'	*croi[–]* (acc.)	Inishcaltra 2
deichenbor, 'set of ten people'	*dechenboir* (gen.)	Inishcaltra 1
mac(c) 'son'	*macc* (dat.)	Inishcaltra 13
	'mac' (nom.)	Inishcaltra *19
	m(ac) (nom.)	Lismore 2
oráit, 'a prayer'	*or(óit) do*	Derrynaflan, Inishcaltra 2, 3, 5-*17, probably Inishcaltra 18, *Inishvickillane, Lismore 4, 5, Monaincha 2, 4, Roscrea *2, Scattery Island, possibly Toureen Peacaun 40
	or(óit) ar	*Ballymorereagh, Monaincha 1, *3, Toureen Peacaun *56
	[or]ait do	?St Berrihert's Kyle
rí, 'king'	*'rig'* (dat.)	Roscrea *2
	'ri' (gen.)	Church Island 2
sacart, 'priest'	*[s]acart* (dat.)	Inishcaltra 12
úa, 'grandson, descendent'	*'u'* (dat.)	Roscrea *2,

	u(a) (dat.)	*Inishvickillane
	[u]a (dat.)	Ardfert
	'ua' (dat.)	Monaincha 1

Adjectives

| cáelrach, 'slender' | caelrac (nom.) | Toureen Peacaun *51 |
| Laignech, 'Leinsterman' | laignech (dat.) | Inishcaltra 4 |

Verbs

| do-gní, 'to make' | do-rigni
(3 sg perfect,
'he made') | Inishcaltra 2 |
| | ·dern[a]d
(prototonic,
sg perfect passive,
'it was made') | Toureen Peacaun 40 |

Definite article

| in, 'the' | i(n) | Inishcaltra 1 |
| | i(n) | Inishcaltra 2 |

Prepositions

do, 'for'	do	Derrynaflan, Inishcaltra 2-3, 5- 17, *Inishvickillane, Lismore 4, 5, Monaincha 2, 4, Roscrea *2, St Berrihert's Kyle, Scattery Island
ar, 'for'	ar	*Ballymorereagh, Monaincha 1, *3, Toureen Peacaun *56
for, 'for'	for	Lismore 1, 3
	'for'	Church Island 2
	f(or)	Church Island 1

Other parts of speech

·i· id est / ed-ón, 'that is'   Inishcaltra 2 (see above **§5.3.2**)

§5.3.6 Proper names

The majority of the stones commemorate individual people and forty-eight complete or nearly complete names are preserved, all of them male. Most of these are fairly common names; no less than a third appear in O'Brien's list of the 100 most frequently attested early Irish names (O'Brien 1973, 232). These are: Bran, Cellach, Cormac, Diarmait, Domnall, Donnchad, Fergus(sán), Fínán, Fintan, Flaithbertach, Fland, Móenach, Muiredach, Murchad, Rechtabrae, and Suibne. Others, however, are rather more unusual, for instance, Dubscule, Findlug, and Laidcenn. The collection of names is thus of some onomastic interest.

Very few of these named people can be identified as figures known from the historical record. There are, however, some indications as to the kind of people they were. Two are explicitly identified as secular dynasts. The slab Roscrea *2 asked for a prayer on behalf of the local king, *rig Ele*, and a similar request was apparently made on the recumbent grave-slab Church Island 2 on behalf of the designated successor of the local king. However, both these slabs are late. Roscrea *2 was probably no earlier than the late eleventh century and Church Island 2 is unlikely to pre-date 1200. The person commemorated in the fragmentary twelfth-century Ardfert inscription was probably a prominent member of the local ruling family and comparison with other inscribed doorways suggests that this may also have been the case with the person commemorated on the fragmentary mid-twelfth-century inscription, Monaincha 4. These architectural inscriptions record the patronage of leading secular figures at the major churches. The erection of ecclesiastical monuments was not, however, the sole preserve of the secular elite. The inscription on the cross Inishcaltra 2 records the name of one of the leading churchmen of his day, presumably because he sponsored its erection.

It is easier to link ecclesiastical rather than secular figures to the funerary monuments. Indeed Swift has argued that many early grave-slabs 'should be seen as commemorating ecclesiastics almost exclusively' (1999, 118). Although few of the people named on the Munster stones can be positively identified, none can be shown to be laymen and some are explicitly identified as ecclesiastical personnel by means of epithets, for example *episcopus* (Inishcaltra 10), *sacart*, 'priest' (Inishcaltra 12); *puer*, '?oblate' (Toureen Peacaun 36). The handful of names where an identification is likely are all prominent ecclesiastics, mostly abbots of the leading houses (see below). A number of Latin-derived names are probably those of clerics, the name assumed on the taking of orders, for instance *Colum* (< *columba* 'dove'), *Martan* (< *Martinus*) and *Domnic* (< *Dominicus*). Less conclusive are a group of compound names which have as their second element the name of a saint in the genitive. The first element is either *Máel-* 'devotee', as in *Máel-Sechnaill*, *Máel-Pátraic*, *Máel-Lugdach* (O'Brien 1973, 229), or *Gilla-* 'servant', as in *Gilla-Críst*, 'servant of Christ', *Gilla-in-Chomded* 'servant of the Lord' (O'Brien 1973, 229-30; Ó Cuív 1986b, 167-8). Although such names have an obvious religious significance, they were also popular among the laity and we cannot assume that their bearers were churchmen.

Swift suggested that the general lack of patronymics on the grave-slabs reflects the clerical status of the people commemorated: 'ecclesiastics, in general, tended to be almost exclusively commemorated without patronymics on grave-slabs – whatever style was adopted for their death-notices in the annals' (1999, 118). We should, of course, be wary of comparing ways of identifying people in what are two very different media, but it is interesting that only two of the Munster grave-slabs give the name of a father. Of these, the son named on Inishcaltra 13 cannot be identified, but the Suibne on Lismore 2 is likely to have been the ninth-century abbot Suibne of Lismore. This need not negate Swift's argument, however, as she demonstrated on the basis of the styles used in the Annals of Ulster that, although 'the majority of notices of ecclesiastics refer to them by their name alone without the use of patronymic

... indications of dynastic descent are important in the case of leaders of the community' (Swift 1999, 114). There are five instances of a person identified, or probably identified, as *úa*, 'grandson, descendent', but all are on lost or damaged stones (Ardfert, *Inishvickillane, Monaincha 1, Roscrea *2 and possibly Church Island 2). On the Roscrea slab the word was probably used to mean 'descendent', as part of the surname Úa Cherbaill. This may also be true of the other examples, although it is 'notoriously difficult to distinguish' between the two usages in sources of this period (Ó Murchadha 1999, 33).

As stated above, very few of the people named in the Munster inscriptions can be identified. Swift has been justifiably critical of attempts to link names on slabs with figures of the same name in the historical record (Swift 1995, 1999; see also Ó Floinn 1995). Nonetheless there are small number of plausible identifications, all of them senior ecclesiastical personnel from major church sites. Such potential links have been considered only if the person with the same name is explicitly linked with the site. Although none is conclusive, the following identifications are tentatively proposed (see the individual entries for details):

Church Island 1: 'Anmchadh', with Anmchad Ua Dúnchada, *ánchara Dé*, 'anchorite of God', who was buried on *Inis Ausail* in 1058

Inishcaltra 2: 'Cathas[ach] *ardse[n]oir hÉrenn*', with Cathasach, *cend crábuid Érénd*, 'the most pious man in Ireland', who died on Inishcaltra in 1111

Lismore 2: 'Suibne m(ac) Conhuidir', with *Suibne nepos Roichlich, scriba 7 anchorita, abbas Liss Moer*, 'Suibne úa Roichligh, scribe and anchorite, abbot of Lismore', who died in 855

Lismore 3: 'Martan', with Martan úa Roichligh, abbot of Lismore, who died in 878

Roscrea 1: 'Rechta[b]ra', with Reachtabhra, abbot of Roscrea, who died in 898

The special nature of the connection between Monaincha and nearby Roscrea means that some consideration might also be given to the possible identification of the following:

Monaincha 1: '[M]áenach [úa Máel]-Lugdac[h]', with Máenach son of Conmhach, abbot of Roscrea, who died in 862

Monaincha 2: 'Bran d[ub]', with Bran son of Colmán, abbot of Roscrea, who died in 929

The eighth-century date tentatively proposed for monuments akin to Inishcaltra 21 (Ó Floinn 1995, 253) opens up the possibility that the Dermait commemorated there is the abbot Diarmait of Inishcaltra who died in 762, but this is speculative. Although neither Cumméne nor Laidcen are firmly linked in any source with Toureen Peacaun (leaving aside the problematic link between Cumméne and a Beccán), the pairing of their names on a single slab (Toureen Peacaun 16) suggests that they may indeed be the famous scholars of these names who died in 661. This need not, however, be the date of the slab. As argued by Moloney (1964), the small slabs at Toureen Peacaun may not be funerary monuments at all but may instead record the names of the dead to be commemorated during Mass. (See Toureen Peacaun, Discussion of small slabs) If so, the identification of Cumméne and Laidcen can provide only a *terminus post quem* for the slab.

List of proper names

The following is a list of the names of people, families and places which appear in the Corpus. It is arranged in three columns. In the first is the name as it appears in one or more of the standard reference works (O'Brien 1976, Ó Riain 1985, or Hogan 1910). In the second column is the name as it actually appears on the stone, followed by a note of the grammatical case in which it is attested, if known. Unverified forms on stones now lost are enclosed in single inverted commas. The third column contains the name and number of the stone or stones on which the name is attested.

Personal names: Old English

Beorhtwine	*Berechtuine* (dat.)	Tullylease 1

Personal names: Old and Middle Irish

Áedlac	*Aedlac* (dat.)	Toureen Peacaun *56
Anmchaid	*Anmchada* (gen.)	Church Island 1
Báethcú	*[B]aed cu[.]* (?nom.).	?Toureen Peacaun 34
Bran(dub)	*Bran [d]–* (dat.)	Monaincha 2
Cathasach	*Cathas[ach]* (dat.)	Inishcaltra 2
Cathgall	*[Cath]g[a]ll* (dat.)	Inishcaltra 7
Cellach	*Chellach* (dat.)	Inishcaltra 6
Conn	'Chunn' (dat.)	Inishcaltra *17
Colcu	*Colgen* (gen.)	Lismore 1
Colum	*Colum* (?nom.)	Gallarus
Cond(—)	*Cond–* (?nom.)	Toureen Peacaun 6
Conodor	*Conhuidir* (gen.)	Lismore 2
Cormac	*Co[r]mac* (dat.)	Lismore 5
Cuimmíne	*Cummene* (nom.).	Toureen Peacaun 16
Delbáeth	*Delbaid* (gen.)	Inishcaltra 13
Diarmait	*Diarmait* (dat.)	Inishcaltra 13
	Derm– (?nom.)	Inishcaltra 21
Domnall	*Domnall* (dat.)	Inishcaltra 12
	Domnall (dat.)	Inishcaltra 15
Domnóc	*[D]om nic* (nom.)	Toureen Peacaun 31
Donngus	*Dongus* (nom.)	Toureen Peacaun 4
Donnchad	*Donnchad* (dat.)	Lismore 4
Dorchaide	'[D]orchide' (nom.)	*Tuamgraney
Dubscule	*Dubscul[e]* (gen.)	Derrynaflan
Dun(—)	*Dun–* (?nom.)	Toureen Peacaun 1
Fergusán	*[Fer]gussan* (?case)	St Berrihert's Kyle
Fidláer	*Fidláer* (nom.)	Toureen Peacaun 2
Fin(—)	*Fin–* (?nom.)	Toureen Peacaun 11
Finán	*Finán* (nom.)	Toureen Peacaun 36
Findlug	*Findlu–* (?nom.)	Toureen Peacaun 5
?Finguine	*(F)ing[a]ne* (dat.)	Inishcaltra 9
Fintan	*[F]inten* (nom.)	Kilfountan

Flaith(—)	*'Flait–'* (?nom.)	Toureen Peacaun *60
Flaithbertach	*(F)laithbertach* (dat.)	Inishcaltra 8
	Fla[ith]bertach (nom.)	Inishcaltra 22
Fland	*Fland* (nom.)	Toureen Peacaun 10
Forf(—)	*Fo[rf]–* (?nom.)	Toureen Peacaun 33
Gilla-in-Chomded	*'Gille in Chomded'*	(gen.) Church Island 2
Gilla-Críst	*Gillu['Crist']* (dat.)	Inishcaltra 10
Laidcenn	*Lad·cen* (nom.)	Toureen Peacaun 16
	'Lodgin' (gen.)	Inishcaltra *19
?Mac-Cu(—)	*Maccu–* (dat.)	Inishcaltra 5
(Mac-Rued)	*'Mac Rued'* (dat.)	*Inishvickillane
	(c.f. *Mac Ruadain:*Ó Riain 1985, p. 158, §710)	
Máel-(—)	*Mae[l]–* (dat.)	Inishcaltra 11
Máel-Pátraic	*Mael Patraic* (dat.)	Inishcaltra 14
Máel-Sechnaill	*Mael Sechnaill* (dat.)	Inishcaltra 16
Martan	*Martan* (gen.)	Lismore 3
Mugrón	*Mogroin* (gen.)	Scattery Island
Máenach	*Moinach* (dat.)	Scattery Island
	Moenach (dat.)	Scattery Island
	[M]aenach (dat.)	Monaincha 1
Muir–	*Muir[–]a[i]th* (?nom.)	Inishcaltra 20
Murchad	*Murchad* (dat.)	Inishcaltra 3
Rechtabra	*Rechta[b]ra* (?nom.)	Roscrea 1
Soadbar	*Soadbar* (nom.)	Toureen Peacaun 19
Soairlech	*Soerlech* (nom.)	Toureen Peacaun 26
Suibne	*Suibne* (nom.)	Lismore 2

Sept names

Úa Cerbaill, 'O'Carroll'	*u Cherbaill* (dat.)	Roscrea *2
Úa Fhogartaich, 'O'Fogarty'	*[u]a F(h)ogar[t]–* (dat.)	Ardfert
Úa Dalaigh. 'O'Daly'	*u(a) Dalac[h]* (dat.)	*Inishvickillane
Úa Máel-Lugdach	*[ua Mael] Lugdac[h]* (dat.)	Monaincha 1

Place names

É(i)le, 'Eile'	*Ele* (gen.)	Roscrea *2
Ériu, 'Ireland'	*hErenn* (gen.)	Inishcaltra 2
Ciarraige, 'Kerry'	*'Ciarraidi'* (gen.)	Church Island 2

§5.3.7 Irish texts: orthography

This is a specialist topic worthy of more detailed study and only a few general observations are offered here. In the manuscripts, vowel length is 'often, though by no means consistently' marked with an acute accent (Thurneysen 1946, p. 20, §26). This appears in *Finán* on Toureen Peacaun 36, and perhaps also in *ú* on *Inishvickillane. In manuscripts the acute accent is also used to mark diphthongs (Thurneysen 1946, p. 20, §26; p. 42, §66). There is a single example in the corpus, in *Fidláer* on Toureen Peacaun 2, where the length marked is of the diphthong *áe* which appears in ligatured form (Thurneysen 1946, p. 18, §24.1). See also **§4.3** above.

Fluctuation in the spelling of diphthongs is nicely reflected in the occurrence of three different forms of the name Máenach. Two of these, M*oinach* and M*oenach* appear on the same stone (Scattery Island) and refer to the same person. The third form, *[M]aenach*, appears on Monaincha 1. For the spelling of this diphthong, see Thurneysen 1946, pp. 42-43, §§66-7).

In manuscript usage the mute letter *h* is purely scribal being 'arbitrarily' prefixed to words, especially short words, beginning with a vowel (Thurneysen 1946, p. 19, §25). It is found twice in the Corpus, in *hErenn* (Inishcaltra 2) and, regardless of the proposed reconstruction, in *hel*[–] (Toureen Peacaun 25).

§5.3.8 Irish texts: lenition
The limited range of texts within the Corpus means that there are only three situations in which the initial mutation known as lenition occurs (see Thurneysen 1946, p. 506, §832; pp. 497-8, §823):

following the preposition *do* 'to, for, on behalf of'
following the preposition *ar* 'before, for'
following the dative *úa* 'grandson, descendent'

In the Corpus the mutation is indicated orthographically in only a minority of cases. These occur mainly on late slabs, probably dating from the eleventh or twelfth century. The lenition of *c* and *t* following *do* is shown by the insertion of *h* on Inishcaltra 2, 6, and *17, while the lenited (silent) *f* in the same position, is indicated by omission on Inishcaltra 8 and 9. The lost slab from *Ballymorereagh is the only example of lenition indicated after *ar*, shown by the insertion of *h* following *t*. However, this slab is poorly recorded and the reading remains somewhat doubtful. The lenition of *c* following the dative *úa* is indicated on the later eleventh- or twelfth-century Roscrea *2 by the insertion of *h*; the lenition of *f* in the same position on the twelfth-century Ardfert stone is indicated by the *punctum delens* (see Thurneysen 1946, p. 24, §33.3). This is consistent with contemporary manuscript practice where 'scribal evidence of lenition is confined to the letters *c t p*, and subsequently *s* and *f* ', and is not indicated at all in the earliest examples (Thurneysen 1946, pp. 141-2, §231; quotation from §231.8).

§5.3.9 Irish texts: dating
The inscriptions in the Irish language range in date from perhaps as early as the seventh or early eighth century, through to the later twelfth century. They therefore reflect the development of the language over this period from Old Irish (pre-900) to Middle Irish (c.900-c.1300). It is hoped that further work by specialists may contribute to the dating of these texts by reference to philological criteria. However, conservative spellings were optionally preserved for a long time after pronunciations had changed, and it is therefore necessary to exercise care when using orthography as a means of dating. A relevant example is provided by the assimilation of -*nd* to -*nn* during the Old Irish period. The spelling -*nn* became common only in the Middle Irish period

(Thurneysen 1946, p. 93, §151). The spelling *bennacht* 'blessing' (Church Island 1) thus indicates a date from the tenth century or later: in fact the inscription might commemorate someone who died in the mid-eleventh century. The older form *bendacht*, however, continued in use. It is seen in epigraphic use, for example, on the mid-eleventh-century inscription on the Stowe Missal Shrine (Michelli 1996, 16-18 and pl. V). Thus, while its appearance on Lismore 1 and 3 could indicate a date in the Old Irish period, it need not necessarily do so. The text on Lismore 3 might in fact commemorate someone who died in 878. Despite this caveat, the conservative spelling *Finten*, for later *Fintan*, on the Kilfountan pillar may well suggest a comparatively early date, perhaps seventh or early eighth century, for the text. This is in accordance with the art-historical evidence for dating this stone.

Orthography is not the only aspect of the texts which is chronologically sensitive. Some of the names themselves have dating implications. The clearest example occurs with names in Gilla- followed by the name of a saint, or similar, in the genitive. The earliest examples of this kind of name date from the ninth century but it became popular in the eleventh century and later (O'Brien 1973, 229-30; Ó Cuív 1986b, 167). This tallies with the dating of the two Munster monuments on which such names were apparently inscribed, although in both cases the texts are now in a poor state of preservation. One of these, Inishcaltra 10, probably contained the name *Gilla-Críst*, 'servant of Christ'. The text on the other, Church Island 2, is now largely illegible but Macalister (1949a, 98) read on it the name *Gilla-in-Chomded* 'servant of the Lord'.

The formula used also varied over time. In general terms the shorter texts are earlier, the longer ones later. The earliest texts, for example Cloghinch, Inishcaltra 20-22, Kilfountan and many from Toureen Peacaun, date mainly from the seventh and eighth centuries and are simple personal names. Texts requesting prayers or blessings, using the standard formulae, appear to date mostly from the ninth century and later, although there is probably some overlap with the name-only texts. Only at the end of the period, in the eleventh and twelfth century centuries, do these simple texts become more developed. However, even these longer texts, for example Inishcaltra 2, Roscrea *2, Church Island 2 (post-1200), are merely slightly augmented forms of the *or*(*óit*) *do* N. formula which, in its basic form, continued in use to the end of the period.

CATALOGUE

Guide to Entries

Each catalogue entry begins with factual information about the monument. The **Monument name** is given in both Irish and English, the English place-name forms being taken from the OS 1:50 000 series of maps, where available, otherwise from the 1" (1:63 360) series. There then follows the **Site name** and the **Townland** name. The **NGR** is given in the form 12345,67891, followed by the **SMR site number**.

The factual information about each stone includes its **Current location**, its **History** and its **Description**. The latter contains the stone's measurements and its present state of preservation; where the information is available, a geological description is included. The **Description** also includes an account of any carving on the stone and the location of the text on the stone. The **Lettering** of the text follows and the **Text** is then transliterated so as to indicate its present reading (see below for the system of transliteration used). The discursive part of each entry includes a suggested **Interpretation** of the text and a **Discussion** of any points of interest relating to text and stone. Any evidence for dating the stone is given here. Each entry contains a **Bibliography**, a comprehensive list of published references to the stone. Under **Examined**, the date(s) on which the stone was visited are given, along with the initials of which author undertook the examination. After all the Entries to stones from one location, a short account of the **Site** is given.

System of transliteration

In the section headed **Text**, a diplomatic transliteration of each text is given. This corresponds to the transliteration given in the **Introduction §5.1** except that in the Entries texts on more than one line are printed as they appear on the stones. In both cases the texts are transliterated into small capitals. Spaces between letters, diacritics and punctuation are included only if they appear on the stones. The following signs are used:

    A indicates a legible letter A
    <u>A</u> indicates a letter A damaged but legible
    [<u>A</u>] indicates a lost or badly damaged letter, probably A
    [.] indicates one lost letter
    [–] indicates lost text within defined limits
    – indicates an indefinite amount of lost text
    A/B indicates two ligatured letters
    . indicates a deliberate dot in the text
    || indicates text divided by ornament on the stone

Substantially the same system is used for the first transliteration under **Interpretation**, except that underlining is omitted and the reading of the text is given in italics. The text is then given in an edited form corresponding to the list of edited texts in the **Introduction §5.2**. The texts are divided into words, the abbreviations are expanded and diacritics are added. Letters which, although lost or damaged, can reasonably be inferred from the context are added. Expanded abbreviations and *h* for lenition are given in round brackets and added letters in square brackets. Where an abbreviation mark appears in the text but it is not clear what it should be expanded to, the abbreviation mark is retained. A translation is then given.

Each Entry is accompanied by a photograph, except in the few cases of lost stones where no photograph exists. An interpretative scale drawing of all extant, and some lost, texts also accompanies each Entry. These drawings were prepared from rubbings made by one of the authors (KF), except in the case of lost stones where there is a good photograph from which the drawings were prepared.

Alternative names

The names given to the stones in the Corpus generally refer to the names of the localities where the stones were found. Where the locality is a town, for example Lismore, there is little ambiguity. However the localities are often rural areas and in these cases a number of names can be possible. The names chosen in the Corpus reflect those most commonly used in earlier work on the stones. The following list gives some alternative names used by earlier scholars but does not include variants that are merely different spellings of the names used in the Corpus.

Annascaul *see* Coumduff
Ardane *see* St Berrihert's Kyle
Blasket Islands *see* Inishvickillane
Cloon Island *see* Castleconnell
Inis Cathaigh *see* Scattery Island
Kildrenagh *see* Loher
Killfinten *see* Kilfountan
Kilpeacan, Killpeacon, Kilpeakaun etc *see* Toureen Peacaun
Knockane *see* Coumduff
Magharee Islands *see* Illauntannig
Teampull Geal *see* Ballymorereagh

Concordances with previous corpora

1. Petrie 1878 and Corpus

Plate II, figs 2, 3, 4 and pp. 3-4 : Camp
Plate III, fig. 5 and p. 5 : Kilfountan
Plate III, figs 6, 7 and p. 5 : Reask 2
Plate IV, fig. 8 and pp. 5-6 : Reask 1
Plate V, fig. 9 and pp. 78 : Kilmalkedar 1

Plate V, fig. 10 and pp. 78 : Gallarus
Plate VIII, fig. 15 and p. 13 : Castleconnell
Plate XVIII, fig. 37 and pp. 256 : Scattery Island
Plate XX, fig. 40 and p. 31 : Lismore 2
Plate XX, fig. 41 and pp. 312 : Lismore 3
Plate XX, fig. 42 and p. 31 : Lismore 1 (not fig. 39, as stated on p. 31)
Plate XXI, fig. 42 and pp. 31-2 : Lismore 5
Plate XXI, fig. 43 and p. 32 : Lismore 4
Plate XXII, fig. 44 and pp. 334 : Toureen Peacaun 5
Plate XXII, fig. 45 and pp. 334 : Toureen Peacaun *60
Plate XXII, fig. 46 and pp. 334 : Toureen Peacaun 2
Plate XXII, fig. 47 and pp. 334 : Toureen Peacaun *58
Plate XXII, fig. 48 and pp. 334 : Toureen Peacaun *59
Plate XXIII, fig. 49 and pp. 35-6 : Monaincha 1
Plate XXIV, fig. 50 and p. 37 : Monaincha 2
Plate XXIV, fig. 51 and p. 37 : Monaincha *3
Plate XXV, fig. 52 and p. 39 : Roscrea 1
Plate XXV, fig. 53 and pp. 3940 : Roscrea *2
Plate XXVI, fig. 54 and pp. 412 : Inishcaltra 2
Plate XXVI, fig. 55 and p. 42 : Inishcaltra *19
Plate XXVI, fig. 56 and pp. 423 : Inishcaltra 1
Plate XXVII, fig. 57 and p. 44 : Inishcaltra 13
Plate XXVII, fig. 58 and p. 44 : Inishcaltra 14
Plate XXVII, fig. 59 and p. 44 : Inishcaltra 8
Plate XXX, fig. 64 and pp. 52-4 : Tullylease 1
Fig. 56a and p. 43 : Inishcaltra *17
Fig. on p. 34 and p. 33 : Toureen Peacaun 40
Page 35, note b : Monaincha 4

2. Macalister 1945, Macalister 1949a and Corpus

Macalister 1945:
CIIC 176 : Camp
CIIC 186 : Kilfountan.

Macalister 1949a:
CIIC 887 : Scattery Island
CIIC 888 : Inishcaltra 1
CIIC 889 : Inishcaltra 2
CIIC 890 : Inishcaltra 3
CIIC 891 : Inishcaltra 4
CIIC 892 : Inishcaltra 5
CIIC 893 : Inishcaltra 6
CIIC 894 : Inishcaltra 7
CIIC 895 : Inishcaltra 8

CIIC 896 : Inishcaltra 9
CIIC 897 : Inishcaltra 10
CIIC 898 : Inishcaltra 11
CIIC 899 : Inishcaltra 12
CIIC 900 : Inishcaltra 13
CIIC 901 : Inishcaltra 14
CIIC 902 : Inishcaltra 15
CIIC 903 : Inishcaltra 16
CIIC 904 : Inishcaltra *17
CIIC 905 : Inishcaltra 18
CIIC 906 : Inishcaltra *19
CIIC 907 : *Tuamgraney
CIIC 908 : Tullylease 1
CIIC 910 : Gallarus
CIIC 911 : *Inishvickillane
CIIC 912 : Kilmalkedar *2
CIIC 913 : Kilmalkedar 1
CIIC 914 : Reask 1
CIIC 915 : Reask 2
CIIC 916 : Church Island 1
CIIC 917 : Church Island 2
CIIC 918 : Castleconnell
CIIC 919 : Toureen Peacaun *51
CIIC 920 : Toureen Peacaun 2
CIIC 921 : Toureen Peacaun 5
CIIC 922 : Toureen Peacaun 14
CIIC 923 : Toureen Peacaun *56
CIIC 924 : Toureen Peacaun 34
CIIC 924A : Toureen Peacaun 39
CIIC 924B : Toureen Peacaun 40
CIIC 926 : Monaincha 1
CIIC 927 : Monaincha 2
CIIC 928 : Monaincha *3
CIIC 929 : Roscrea 1
CIIC 930 : Roscrea *2
CIIC 933 : Lismore 1
CIIC 934 : Lismore 2
CIIC 935 : Lismore 3
CIIC 936 : Lismore 4
CIIC 937 : Lismore 5
CIIC 938 : Lismore 6
CIIC 940 : *Shanakill

Further stones from Toureen Peacaun were found too late for inclusion within Macalister's sequence (Macalister 1949a, p. 101). These he listed on p. 213 and numbered 1 to 19:

 1 : Toureen Peacaun 31
 2 : Toureen Peacaun 3
 3 : Toureen Peacaun 25
 4 : Toureen Peacaun 33
 5 : Toureen Peacaun 19
 6 : Toureen Peacaun 26
 7 : Toureen Peacaun *48
 8 : Toureen Peacaun *52
 9 : Toureen Peacaun 7
10 : Toureen Peacaun 15
11 : Toureen Peacaun *47
12 : Toureen Peacaun 18
13 : Toureen Peacaun 1
14 : Toureen Peacaun *57
15 : Toureen Peacaun 16
16 : Toureen Peacaun 10
17 : Toureen Peacaun 6
18 : Toureen Peacaun 4
19 : Toureen Peacaun 13

In addition Macalister mentions *Ballymorereagh and *Moorestown without assigning them numbers (Macalister 1949a, pp. 95 and 97 respectively).

COUNTY CLARE

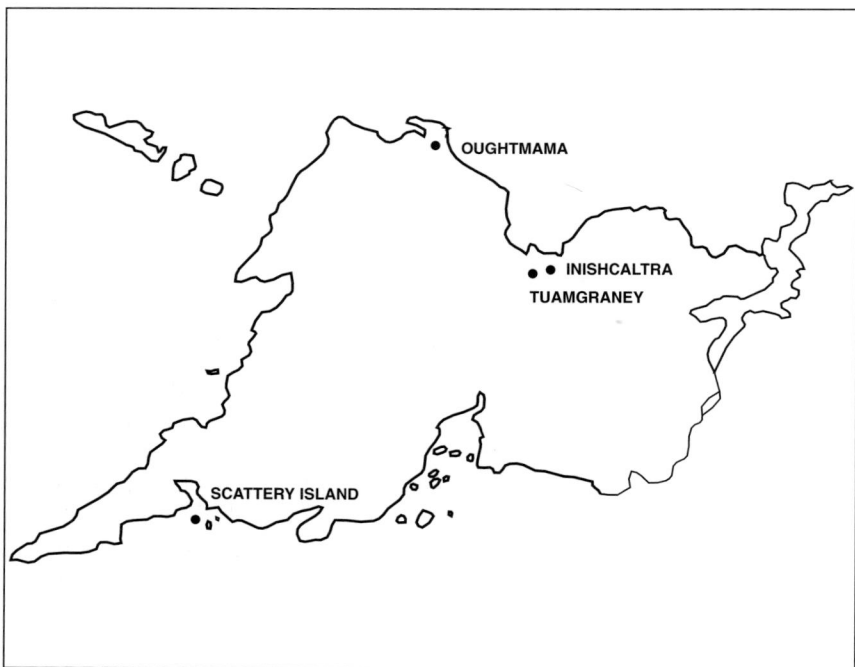

Early Christian inscribed stones of County Clare

INISHCALTRA: INIS CEALTRA

Site name Saints' Graveyard
Townland Inishcaltra or Holy Island
NGR 16987,18489
SMR site no. CL029-00901-

Of the eighty or more carved stones known from this important island monastery, twenty-two are inscribed. These comprise a cross base (no. 1), a free-standing cross of early twelfth-century date (no. 2), three small cross-incised slabs inscribed with single personal names (nos 20-22), one large cross-less slab (no. 5), and sixteen large recumbent cross-slabs (nos 3-4, 6-19) of which two are lost. All the pieces were first noted in or near the Saints' Graveyard, although since 1879 a number have been moved. Some of the large slabs appear to be in their original position.

Inishcaltra 1: cross-base

CURRENT LOCATION
This stone is in the south-west corner of the Saints' Graveyard, apparently *in situ*.

HISTORY

The first person to record the stone in detail was apparently Wakeman who stated: 'Many years ago it was my fortune ... to meet with the base of a cross bearing a very curious record, which I carefully copied. The drawing then made was, with others, subsequently presented by me to the late Dr. Petrie' (Wakeman 1885-86, 268). This is presumably the drawing made in 1837 to which Petrie referred and which he reproduced in 'corrected' form (Petrie 1878, 43 and pl. XXVI, fig. 56). In 1865

Brash re-visited the island (Brash 1866, 21) and examined the stone which was in the 'burial-ground' (Brash 1866, 19). In 1880 the stone was described as 'in graveyard' and shown in the plan as in the graveyard of St Caiman's [*sic*] church (Deane 1880, pls 1, 2). The stone remains in the graveyard, in the same position as Deane recorded it.

DESCRIPTION

The current maximum dimensions of the cross-base are:
L. 81 cm, W. 127 cm, H. 27 cm.
The cross-base is now split through the socket into two pieces. Only the top few centimetres of the sides are shaped, which suggests that it was intended to be imbedded in the ground. The upper surface is dressed and is of a trapezoidal shape; since the south-west corner has been chamfered, it is, strictly speaking, a five-sided rather than a four-sided figure. A groove on the upper surface forms a flat perimeter moulding. The oblong socket for the cross is set parallel to the longest side but the cross itself is missing and has been so from the time of the earliest reports (Macalister 1916-17, 146). The text is incised in one horizontal line and is complete. It is set along the longest (west) side beginning in the north-west corner

LETTERING

The text uses half-uncial script with a maximum letter H. of 7 cm. The text is worn but legible.

TEXT

+ILAD ĪDECHENBOIR

INTERPRETATION

The text is in Irish and reads +*ilad īdechenboir* for + *ilad i(n) dechenboir*, 'tomb of the ten persons', with *ilad* (nom.), 'a tomb, sepulchre, or burial cairn' (*DIL s.v. ailad*, see also Thurneysen 1946, p. 52, §80), and *in dechenboir* (gen.) 'the set of ten people' (*DIL s.v. deichenbor*). (See the **Introduction §4.3** for a discussion of the initial cross and the suspension mark).

DISCUSSION

The cross-base is surrounded by a low kerb of upright stones and stands in the south-east corner of the small rectangular area thus delineated. The area appears to have been cleared since Macalister described it as 'what seems to be a low carn, covered with earth, and grass-grown' (1916-17, 147). Some of the packing stones under the cross-base are now visible and there are other large loose stones protruding from the ground. Macalister was authoritatively informed that during the Board of Works' clearance 'a large number of small rounded stones, about the size and shape of a turkey's egg, were here found' (Macalister 1916-17, 147). This is consistent with this being a grave or *leacht*-type structure.

The identity of the ten persons here commemorated is not known. Macalister looked to local history and suggested they were 'ten victims of some notorious raid or massacre', for instance, the burning of Inishcaltra by Vikings recorded in 836 (1906, 309). Petrie, however (1878, 43), drew a comparison with two slabs from St Brecan's churchyard on Aran Mór, Co. Galway, which commemorate enumerated but unnamed persons. One commemorates *UII romani* 'seven Romans' (Macalister 1949a, no. 534, pp. 6-7 and pl. I, fig. 534) while the other requests *or(óit) ar II canoin* 'a prayer for (the) two canons' (Macalister 1949a, no. 535, p. 7 and pl. II, fig. 535). The former might mark the grave of seven local *romani* (perhaps adherents to the Roman side in the seventh-century Paschal controversy), but is more plausibly seen as a dedication to the 'Seven Brothers', a group of seven second-century Roman martyrs culted on 10 July. It should be noted that *ailad* can also mean a penitential station (*DIL s.v.*). Other monuments dedicated to saints include a high cross from Kells, Co. Meath, inscribed on its base *Patricii et Columbae crux* (Macalister 1949a, no. 587, pp. 36-7 and pls.), another cross-slab from St Brecan's, Aran Mór, which was apparently dedicated to the site's eponym *S(an)c(t)i Brecani* (Macalister 1949a, no. 531, p. 5 and pl. II, fig. 531), and the Kilfountan pillar.

The lettering of the text is large and consistent in size but the spacing between letters increases towards the end of the text, as if the inscriber had then realised that there was ample room available. The text does not, in fact, fill the whole of the available line. Macalister suggested this was the reason the corner had been chamfered: 'a rather clumsy device to hide the asymmetry produced by this error of judgment' (1916-17, 146). The inscriber may not, however, have intended to fill the whole line; indeed it seems more likely that the text was incised on the finished cross-base, rather than that the base and its moulding were shaped after the text was cut.

BIBLIOGRAPHY
Brash 1866, 19-20
Quin, E. R. W. 1877, 57
Petrie 1878, 42-3 and pl. XXVI, fig. 56
Deane 1880, pl. 1; pl. 2, fig. at bottom of page
Wakeman 1885-86, 268
Allen 1889, 120
Lenihan 1889, 164
Westropp 1900-02, 124, 156

Macalister 1906, no. 12, pp. 308-9 and fig. 11
Crawford 1907, 204
Macalister 1916-17, no. 11, pp. 146-7 and pl. XVI, fig. 1
Macalister 1949a, no. 888, p. 88 and pl. XXXVIII, fig. 888
Lionard 1961, fig. 2.6
Higgitt 1986, 127, 147
Killanin and Duignan 1989, 250
Harbison 1992, 98, 361, 395 and fig. 1016
OS Letters unpublished 1928, 195-6 and fig.

EXAMINED
July 1996 (KF)

Inishcaltra 2: free-standing cross

CURRENT LOCATION
This stone, known from its current location as the 'East Cross', is inside the ruins of St Caimin's church, set upright and cemented against the north wall of the nave.

HISTORY

Petrie was the first to record part of this stone. He said that Wakeman drew it for him but since Petrie initialled the drawing he reproduced, he presumably redrew it from Wakeman's drawing (Petrie 1878, 42 and pl. XXVI, fig. 54). Petrie recorded that 'the inscription has now disappeared' (Petrie 1878, 41), but whether he meant the stone or just the text is unclear. Neither Wakeman nor Petrie recognised this stone as the arm of a cross and Petrie suggested that it might have been part of a cross-base (Petrie 1878, 41-2). According to Macalister (1916-17, 147), the cross was discovered 'smashed in pieces' by the Board of Works in 1879-80 and was reconstructed then. Deane, however, did not mention the reconstruction work (1880, 73) but described the cross as having been 'found in vicinity of St. Caiman's Church' (Deane 1880, pl. 7). In May 1906 the cross was 'in St. Caimin's Church' (Macalister 1906, 309). However Macalister did not then realise that Petrie's stone was part of the cross (Macalister 1906, 310). At his later visits, between 1909 and 1915, Macalister had an opportunity to examine the cross and realised that Petrie's stone was its left arm (Macalister 1916-17, no. 15, p. 147). The cross was then on the north side of the nave of St Caimin's church (Macalister 1916-17, 144, 147) where it remains today.

DESCRIPTION

The current dimensions of the cross are:

H. 159 cm, W. (across arms) 97 cm, T. 8 cm.

This monolithic free-standing ring-less cross has semi-circular armpits and, at its base, rectangular panels on either side of the shaft. It is broken into four pieces, with fractures at the top and bottom of the shaft and separating the left arm from the cross-head. Most of the left side-panel at the base is missing. The outline of the cross is delineated by a continuous roll moulding. The surface is severely abraded but it is clear that the arms and shaft of the cross were elaborately decorated with various kinds of interlace. Macalister made a careful attempt at reconstructing the interlace and other designs (1916-17, no.15, p. 148 and pl. XVII). All that can be seen on the left side-panel are two boss-like objects, but on the right panel there is a quadruped, perhaps a unicorn, with the leg of a devoured human protruding from its mouth (Harbison 1992, 98, and pls 317 and 1015). The narrow face on the end of the right arm is decorated with rectilinear ornament but the equivalent surface on the left arm is worn away. The back of the cross is not visible; Macalister described it as 'quite plain' (1916-17, 148).

The text is incised on the two narrow faces of the cross. On both faces the text starts at the outer edge of the underside of the cross-arm and reads in a continuous line round the hollow of the armpit and down the shaft to the point where the shaft joins the side panel. Both lines read left-to-right downwards; the left text has the bottoms of its letters to the back of the cross, and the right text has the bottoms of its letters to the front of the cross. Letters have been lost from both lines where the pieces of cross have been cemented together. There was less cement when Macalister read the text, but there were metal clamps (labelled 'Holdfast' on his drawing) which obscured sections now visible (1916-17, pl. XVII). The ends of both lines are obscured by cement where they join the side-panels.

LETTERING

The text uses half-uncial script with a maximum letter H. of 3.5 cm and is badly worn in places.

TEXT

 Right: Ō R̄ DOARDSE[N̲]OIR HERENN ·I· DO CATHAS[A̲]

 Left: Ō R̄ DO TH[–Q̲] DORIGN ĪĪCRO̶─

INTERPRETATION

The two lines are part of a single text in Irish but there is no indication which is to be read first. The right-hand line of text reads reads *ōr doardse[.]oir herenn ·i· do cathas[a]–*. The lost letter in the second line probably reads *n*. Macalister read *-ch* at the end of the line but admitted that the last two letters were 'almost invisible' (1916-17, 149 and pl. XVII). Taking this as the likely reading the line may be expanded to *or(óit) do ardse[n]óir hErenn i(d est) do Cathas[ach]*, 'a prayer for the chief elder of Ireland, that is, for Cathas[ach]'. The symbol ·i·, an abbreviation for Latin *id est* 'that is', is frequent in manuscripts but rare in epigraphy (see the

Introduction §§4.3, 5.3.2 for further discussion). Irish scribes often read it simply as *id*, and rendered it in Irish by *ed-ón* 'that' (Thurneysen 1946, p. 25, §35).

The left-hand line of text reads *ōr do th[–o.] dorigniī croi–* for *or(óit) do Th[–o.] do rigni i(n) croi–*, 'a prayer for T[–] who made this cross'. Macalister described this line of text as less easy to read than the other line but took the final word as *crois[s]* 'cross'. He read the personal name as *Thor[n]oc*, that is Tórnóc, a diminutive of Tórna (Macalister 1916-17, 149). The lenition of the name beginning *T[–]* following *do* is indicated by the insertion of *h* but the equivalent lenition of *Cathas[ach]* is not indicated orthographically. (For discussion of both the *or(óit) do* formula and lenition, see the **Introduction §§5.3.4, 5.3.8**).

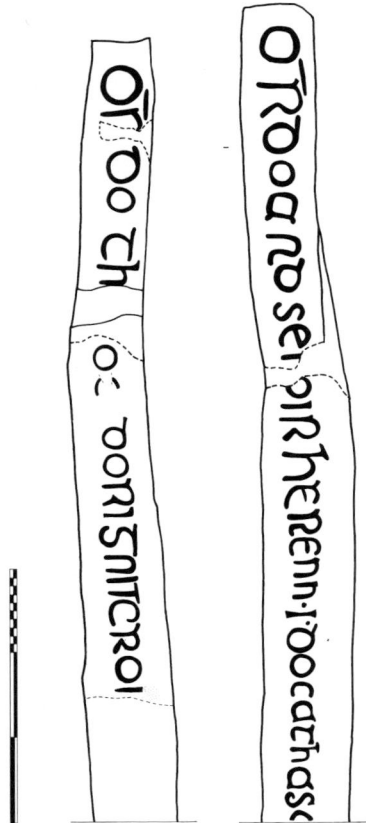

DISCUSSION

As Harbison noted, this cross, 'though squatter in its proportions', is of the same type as the adjacent 'West Cross' (1992, 98). Both seem too thin to stand without support. In Harbison's opinion, although the shape of these crosses and aspects of their decoration conformed to the style of earlier crosses, they were 'more likely to represent a revival of earlier styles', consistent with the early twelfth-century date

proposed by Macalister (Harbison 1992, 361). Higgitt has argued that the
positioning of inscriptions on Irish crosses reflects a liturgical habit of kneeling
before them to pray (Higgitt 1986, 142-3). The arrangement of text on this cross
would support his argument for the inscriptions are invisible as one stands directly
in front of the cross, but are more easily read from below. Taken together, the two
lines of text may be compared with the two- and three-part texts on contemporary
metalwork reliquaries. These use the *or(óit) do* formula to record the
commissioners of the work (always the first part) and the craftsmen who made
them (always the last part), with an optional middle part recording other
interested parties (Michelli 1996). Variants are found on stone on the two crosses
from Tuam commissioned by king Toirdelbach Ua Conchobair (reigned 1106-56),
(Macalister 1949a, nos 522-3, pp. 2-3 and pl. I, figs 522-3) and on the doorways of
Romanesque churches at Freshford, Co. Kilkenny (Macalister 1949a, no. 569, p.
24 and fig.) and Killeshin, Co. Laois (Macalister 1949a, no. 574, pp. 26-8 and pl.
VI).

The identity of the commissioner is not certain. There are several eminent
clerical Cathasachs recorded in the Annals. These include, for instance, Abbot
Cathasach of Mungret, *cinn clérech fear Muman* 'head of the clergy of Munster',
whose death is recorded *s.a.* 1070 (Annals of the Four Masters: O'Donovan 1851,
896-7), and Cathasach *coarb* of Patrick, *suí-espucc Gaoidel* 'the most distiguished
bishop of the Irish', whose death is recorded *s.a.* 957 (Annals of the Four Masters:
O'Donovan 1851, 676-7). Although the date of the latter could be thought more
consistent with the art history, there is, as Macalister conceded, nothing to link
him with Inishcaltra (Macalister 1916-17, 149). The only Cathasach with an
explicit connection to the island is the Cathasach, *cend crábuid Érénd*, 'the most
pious man in Ireland', whose death on Inishcaltra is recorded *s.a.* 1111 (Annals of
Inisfallen: Mac Airt 1951, 268-9), not in 1094, as stated by Macalister (1916-17,
149). Comparison with the reliquaries and the Tuam crosses suggests that
Inishcaltra 2 is unlikely to be funerary but is more likely to have been
commissioned by Cathasach before his death. It is interesting to note that a decade
or so later, the Cross of Cong (made *c.*1123-34) was commissioned by another
senóir Érend, Muredach Ua Dubthaig (Michelli 1996, 26-8).

BIBLIOGRAPHY
Petrie 1878, 41-2 and pl. XXVI, fig. 54
Deane 1880, pl. 7
Macalister 1906, nos 17, 18, p. 310
Crawford 1907, 203
Crawford 1908, 276-7 and fig.
Crawford 1912, 229
Macalister 1916-17, no. 15, 147-9, pl. XVII and pl. XXV, fig. 1
Henry 1933, vol. 1, 18-20; vol. 2, pl. 101
Macalister 1949a, no. 889, p. 89 and pl. XXXIX, figs 889
Lionard 1961, 117
Gwynn and Gleeson, D. F. 1962, 28-9

Weir 1980, 108
Higgitt 1986, 127-9, 147
Killanin and Duignan 1989, 250
Harbison 1992, no. 119, pp 98, 318, 325, 361, 366, 383 and figs 317, 1015

Detail of left side

Detail of right side, underside of arm

Detail of underside of arm and upper part of shaft

Inishcaltra 2: details of lettering

Hughes and Hamlin 1997, 91
Cronin 1998, 143
Rynne 1998, 127
de Paor in preparation, list 1, fig. 24

EXAMINED
July 1996 (KF)

Inishcaltra 3: large cross-slab

CURRENT LOCATION
This stone is inside the ruins of St Caimin's church, set upright and cemented against the south wall of the nave at its west corner.

HISTORY
In 1880 this stone was lying in the chancel of St Caimin's church (Deane 1880, pl. 6, stone no. 2, fig. and on plan). Macalister described this as 'the south side of the altar of St. Caimin's church' (Macalister 1916-17, 153) although by then it was on the south side of the nave (Macalister 1916-17, 144, 153).

DESCRIPTION

The current dimensions of the stone are:

H. 96 cm, W. 48 cm, T. 6 cm.

The stone is a recumbent cross-slab now broken into two pieces. This damage is not shown in any of Macalister's drawings and may therefore be of relatively recent date. The small circular dent on the lower part of the left terminal was, however, shown by Deane (1880, pl. 6, stone no. 2). Otherwise the stone is in good condition and is complete. The face is dressed and contains an incised outline Latin cross with squared expanded terminals and square expansions at the armpits. The text is complete. It is incised in one horizontal line above the head of the cross and upside down with respect to it. The cross and inscription together occupy the whole of the carved face with the side arms and shaft touching the edge of the slab. The carving is well preserved.

LETTERING

The text is legible and uses half-uncial script with a maximum letter H. of 4 cm.

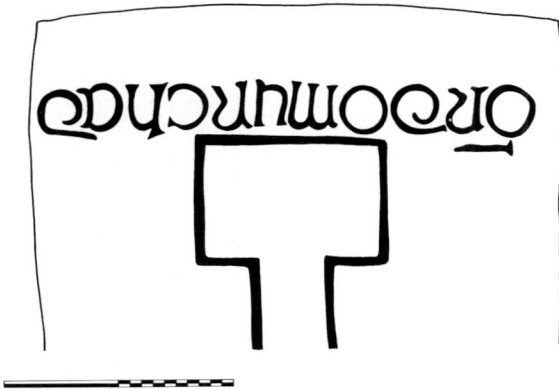

TEXT

ŌR̄DOMURCHAD

INTERPRETATION

The text is in Irish and reads *ōr̄domurchad* for *or(óit) do Murchad*, 'a prayer for Murchad'. (For discussion of the *or(óit) do* formula, see the **Introduction §5.3.4**).

DISCUSSION

This is among the smallest of the large cross-slabs and is comparatively squat. Unlike most of the other large slabs, the cross here does not have a base as such: the expansion at the end of the shaft is no wider than the expansions at the other terminals. With one exception (Macalister's no. 70) which differs in other major respects, this is the only large slab with square expansions at the crossing, although the feature is found on the small slabs 21 and 22 (which have much longer and thinner arms). Murchad has not been identified.

BIBLIOGRAPHY

Deane 1880, pl. 6, stone no. 2
Macalister 1906, no.15, p. 310 and fig. 14
Macalister 1916-17, no. 30, p. 153 and pl. XXII, fig. 10
Macalister 1949a, no. 890, p. 89 and pl. XXXVIII, fig. 890
Lionard 1961, 113 and fig. 10.12
Weir 1980, 108
de Paor in preparation, list 1, fig. 17

EXAMINED
July 1996 (KF)

Inishcaltra 4: large cross-slab

CURRENT LOCATION
This stone is in the Dúchas depot in Athenry.

HISTORY
The stone was first recorded by Deane in 1880 when it was lying in the graveyard, presumably *in situ*, in the middle of a row at its western edge, near the chancel of St Caimins's Church (Deane 1880, 73 and pl. 1, fig. E). In 1889 Lenihan reported that the stone was lost: 'Unfortunately this stone disappeared in the summer of 1888' (Lenihan 1889, 164n). However, the stone was lying in the graveyard in 1906 and Macalister argued that it was in the place where Deane had described it (Macalister 1906, 303-4). Macalister was clearly right in suggesting that Lenihan's report, substantiated by Wakeman's account (1890-91a, 274), referred to a different, and probably more portable, stone. In 1916-17 Macalister reported the stone as still in the location described by Deane (Macalister 1916-17, 144, 153 and pl. XV). It was subsequently moved and in August 1982 was exhibited at Mountshannon, Co Clare; when the exhibition ended, the stone was placed for safe-keeping in the Dúchas depot in Athenry (Pat Herity, pers. com.).

DESCRIPTION
The current dimensions of the stone are:
H. 160 cm, W. 59 cm, T. 6 cm.
The stone is a large recumbent cross-slab in good condition and is complete. The face is dressed and contains a ringed Latin cross in false relief. All four terminals have semi-circular expansions, that of the shaft being internally divided to form two petals. The armpits are curved hollows and there is a four-pointed recess at the centre of the cross. To the right of the cross are incised the outline of two shod foot-prints, facing the top of the slab, the left one in the upper right quadrant and

the right one in the lower right quadrant. The text is complete. It is incised in two off-set horizontal lines above the head of the cross and upside down with respect to it.

LETTERING
The text is legible and uses half-uncial script with a maximum letter H. of 6 cm.

TEXT

    COSCRACH

    LAIGNECH

INTERPRETATION

The text is in Irish and reads *Coscrach Laignech*, 'Cosgrach the Leinsterman'.

DISCUSSION

There are a number of unusual features about this slab. The form of the cross is unique at Inishcaltra. As Macalister pointed out, the base echoes the upper half of the design at the crossing. The foot-prints are also unparalleled on a cross-slab. Macalister suggested that they might indicate that the person commemorated died while on pilgrimage to the island (1916-17, 153). They might be indicative of his origin as an outsider, which is made explicit by the epithet *Laignech*. The use of such an ethnic label is not found anywhere else in Ireland. It may be significant that no prayers are asked on his behalf, this being the only large inscribed cross-slab on the island to lack the *or(óit) do* formula.

Attempts have been made, for example by Lionard (1961, 162), to identify Coscrach on the stone with the Coscrach *truaghán*, 'the wretched', anchorite of Inishcaltra, whose death is recorded s.a. 898 (Annals of the Four Masters: O'Donovan 1851, 556-7). Macalister maintained that this was rather early for the style of the slab, preferring instead to identify him as the much later Coscrach, son of Angid and Bishop of Killaloe, who died in 1038 (Macalister 1906, 305). Inishcaltra and Killaloe were certainly closely linked but a Leinster origin for this Coscrach is unproven and the name is not uncommon. The identification remains uncertain.

BIBLIOGRAPHY
Deane 1880, 73 and pl. 1, fig. E
Lenihan 1889, 164n and fig.
Wakeman 1890-91a, 274
Macalister 1906, no. 1, pp. 303-6 and fig. 1
Crawford 1912, 229
Macalister 1916-17, no. 31, p. 153 and pl. XX, fig. 6
Macalister 1949a, no. 891, p. 89 and pl. XXXVIII, fig. 891
Lionard 1961, 149, 162 and fig. 18.3
Weir 1980, 108
Swift 1999, 113
de Paor in preparation, list 2, fig. 9

EXAMINED
July 1996 (KF)

Inishcaltra 5: large plain slab

CURRENT LOCATION
This stone is in the Saints' Graveyard, apparently *in situ*, in the middle of a composite kerbed structure of three (formerly five) recumbent slabs.

Saints' Graveyard, Inishcaltra: composite kerbed structure of recumbent slabs (L to R: nos 7, 11, 5, 10)

HISTORY

The stone was first recorded by Deane in 1880 when it was lying in the graveyard in its present position (Deane 1880, pls 1, 2, fig. T).

DESCRIPTION

The current dimensions of the largest piece of stone are:

H. 48 cm, W. 46 cm, T. 6 cm. The complete length would have been *c.* 145 cm. The stone is a large recumbent slab, now broken into three large pieces with several small pieces missing. The stone appears to have been damaged quite considerably since it was first recorded. Deane's drawing shows the stone as complete although in three pieces, one large and two small (Deane 1880, pl. 2, fig. T). Macalister illustrated the stone in two pieces, one large and one small, with a small piece missing (Macalister 1916-17, pl. XX, fig. 9). The large piece has now broken in two and has lost a corner. There is no record or present trace of any carving other than the text and it appears likely that the slab was never decorated. The text is inscribed on what is now the middle one of the three main pieces of stone. The text is incised in a single line along the long axis of the stone. If the west end is taken as the top, it reads vertically down the stone with the bottoms of the letters to the viewer's left. The text is incomplete at the end.

LETTERING

The text uses half-uncial script with a maximum letter H. of *c.* 5 cm. The text is now slightly deteriorated.

TEXT

ŌR̄ DOMACCU[.]–

INTERPRETATION

The text is in Irish and reads ŌR̄ *domaccu–* for *or(óit) do Maccu–*, 'a prayer for Maccu–'. Following the U there is part of the vertical stroke of the next letter (perhaps an I, less probably a U, M or N). After consideration, Macalister dismissed this as 'a mere flaw' (1916-17, 154), but on balance it does appear to be part of a letter. The bottom of the stroke is lost in a patch of wear and the surface of the stone to the right is abraded and no further letters can be read. If this reading is correct, the name could have been one of several beginning 'Mac-Cui', for example Mac-Cuill, Mac-Cuilind, or Mac-Cuirp. (See the **Introduction § 5.3.4** for discussion of the *or(óit) do* formula).

DISCUSSION

The person commemorated has not been identified. As Macalister pointed out, this is the only inscribed stone on the island that contains no cross (Macalister 1916-17, 154). It is part of a compartmentalised grave monument which consisted of a row of five large, recumbent slabs laid parallel and separated from one another by long, low slabs set on edge. Similar edging slabs flanked the head and foot of the row and its outer ends. The southern end of the monument is now rather broken and two recumbent stones are missing. The other three slabs are broken but missing only small pieces. Inishcaltra 5 lies between stones nos 10 and 11. If, as seems likely, this is an original monument, we may assume that the three are more or less contemporary. Stones nos 10 and 11 have virtually identical cross forms, with their heads to the west, with one- and two-line horizontal texts at the west end. This slab, however, contains a text reading vertically down the slab in a single line. Four other slabs from the site have vertically disposed texts; of these, three read down as here (nos 12, 15 and 18) and only one (stone no. 6) has a text reading upwards.

BIBLIOGRAPHY
Deane 1880, pls 1, 2, fig. T
Macalister 1906, no. 9, p. 307 and fig. 8
Macalister 1916-17, no. 32, p. 154 and pl. XX, fig. 9
Macalister 1949a, no. 892, p. 89 and pl. XL, fig. 892
de Paor in preparation, list 2, fig. 31

EXAMINED
July 1996 (KF)

Inishcaltra 6: large cross-slab

This stone is in the Saints' Graveyard, apparently *in situ*. It lies towards the north-east corner of the graveyard and is partially turfed over.

HISTORY

The stone was first recorded by Deane in 1880 when it was lying in the graveyard (Deane 1880, pls 1, 2, fig. W). The stone remains in this position. Macalister noted that the slab had 'recently been defaced by having been utilized as a table on which to mix mortar' when a new cross was being erected (Macalister 1916-17, 155).

DESCRIPTION

The current dimensions of the stone are:
H. 121 cm, W. 80 cm, T. *c.* 7 cm visible. The length of the complete stone would have been *c.* 193 cm.
The stone is a large recumbent cross-slab and is incomplete. When first recorded it was broken in two pieces with one considerable piece, and several smaller ones, missing (Deane 1880, pl. 2, fig. W). The lower of the two large pieces is now missing and the extant portion has suffered some damage to its surface. The face is dressed and is incised with an outline Latin cross. Earlier drawings of the missing portion record that the shaft ended in a rectangular base, open at the bottom

where it met the end of the slab. The text is complete and is incised in one vertical line up the stem of the cross with the bottoms of the letters to the viewer's right. The text begins near the top of the shaft and continues into the upper arm.

LETTERING

The text is legible and uses half-uncial script with a maximum letter H. of 5 cm.

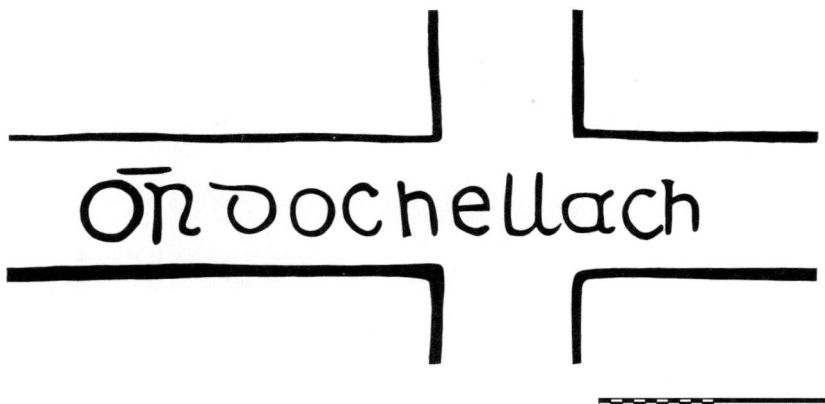

TEXT

ŌR̄ DOCHEL̲L̲ACH

INTERPRETATION

The text is in Irish and reads ŌR̄ *dochellach* for *or(óit) do Chellach*, 'a prayer for Cellach'. As on stone no. 17, the lenition of *c–* following *do* is indicated by the insertion of *h* (See the **Introduction §§5.3.4, 5.3.8** for discussion of both the *or(óit) do* formula and the indication of lenition).

DISCUSSION

Cellach has not been identified. This is one of five stones from the site with a vertically disposed text and the only one to read upwards. Although several slabs, inscribed and uninscribed, have crosses with rectilinear bases, this is the only one with straight rather than curved armpits.

BIBLIOGRAPHY

Deane 1880, pls 1, 2, fig. W
Macalister 1906, no. 11, p. 308 and fig. 10
Macalister 1916-17, no. 35, p. 155 and pl. XXI, fig. 8
Macalister 1949a, no. 893, p. 89 and pl. XL, fig. 893
Lionard 1961, fig. 6.2
de Paor in preparation, list 2, fig. 35

EXAMINED
July 1996 (KF)

Inishcaltra 7: large cross-slab

CURRENT LOCATION

This stone is in the Saints' Graveyard, apparently *in situ*. It lies immediately south of the composite structure of recumbent slabs.

HISTORY

The stone was first recorded by Deane in 1880 when it was lying in the graveyard (Deane 1880, pls 1, 2, fig. R). The stone remains in this position.

DESCRIPTION

The current dimensions of the stone are:
H. 155 cm, W. 50 cm, T. 8 cm.
The stone is a large recumbent cross-slab and is complete except for small pieces broken off its extremities. The face is dressed and is carved in relief with a tall Latin cross on a concave-sided trapezoid base. The arms are short and do not reach the sides of the slab. At the east end of the slab, above the cross and of a piece with it, is a panel which extends the full width of the cross. It contains the text incised in two horizontal lines, upside down with respect to the cross. The stone is now broken at the top right corner, with the loss of the beginning of the text. The drawings by Deane and Macalister show that the stone was then intact at this corner (Deane 1880, pl. 2, fig. R; Macalister 1916-17, pl. XX, fig. 3).

LETTERING

The text is highly deteriorated; it probably uses half-uncial script with a maximum letter H. of *c.* 4 cm.

TEXT

–R̲D̲O̲[C̲A̲..]G̲
–[A̲]L̲

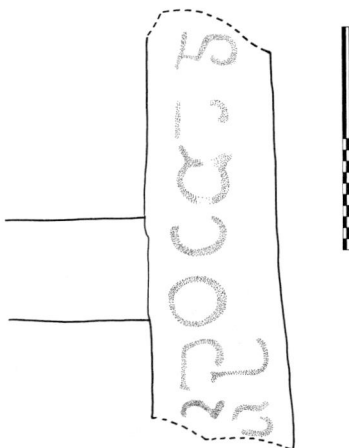

INTERPRETATION

The text is in Irish and reads *–rdo[ca..]g [–a]l* which, on the testimony of
Macalister, may be reconstructed as for *[o]r(óit) do [Cath]g[a]l* 'a prayer for Cathgal'.
However Macalister admitted that the text was 'difficult to decipher, especially the
th, which is scarcely traceable' (Macalister 1916-17, 155). (See the **Introduction
§5.3.4** for discussion of the *or(óit) do* formula).

DISCUSSION

This slab is immediately adjacent to and parallel with the composite grave-
monument discussed above. It is, however, outside the kerb and longer than the
monument is wide. It is clearly, therefore, not part of this structure. The form of
the cross is also seen on two uninscribed slabs (Macalister 1916-17, nos 42 and 44,
p. 155, pl. XXII, fig. 4 and pl. XIX, fig. 1) and, with semi-circular hollow rather
than straight armpits, on two inscribed slabs (nos 8 and 9). The slab is exceptional
in having the head of its cross (and its text) at the east end. It is the only inscribed
slab currently oriented in this direction. Macalister suggested that the distinction
might be because it was the grave of a layman (1916-17, 155), but there is no basis
for identifying Cathgal; moreover no other examples are known to us of the slabs
of layman oriented east-west in distinction to clerics oriented west-east.

BIBLIOGRAPHY

Deane 1880, pls 1, 2, fig. R
Macalister 1906, no.7, p. 307
Macalister 1916-17, no. 45, p. 155 and pl. XX, fig. 3
Macalister 1949a, no. 894, p. 89 and pl. XL, fig. 894

Lionard 1961, 106 and fig. 6.3
de Paor in preparation, list 2, fig. 29

EXAMINED
July 1996 (KF)

Inishcaltra 8: large cross-slab

CURRENT LOCATION

This stone is inside the ruins of St Caimin's church, set upright and cemented against the south wall of the nave, third from the west corner.

HISTORY

This stone was first recorded by Petrie who published a drawing made by Stokes 'from a rubbing made of the stone in the churchyard of Iniscealtra by the late Earl of Dunraven' (Petrie 1878, 44 and pl. XXVII, fig. 59). In 1880 the stone was in the graveyard but not *in situ* (Deane 1880, pl. 2, bottom of page). The stone was inside the church when Macalister saw it, on the south side of the nave in its current position (Macalister 1916-7, 144, 156).

DESCRIPTION

The current dimensions of the stone are:
H. 119 cm, W. 42 cm, T. *c.* 16 cm.
The stone is a large recumbent cross-slab, complete and in quite good condition. The face is dressed and is incised with an outline Latin cross with semi-circular

hollowed armpits. The cross stands on a trapezoid base which has concave sides and is open below. The text is complete and is incised in two horizontal lines above the top of the cross and upside down with respect to it.

LETTERING
The text is legible and uses half-uncial script with a maximum letter H. of c. 4 cm.

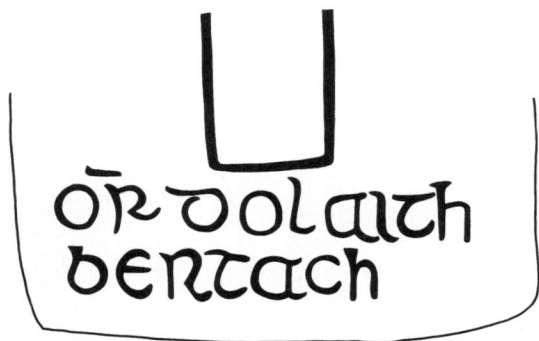

TEXT
O̅R̅ DOLAITH
BERTACH

INTERPRETATION
The text is in Irish and reads *o̅r̅ dolaith bertach* for *or(óit) do (F)laithbertach*, 'a prayer for Flaithbertach'. The lenition of *f–* after *do* is indicated by omission (See the **Introduction §§5.3.4, 5.3.8** for discussion of both the *or(óit) do* formula and the indication of lenition).

DISCUSSION
Flaithbertach has not been identified. The same name is inscribed on stone no. 22 and the form of cross used is identical to that on stone no. 9.

BIBLIOGRAPHY
Petrie 1878, 44 and pl. XXVII, fig. 59
Deane 1880, pl. 2, fig. at bottom of page
Macalister 1906, no. 14, p. 309 and fig. 13
Macalister 1916-17, no. 52, p. 156 and pl. XIX, fig. 5
Macalister 1949a, no. 895, p. 90 and pl. XXXVIII, fig. 895
Lionard 1961, 115, 148 and fig. 11.8
de Paor in preparation, list 1, fig. 14

EXAMINED

July 1996 (KF)

Inishcaltra 9: large cross-slab

CURRENT LOCATION

This stone is in the Saints' Graveyard, apparently *in situ*. It lies to the south of Teampal na bhFear nGonta and is partially turfed-over.

HISTORY

The stone was first recorded by Deane in 1880 when it was lying in the graveyard (Deane 1880, pls 1, 2, fig. O). The stone remains in this position.

DESCRIPTION

The current dimensions of the stone are:
H. 91 cm, W. 61 cm, T. 4 cm. The length of the complete stone would have been c. 145 cm.
The stone is a large recumbent cross-slab, now broken and incomplete. Deane recorded the stone as largely complete although one considerable piece was missing from the bottom and some smaller pieces from the sides; the stone is shown with a large crack across it (Deane 1880, pl. 2, fig. O). The drawing by de Paor shows the stone as having one large piece and four small ones with various

small pieces lost (de Paor in preparation, list 2, fig. 20). All that is now visible is the one large piece, apparently broken along the crack shown by Deane, and this piece is itself broken into two. The face is dressed and is incised with an outline Latin cross with semi-circular armpits on a base which Deane and Macalister depict as trapezoid with concave sides, open at the bottom (Macalister 1916-17, pl. XIX, fig. 7). Most of the text is incised in one horizontal line across the top of the cross (that is, the west end), with one letter inside the upper arm of the cross. The final letter, E, is set above the penultimate letter, presumably due to lack of space. The text is complete and is set upside down with respect to the cross.

LETTERING

The text uses half-uncial script with a maximum letter H. of *c*. 6 cm. The text is rather deteriorated.

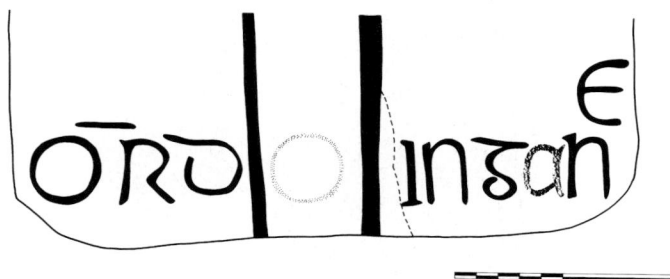

TEXT

O̅R̅ D || [O] || ING[A]N
E

INTERPRETATION

Taking the lower line first, the text, which is in Irish, reads *o̅r̅ d [o] ing[a]n e*. This is presumably for *or(óit) d[o] (F)ing[a]ne*, 'a prayer for Fing[a]ne', with the lenition of *f–* after *do* indicated by omission (See the **Introduction §§5.3.4, 5.3.8** for discussion of both the *or(óit) do* formula and the indication of lenition).

DISCUSSION

Fing[a]ne has not been identified. This slab lies alongside stone no.15 and parallel with no. 18, further along the same row. The form of cross is identical to that on stone no. 8.

BIBLIOGRAPHY

Deane 1880, pls 1, 2, fig. O
Macalister 1906, no. 5, pp. 306-7 and fig. 5
Macalister 1916-17, no. 53, pp. 156-7 and pl. XIX, fig. 7
Macalister 1949a, no. 896, p. 90 and pl. XXXVIII, fig. 896

Lionard 1961, 115 and fig. 11.7
de Paor in preparation, list 2, fig. 20

EXAMINED
July 1996 (KF)

Inishcaltra 10: large cross-slab

CURRENT LOCATION
This stone is in the Saints' Graveyard, apparently *in situ*. It lies at the northern end
of the composite kerbed structure of three (formerly five) recumbent slabs.

HISTORY
The stone was first recorded by Deane in 1880 when it was lying in the graveyard
(Deane 1880, pls 1, 2, fig. U). The stone remains in this position.

DESCRIPTION
The current dimensions of the stone are:
H. 145 cm, W. 42 cm, T. 10 cm.

The stone is a large recumbent cross-slab, broken into two pieces and with several pieces missing. Deane showed damage only at the lower right side (Deane 1880, pl. 2, fig. U), but by the time Macalister illustrated the stone, a piece at the top right corner, containing some of the text, had apparently also become separated (Macalister 1916-17, pl. XXII, fig. 1). The drawing by de Paor shows this piece as missing (de Paor in preparation, list 2, fig. 32) but part of the missing piece is now there, placed in its original position. The face is dressed and is incised with an outline Latin cross with semi-circular armpits and a square base, open at the bottom. The text is incised in two horizontal lines above the top of the cross (that is, the west end) and is set upside down with respect to the cross. The text is now incomplete where part of the stone is lost.

LETTERING

The text uses half-uncial script with a maximum letter H. of 6 cm. The text is slightly deteriorated.

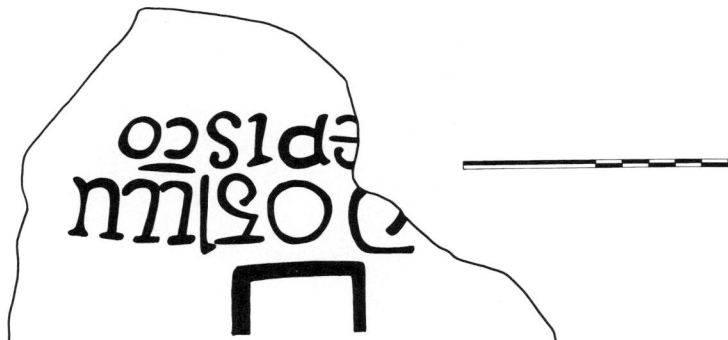

TEXT

   –DOGILLU
   –EPISCŌ

INTERPRETATION

The text is in Irish a nd reads *–dogillu –episcō*. Deane's drawing shows the stone intact with the text apparently reading *ordogilu criepisco* (Deane 1880, pl. 2, fig. U). It is not clear why only one *l* is shown in the first line, unless this is an error. When Macalister examined the stone, the missing piece was apparently still in place although separated from the rest (Macalister 1916-17, pl. XXII, fig. 1). Macalister's reading accords with Deane's, although Macalister read both letters *l* in the first line and saw three abbreviation marks, above the first word and the last two (Macalister 1916-17, 157). From these earlier drawings the text can be reconstructed as *[or(óit)] do Gillu[Cristi] episco(po)*, 'a prayer for Gilla-Crist bishop'. (See the **Introduction §5.3.4** for discussion of the *or(óit) do* formula).

DISCUSSION

Bishop Gilla-Críst cannot be identified. It is interesting to note that the Latin form of his title, *episco(pus)*, was used in preference to the Irish, *epscop*. This title is not common but does occur on two stones from Clonmacnoise. One commemorates *Máel-Iohain ēp̄s̄*, where the title could be Latin or Irish (Macalister 1949a, no. 620, p. 45 and pl. XIII, fig. 620). The other certainly uses the Irish title and commemorates *Epscop Dathal* (Macalister 1949a, no. 640, p. 47 and pl. XV, fig. 640).

This slab is part of a compartmentalised grave monument which consisted of a row of five large recumbent slabs laid in parallel and separated from one another by long, low slabs set on edge. Similar edging slabs flanked the head and foot of the row and its outer ends. The southern end of the monument is rather broken and two recumbent stones are missing. The other three slabs are broken but lack only small pieces. Inishcaltra 10 is at the northern end of the group next to the cross-less slab no. 5. The following slab (no. 11) is incised with a very similar form of cross although the cross on this narrower slab no. 10 is slimmer, with an elongated upper arm. Both slabs have horizontal texts at the west end above the top of the cross, while the text on the middle slab, no. 5, reads vertically downwards. All are inscribed with the *or(óit) do* formula. If, as seems likely, this is an original monument we may assume that these three slabs are more or less contemporary.

BIBLIOGRAPHY

Deane 1880, pls 1, 2, fig. U
Macalister 1906, no. 10, pp. 307-8 and fig. 9
Macalister 1916-17, no. 58, p. 157 and pl. XXII, fig. 1
Macalister 1949a, no. 897, p. 90 and pl. XXXIX, fig. 897
Swift 1999, 112-13
de Paor in preparation, list 2, fig. 32

EXAMINED

July 1996 (KF)

Inishcaltra 11: large cross-slab

CURRENT LOCATION

This stone is in the Saints' Graveyard, apparently *in situ*. It lies at the southern end of a composite kerbed structure of three (formerly five) recumbent slabs.

HISTORY

The stone was first recorded by Deane in 1880 when it was lying in the graveyard (Deane 1880, pls 1, 2, fig. S). The stone remains in this position.

DESCRIPTION

The current dimensions of the stone are:
H. 139 cm, W. 56 cm, T. 9 cm.
The stone is a large recumbent cross-slab, complete except for a small piece broken off the bottom left corner and a more substantial piece off the top right corner; unfortunately text is lost from the missing top corner. The stone is in substantially the condition that it was when Deane drew it (Deane 1880, pl. 2, fig. S). The face of the slab is dressed and is incised with an outline Latin cross with semi-circular armpits and a square base, closed at the bottom. The text is incised in one horizontal line above the top of the cross (that is, the west end), and is set upside down with respect to the cross. The text is now incomplete where part of the stone is lost.

LETTERING

The text is legible and uses half-uncial script with a maximum letter H. of 6 cm.

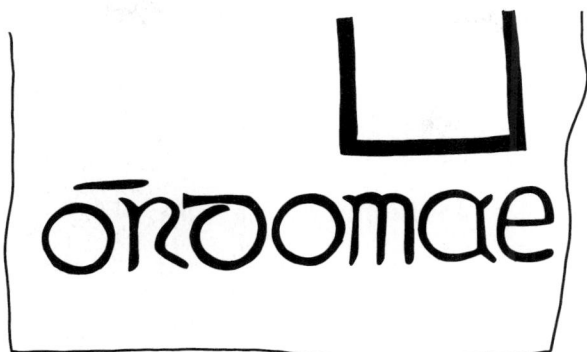

TEXT

ŌR̄DOMAE–

INTERPRETATION

The text is in Irish and reads *ōr̄domae–* for *or(óit) do Máe–*, 'a prayer for Máe–'. Macalister read the letter after *mae* as *l* (Macalister 1916-17, 157); this is what we might expect, to form a personal name of the type *Máel–*. However there is no sign of the letter *l* on the stone today, nor is it shown on Deane's drawing (Deane 1880, pl. 2, fig. S). (See the **Introduction §5.3.4** for discussion of the *or(óit) do* formula).

DISCUSSION

The person commemorated cannot be identified. This slab is part of a compartmentalised grave monument which consisted of a row of five large recumbent slabs laid in parallel and separated from one another by long, low slabs set on edge. Similar edging slabs flanked the head and foot of the row and its outer ends. The southern end of the monument is now broken and two recumbent stones are missing. The other three slabs are broken but missing only small pieces. This slab is at the southern end of the group next to the cross-less slab no. 5. The slab at the northern end, stone no. 10, has a very similar form of cross to this stone. Both slabs have horizontal texts at the west end above the top of the cross, while the text on the middle slab, no. 5, reads vertically downwards. All are inscribed with the *or(óit) do* formula. If, as seems likely, this is an original monument, we may assume that these slabs are more or less contemporary.

BIBLIOGRAPHY

Deane 1880, pls 1, 2, fig. S
Macalister 1906, no. 8, p. 307 and fig. 7
Macalister 1916-17, no. 59, p. 157 and pl. XXII, fig. 2

Macalister 1949a, no. 898, p. 90 and pl. XXXVIII, fig. 898
Lionard 1961, 115 and fig. 11.6
de Paor in preparation, list 2, fig. 30

EXAMINED

July 1996 (KF)

Inishcaltra 12: large cross-slab

CURRENT LOCATION

This stone is in the Saints' Graveyard, apparently *in situ*. It lies beside the west door of the ruined Teampal na bhFear nGonta and is partially turfed over.

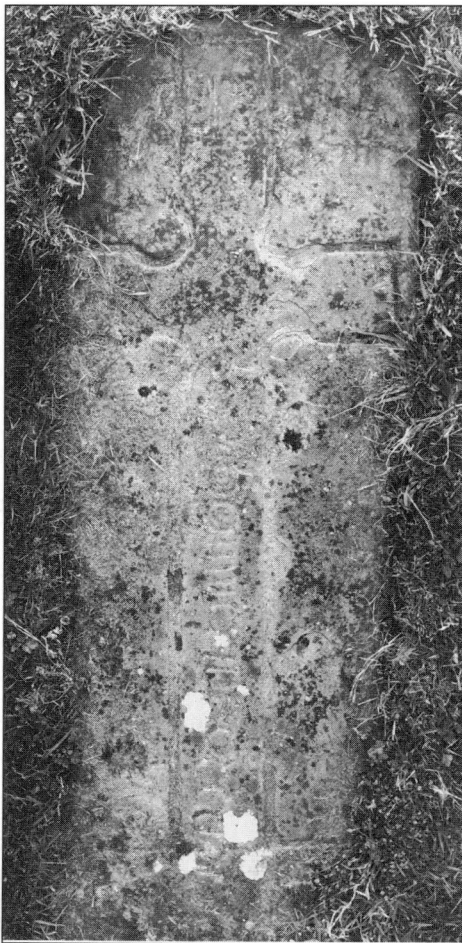

HISTORY

The stone was first recorded by Deane in 1880 when it was lying in the graveyard (Deane 1880, pls 1, 2, fig. K). The stone remains in this position.

DESCRIPTION

The current dimensions of the stone are:
H. 127 cm, W. 51 cm, T. 8 cm visible.
The stone is a large recumbent cross-slab, complete but with some delamination of the carved surface. It is in substantially the condition that it was when Deane drew it (Deane 1880, pl. 2, fig. K, see also Macalister 1916-17, pl. XXII, fig. 3). The face of the slab is dressed and is incised with an outline Latin cross with semi-circular hollow armpits. It stands on a rectangular base, open below, with a faint line separating the shaft from the base. There is a broad recessed band round the perimeter of the slab. The head of the cross is to the west and the text, which is complete, is incised in one vertical line down the shaft with the bottoms of the letters to the viewer's left. The text begins at the top of the shaft and ends within the base. The penultimate letter straddles the line at the bottom of the shaft.

LETTERING

The text uses half-uncial script with a maximum letter H. of *c.* 5 cm. The text is slightly deteriorated.

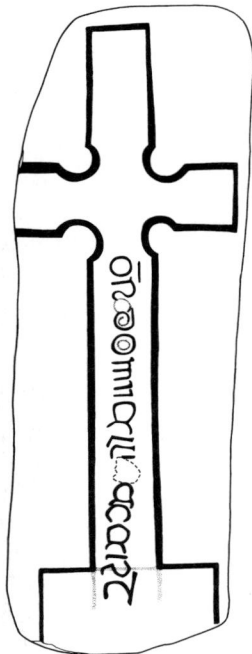

TEXT

ŌR̄DOMNALL[–]ACART

INTERPRETATION

The text is in Irish and reads ōr̄domnall[–]acart for or(óit) [do] Domnall [s]acart, 'a prayer for Domnall the priest'. The do has been omitted, presumably through haplography, and an attempt has been made to correct the error. There is the faint trace of the round bowl of a letter (D or O) following the first R but this has not been finished. Macalister suggested that the omitted DO had been supplied in smaller letters above the existing letter D (Macalister 1916-17, 157 and pl. XXII, fig. 3), but this appears to be damage to the stone, not further lettering. It is possible, however, that the missing letters have been added inside the D and O of the main text. Macalister read the final word as sacart, 'priest', with the S on its side. The letter read by Macalister as S is now illegible but this interpretation is contextually likely. (See the **Introduction §5.3.4** for discussion of the or(óit) do formula).

DISCUSSION

The form of the cross is paralleled on stones nos 10 and 11 and on a number of uninscribed slabs (Macalister 1916-17, pl. XXII). The feature of the line separating shaft from base is found on inscribed slab no. 14, although the sides of its base are not parallel as here. The omission of do and the clumsy over-laying of text and base-line suggests a certain lack of planning by the inscriber. This is one of two slabs indicating the clerical office of the person commemorated, the other being no. 10; see also the free-standing cross, no. 2. Domnall the priest has not been identified.

BIBLIOGRAPHY

Deane 1880, pls 1, 2, fig. K
Macalister 1906, no. 3, p. 306 and fig. 3
Macalister 1916-17, no. 60, p. 157 and pl. XXII, fig. 3
Macalister 1949a, no. 899, p. 90 and pl. XL, fig. 899
Lionard 1961, 115 and fig. 11.9
Swift 1999, 112-13
de Paor in preparation, list 2, fig. 15

EXAMINED

July 1996 (KF)

Inishcaltra 13: large cross-slab

This stone is inside the ruins of St Caimin's church, set upright and cemented against the north wall of the nave in its west corner.

HISTORY

The stone was first recorded in 1837 when Wakeman drew it for Petrie (Petrie 1878, 44 and pl. XXVII, fig. 57). In 1880 the stone was in the graveyard but not *in situ* (Deane 1880, pl. 2, fig. at bottom of page). The stone was inside the church, in its present position on the north side of the nave, when Macalister saw it (Macalister 1916-7, 144, 158).

DESCRIPTION

The current dimensions of the stone are:
H. 149 cm, W. 59 cm, T. 7 cm.
The stone is a large recumbent cross-slab, complete and well-preserved. The face of the slab is dressed and is incised with an outline Latin cross with semi-

circular hollow armpits and open terminals. There is a pellet in each of the four hollows. The cross rests on a rectangular base, open below. The outline of the cross is formed by a broad flat band which makes the cross itself stand out in false relief. The text is complete; it is incised in two horizontal lines above the cross and inverted with respect to it.

LETTERING

The text is legible and uses half-uncial script with a maximum letter H. of 4 cm. The form of the M of *macc*, with the left-hand stroke curving round to meet the middle stroke, is unusual.

TEXT

ŌR̄DODIARMAIT
MACCDELBAID

INTERPRETATION

The text is in Irish and reads ōr̄*dodiarmait maccdelbaid* for *or(óit) do Diarmait macc Delbaid*, 'a prayer for Diarmait macc Delbaid'. (See the **Introduction §5.3.4** for discussion of the *or(óit) do* formula).

DISCUSSION

This fine cross is a variant of a form common on Inishcaltra (Macalister 1916-17, pl. XXII). It is the only slab at the site to give the filiation of the deceased. The Annals record the names of two Diarmaits associated with Inishcaltra. The later Diarmait, whose death is recorded *s.a.* 951, was a bishop but his father's name is given as *Caicher* (Annals of the Four Masters: O'Donovan 1851, 668-9). The filiation of the earlier Diarmait, an abbot, is not given but his death, recorded *s.a.* 762, seems rather early for a slab of this form (Annals of Inisfallen: Mac Airt 1951, 112-13). We cannot follow Lionard in ascribing a mid-eighth century date to this slab (1961, 159) and Diarmait macc Delbaid remains unidentified.

BIBLIOGRAPHY

Petrie 1878, 44 and pl. XXVII, fig. 57
Deane 1880, pl. 2, fig. at bottom of page
Macalister 1906, no. 13, p. 309 and fig. 12
Macalister 1916-17, no. 62, p. 158 and pl. XX, fig. 5
Macalister 1949a, no. 900, p. 90 and pl. XL, fig. 900
Lionard 1961, 115, 148, 159 and fig. 11.5
Swift 1999, 113
de Paor in preparation, list 1, fig. 20

EXAMINED

July 1996 (KF)

Inishcaltra 14: large cross-slab

CURRENT LOCATION

This stone is in the Dúchas depot in Athenry.

HISTORY

According to Petrie, the stone was 'in the churchyard' in 1837 when Wakeman drew it for him (Petrie 1878, 44 and pl. XXVII, fig. 58). In 1880 Deane recorded the stone as 'Tomb Stone found in church' (Deane 1880, pl. 6, stone not numbered). The stone was still inside the church when Macalister saw it, on the south side of the nave (Macalister 1916-17, 144, 158). In August 1982 it was exhibited at Mountshannon, Co Clare, and when the exhibition ended, was placed for safe keeping in the Dúchas depot in Athenry (Pat Herity, pers. com.)

DESCRIPTION

The current dimensions of the stone are:
H. 96 cm, W. 38 cm, T. 6.5 cm.
The stone is a large recumbent cross-slab of slightly irregular shape. It is complete and well-preserved although the edges have crumbled a little. Deane's drawing suggests that the slab was in substantially the same state then as now (Deane 1880, pl. 6). The face of the slab is dressed and is deeply incised with an outline Latin cross with semi-circular armpits which rests on a trapezoid base. The shaft is separated from the base by a horizontal line. The slab tapers to the foot which has irregularly chamfered corners. The cross-base has been shaped to fit neatly into the available space. The text is complete; it is incised in two horizontal lines above the cross and is inverted with respect to it.

LETTERING

The text is legible and uses half-uncial script with a maximum letter H. of 3.5 cm. The lettering is carefully laid out to ensure that the lower line, although consisting of fewer characters, fills the same space as the upper line.

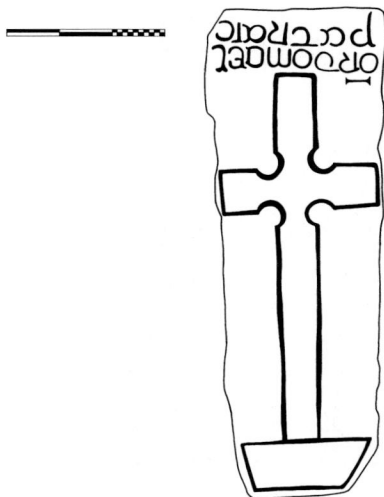

TEXT

ŌṞDOMAEL
PATRAIC

INTERPRETATION

The text reads ōṛdomael patraic for or(óit) do Máel Pátraic, 'a prayer for Máel Pátraic'. (See the **Introduction §5.3.4** for discussion of the or(óit) do formula).

DISCUSSION

This is one of the smaller and narrower of the large slabs at Inishcaltra. The form of the cross used is essentially the same as that found on slabs nos 10, 11 and 12 and is closely related to the cross on slab no. 13. The feature of the short line dividing the shaft and base recurs on slab no. 12. Máel Pátraic has not been identified.

BIBLIOGRAPHY

Petrie 1878, 44 and pl. XXVII, fig. 58
Deane 1880, pl. 6, stone not numbered
Macalister 1906, no. 16, p. 310 and fig. 15
Macalister 1916-17, no. 63, p. 158 and pl. XIX, fig. 8
Macalister 1949a, no. 901, p. 91 and pl. XXXVIII, fig. 901
Lionard 1961, 115 and fig. 11.14
de Paor in preparation, list 1, fig. 5

EXAMINED

July 1996 (KF)

Inishcaltra 15: large cross-slab

CURRENT LOCATION

This stone is in the Saints' Graveyard, apparently in situ. It lies to the south of Teampal na bhFear nGonta and is partially turfed over.

HISTORY

The stone was first recorded by Deane in 1880 when it was lying in the graveyard (Deane 1880, pls 1, 2, fig. N). The stone remains in this position.

DESCRIPTION

The current dimensions of the stone are:
H. 177 cm, W. 52 cm, T. 6 cm.
The stone is a large recumbent cross-slab, complete but now in a poor state of preservation. The face of the slab is incised with an outline Latin cross with semi-circular hollow armpits. The head of the cross is to the west. The lower part of the shaft is now very worn but the drawings by Deane and Macalister show the cross standing on an incised and roughly triangular base. These drawings also show two horizontal lines running from each side of the cross, just above the base, to the edges of the stone (Deane 1880, pl. 2, fig. N; Macalister 1916-17, pl. XX, fig. 1). The text is now incomplete. It is incised in one vertical line down the shaft of the cross with the bottoms of the letters to the viewer's left.

LETTERING

The text uses half-uncial script with a maximum letter H. of *c*. 5 cm. The text is now rather deteriorated.

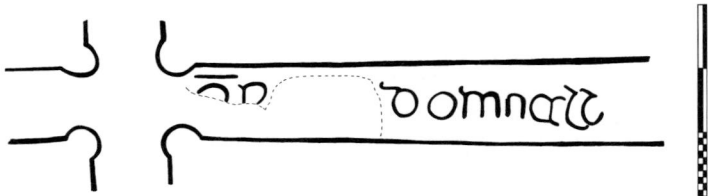

TEXT

O̅R̅ [–] ᴅOMNALL

INTERPRETATION

The text is in Irish and reads *o̅r̅ [–] domnall* for *or(óit) [do] Domnall*, 'a prayer for Domnall'. (See the **Introduction §5.3.4** for discussion of the *or(óit) do* formula).

DISCUSSION

This slab lies immediately to the south of slab no. 9 and parallel to slab no. 18 which lies further to the north in the same row. Stone no. 15 is comparatively long and slim. The form of the cross used is similar to that on stone no. 8, although the side arms do not extend to the edge of the slab. In this respect it is closer to the cross on slab no. 7 which, however, does not have hollow armpits. Domnall has not been identified.

BIBLIOGRAPHY

Deane 1880, pls 1, 2, fig. N
Macalister 1906, no. 4, p. 306 and fig. 4
Macalister 1916-17, no. 66, p. 158 and pl. XX, fig. 1
Macalister 1949a, no. 902, p. 91 and pl. XL, fig. 902
Lionard 1961, 115 and fig. 11.12
de Paor in preparation, list 2, fig. 19

EXAMINED

July 1996 (KF)

Inishcaltra 16: large cross-slab

CURRENT LOCATION

This stone is in the Saints' Graveyard, apparently *in situ*. It lies at the western edge of the graveyard and is partially turfed over.

HISTORY

The stone was first recorded by Deane in 1880 when it was lying in the graveyard (Deane 1880, pls 1, 2, fig. F). The stone remains in this position.

DESCRIPTION

The current dimensions of the stone are:
H. 116 cm, W. 43 cm, T. 5 cm visible.
The stone is a large recumbent cross-slab, complete except for a piece lost from the top right corner. The face of the slab is dressed and is incised with an outline Latin cross with semi-circular hollow armpits. The upper arm and shaft are open. The side arms meet the framing lines which run the length of the slab. The cross sits on a base of unusual shape carved in low relief; it consists of an inverted triangle with large flat bosses at the upper corners and rounded apex below. The end of the slab is shaped to a rounded point. The text is incised in two horizontal lines across

the top of the cross with the H inside the open cross-arm. A small part of the text is lost where the corner of the stone is broken off; the earliest drawing shows this corner missing (Deane 1880, pl. 2, fig. F).

LETTERING

The text uses half-uncial script with a maximum letter H. of *c.* 5 cm. The text is slightly deteriorated.

TEXT

S̲E̲C̲ || H̲ || N̲A̲ILL
[–]DOMAEL

INTERPRETATION

The text is in Irish. Taking the lower line first, the text reads *[–]domael sec h naill* for *[or(óit)] do Máel Sechnaill*, '[a prayer] for Máel-Sechnaill'. (See the **Introduction §5.3.4** for discussion of the *or(óit) do* formula).

DISCUSSION

This is one of the shorter of the large recumbent cross-slabs. The cross is markedly slim and the form of the base unique. The use of a frame is also somewhat unusual. Only two other inscribed slabs (nos 17 and 18) have a frame, although there are several uninscribed slabs which do (see for example Macalister 1916-17, pl. XIX, fig. 9 and pl. XX, figs 4, 7). As with stone no. 9, the text on this stone is placed not above the cross but across its upper arm, with a letter inside the cross-arm. Three other inscribed slabs contain two-line texts in which the person's name is split over two lines (slabs nos 8, 10, 14) but this is the only one to have the second line above the first. It is possible that the inscriber was unsure as to whether there was sufficient space for two lines beyond the cross, and so carved the second line above rather than below the first. Máel-Sechnaill has not been identified.

BIBLIOGRAPHY

Deane 1880, pls 1, 2, fig. F
Macalister 1906, no. 2, p. 306 and fig. 2
Macalister 1909, 68
Macalister 1916-17, no. 67, p. 159 and pl. XIX, fig. 11
Macalister 1949a, no. 903, p. 91 and pl. XXXVIII, fig. 903
Lionard 1961, 115-16, 148 and fig. 11.11
de Paor in preparation, list 2, fig. 11

EXAMINED

July 1996 (KF)

Inishcaltra 17: medium-sized cross-slab

CURRENT LOCATION

This stone is now lost.

HISTORY

The stone was first recorded in 1842 by Wakeman who drew it for Petrie (Petrie 1878, 43). However the drawing reproduced by Petrie (fig. 56a: see illustration below) is signed 'Jewitt' and is identical to the similarly signed drawing reproduced by Quin (Quin, C. W. 1865, 164 and fig.). This drawing was also reproduced by E. R. W. Quin, who noted that the drawing had been made by L. Galway and engraved by D. Jewitt (Quin, E. R. W. 1877, ix, 57). In 1865 the stone was in Adare Manor. Quin stated that it 'was brought, some years ago, from Inis-cealtra' (Quin, C. W. 1865, 164 and fig.). Macalister recorded that the stone had been taken to Adare Manor but that he himself had not seen it (Macalister 1916-17, 161-2). In 1949 he repeated that the stone was at Adare (Macalister 1949a, 91), as did Lionard in 1961 (Lionard 1961, 129n), although it is not certain if Lionard had independent information or was repeating Macalister's statement. There is no trace of the stone at Adare Manor, now a hotel, and it must be assumed to be lost.

DESCRIPTION

The description, lettering and text are taken from the drawing reproduced by Quin (Quin, C. W. 1865, 164 and fig.). Quin gave the dimensions of the stone as '2 ft. long, by 1 ft. 6 in. broad' (Quin, C. W. 1865, 164), that is, 60 cm by 45 cm.

Quin's drawing shows the stone as broken at the top. The illustrated face contained a Latin cross formed from two strands of interlace with a triquetra knot at its extremities; however the upper limb of the cross was almost entirely missing. The cross was set inside a single-line rectangular frame. The text was set below the cross outside the frame in one horizontal line and appears from the drawing to have been complete.

LETTERING

The text used half-uncial script and appears from the drawing to have been quite legible. The letter H. is not known.

TEXT

ŌR̄DOCHUNN

INTERPRETATION

The text was in Irish and read ōr̄dochunn for or(óit) do Chunn, 'a prayer for Conn'. As on stone no. 6, the lenition of c– following *do* is indicated by the insertion of *h* (See the **Introduction §§5.3.4, 5.3.8** for discussion of both the or(óit) do formula and the indication of lenition).

DISCUSSION

To judge from the extant design, this slab when complete would have been similar in size to the small cross-slabs (nos 20-22). Like them it is carved with a cross of elaborate form enclosed by a frame. Unlike them its text is of the or(óit) do formula, not simply a personal name. The form of the interlace cross is identical to that on the much larger inscribed slab from Scattery Island, at the mouth of the Shannon.

Conn has not been identified. Macalister (1916-17, 162n) suggested Conn ua Sinnaich, whose death on Inishcaltra is recorded in the Annals of Inisfallen *s.a.* 1033 (Mac Airt 1951, 200-201), not in 1016 as Macalister stated. However, an eleventh-century date seems rather late for a cross of this type. Quin considered the stone 'as containing the name of Quin' (Quin, C. W. 1865, 164) which may explain why only this stone was removed from Inishcaltra to Adare Manor, the seat of the Quin family.

BIBLIOGRAPHY

Quin, C. W. 1865, 164 and fig.
Quin, E. R. W. 1877, 57 and fig.
Petrie 1878, 43 and fig. 56*a*
Wakeman 1891, 183 and fig.
Macalister 1906, no. 20, pp. 305, 310
Crawford 1912, 229
Macalister 1916-17, no. 81, pp. 161-2 and pl. XXIV, fig. 3
Macalister 1949a, no. 904, p. 91 and pl. XXXVIII, fig. 904
Lionard 1961, 129 and fig. 26.5

Inishcaltra 18: large cross-slab

CURRENT LOCATION

This stone is in the Saints' Graveyard, apparently *in situ*. It lies near the southern entrance of Teampal na bhFear nGonta and is partially turfed over.

HISTORY

The stone was first recorded by Deane in 1880 when it was lying in the graveyard (Deane 1880, pls 1, 2, fig. Q). The stone remain in this position.

DESCRIPTION

The current dimensions of the stone are:
H. 176 cm, maximum W. 45 cm. The stone is so far into the ground that its thickness cannot be measured.
The stone is a large recumbent cross-slab which tapers to the foot. It is complete but in a poor state of preservation. The face of the slab is dressed and is incised with a double-outline Latin cross with semi-circular hollow armpits. Traces of ornament can be made out in the upper quadrants. This is a chequered pattern formed from stepped lozenges with cruciform cores. A single such stepped lozenge occupies the extreme top of the upper cross-arm before the first letter of the inscription. The long axes of the slab, at least, appear to have been framed with a single line. Only parts of the top three cross-arms and the top of the shaft can now be made out. The drawings by Deane and Macalister suggest that even then it was very worn (Deane 1880, pl. 2, fig. Q; Macalister 1916-17, pl. XXIII, fig. 6). The text is incised inside the top of the upper cross-arm (that is, the west end of the slab). It is in one line and reads vertically down the shaft with the bottoms of the letters to the viewer's left. Only that part of the text above the cross-arms is now visible.

LETTERING

The text probably uses half-uncial script with a maximum letter H. of *c.* 5 cm. The text is highly deteriorated and little of it can be read.

TEXT

O̅R̅ –

INTERPRETATION

The text begins o̅r̅– for or(óit) –, but the rest is illegible. The text has always been very worn. Macalister suggested that the first three of the lost letters might possibly have read dog but described them as 'the merest ghosts' (Macalister 1916-17, 160). They are no longer discernible. The text is in Irish and is likely to have begun or [do –] for oróit [do –], 'a prayer for –'. It could have continued with a personal name beginning with G.

DISCUSSION

The stone is a long thin slab, elaborately decorated, which lies towards the northern end of the same row as slabs nos 9 and 15. Related patterns of stepped or cruciform lozenges are found on some uninscribed slabs (see, for example, Macalister 1916-17, pl. XXIII, fig. 5 and pl. XXIV, fig. 6) but, as Macalister noted, this is the only one of the elaborately ornamented slabs to be inscribed (Macalister 1916-17, 160). Lionard linked these kinds of pattern to designs on eleventh-century metalwork (1961, 149). Two other inscribed slabs (stones nos 12, 15) have texts running vertically down the cross-shaft, although these have texts which begin at the top of the shaft but not, as here, at the top of the upper arm.

BIBLIOGRAPHY

Deane 1880, pls 1, 2, fig. Q
Macalister 1906, no. 6, p. 307 and fig. 6
Macalister 1916-17, no. 74, p. 160 and pl. XXIII, fig. 6
Macalister 1949a, no. 905, p. 91 and pl. XL, figs 905
Lionard 1961, fig. 11.10
de Paor in preparation, list 2, fig. 22

EXAMINED

July 1996 (KF)

Inishcaltra 19: small cross-slab

CURRENT LOCATION

This stone is now lost.

HISTORY

This stone was already lost when it was first recorded in print in 1878; the drawing reproduced there was a 'rough sketch' found by Stokes amongst Petrie's papers (Petrie 1878, 42 and pl. XXVI, fig. 55: see illustration below). Although Macalister is clearly wrong in suggesting that this stone might have been the one described by Lenihan as having been stolen from Inishcaltra in 1888 (see **Inishcaltra 4, History** and Macalister 1906, 304-5), it is indeed possible that it was stolen from the island at some time before 1878.

DESCRIPTION

The description, lettering and text are taken from the drawing published by Petrie (Petrie 1878, pl. XXVI, fig. 55: see illustration below). The size of the stone is unknown since no dimensions are given by Petrie and there is no scale on the drawing.

The stone appears to have been roughly square in shape. The illustrated face contained an equal-armed cross inside a two-line circular frame. Each arm of the cross ended in a pair of inwardly-disposed scrolls. The text was in two lines set horizontally within the top two quadrants of the cross, reading across the vertical limb of the cross. From the drawing, the text appears to have been complete.

LETTERING

The text used half-uncial script and is shown on the drawing as quite legible. The letter H. is not known.

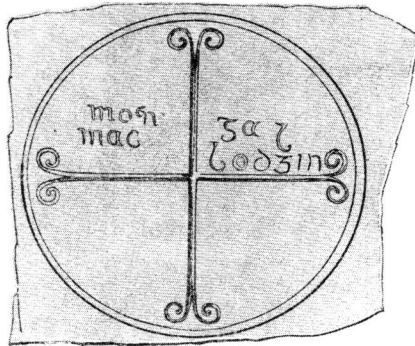

TEXT

MOE/N || GAL
MAC || LODGIN

INTERPRETATION

From the drawing the text appears to have read *moen gal mac lodgin* for *Moengal mac Lodgin*, 'Móengal son of Lodgin' or 'Móengal son of Ladgin'. Petrie suggested that the second name had been incorrectly read, although the suggestion of a Mr Hennessy is also given, that this name might be a form of the name Laidgen (Petrie 1878, 42).

DISCUSSION

One of the small uninscribed cross-slabs is similar to this one, being incised with an equal-armed cross set in a circle (Macalister 1916-17, pl. XVI, fig. 6). It cannot, however, be stone no. 19 as it is uninscribed and there are no scrolls at its terminals. The form of the cross on slab no. 19 is similar to a number of early examples found on the Dingle and Iveragh peninsulas (Sheehan 1990, 160). From

Petrie's sketch the lettering seems somewhat insubstantial and poorly laid out. The lettering might be secondary, although it may have been similar to that on the small cross-slabs, especially nos 20 and 22 which have text laid out in the upper quadrants of the cross. The lack of the *or(óit) do* formula is worthy of note, as is the indication of filiation. Móengal has not been identified.

BIBLIOGRAPHY

Petrie 1878, 42 and pl. XXVI, fig. 55
Crawford 1912, 229
Macalister 1906, no.19, pp. 304-5, 310
Macalister 1916-17, no. 82, p. 162
Macalister 1949a, no. 906, p. 91
Lionard 1961, 106 and fig. 8.11

Inishcaltra 20: small cross-slab

CURRENT LOCATION

This stone is inside the ruins of St Caimin's church. It is set sideways and cemented to the south wall of the nave, second from its east end.

HISTORY

This stone was first recorded in 1880 when it was in the graveyard but not *in situ* (Deane 1880, pl. 2, fig. not numbered, between figs F and U). The stone was inside the church, on the south side of the chancel, when Macalister saw it, but apparently he did not notice the text (Macalister 1916-7, 144, 151).

DESCRIPTION

The current dimensions of the stone are:
H. 67 cm, W. 47 cm, T. 9 cm.
The stone is complete. One face is dressed and incised with a double outline cross of unusual form: an equal-armed cross with semi-circular armpits, combined with a smaller saltire with circular expansions at its terminals. The whole is enclosed within a double frame and the four limbs of the equal-armed cross touch the frame. Where the right and left arms meet the frame there are four double outline billets. The text is complete; it is incised in one horizontal line, divided between the two upper quadrants of the cross.

LETTERING

The text uses half-uncial script with a maximum letter H. of 3 cm. The M is unusual in shape with the side arms curling round to almost meet the medial arm at the bottom. The text is now rather deteriorated.

TEXT

MUIR[–] || A[I]TH

INTERPRETATION

The text reads *muir[–]a[i]th*. The first four letters are reasonably clear, the final two a little less so, but the middle letters are very uncertain. If the penultimate letter were a C rather than a T, then the text could be a form of the male personal name *Muiredach*. The genealogies preserve a female name *Muiriath* (O'Brien 1976, p. 18, §118 a 16), but there appear to be too many letters on the stone for this, and the commemoration of a female would be unexpected. There does not appear to be room for *Muirchertach*.

DISCUSSION

This stone, along with stones nos 21 and 22, form a separate group from the large recumbent slabs. Their common features are, firstly, the slabs are small, irregularly shaped and more square than oblong; secondly, the crosses are equal-armed or short Latin crosses, enclosed in a frame; thirdly, the texts consist of a personal name only, inscribed in the quadrants of the cross or to the side of frame. Similar monuments are also found at Clonmacnoise, where Ó Floinn noted over thirty examples of this type, labelled 'Type A' (1995, 252-3). Ó Floinn acknowledged the hazards of attempting to date these slabs on the basis of coincidences of name recorded in the Annals, a point forcefully reiterated by Swift (1995, 245-9; 1999, 111-18). There is, however, additional circumstantial evidence to suggest that this type of slab was current in the mid-eighth century, although it may been in use earlier and continued later (Ó Floinn 1995, 253). *Muiredach*, if indeed that is the correct reading, has not been identified.

BIBLIOGRAPHY
Deane 1880, pl. 2, fig. not numbered, between figs F and U
Macalister 1916-17, no. 20, p. 151 and pl. XVI, fig. 7
de Paor in preparation, list 1, fig. 7

EXAMINED
July 1996 (KF)

Inishcaltra 21: small cross-slab

CURRENT LOCATION

This stone is inside the ruins of St Caimin's church. It is set upright and cemented to the south wall of the nave, fourth from its east end.

HISTORY

This stone was first recorded in 1880 when it was in the graveyard but not *in situ* (Deane 1880, pl. 2, fig. not numbered, between figs H and S). The stone was inside the church, on the north side of the chancel, when Macalister saw it, but apparently he did not notice the text (Macalister 1916-7, 144, 152). Lionard also failed to record the text (Lionard 1961, fig. 10.8).

DESCRIPTION

The current dimensions of the stone are:
H. 39 cm, W. 53 cm, T. 5 cm.
The stone is complete. One face is dressed and is incised with an equal-armed cross with slim arms and square expansions at the terminals and crossing. It is enclosed by a double outline frame. The upper right quadrant is filled with an interlace knot and there is a key pattern filling the lower right quadrant. The two quadrants on the left are filled with the same pattern, a hybrid key pattern with an interlace loop. All four patterns have a strong diagonal axis which forms a saltire in the angles of the main cross. The text is incised in one horizontal line and is probably complete. It is set outside and to the right of the frame, just below the cross-arm of the cross.

LETTERING

The text uses half-uncial script with a maximum letter H. of *c.* 2.5 cm. The text is now rather deteriorated.

TEXT
    DERM–

INTERPRETATION

The text reads *derm–* followed by two or perhaps three letters, possibly AIT, UIT, or AD. It is likely to be a form of the male personal name *Dermait* (*Diarmait*).

DISCUSSION

See above (Inishcaltra 20) for discussion of this type of monument. If the mid-eighth-century date proposed is broadly correct, it is tempting to link this monument with the Abbot Diarmait of Inishcaltra whose death is recorded in the Annals of Inisfallen *s.a.* 762 (Mac Airt 1951, 112-13).

BIBLIOGRAPHY

Deane 1880, pl. 2, fig. not numbered, between figs H and S
Macalister 1916-17, no. 27, p. 152 and pl. XVI, fig. 14
Lionard 1961, 112 and fig. 10.8
de Paor in preparation, list 1, fig. 9

EXAMINED

July 1996 (KF)

Inishcaltra 22: small cross-slab

CURRENT LOCATION

This stone is inside the ruins of St Caimin's church. It is cemented in an inverted position to its south wall, fifth from the east end.

HISTORY

The stone was apparently found by de Paor, probably between 1970 and 1972 during his excavations at Inishcaltra. His drawing shows the slab inverted, suggesting he was unable to decipher the text (de Paor in preparation, list 1, fig. 10).

DESCRIPTION

The current dimensions of the stone are:
H. 51 cm, W. 33 cm, T. 6 cm.
The stone is complete. One face is dressed and incised with an outline Latin cross with square expansions at the terminals and crossing. The cross, which is only slightly taller than it is broad, is enclosed in a double outline frame. The text is incised in two horizontal lines and is complete. It is set inside the upper two quadrants of the cross.

LETTERING

The text uses half-uncial script with a maximum letter H. of 3 cm. The text is now rather deteriorated.

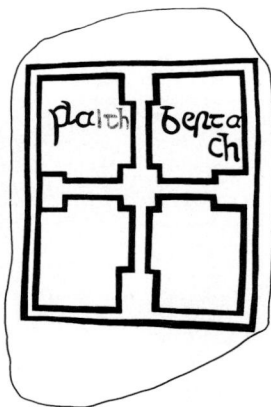

TEXT

FLA[ITH] || BERTA
CH

INTERPRETATION

The text reads *fla[ith] berta ch* for *Fla[ith]bertach*, the male personal name.

DISCUSSION

See above (Inishcaltra 20) for a discussion of this type of monument. Inishcaltra 22 bears a clear resemblance to a series of small grave-markers from Hartlepool and to a lesser extent Lindisfarne (Cramp 1984, pp. 98-101, pls 84-5; pp. 202-6, pls

199-201; Okasha 1971, nos 45-50, pp 77-9 and figs; nos 75-84, pp 94-7 and figs). Flaithbertach has not been identified. According to Hamlin, de Paor also found a stone containing a *chi-rho* (Hamlin 1972, 26; see also de Paor 1977, 99 and fig. 23; Herity 1995 and pl. 6, fig. 1). There is no drawing of any stone with a *chi-rho* amongst de Paor's later drawings, although it is possible that the stone referred to is the small cross-incised slab included there (de Paor in preparation, list 1, fig. 11).

BIBLIOGRAPHY
de Paor in preparation, list 1, fig. 10

EXAMINED
July 1996 (KF)

SITE
The island of Inishcaltra lies in Lough Derg, close to the west shore, some twelve km north of Killaloe. Between 1849 and 1899 the island was in Co. Galway (the background to its transfer and return is given by Macalister 1916-17, 115-16). The monastic site on Inishcaltra was traditionally founded by St Caimin in the first half of the seventh century, but there are annalistic references to ecclesiastical activity at the site in the mid-sixth century. From the mid-eighth century there are annalistic references to abbots and other ecclesiastical personnel, references which continue intermittently until the beginning of the eleventh century. The island was sacked by Vikings in 836 and again in 922. Little is known of the site in the early centuries but by the tenth century it was clearly a major centre. In the eleventh century it was apparently an important cemetery since in 1076 Gormlaith, wife of Tairdelbach ua Briain, was brought to the island for burial (Annals of Inisfallen: Mac Airt 1951, 232-3). The last reference to the site before the fourteenth century is apparently the death recorded there *s.a.* 1111 of Cathasach *cend crábuid Érénd* (see above under Inishcaltra 2). For a summary of the early historical material relating to Inishcaltra, see Macalister 1916-17, 94-107.

   The physical remains on the island consist of the ruins of four churches (St Brigid's, St Caimin's, St Mary's and St Michael's), a round tower, a cell, Teampull na bhFear nGonta, a holy well, a network of earth-works, a small rectangular building of unknown purpose and a landing stage. The churches remained in use during the medieval period: St Brigid's church contains some Romanesque work, there are some late medieval tombstones and St Mary's church has a fifteenth-century window. St Caimin's is an early rectangular building (with corner *antae*) to which a Romanesque chancel has been added (Macalister 1916-17, 122). For a detailed discussion see Macalister 1916-17, 116-143. There are two graveyards, a larger one, 'the Saints Graveyard' to the east of St Caimin's church, and a smaller one beside St Mary's. These are still in use. The enclosing wall of the Saints' Graveyard was ruinous by the 1860s and the current wall was built in 1875. Most of the sculptured stones on the site are still in their earliest recorded, and presumably original, positions. Of the stones gathered into the ruined church of St

Caimin by the Board of Works in the nineteenth century, most came from the Saints' Graveyard although some came from St Mary's. Macalister lamented that no record was kept of which stones came from where (1916-17, 114-15) but it seems that none of the inscribed stones are in this category.

In addition to a number of architectural fragments there are, or were, five *bullaun* stones, thirteen cross-bases or socketed stones (one inscribed), four free-standing crosses (one inscribed) and about eighty carved slabs (twenty inscribed). The slabs were catalogued and illustrated by Macalister 1916-17, 150-163. The slabs fall into two main groups: a smaller group consisting of small, irregularly shaped slabs with elaborate, mostly equal-armed crosses, and a more numerous group of large recumbent grave-covers. Of the latter, about half are incised with full-length Latin crosses while the remainder are plain. Macalister thought they had always been so (1916-17, 144), but it is possible that some at least of the more weathered slabs were originally decorated and/or inscribed. Most of the slabs are oriented with their head to the west.

In the nineteenth century a number of antiquarians visited the island, including Wakeman who drew at least three of the stones in 1837 and 1842 (Petrie 1878, 43-4). In 1852, and again in 1865, Brash visited Inishcaltra (Brash 1866, 21). On his first visit Brash had observed 'in the church [that is, the ruins of St Caimin's church] and around it a number of slabs, with quaint crosses of ancient type, and inscriptions in Irish characters'; by 1865 these had 'all disappeared' except for one uninscribed cross-slab in the chancel (Brash 1866, 15). This uninscribed cross-slab is illustrated by de Paor and shown by him as in the nave of the church (de Paor in preparation, list 1, fig. 25). Presumably the inscribed slabs that Brash had seen in and around the church in 1852 had by 1865 either been moved to the graveyard or covered in 'a mass of rubbish' (Deane 1880, 73). In 1879-80 considerable clearance and repair work was carried out on the island by the Board of Works and many of the inscribed stones were then noticed for the first time (Deane 1880, 73). De Paor conducted extensive excavations on the island between 1970 and 1980 but these remained unpublished at his untimely death (de Paor, in preparation).

GENERAL DISCUSSION

Inishcaltra is one of the small number of important and wealthy Gaelic monasteries which have more than a handful of carved or inscribed grave-slabs. Although there are not as many at Inishcaltra as at Clonmacnoise, Gallen or Iona, the Inishcaltra collection is important because so many of its slabs have been preserved *in situ*. This is in marked contrast to Clonmacnoise, where the majority of slabs have been recovered from secondary locations (often within more modern graves). The Inishcaltra slabs are laid out in closely packed rows oriented with, in most cases, the head to the west (an exception is stone no. 7). Closer study of the slabs and their relative positions may give some clues as to their relative chronology and the growth of the graveyard. A group of slabs near the northern edge of the enclosure, including stones nos 5, 10 and 11, is of particular interest. These are joined together by long, low slabs set on edge at the head and foot and separated by similar slabs placed to form individual compartments.

Of the fifteen inscribed large recumbent slabs (see pp. 105–6), five have texts disposed along the long axis of the slab, that is, vertically. One of these slabs, no. 5, has no cross but reads from the west end down. Of the cross-incised examples, three read down the shaft (nos 12, 15, 18) and only one (no. 6) reads up the shaft. The other inscribed recumbent slabs have the text inscribed across the stone, that is, horizontally, in either one or two lines, depending on the length of the text and the width of the slab. The ten stones with horizontal texts (nos 3, 4, 7, 8, 9, 10, 11, 13, 14, 16) all have the text placed at the end of the slab above the head of the cross and inverted relative to it. The examples which are still *in situ* give us some sense of how these stones functioned as monuments. Since the inscription lay at the west end, someone kneeling to pray at the head of the slab would face east down the length of the slab (over the body) and be able to read the text the right way up. With one exception (no. 4), all of the large recumbent slabs are inscribed with the formula *or(óit) do N.*, 'a prayer for N.', which is found throughout Ireland. The position of the cross on these ten slabs with horizontal texts makes it clear that the inscription was part of the original design, not a later addition. One of them (stone no. 7) has indeed a special panel for the text.

The large recumbent slabs vary somewhat in size and shape. The shortest complete slab is 96 cm long and the longest 177 cm, with the average around 140 cm. The widths vary between 38 cm and 61 cm. All the slabs are thus large enough to cover a grave. All are straight-sided and carefully shaped. Lionard commented that their 'severely rectangular shape is very unusual in Irish grave-slabs' and contrasts them with the typically irregular shape of the slabs from Clonmacnoise (Lionard 1961, 148). Some of the slabs, most notably no. 18, taper towards the foot, a feature suggesting a later, possibly twelfth-century, date.

Our state of knowledge regarding the dating of this class of monument is still rudimentary. Nevertheless, the large recumbent slabs at Inishcaltra share several features of shape, cross-form and script which, taken together, imply that most are no earlier than the tenth century, and that the majority may belong to the twelfth century (see Macalister 1916-17, 150-51; Lionard 1961, 149). This, again, is in contrast to Clonmacnoise, where most of the slabs are thought to date from the eighth to the tenth centuries (Ó Floinn 1995, 254). As Ó Floinn noted, only five of the 700 or so slabs at Clonmacnoise have the tapering trapezoidal shape characteristic of the twelfth and thirteenth centuries (1995, 258).

The small slabs constitute a separate group. There are some twelve of these recorded from the site. They are irregularly shaped, typically measuring 60 cm by 40 cm, and are carved with finely executed crosses. The crosses are mostly equal-armed or cross-of-arcs and are usually enclosed within a frame. Each of the extant crosses is of a design unique at the site. Four of the small slabs, nos 19-22, are or were inscribed, in each case the text consisting of a personal name only. This class of monument is found elsewhere, notably at Clonmacnoise (Ó Floinn's 'Type A'), and can probably be dated between the mid-eighth and the mid-ninth century (Ó Floinn 1995, 252-3). These slabs could not have stood in the ground without obscuring some of the carving and they therefore seem likely to have been recumbent. Like the later large recumbent slabs, they were probably funerary monuments laid over graves.

Ó Floinn (1995, 253) noted that 'Type A' slabs are only found from Clonmacnoise and Gallen. The identification of the type at Inishcaltra therefore has important implications for understanding the relationships between monasteries at this period. Macalister commented on the similarity between one of the uninscribed slabs from Inishcaltra and some of the Clonmacnoise slabs (Macalister 1916-17, 152-3). Further parallels can be seen between the form of the cross on Inishcaltra 4 and that on several of the Clonmacnoise slabs (see Lionard 1961, fig. 19).

One slab, Inishcaltra *17, falls between the two groups. It was closer in size to the small slabs but more akin to the large slabs in shape and text; it may also fall between them in date. The other two inscribed stones are Inishcaltra 1 and 2. The text on no. 2, the free-standing cross, probably commemorates an act of patronage, while that on no. 1 labels the monument. Both texts can be seen as authenticating the monuments and, perhaps, as placing them in a liturgical context. In one way or another, all the inscribed texts on the Inishcaltra stones can be viewed as calls to prayer.

The persons commemorated in the texts are all men. In the few cases where status is indicated, these men are ecclesiastics: a bishop (no. 10), a priest (no. 12), chief elder (no. 2). Some of the personal names, for example Gilla-Críst (no. 10) and Máel Pátraic (no. 14), also suggest ecclesiastical personnel. The lack of patronymics is also consistent with eccelsiastics but the two instances where filiation is stated need not imply a secular commemorand. Instead Swift tentatively suggested that the rare instances at Clonmacnoise of grave-slabs with patronymics might commemorate clerics of the scholarly grades (Swift 1999, 116-17). None of the people commemorated at Inishcaltra can be indentified with certainty, but the most secure identification is that of Cathasach on stone 2; he may have been the Cathasach whose death on the island is recorded *s.a.* 1111.

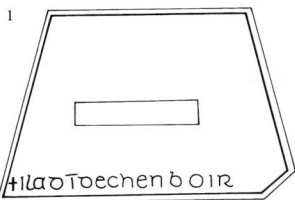

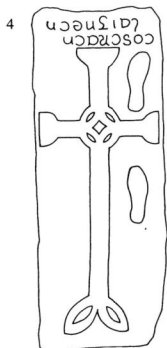

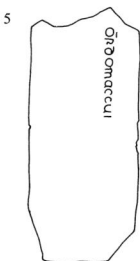

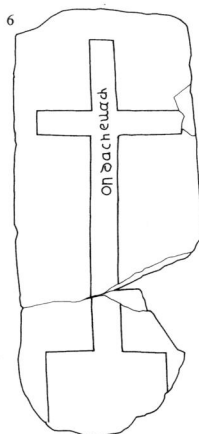

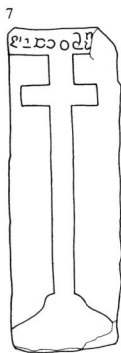

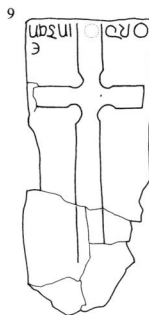

The inscribed stones of Inishcaltra, to a common scale

0 – 50cms

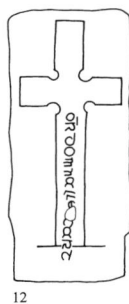

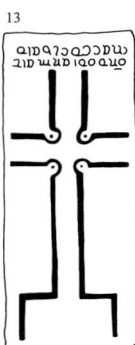

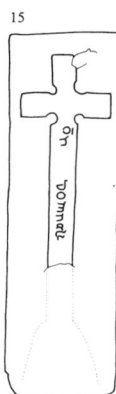

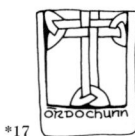

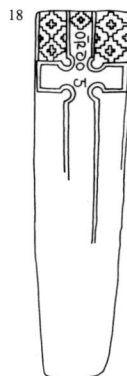

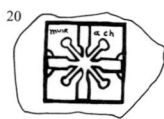

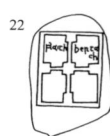

The inscribed stones of Inishcaltra, to a common scale

0 – 50cms

OUGHTMAMA: UCHT MAMA

Site name Church of the Three Colmans
Townland Oughtmama
NGR 12549, 21023
SMR site no. CL003-03201-

One or more inscribed slabs were noted in the late nineteenth century at this early ecclesiastical site. They are now lost and no details are recorded.

CURRENT LOCATION

The stones are now lost.

HISTORY

In 1895 Westropp mentioned that there were 'Several defaced tombs of early date' lying in the chancel of the west church at Oughtmama. One of these bore 'a fragmentary Irish inscription' (Westropp 1895, 284). Westropp's account is in the present tense and the clear implication is that he himself saw the stone, although this is not actually stated. This is made more likely by the fact that neither of the two authorities he cites (Brash 1875 and Quin, E.R.W. 1875-77) mentioned it. Windele visited Oughtmama in September 1861 but made no mention of any inscribed stones (Windele MSS, 12.K.27, p. 506). In a later publication, Westropp noted that 'several slabs, with defaced Irish inscriptions, lie in the chancel' (Westropp 1900-02, 130). Crawford's account (1912, 228) appears to be dependent on Westropp's earlier publication. Killanin and Duignan mentioned 'defaced early gravestones' (1989, 117). In 1992 Swinfen noted that, 'Late in the nineteenth century, when cleaning up the interior of the largest church, the Board of Works found several slabs with carved crosses and Irish inscriptions. None are [sic] in sight today' (Swinfen 1992, 103).

DESCRIPTION

No dimensions, descriptions nor illustrations of the stones have survived.

LETTERING

The script used is not known.

TEXT AND INTERPRETATION

Westropp stated that the text was (or texts were) in Irish but no further details are known (Westropp 1895, 284; 1900-02, 130).

DISCUSSION

In view of the paucity of information, further discussion is impossible.

BIBLIOGRAPHY

Westropp 1895, 283-4
Westropp 1900-02, 130
Crawford 1912, 228
Swinfen 1992, 102-3
Killanin and Duignan 1989, 117

SITE

The early Christian site of Oughtmama is on the northern edge of the Burren, *c.* one km to the south-east of the late twelfth-century Cistercian abbey of Corcomroe. The only physical remains of the early monastery are three ruined churches, the largest and most westerly of which is of nave-and-chancel plan with a flat-headed doorway and a plain Romanesque arch (Harbison 1975, 47). It was in the chancel of this church that Westropp recorded the inscribed slab(s) (Westropp 1895, 284; 1900-02, 130). Traditionally the site is associated with St Colman but little is known of its early history.

SCATTERY ISLAND: INIS CATHAIGH

Site name Teampall Seanáin, St Senan's Church
Townland Scattery Island
NGR 09716, 15232
SMR site no. CL067-02401-

A large recumbent cross-slab, of possibly ninth- or tenth-century date, lies probably *in situ* at this important island monastic site.

CURRENT LOCATION

The stone lies, probably *in situ*, a short distance beyond the west wall of the enclosure known as Leaba Seanáin, to the west of the ruins of Teampall Seanáin, on Scattery Island.

HISTORY

The stone was first recorded and drawn by Windele when he visited the island in July 1855; it was then 'a few feet W of Leaba Senan little ch[urch]' (Windele MSS 12.K.27, p. 139). A drawing of the stone was made by Stokes in 1872 (Petrie 1878, 26 and pl. XVIII, fig. 37). The stone was then 'in the churchyard', although which churchyard is not specified (Petrie 1878, 26). In 1896 Westropp drew the stone, which was lying 'near Temple Senan' (Westropp 1897a, 285), that is, just outside St Senan's church. These descriptions all appear to refer to the slab's current location. Macalister (1949a, 88) stated that he had not examined this stone himself; it is also far from certain that all subsequent people who wrote about the stone had seen it.

DESCRIPTION

The current dimensions of the stone are:
H. 159 cm, W. (maximum) 60 cm.
Since the stone is set flush with the ground, its thickness cannot be measured. The stone is a large recumbent cross-slab of irregular shape, intact and well-preserved. It is oriented north-west / south-east with the head to the north-west. The slab is incised with a Latin cross formed of a two-strand interlace with triquetra knots at each of the terminals. The knot at the base of the shaft is slightly larger than the others. Text a is incised in a single horizontal line above the head of the cross. Text b is incised in four horizontal lines, inverted relative to the cross and to text a. The first two lines are below the foot of the cross, the third line is to the right of the shaft and the fourth line is above the cross on both sides of the shaft. Both texts are complete.

LETTERING

Both texts use half-uncial script and both are legible although worn in places. Text a has smaller lettering than text b; the maximum letter H. of text a is 6 cm and of text b is 14 cm.

TEXT

a   ŌR̄DOMOINACH
b   ŌR̄ DO
    MOENACH
    AITE
    MOG | | ROIN

INTERPRETATION

Text a reads: *ōr̄domoinach* for *or(óit) do Moínach*, 'a prayer for Moínach'. Text b reads: *ōr̄ do moenach aite mog roin* for *or(óit) do Móenach aite Mogróin*, 'a prayer for Móenach tutor of Mogrón'. *Moínach* and *Móenach* are variant spellings of the same name. In an ecclesiastical context, *aite* can mean 'tutor, teacher' (*DIL* s.v.). (See the **Introduction §5.3.4** for discussion of the *or(óit) do* formula).

DISCUSSION

The layout of the carving on this large slab confirms that it was intended as a recumbent monument. As Petrie observed, the relative positions of the inscriptions indicate that text a was the first of the two texts (1878, 26). He thought text b was linguistically later. Macalister thought it 'an orthographical correction' (1949a, 88). The two spellings *Moínach/Móenach* are, however, simply variants with no chronological significance: for the spelling of the diphthong see Thurneysen 1946, pp. 42-43, §§66-7. A third spelling of the same name, *Máenach*, is found on Monaincha 1.

Text b gives the additional information that Moínach was the tutor of Mogrón, but this can scarcely have been the main reason for inscribing this text, since this information could have been added to the end of text a without difficulty. The inverted orientation of text b may be significant. It was suggested above that the layout of text on the large recumbent slabs at Inishcaltra might reflect a devotional practice whereby a person knelt to pray at the head of a grave and, facing east across the body, was then able to read an inverted text the right way up. The second inscription on the Scattery Island slab would facilitate the same practice. Its letters are larger than those of text a and the letters of the furthest lines are larger than those of the nearer lines; thus it is easily read from the head of the slab.

In size, the Scattery Island slab is akin to the large recumbents at Inishcaltra, but its irregular outline contrasts with their carefully shaped straight sides. It is unlike them also in that its cross does not run the full-length of the slab. The cross and text a on the Scattery Island slab resemble the third of the three main types of memorial slab at Clonmacnoise, Ó Floinn's 'Type C' (Ó Floinn 1995, 254-5 and fig. 1). These have *or(óit) do* texts inscribed in horizontal lines above, across or on either side of the upper arms of the cross. This class cannot be closely dated but is likely to belong to the later ninth and tenth centuries. It is also found at other sites associated with Clonmacnoise, such as Gallen, Inisbofin and Clonfert (Ó Floinn 1995, 255). The form of the cross, interlace with triquetra knot terminals, is found on the lost slab Inishcaltra 17 and on the two lost slabs from Tuamgraney, one of which was inscribed. Variants of this form of cross appear elsewhere, for example on two slabs from Glendalough (Macalister 1949a, nos 878, 881, pp. 81-2 and pl. XXXVII, figs 878, 881), and at Clonmacnoise (Macalister 1949a, no. 720, p. 56 and pl. XXXI, fig. 720).

The vast majority of people commemorated on slabs with the *or(óit) do* formula are identified by their given name only (Swift 1999, 113). The tiny minority for whom filiation is indicated are recorded as the sons or grandsons of named fathers and grandfathers. The Scattery Island slab is unique in identifying someone by means of a fosterage relationship. It is unique also, in that the person identified is the senior party in the dyad. Given the ecclesiastical context of the monument, the relationship is likely to have been that of tutor and pupil, a relationship explicitly conceived of in terms of fosterage (*DIL s.v. aite*). Neither *Moínach/Móenach* nor *Mugrón* have been identified. Text b could have been added by Mugrón himself as a pious gesture to his former teacher, a gesture which would itself prompt prayers on his own behalf also. Alternatively, if Mugrón had gone on to become a particularly prominent churchman, the community at Scattery might have supplied the additional information to enhance the deceased's, and thereby their own, prestige. In neither case need there have been a long interval between the carving of the two texts. The position of the second text could, however, reflect an innovation in devotional practice.

BIBLIOGRAPHY

Petrie 1878, 25-6 and pl. XVIII, fig. 37
Westropp 1897a, 285 and fig.
Westropp 1900-02, 170
Crawford 1912, 229
Macalister 1949a, no. 887, 88
Lionard 1961, 129
Harbison 1975, 49
Killanin and Duignan 1989, 226
Swift 1999, 113
Windele MSS 12.K.27, p. 139

EXAMINED

July 1997 (KF)

Scattery Island, at the mouth of the Shannon near Kilrush, has been an ecclesiastical centre since early times. A monastery was reputedly founded here by St Senan in the sixth century, but suffered under the Vikings in the ninth and tenth centuries. Its subsequent fortunes fluctuated until it was largely destroyed in Tudor times (see Harbison 1975, 49; Gwynn and Hadcock 1970, 96-7; Kenney 1979, 364-6). There are visible today the remains of the monastery, including a round tower, of the cathedral and of three other medieval churches. One of these, Teampall Seanáin, or St Senan's church, stands on higher ground to the north of the main group of buildings.

Near the inscribed slab, set against the west wall of the enclosure as a bench, is a large block of gritstone with 'ogham-like scores' (Westropp 1897a, 285). This stone was not included by Macalister in his corpus (Macalister 1945, 1949a). Close examination suggests that it is indeed a much-battered ogham stone. The stone is about 200 cm long, 60 cm wide and 14 cm thick with the inscription cut along the upper outer edge. Faint traces of individual strokes are discernible at various points but the best preserved section is towards the left end where the remains of five neatly parallel strokes of equal length, 6 cm long and 2 cm apart, are visible on the upper surface. These form an ogham letter N. Further to the left, following a gap, are the remains of four similar strokes on the upper surface, an S or part of an N. Ogham stones are not uncommon on early ecclesiastical sites in the peninsulas of the south-west (Moore 1998, 23-5 and fig. 4.1) and one has also been found at Clonmacnoise (Manning and Moore 1991, 10-11 and figs). Petrie also noted an uninscribed cross-slab near Tobar Seanáin, St Senan's well (1878, 25-6) but this has now disappeared.

TUAMGRANEY: TUAIM GRÉINE

Site name Tuamgraney churchyard
Townland Tuamgraney
NGR 16375, 18290
SMR site no. CL028-05802-

A medium-sized recumbent cross-slab, of possibly ninth- or tenth-century date, was found at this early monastic site.

CURRENT LOCATION

The stone is now lost.

HISTORY

The stone was first recorded by Westropp who drew it in 1909 (Westropp 1909, 397 and fig.: see illustration below). Along with another, apparently uninscribed, cross-slab, it was 'unearthed in digging graves' in the churchyard at Tuamgraney and was then still in the graveyard (Westropp 1909, 397). The uninscribed stone was then still partly in the ground and Westropp's drawing suggests that the inscribed one may also have been so. It was still in the graveyard in 1912 (Crawford 1912, 228). In 1947 Macalister recorded that when, some time previously, he had been unable to find the stone at the site, he had sought the assistance of Dr Edward MacLysaght (the authority on Irish names and family history) who had a local connection (Macalister 1947, 156). After an extended search MacLysaght found the slab and sent Macalister a sketch. He took what Macalister described as 'steps to secure that the stone will now be properly cared for on its own site' (1947, 156). The East Clare Heritage Society has copies of correspondence from June 1944 concerning responsibility for the cross-slabs, which presumably arose from MacLysaght's intervention. A letter from H. G. Leask, dated 7 June 1944, explained that the slabs could not be taken into state care since the graveyard was controlled by Clare County Council. The stones were taken to a nearby house where they stayed for some time but then were lost, probably in the 1950s. The East Clare Heritage Society made an extensive search for them but eventually abandoned it as fruitless (Gerard Madden, pers. com.).

DESCRIPTION

The dimensions are taken from Crawford 1912, 228 with reference to the figure in Westropp 1909, 397:
H. *c.* 60 cm, W. *c.* 50 cm, T. unknown.
The description and text are taken from Westropp 1909, 397 and fig. The stone was a slab, apparently broken at the top and either broken at the bottom or set in the ground. One face was incised with a Latin cross formed of a two-strand

interlace, with triquetra knots at the three visible terminals. The text was set in one line in the top left quadrant of the cross, parallel to the upper arm of the cross. It read vertically downwards, with the bottom of the letters to the viewer's left. It is uncertain whether or not the text was complete.

LETTERING

The text used half-uncial script and was legible. The maximum letter H. was *c.* 6.5 cm.

TEXT

[.]ORCHIDE

INTERPRETATION

The text appears to have read *[.]orchide.* Westropp's sketch could permit the third letter to be read as s but MacLysaght interpreted it as R. The first letter was 'rather obscure' (Macalister 1947, 156). Westropp interpreted it as C but MacLysaght read it as D. Westropp's reading gives no obvious sense but MacLysaght's yields *[d]orchide. Dorch(a)ide* is a rare male personal name meaning 'dark', 'gloomy' (c.f. *sorchaide* 'bright', 'brilliant'). It is attested in *Cath Finntrága* where there is a reference to a *Druimdherg mac Dolair mic Dorchaidhi* (Meyer 1885, p. 39, lines 719-20; see also *DIL s.v. dorchaide*). The related name *Dorche,* also rare, is attested in the genealogies (O'Brien 1976, p. 308, §160 b 25).

DISCUSSION

Westropp's sketch shows a straight-sided slab with a slightly uneven upper edge. His rendering of the lower edge is somewhat ambiguous: the stone appears to be sunk into the ground but it could be broken. Macalister reported that MacLysaght's sketch (not reproduced) agreed with Westropp's. Since the slab had been moved when MacLysaght saw it, we may assume that little, if any, of the slab was obscured in Westropp's sketch. It may be that the upper edge was intact and only the bottom edge broken. In order to complete the cross design perhaps a third more of the slab would be needed, implying that it was originally up to *c.* 90 cm long. In size it may be compared with the lost slab Inishcaltra 17 which bore an identical cross. The design that appeared on the second, now lost, slab from Tuamgraney, is seen also on the inscribed slab from Scattery Island (see above).

In the use of an expanded cross-form and the vertical position of the text, the Tuamgraney slab resembles the slabs of the second of the three main groups at Clonmacnoise (Ó Floinn's 'Type B') which have been tentatively dated to the later ninth and tenth centuries (Ó Floinn 1995, 254). The vertical texts on the Clonmacnoise slabs read downwards, which would confirm that it is the base of the Tuamgraney cross which is missing. With only one doubtful exception, however, all the 'Type B' slabs are inscribed with the *or(óit) do* formula while the single-name-only formula predominates among the earlier 'Type A' slabs (Ó Floinn 1995, 253, Table 2). 'Type B' slabs are found at a number of other sites in the vicinity of Clonmacnoise and Ó Floinn suggested that it might be possible to use the distribution of this class of monument 'to indicate the extent of Clonmacnoise influence in the midlands during the 10th century' (1995, 254). Thus the Tuamgraney slab may provide archaeological support for a connection which is well attested in the historical record. Unfortunately (D)orchide, if the interpretation is correct, cannot be identified.

BIBLIOGRAPHY

Westropp 1909, 397 and fig.
Crawford 1912, 228
Macalister 1947, 156
Macalister 1949a, no. 907, p. 92
Lionard 1961, 129

SITE

Tuamgraney, by the shores of Lough Derg, 6.5 km from Inishcaltra, was an important monastery reputedly founded by St Cronán, perhaps the Cronán, abbot of Clonmacnoise who died in 638. There were continuing close connections with Clonmacnoise; several coarbs of Cronán in the tenth, eleventh and twelfth centuries were also coarbs of Ciarán of Clonmacnoise. The obits of several lectors of Tuamgraney in the first quarter of the eleventh century attested to the site's importance as a centre of learning (see, for example, Annals of Inisfallen 1010, 1020: Mac Airt 1951, 180-1, 188-9). A church and round tower were supposedly built in the tenth century. No trace of the round tower remains but the church contains some early features, perhaps dating from the tenth century, as well as some twelfth-century work, and is 'probably the oldest Irish church still in use' (Harbison 1975, 50). For historical references to the site, see Gwynn and Hadcock 1970, 46.

COUNTY CORK

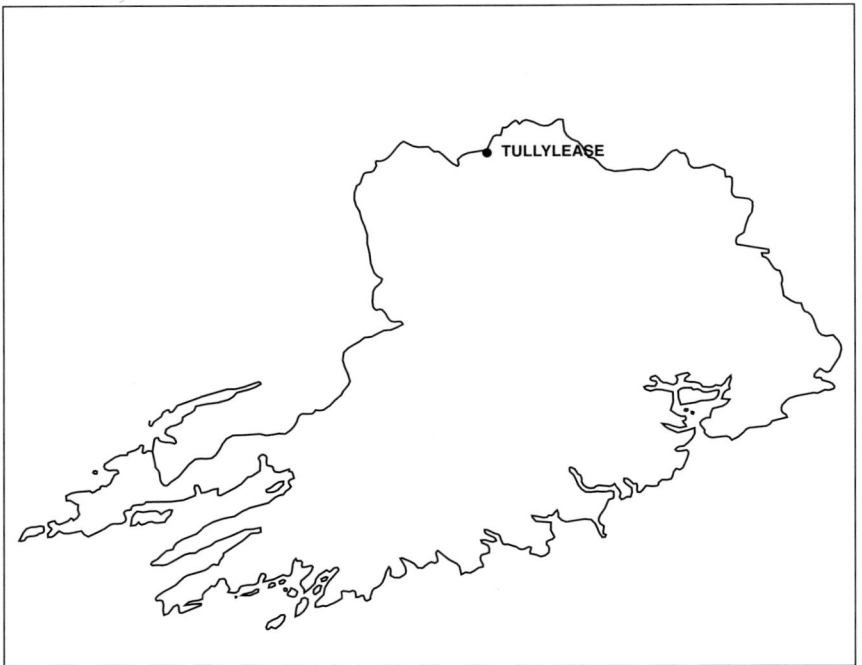

Early Christian inscribed stones of County Cork

TULLYLEASE: TULACH LÉIS

Site name Tullylease
Townland Tullylease
NGR 13594, 11870
SMR site no. CO006-00605

In addition to at least thirteen uninscribed carved stones of early Christian date, this small monastery with Anglo-Saxon associations has produced five inscribed stones: a cross-slab dating from the mid-eighth century, and fragments of four others.

Tullylease 1: medium-sized cross-slab

CURRENT LOCATION
The stone is fastened on to the south wall of the ruined church at Tullylease. It is set immediately above the recess in the wall and is protected by a small wooden roof.

HISTORY
The stone was first mentioned by Windele who visited Tullylease in May and October 1851. The stone was then 'placed upright against the Wall', that is, the interior east wall of the old church (Windele MSS 12.I.10, p. 224; White 1921, 270). Unfortunately the drawing made by Windele in 1851 has not survived.

Reeves described the stone as leaning against the same wall (Reeves 1858, 272) and Coleman saw it in the same position (Coleman 1895, 65). During the repair work of 1933-34, the stone was 'secured in position on a new base'. (This information is contained in *Extract from 102nd Report 1933-34 of the Commissioners of Public Works*. A copy of this document was kindly supplied by Dúchas). This presumably refers to the stone's being clamped to the wall against which it had previously been leaning. The stone remained in this position until September 1993 when it was moved to its present location by the OPW.

DESCRIPTION

The current dimensions of the stone are:
H. c. 95 cm, W. c. 63 cm, T. c. 7 cm.
The stone is a rectangular cross-slab, complete except for two corners which are now damaged. The slab was apparently intended to be erect (Henderson and Okasha 1992, 15-16). The sides and back are plain but the face contains a framed, shafted Greek cross with U-shaped expansions. It is ornamented partly in relief but mainly in incision with fret-patterns, spiral patterns and interlace. (For a full description of the decoration, see Henderson and Okasha 1992, 15-17). There are two texts on the face of the stone: text a is incised horizontally in the top right corner and text b is incised in the two lower quadrants of the cross. Text b is set in three horizontal lines, the first two interrupted by the shaft of the cross, the third only in the left quadrant. Text a is probably incomplete but text b is complete.

LETTERING

The texts are both in half-uncial script and both are legible. The maximum letter H. is c. 3.5 cm.

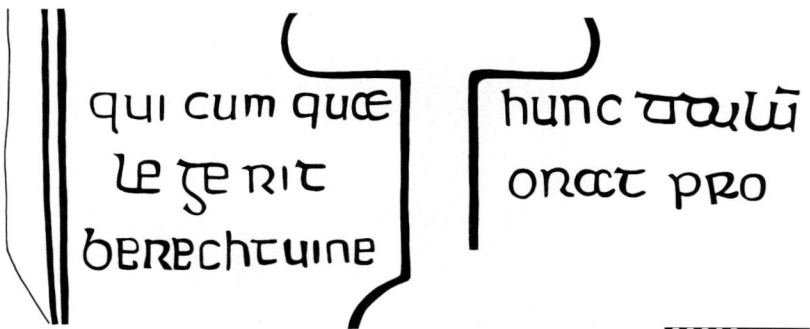

TEXT

a   XP̄S
b   QUI CUM QUA/E ‖ HUNC T/IT/UL/Ū
    L/E G/E RIT ‖ ORAT PRO
    BERECHTUINE

INTERPRETATION

Text a reads *xp̄s* for *Chr(istu)s*. This text is set in the top right corner of the face of the stone and the corresponding left corner is broken off. As first suggested by Reeves (1858, 273), the lost corner is likely to have contained the abbreviation *ihs* for *[Ihesus]*.

Text b reads *qui cum quae hunc titulū le ge rit orat pro berechtuine*. This is for *quicumquae hunc titulu(m) legerit orat pro Berechtuine* 'whoever will [or might] have read this inscription, let her/him pray [or pray] for Berechtuine'. *Orat* is probably an error for *oret* 'may he/she pray', as occurs elsewhere in Hiberno-Latin, or possibly for the imperative *orate* 'pray'. *Legerit* could be an error for *legit* 'reads' but as it stands could be either future perfect 'will have read' or, perhaps, perfect subjunctive 'might have read'. The *titulum* may refer to the whole inscription or, more specifically, only to text a.

DISCUSSION

A parallel for text a is provided by the the late Pictish cross-slab from St Donnan's, Eigg, which has IHU XPI incised in its top left and right corners respectively (Runciman 1933, 65 and fig. 3). There are stones in Wales with similar texts to text b (Nash-Williams 1950, no. 182, pp. 29, 40, 123-25; no. 125, pp. 18-20, 26, 100-2). Some manuscript colophons are also similar, for example the Macregol Gospels (Oxford, Bodleian Library, MS Auct. D.2.19 (S.C. 3946), fol. 169v). The personal name *Berechtuine* is a form of the common Old English masculine name *Beorhtwine*. (For a full discussion of the texts on this stone, see Henderson and Okasha 1992, 8-12, 13-15).

Tullylease has been associated with the Anglo-Saxons since at least the eleventh century (Henderson and Okasha 1992, 10) but the name *Beorhtwine* cannot be associated with any historical person. Henderson and Okasha suggested a possible context for all the Tullylease sculpture 'in the middle of the eighth century' (Henderson and Okasha 1992, 32).

BIBLIOGRAPHY

Reeves 1858, 268, 272-3 and fig.
Brash 1874-75, 321-2
Westwood 1876-79, 145
Petrie 1878, 52-4 and pl. XXX, fig. 64
Graves 1883-84, 46
Allen 1887, 84, 113-15 and fig. 20.2
Allen 1889, 117-18, 121, 127, 175
Coleman 1895, 61-8 and fig.
(-) 1897, 157
Allen 1903, 302 and fig.
Allen 1904, 181
Cochrane 1912, 132
Crawford 1912, 229-30
White 1920, 268
White 1921, 269-72
Crawford 1926a, 9-10, 32 and figs
Henry 1933, vol. 1, 22, 107, 139-40; vol. 2, pl. 47.2
O'Briain 1935, cols 354-5
Leask 1938, 101-8 and pl. XIII
Ryan, J. 1938, 111-12
Henry 1940, 113
Macalister 1949a, no. 908, pp. 92-4 and fig.
Nash-Williams 1950, 29, 140
Lionard 1953, 12-13
Radford 1956, 334
Lionard 1961, 141-3, 154-5 and pl. XXXI.1
Evans 1966, 84
Ó hÉailidhe 1967, 104
Thomas 1971, 127
Harbison 1975, 18, 61
Weir 1980, 120 and fig.
Hamlin 1985, 294
Higgitt 1986, 128, 140-1
Brown 1989, 160 and pl. 8
Killanin and Duignan 1989, 136 and fig.
Ó Cróinín 1989, 199-201 and pl. 8
Ryan, M. 1989, 127 and fig. 3
Edwards 1990, 170
Herity 1990, 215 and fig. 4
Higgitt 1990, 159-60 and fig. 5
Henderson and Okasha 1992, no. 1, pp. 1-36 and pls Ia, II and IVb
Okasha 1992, no. 208, pp. 56-7 and pl. VIId
Manning 1995, 36 and photo 17
Harbison 1997, 37-8

Henderson and Okasha 1997, 9
Higgitt 1997, 69, 72 and pl. 1
Hughes and Hamlin 1997, 91, 121
Thomas 1998, 191, note 3
Windele MSS 12.I.10, p. 224

EXAMINED

On numerous occasions between February 1989 and April 1998 (EO); May 1996 (KF)

Tullylease 2: fragmentary slab

CURRENT LOCATION

The stone is in the National Museum of Ireland, reg. no. 1933:3319.

HISTORY

The stone was probably seen by Windele in 1851. He illustrated a stone without description in the text but with a caption stating: 'Fragment stone, small size in church' (Windele MSS 12.I.10, p. 244). Although his drawing shows only two lines of text, it seems likely that he was referring to this stone. If he was not illustrating this stone, then there must have been another stone, now lost, inscribed with what appears to be a Latin text. The stone seems to have been lost sight of until December 1933 when it was deposited in the NMI. It is likely that this stone was among those referred to by Leask when he said that during repair work undertaken in 1933-34 'most of the memorials to be described came to light, some in the actual fabric of the building and others in the soil within and around it' (Leask 1938, 101). Concrete casts of several stones, including this one, were made and fixed to the interior south wall of the church, where they remain.

DESCRIPTION

The current dimensions of the stone are:
H. c. 13.5 cm, W. c. 14 cm, T. c. 2.2 cm.
The stone is a fragment of a slab of unknown form incised with a section of a margin or frame and parts of four lines of text on its face. The letters are set horizontally on the left of the stone within the margin or frame.

LETTERING

The text is in half-uncial script and is legible. The maximum letter H. is c. 2.5 cm.

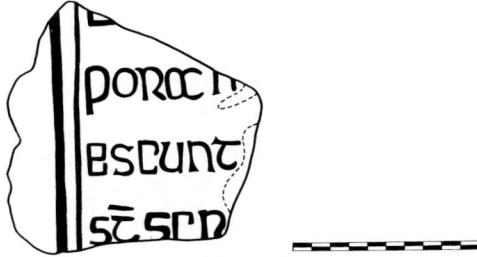

TEXT

[.]–
PORA[.]–
ESCUNT[.]–
S̄T̄ SCR–

INTERPRETATION

The text reads –*pora [-]escunt [-] s̄t̄ scr–* for –*pora [-]escunt [-] s(un)t scr–*. The incised margin indicates that nothing is lost from the beginning of each line. The last letter in the second line could read *n*, or perhaps *i* followed by the beginning of another letter. The group of letters reading *escunt* suggests that the text is in Latin. The group *s̄t̄* is probably for *sunt*, an abbreviation that occurs fairly commonly in manuscripts; alternatively, it could be the end of a longer word ending in -*sunt*.

Leask said that the text could 'be restored or completed by reasonable inference from the words that remain' (Leask 1938, 108); his restoration read:

quorum cor
PORA hic requi-
ESCUNT et nomina (or eorum?)
ST (*i.e.*, sunt) SCRipta in
libro vitae.

Unfortunately no complete word of the text now remains and we have no way of knowing how many letters are lost from each line. Leask's reconstructed text has to be treated as conjectural and we must conclude that the text on the stone is too fragmentary to be interpreted.

DISCUSSION
Windele's drawing (Windele MSS 12.I.10, p. 244), which is probably of this stone, shows a text reading:

BUS OMN | S̄CIS A[.]

If this drawing is not an attempt at stone no. 2, then there must have been a further piece of stone, now lost, which also had a text inscribed on it, probably in Latin.

It is possible that this fragmentary stone was part of a medium-sized cross-slab similar to Tullylease 1. Henderson and Okasha suggested a possible context for all the Tullylease sculpture 'in the middle of the eighth century' (Henderson and Okasha 1992, 32).

BIBLIOGRAPHY
Leask 1938, 101-8 and fig. 4b
Henderson and Okasha 1992, no. 11, pp. 1-36 and pl. Ic
Windele MSS 12.I.10, p. 244

EXAMINED
October 1990 (EO); July 1996 (KF)

Tullylease 3: fragmentary cross-slab

CURRENT LOCATION
The stone is in the National Museum of Ireland, reg. no. 1933:3322.

HISTORY

It is likely that this stone was among those referred to by Leask when he said that during repair work undertaken in 1933-34 'most of the memorials to be described came to light, some in the actual fabric of the building and others in the soil within and around it' (Leask 1938, 101). Concrete casts of several stones, including this one, were made and these were fixed to the interior south wall of the church, where they remain. The stone was deposited in the NMI in December 1933.

DESCRIPTION

The current dimensions of the stone are:
H. *c.* 21.5 cm, W. *c.* 18.5 cm, T. *c.* 4.5 cm.
The stone is part of a cross-slab of unknown form. The remaining fragment contains on its face most of the upper arm of a framed cross with part of a text beside it. The text is set horizontally in the upper left quadrant of the cross-slab and consists of the ends of two lines of text.

LETTERING

The remaining letters are in half-uncial script and are legible. The maximum letter H. is *c.* 1.8 cm.

TEXT

–DANT
–[..][̄]

INTERPRETATION

The text reads –*dant* –, the suprascript line at the end presumably indicating an abbreviation. The text is, however, too fragmentary to be interpreted and it is not even certain what language was used. Further text may well have been lost from other quadrants of the cross.

DISCUSSION

On account of the similarity of their design, Leask suggested that this stone and Tullylease 5 might have been part of the same monument (Leask 1938, 106). Since Tullylease 5 was apparently also inscribed in the upper left quadrant, this would imply a long text. In view of the fragmentary nature of the texts on both stones, and since stone no. 5 is lost, it is not now possible to decide if these two stones came from the same monument. It is possible that this stone, either with or without Tullylease 5, was part of a medium-sized cross-slab similar to Tullylease 1. Henderson and Okasha suggested a possible context for all the Tullylease sculpture 'in the middle of the eighth century' (Henderson and Okasha 1992, 32).

BIBLIOGRAPHY

Leask 1938, 101-8 and fig. 4c
Henderson and Okasha 1992, no. 12, pp. 1-36 and pl. Ib

EXAMINED

October 1990 (EO); July 1996 (KF)

Tullylease 4: fragmentary slab

CURRENT LOCATION

The stone is in the National Museum of Ireland, reg. no. 1930:186.

HISTORY

The stone was found by John Linehan of Ballinaguila, Tullylease, 'resting on the top' of stone no. 1. (Information about this stone is contained in a document kept in the NMI who kindly supplied a copy). It is not clear when Linhan found the stone but he handed it to Leask in July 1930, and Leask deposited it in the NMI in the same month.

DESCRIPTION

The current dimensions of the stone are:
H. *c.* 8 cm, W. *c.* 11.5 cm, T. *c.* 2.5 cm.
The stone is an undecorated fragment that contains parts of three lines of text
incised horizontally on its face.

LETTERING

The text uses half-uncial script but only the second line contains any
completely legible letters. The maximum letter H. is *c.* 1.5 cm.

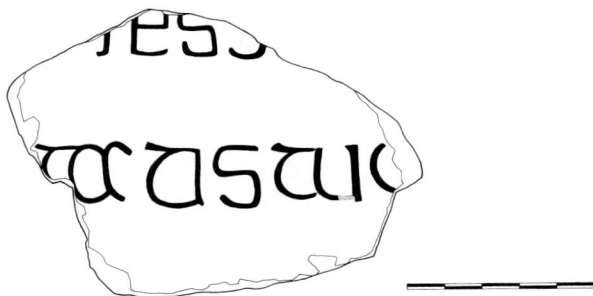

TEXT

[–]ES[.]–
[–]ATISTU[–]
[–]

INTERPRETATION

The text reads *–es[–]atistu–*. The lost letter at the end of the second line might
have been D and the second line would then read, *–[t]atistu[d–]–*. If this text is
in Latin, as seems probable, it could have contained the end of a word *–[t]atis*
followed by *tu [d]–* or *tu[d]–*; alternatively it may have contained the word
istu[d] 'this'. No further interpretation of this text is possible.

DISCUSSION

In form and size the letters resemble those on Tullylease 2, but there is
insufficient evidence to conclude that the two stones formed part of the same
monument. It is possible that this fragmentary stone was part of a medium-sized
cross-slab similar to Tullylease 1. Henderson and Okasha suggested a possible
context for all the Tullylease sculpture 'in the middle of the eighth century'
(Henderson and Okasha 1992, 32).

BIBLIOGRAPHY

Leask 1938, 101-8 and fig. 4d
Henderson and Okasha 1992, no. 13, pp. 1-36 and pl. Id

October 1990 (EO); July 1996 (KF)

Tullylease 5: fragmentary cross-slab

CURRENT LOCATION

The stone is now lost.

HISTORY

Leask (1938, 106) recorded that this stone was found in 1894 but had subsequently been lost. He reproduced a sketch which was 'on record' (Leask 1938, 106); this drawing cannot now be located but Leask's reproduction appears below.

DESCRIPTION

The dimensions of the stone are not known. The description and text are taken from Leask 1938, 106 and fig. 4a, illustrated above. The stone was probably part of a cross-slab, containing, when found, only part of the left cross-arm with a single line of text above it. The design of the cross appears very similar to that on Tullylease 3. The text appears to have been set horizontally but the letters are shown as damaged.

LETTERING

From Leask's drawing, the text appears to have been in half-uncial script.

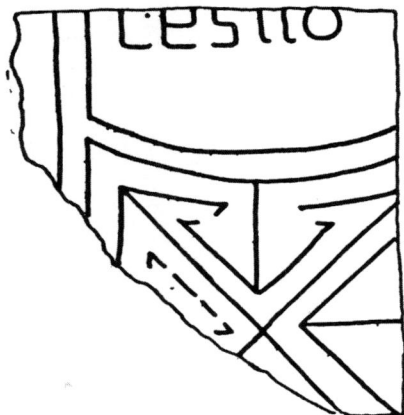

TEXT

–[C]ES[...]–

INTERPRETATION

The text appears to have read –[c]es–. If the first letter was not C it could possibly have been T. The first two lost letters are uncertain but the third could have been B, D or O. The text is too fragmentary to be interpreted and it is not even certain what language was used.

DISCUSSION

On the possible relationship between this stone and Tullylease 3, see above. Henderson and Okasha suggested a possible context for all the Tullylease sculpture 'in the middle of the eighth century' (Henderson and Okasha 1992, 32).

BIBLIOGRAPHY

Leask 1938, 101-8 and fig. 4a
Henderson and Okasha 1992, no. 14, pp. 1-36 and pl. Ie

SITE

Traditionally Tullylease has been associated with St Berichter or St Bercert who might have been a seventh-century Saxon. However, the first historical association of a Bercert at Tullylease occurs in the eleventh-century Notes to the *Martyrology of Oengus* (Stokes, W. 1905, 258-9). Subsequently the cult of St Berichter at Tullylease appears to have grown in importance (see Henderson and Okasha 1992, 10-12 and references given there). In the Annals of Inisfallen *s.a.* 1059 the death is recorded of an *erenach* of Tulach Léis, Dúnadach Úa hInmainéin, (Mac Airt 1951, 218-9). At some time before 1170 an Augustinian priory was founded on the site (Gwynn and Hadcock 1970, 156, 197, 408). The physical remains of the old church at Tullylease date from the twelfth to the fifteenth century. In addition to the five inscribed cross-slabs and cross-slab fragments, there are twelve or more uninscribed cross-slabs or fragments of slabs known from Tullylease; there is also a decorated quern-stone of early medieval date (Henderson and Okasha 1992, 1-36; Henderson and Okasha 1997, 9-17).

COUNTY KERRY

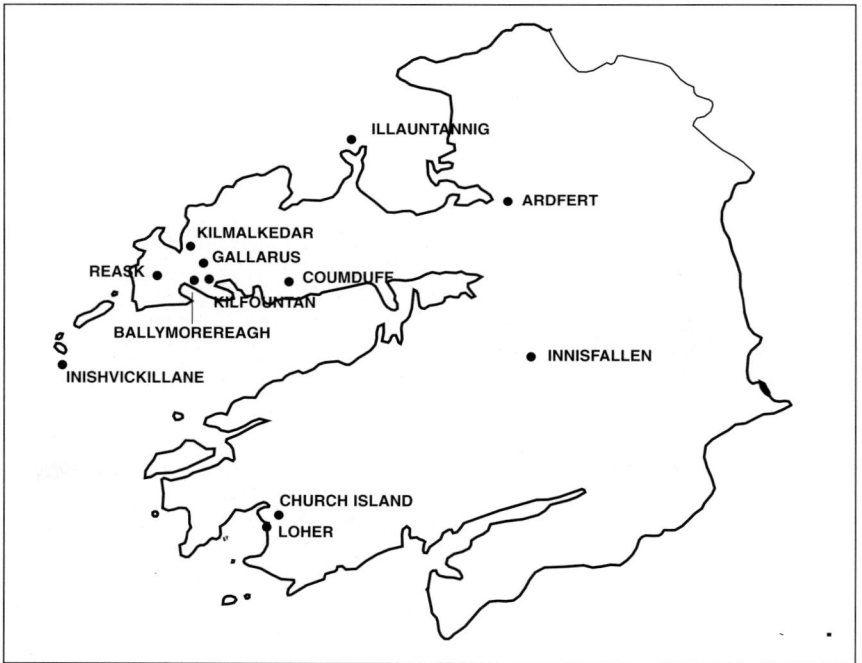

Early Christian inscribed stones of County Kerry

ARDFERT: ARD FHEARTA

Site name Templenahoe
Townland Ardfert
NGR 07854,12114
SMR site no. KE020-046---

The text, a small portion of a longer text, is inscribed on an architectural feature, a twelfth-century voussoir, re-used in the late twelfth-century church.

CURRENT LOCATION

The inscribed block is built into the interior face of the choir arch of the ruined Romanesque structure of Templenahoe, Ardfert. It is in an inverted position, against the corner with the south wall, its lower edge 1.6 m above the current ground level; see illustration on p. 133.

HISTORY

The inscription was first recognised by Fionnbarr Moore during his OPW excavations at the neighbouring cathedral. Toal included a tentative reference in her survey (Toal 1995, 251), but there is no other mention of the stone in print. The authors are most grateful to Fionnbarr Moore for alerting them to the existence of this stone in advance of his publication of the site.

DESCRIPTION

The current dimensions of the stone are:
H. 9.5 cm, W. 25 cm, T. 3 cm visible.

Since the stone is built into the wall, only part of the thickness of the stone is visible. The stone is one of a number of architectural blocks carved from a distinctive grainy red sandstone, which can be seen incorporated into the predominantly grey masonry of the current structure. The slightly curving long edges and wedged-shaped short edges indicate that the piece served as a voussoir, the component block of an arch. In what follows, the block is described as if upright, that is, rotated 180 degrees from its current position. The text is incised in a single horizontal line along the long axis of the stone and covers most of its visible surface. It comprises a section of a longer text which would have continued on the preceding and succeeding blocks.

LETTERING

The text uses half-uncial script and the maximum letter H. is 4 cm. All the letters are damaged: the first lacks its left edge and the remaining ones have each lost at least part of their upper edge, the outer third of the visible surface of the stone having de-laminated. The indication of lenition by the use of a *punctum delens* is unusual in epigraphy.

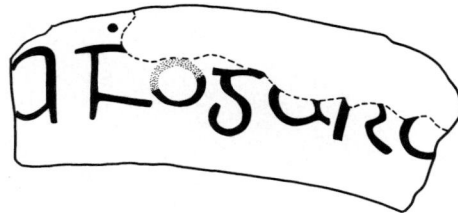

TEXT

|| A̲ḞOGA̲R[.] || (edge of stone)

INTERPRETATION

The text reads -*aḟogar[.]*–for –*[u]a F(h)ogar[t]*–. The final letter is doubtful: the traces appear to be the lower half of a curved T or C or, less probably, the incomplete bowl of a D or an O. From the context, a T might be expected but any horizontal stroke has been lost. There is a well-formed dot above the F which appears intentional and is doubtless intended as the *punctum delens*, the regular indication of lenition of F and S in manuscripts from the Old Irish period onwards (Thurneysen 1946, p. 24, §33). The initial A is most plausibly interpreted as the final letter of *ua* 'descendent of' causing lenition of the following *f*. (See the discussion of lenition in the **Introduction §5.3.8**).The text can then be interpreted as – *[u]a F(h)ogar[t]*–, '– descendent of Fhógar[tach]'.

DISCUSSION

The male personal name *Fogartach*, 'one who inflames', is well-attested in the genealogies (O'Brien 1976, 653). It was, for example, borne by the eighth-century high-king Fogartach mac Néill. The name is frequently confused in the sources with the personal name *Fócarta* (*Fócartach*), from the adjective *fócarthach* 'proclaimed', hence 'one who is proclaimed an outlaw' (*DIL s.v.*). This latter name, in use as a personal name from the early period (Ó Corráin and Maguire 1990, 106), is the origin of the surname *Ua Fógartaich* (modern Ó Fógartaigh, O'Fogarty) (MacLysaght 1997, 112). The Uí Fógartaich were a sept of the Dál Cais, based in north Tipperary but also prominent in north and

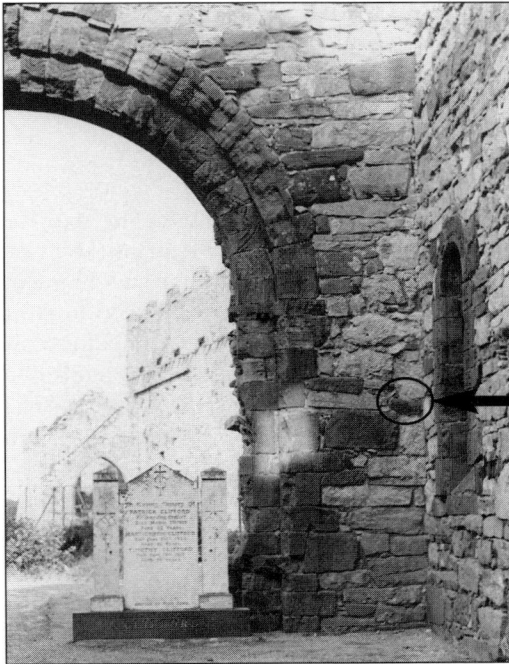

east Munster (MacLysaght 1997, 112; de Bhulbh 1997, 195). By analogy with contemporary architectural inscriptions (see below), one might expect the Ardfert text to have recorded the name of the secular magnate under whose auspices the church was constructed. This may indeed have been the case: Clann Fogartaich, the descendents of Fogartach mac Báeth, are listed in the genealogies as a sub-group of the Ciarraige (O'Brien 1976, p. 313, §161 a 15).

The current structure at Templenahoe was built sometime before 1190 by Bishop O'Conarchy and incorporates the remains of earlier churches (Toal 1995, 251). The inscribed fragment is not *in situ*, and presumably comes from an earlier building. It may be compared with the inscribed doorway at Monaincha, Co. Tipperary (Monaincha 4), as well as with those at Freshford, Co. Kilkenny (Macalister 1949a, no. 569, p. 24) and at Killeshin, Co. Laois

(Macalister 1949a, no. 574, pp. 26-8). Only at Freshford, however, does the text run across voussoirs. All four stones probably date from the twelfth century. The other three open with the phrase *or(óit) do* and, although Monaincha 4 is largely illegible, the others go on to record the patronage of the secular magnates under whose auspices the churches were built. The extant fragment from Ardfert seems to incorporate the name of a local lordly dynasty, so the text may have been of similar form when complete. Other pieces of the inscription, as yet unidentified, may well be incorporated elsewhere in the fabric of the current church.

BIBLIOGRAPHY
Toal 1995, 251

EXAMINED
July 1996 (KF)

SITE
Traditionally Ardfert has been associated with the sixth-century St Brendan and St Erc but there are no early Christian remains extant except for an ogham stone. Throughout the medieval period Ardfert was an important ecclesiastical centre, and the see of a diocese (now part of Kerry) from the twelfth century. Today there are the remains of several medieval buildings and there was a round tower until it fell down *c.* 1770. The ruined St Brendan's cathedral contains twelfth-century and later work. Templenahoe (*Teampall na hÓige* 'church of the Virgin'), north-west of the cathedral, was completed some time before 1190, by Bishop O'Conarchy, who died in 1193 (Toal 1995, 251). Incorporated in its walls are the ruined remains of earlier churches. Although it is now in ruins, some fine Romanesque work remains.

BALLYMOREREAGH: AN BAILE RIABHACH

Site name Teampall Geal
Townland Ballymorereagh
NGR 04046, 10278
SMR site no. KE043-14001-

This rather doubtful small cross-slab came from an early ecclesiastical site which also produced an ogham stone and other cross-incised stones.

CURRENT LOCATION
The stone is now lost.

> man in his position appearing as a practising artist : such persons usually engage professional skill for the works of art which they patronize.
>
> ## COUNTY OF KERRY
>
> ### BARONY OF CORKAGUINEY
>
> Among a number of small cross-signed slabs in and around the little oratory called *Teampull Geal* there is one, o′ 10¼″×o′ 10¼″×o′ 1½″, lying on the window-sill. On one face is an equal-armed cross with expanding ends. In the cantons the letters
>
> | | |
> |----|----|
> | O | R |
> | AR | TH |
>
> seem to be traceable, but the face of the stone is badly battered, and the whole is so uncertain that I do not enumerate it in the series. There is a plain equal-armed cross on the back of the stone.
>
> ¹ I retain this technical term as it stands : a discussion of its meaning would be outside the scope of the present work.

HISTORY

The stone was recorded by Macalister as 'lying on the window-sill' of the oratory Teampall Geal at Ballymorereagh (Macalister 1949a, 95). It subsequently disappeared and was recorded as missing by Cuppage (Cuppage *et al.* 1986, 270).

DESCRIPTION

The dimensions, description and text are taken from Macalister 1949a, 95 below :(see illustration)
H. *c.* 26 cm, W. *c.* 26 cm, T. *c.* 4 cm.
The stone was a thin square slab, carved on both faces. It is unclear whether or not it was complete when seen by Macalister. On the back was an equal-armed cross. On the front, which Macalister described as 'badly battered' (Macalister 1949a, 95), was another equal-armed cross with expanded terminals. The text, which may or may not have been complete, was arranged in two horizontal lines across the four quadrants created by the cross-arms.

LETTERING

Macalister gave no indication as to the form of script used and, in view of his doubt about the inscription (he said only that the letters 'seem to be traceable'), the text was probably highly deteriorated, if indeed it was genuinely lettering.

TEXT

O ‖ R
AR ‖ TH

INTERPRETATION

If the text really read as above, *o r ar th* could be for *or(óit) ar Th–*, 'a prayer for' followed by a personal name beginning with *Th*. Macalister, however, was doubtful about this stone (see below).

DISCUSSION

Cuppage listed and illustrated nine cross-marked stones from the site but none is similar in shape or dimensions to the slab described by Macalister (Cuppage *et al.* 1986, 268-71). The possibility that the text has entirely disappeared from an existing stone can therefore be ruled out and we must conclude that the inscribed stone is lost. Macalister, not renowned for his caution in accepting texts as genuine, was doubtful about this stone, describing it as 'so uncertain that I do not enumerate it in the series' (Macalister 1949a, 95).

BIBLIOGRAPHY

Macalister 1949a, 95 and fig.
Cuppage *et al.* 1986, 270

SITE

The site, also known as Teampall Mhanacháin (Templemanaghan), has a commanding view across Dingle harbour. The remains consist of a dry-stone oratory (standing to a height of 2.75 m in places), the foundations of some dry-stone huts, a souterrain, a burial ground and the remains of a sub-circular enclosure. There are several cross-incised boulders and small slabs standing in the burial ground and in front of the oratory is a large ogham-inscribed pillar (1.75 m tall). In addition to the ogham inscription on its north-east angle, the stone is incised with two equal-armed crosses, but there is absolutely no trace of the half-uncial inscription FECT QUENILOC which Macalister claimed to have seen next to the ogham (1945, no. 170, pp. 163-4 and fig.). Nothing is known of the early history of the site.

CHURCH ISLAND (LOUGH CURRANE): OILEÁN AN TEAMPAILL

Site name St Finan's Church
Townland Termons
NGR 05323, 06689
SMR site no. KE098-03901-

There are two inscribed cross-slabs from this important island ecclesiastical site which also has nine related but uninscribed monuments. One of the two is a large cross-slab which may commemorate a known cleric of the mid-eleventh century. The other, a recumbent grave-cover of later medieval date, contains the remains of a long text recorded more fully in the early twentieth century.

Church Island 1: large cross-slab

CURRENT LOCATION

The stone stands upright on a *leacht*-like structure, outside and immediately to the north of the chancel of the ruined Romanesque church.

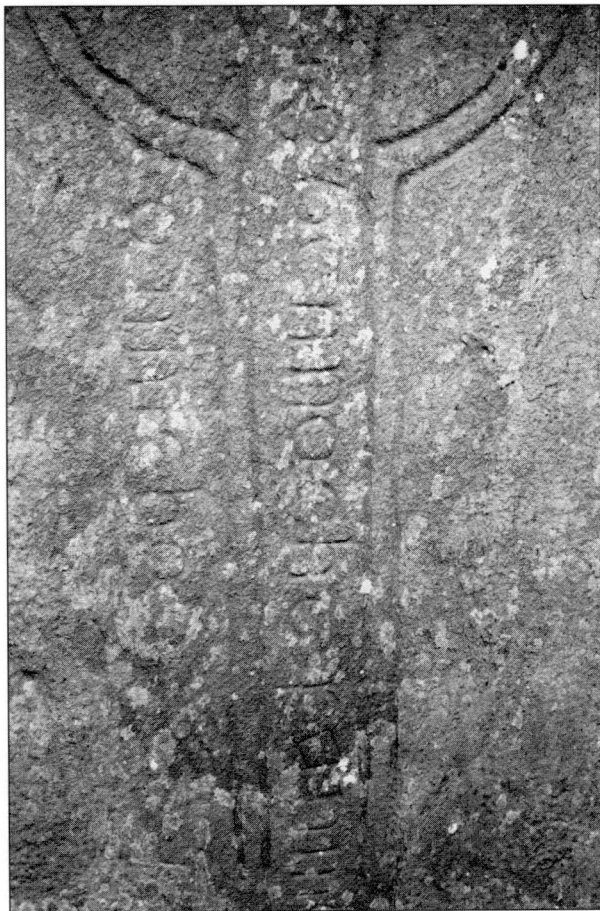

HISTORY

The stone was first recorded by Lynch in 1908 when it was described as standing 'To the north of the church' (Lynch, P. J. 1908, 374), presumably in its present position. O'Sullivan and Sheehan (1996, 319) suggested that it was erected here by the OPW during work on the site in 1883.

DESCRIPTION

The current dimensions of the stone are:
H. 161 cm, W. 60 cm, T. *c.* 8 cm.

The stone is a decorated slab of purplish sandstone which tapers slightly towards the base. On the finely dressed main face is incised a full-length outline Latin cross with a tapering shaft which continues below current ground level. A single line rings the cross-head and the whole cross is silhouetted by a continuous line. Related designs of outlined ringed crosses are found on four uninscribed slabs of similar size from the site. There are three parts to the inscription. The first two, texts a and b, are arranged horizontally in the four arms of the cross-head leaving the crossing bare. The third part, text c, consists of two parallel vertical lines one inside and the other to the left of the shaft. These read downwards with the bottoms of the letters to the viewer's left. There is no reason to doubt that these three texts are contemporary and form a single unified design. All the texts are complete.

LETTERING

Text a has *alpha* as a form of a capital A, but the *omega* is a form of non-capital Greek ω. The forms of both letters are unusual but not unparalleled. The capital A with x-shaped bar may be compared with similar forms on slabs from Toureen Peacaun (nos 8 and 22). As Lynch noted (Lynch, P. J. 1908, 377, 380), a similar form of the *omega* occurs on an eighth-century cross-slab from Hartlepool, Co Durham (Okasha 1971, no. 48, p. 78 and pl. 48: the stone Lynch refers to is in Durham Cathedral, not the British Museum). The script of texts b and c is half-uncial. All three texts are legible with a maximum letter H. of 5 cm.

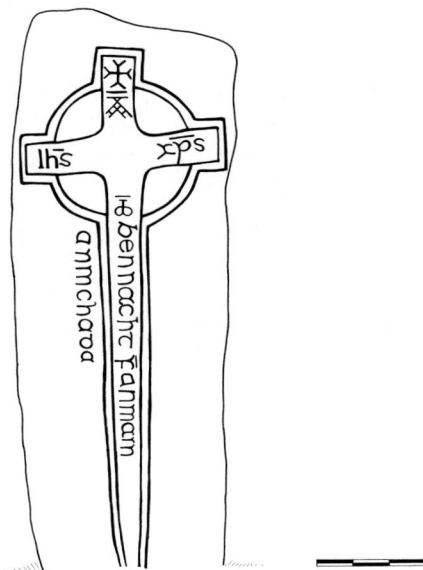

TEXT

a   + | A̅ | ω̅
b   IH̅S XP̅S
c   BENNACHT F̄ ANMAIN
    ANMCHADA

INTERPRETATION

Text a reads + A̅ ω̅ for + *a(lpha) o(mega)*, the first and last letters of the Greek alphabet, which constitue a *nomen sacrum* of Christ. The reference is to the book of Revelations, for example Revelations 22:13. *Alpha* and *omega* are also found on the Loher stone (see the discussion in the **Introduction §5.3.3**).

Text b reads *ih̅s xp̅s* for *Ih(esu)s Chr(istu)s*. These are the usual abbreviations for the Latin *Iesus* and *Christus*. Part of this *nomen sacrum* is also found on the cross-slab Tullylease 1 (for further discussion, see the **Introduction §5.3.3**).

Text c reads *bennacht f̄ anmain anmchada* for *bennacht f(or) anmain Anmchada* 'a blessing on the soul of Anmchadh'. The formula *bennacht for anmain* is much less common than the *oróit do*. The only other examples in Munster are on two slabs from Lismore, nos 1 and 2, and possibly Church Island 2. (For further discussion of this formula, see the **Introduction §5.3.4**).

DISCUSSION

The male name Anmchadh was popular in the early medieval period, especially in the southern half of Ireland (Ó Corráin and Maguire 1990, 23). Sheehan (1990, 173) suggested that Anmchadh may be the Anmchad Ua Dúnchada whose burial on Inis Ausail is recorded *s.a.* 1058 in the Annals of Inisfallen (Mac Airt 1951, 218-9). Nothing else is known of this important ecclesiastic, though, as Sheehan noted, his surname links him to the Eoganacht dynasty of Ua Donnchada. Unfortunately, the identification of Inis Ausail remains uncertain (Mac Airt 1951, 542).

BIBLIOGRAPHY

Lynch, P. J. 1908, 374-80, pl. and figs
Crawford 1912, 239
Crawford 1926a, 45 and fig. 9, O
Crawford 1926b, 43
Macalister 1949a, no. 916, pp. 97-8 and pl. XLIII, fig. 916
Lionard 1961, 98, 138-9 and fig. 16.7
Henry 1965, 56
Harbison 1975, 118
Barrington 1976, 181, 274
Weir 1980, 162
Killanin and Duignan 1989, 304
Sheehan 1990, 164, 171-4 and fig. 7b
O'Sullivan and Sheehan 1996, 319-20 and fig. 211b

EXAMINED

July 1998 (KF)

Church Island 2: large cross-slab

CURRENT LOCATION

The stone lies outside the ruined church, 4 m west of the doorway, beside a *leacht*.

HISTORY

The stone was first recorded by Lynch in 1908. It was then 'Outside the door of the church, on a level with the sod ... set within a rough stone kerbing'; it was broken but 'the parts have been laid together' (Lynch, P. J. 1908, 380).

DESCRIPTION

The current measurements of the stone are:

H. 158 cm, W. 34 cm (maximum), T. *c.* 5 cm.

The stone is a long thin trapezoidal slab of slate, broken in two pieces. A small triangular area of the surface has been lost at the break. The slab is carefully shaped and dressed. It is incised with a full-length outline Latin cross framed by a double line round the perimeter of the slab. The cross joins the frame at all four extremities. The text is set vertically along the long axis of the cross starting at the top of the upper arm and apparently continuing the entire length of the shaft. It reads vertically downwards in one line with the bottoms of the letters to the viewer's left. The initial cross and first letter are clear but the rest of the surface of the slab is badly damaged. The text has now all but disappeared although sufficient traces remain to indicate that it did once continue down the stone.

LETTERING

The text is probably in half-uncial script but is now largely illegible. The maximum letter H. is 3 cm.

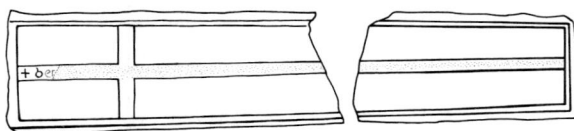

TEXT

+ BE[N]–

INTERPRETATION

The text reads +*be[n]*–, presumably the beginning of + *be[nnacht]* –, but the rest is now lost. Previous scholars were able to read much more of the original text. Lynch published a drawing based on his rubbing from which the following reading may be reconstructed: + *bennoct f̄ anmain gille inchomded ibuicne adbur [.]ine[.] ndod [...]uc* [break] *iabunī deis fein ascoarge s atnote [–] eina[–] nan [.] roig[..] [..]* – He noted that towards the end 'the letters became very small, with – probably – many abbreviations' (Lynch, P. J. 1908, 380). Lynch misinterpreted as O the A of *bennacht* and the final A of *Anmchada* in the Church Island 1 inscription, and he appears to have done the same thing here in *bennocht*. Other Os in his reading of this text are therefore also suspect. Lynch described the letters following *adbur* as 'obscure, uncertain, and defective' (1908, 380) and little confidence can be placed in his reading of this final section.

Macalister published his own drawing of the slab showing the letters closer together than in Lynch's drawing but the two readings agree quite closely up to the end of *adbur* and their readings may be taken as providing some corroboration for each other. Macalister read the letters following *adbur* as *ri ciarraidi*, taking him up almost to the break in the stone. He offered no interpretation of the lettering beyond the break which he described as 'in scratches so fine and so badly worn that I found it quite beyond my powers to decipher them' (Macalister 1949a, 98). The readings of Lynch and Macalister suggest that the text may have begun: + *bennacht f(or) anmain Gille-in-Chomded í Buicine adbur* ...'a blessing on the soul of Gilla-in-Choimded ua Buicine *adbur* ... (that is, one designated or expected to hold a particular office)'.

DISCUSSION
Macalister read two further texts on this stone, both set parallel to the text inside the cross-shaft. In the top right quadrant of the cross he read īhs xp̄s, the *nomina sacra*. In the top left quadrant, in small lettering, he read *maria* which he thought was a later addition (Macalister 1949a, 98). Macalister was the first to observe these two texts and, unfortunately, it is now impossible to evaluate his claim as the surface of the stone in these areas has entirely worn away. It is possible the two texts represented graffiti carved by later pilgrims to the grave.

The slab is a recumbent grave-cover of recognisable medieval type. Its trapezoidal shape and use of slate are two features which point to a date after AD1200, the end date of this corpus. The stone is, however, included here because in several respects it perpetuates established early medieval practice. In using insular rather than gothic script, the vernacular rather than Latin, and apparently including the long-established *bennacht for anmain* formula, this stone is drawing on older epigraphic traditions.

BIBLIOGRAPHY
Lynch, P. J. 1908, 380 and fig.
Crawford 1912, 239
Crawford 1926b, 43
Macalister 1949a, no. 917, pp. 97-8 and fig. on p. 99
Lionard 1961, 107, 138 and fig. 7.4
Harbison 1975, 118
Barrington 1976, 181, 274
Weir 1980, 162
Killanin and Duignan 1989, 304
Sheehan 1990, 171-4
O'Sullivan and Sheehan 1996, 320 and fig. 209

EXAMINED
July 1998 (KF)

SITE
Church Island is located at the north end of Lough Currane. According to tradition, St Finan Cam founded a monastery on the island in the sixth century (Gwynn and Hadock 1970, 31), but there are no structural remains that certainly

date from the early Christian period (see O'Sullivan and Sheehan 1996, 316-22). The existing remains include the foundations of various houses, some of modern date, and, at the north end of the island, St Finan's cell. At the east end of the island are the ruins of St Finan's church, the earliest parts of which probably date from the twelfth century (O'Sullivan and Sheehan 1996, 316-9). There are also three examples of a *leacht*, three pillar stones and some fragments of Romanesque architectural sculpture. Altogether eleven cross-slabs, including the two inscribed ones, are preserved on the island, the greatest concentration in the Iveragh peninsula. Macalister considered that a third slab, which now lies next to Church Island 2, had been inscribed but had become largely illegible (Macalister 1949a, 98). However there is now no sign of any text on this stone (O'Sullivan and Sheehan 1996, 320 and fig. 211c). Art-historical parallels suggest that most of the extant slabs date from the eleventh and twelfth centuries. The late date of this 'impressive' group led Sheehan to suggest that 'the floruit of Church Island as one of the major ecclesiastical centres of Iveragh lay towards the end of the Early Historic period and culminated, perhaps, with the erection of its impressive Romanesque church in the twelfth century' (1990, 174).

COUMDUFF: AN COM DUBH

Site name Knockane
Townland Coumduff
NGR 05796,10346
SMR site no. KE044-053---

This small fragment of a slab, incised with traces of letters, came from a site which also produced a cross-incised stone.

CURRENT LOCATION
The stone is now lost.

HISTORY
The stone was found at Coumduff by Patrick Scannell at some time before 1939 and was given to O'Connell during his work on the Kerry Archaeological Survey (O'Connell 1939, 45-6). It was presented to University College Cork by James Carroll of Abbeydorney, Co Kerry, in 1938-39: it is listed amongst those items presented to the Museum of University College Cork in the twelve months preceding 1 June 1939, a list signed by Seán P. Ó Ríordáin, the Professor of Archaeology (document preserved in the College Archives). The whereabouts of the stone was said to be 'not known' in 1986 (Cuppage *et al.* 1986, 280). Enquiries around University College Cork have failed to elicit either the stone or any further account of it.

DESCRIPTION

The dimensions, description and text are taken from the description and illustration, taken from a rubbing, in O'Connell 1939, 45-6, illustrated below. Since O'Connell gave only the measurement of the thickness of the stone, it may be assumed (though this is not stated) that the rubbing was reproduced full size. In this case the dimensions were:

H. *c.* 13 cm, W. *c.* 10 cm, T. *c.* 7 cm.

The stone was a 'fragment' described as 'evidently part of a flag-stone' (O'Connell 1939, 46). The face of the stone, the only one described and illustrated, contained no carving but had four letter-like shapes incised in two lines. The letters of the upper line were less deeply incised than those of the lower line.

LETTERING

None of the letters is clearly legible and it is uncertain what script was used. The maximum letter H. was probably (with the proviso mentioned above) *c.* 5.5 cm.

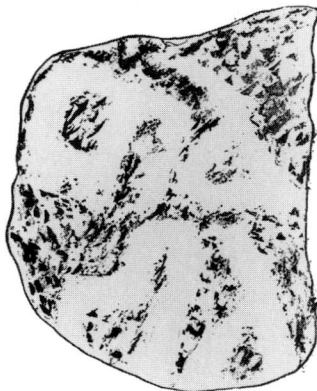

TEXT

The reading of the text is not clear.

INTERPRETATION

O'Connell described the first two letters as '"a"-like figures' and saw traces of what might have been a third (O'Connell 1939, 46). From his illustration, a reading *-aa-* or *-ga-* seems possible but it is hard to discern a third letter. O'Connell described the letters of the lower line as 'resembling ... those of some early Greek alphabets' (O'Connell 1939, 46) and his illustration shows what could be a reversed R and a *lamda*-shape. However these could equally well be read as *-ba-*, or indeed *-ra-*, in either case with the first letter reversed. In view of these uncertainties, and with the stone now lost, no text is now recoverable.

DISCUSSION

There is insufficient evidence to classify this lost and fragmentary slab.

BIBLIOGRAPHY
O'Connell 1939, 45-6 and fig.
Cuppage *et al.* 1986, 280.

SITE

The site 'occupies an area of open ground in the centre of the village of Knockane' (Cuppage *et al.* 1986, 280). It appears to be an early Christian site, although of uncertain extent and nature. In addition to four sub-megalithic cists of uncertain date, probably graves and possibly Bronze Age, there was found an early Christian cross-incised stone with a *chi-rho* on the upper arm of the cross. Cuppage noted that a loom-weight was found on the site at the same time as the inscribed fragment (Cuppage *et al.* 1986, 280).

GALLARUS: GALLROS

Site name Gallarus
Townland Gallarus
NGR 03933, 10486
SMR site no. KE042-07104-

The cross-incised pillar from this early ecclesiastical site is of an early type.

CURRENT LOCATION

The stone stands at the head of a *leacht* type of structure, to the north-east of the oratory.

HISTORY

The stone was examined and drawn by Chatterton in 1838. She described it as outside the oratory and 'Near the east end', adding that it was not upright but 'in a slanting position' (Chatterton 1839, 137). Windele saw it in June of the same year and described its location as 'at the NE angle of the Cell in the little burying ground attached' (Windele MSS 12.C.11, p. 199). Windele and Chatterton both gave the height of the stone as four feet, comparable to its height today. In 1878 Petrie said the stone was 'at the east end of the oratory' and his illustration suggests that the stone was still in the position described by Chatterton and Windele (Petrie 1878, 7 and fig. on p. 8); in 1898 the stone was still 'close to the Oratory ... on the north-east side' ((-)1892, 151). In 1949 Macalister described the stone as 'Formerly prostrate, but now standing in the graveyard surrounding the ancient oratory' (Macalister 1949a, 96). Photographs published by Barrington (1979) and by Weir (1980) show the stone surrounded by grass but by 1986 it had been placed in its present position, set in a bed of stones (Cuppage *et al.* 1986, 289 and pl. XIV).

DESCRIPTION

The current dimensions of the stone as it stands in the ground are:
H. *c.* 111 cm, W. *c.* 30 cm, T. *c.* 10 cm.
The stone is a tall, slim pillar, apparently intact, incised on one face only. Part of the surface at the top of the stone has been lost, but this may be ancient damage. The lower half of the carved face is more weathered than the upper, especially on the left side. The upper third of the face is occupied by a large equal-armed cross set in a circle. The top arm projects beyond the rim and the side arms swell at the point of intersection and continue a little beyond. Below the cross head is a vertical stem which is intersected near its foot by a long horizontal stroke. In the area above this cross-stroke, to left and right of the stem, is a somewhat confused arrangement of curved and straight lines. Some of this was previously interpreted as part of the text (see for example Petrie 1845, 131 and fig.). Although the first character on the right appears similar to the L of the text, the reading LIE cannot be supported and Macalister correctly dismissed it (1949a, 96). Beneath these decorative lines is incised a two-line text, reading vertically downwards with the bottoms of the letters to the viewer's left.

LETTERING

The text is in insular script, possibly minuscule, and is rather deteriorated. The maximum letter H. is 9 cm.

TEXT

COLUM
[....]MEC̲

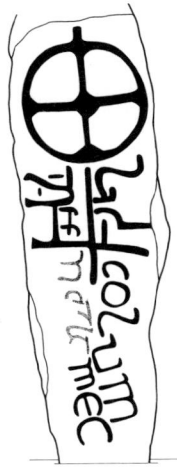

INTERPRETATION

The text now reads *colum [–]mec* with four or five letters lost from the lacuna. The first line comprises the personal name *Colum*, from Latin *columba* 'dove', a popular name in early medieval Ireland, borne by both men and women, including numerous saints. The second line remains uncertain. Macalister read it as *mac dinet*, although he admitted that the letters A and C were 'very faint', the D 'barely traceable' and the T might have been C (Macalister 1949a, 96). Macalister's IN is more plausibly interpreted as M and, although the E is clear, the final letter appears to be a C not T.

DISCUSSION

The person named in the text has not been identified. The decorative arrangement on the stone may be compared with the simpler s-shaped carvings which flank the stem of the cross on the stone from Caherlehillan on the neighbouring Iveragh peninsula (stone 2: O'Sullivan and Sheehan 1996, 265 and fig. 163, b). It is possible that both are debased examples of a motif seen more clearly on a cross-slab from Reask (stone H: Fanning 1981, 145-7, fig. 31 and pl. XI), namely a pair of birds flanking a cross. This motif, although extremely rare in insular art, is widespread on the Continent and can be seen on inscribed memorial slabs of the fifth, sixth and seventh centuries in Gaul and Spain (see for example Le Blant 1856). Sometimes the birds are peacocks (symbolising immortality), sometimes doves. The birds, interpreted as the souls of the faithful, are shown flanking *chi-rho* monograms, Latin or equal-armed crosses, or images of the true vine. The motif is also seen in manuscripts (for instance, the mid-eighth century Gelasian Sacramentary, Biblioteca Apostolica Vaticana, Rome. Reg. Lat. 316, fol 3v). The debased form of the Gallarus and Caherlehillan designs suggests a model far removed from these de luxe examples. Sheehan drew attention to two nearby examples of a closely related motif (a single peacock above the cross), on the same cross-slab from Caherlehillan and a lost slab from Killogrone, near Caherciveen. As he says, these examples strengthen 'the distribution of such introduced motifs in south-western Ireland' (Sheehan 1990, 169).

BIBLIOGRAPHY

Chatterton 1839, 137-9 and fig.
Petrie 1845, 130-1 and fig.
Fitzgerald 1854-55, 200
Petrie 1878, 7-8 and pl. V, fig. 10
Ferguson 1879, 39, 43
Allen 1887, 105
(-) 1890-91, 619-20 and fig.
Allen 1892, 275 and fig. on p. 270
(-) 1892, 151 and fig. on p. 147
Westropp 1897b, 298
Macalister 1902, 60n
Crawford 1912, 233
Macalister 1949a, no. 910, p. 96 and pl. XLI, fig. 910
Evans 1966, 130
Harbison 1970, 43-4, 48 and pl. V, A
Harbison 1975, 110
Barrington 1976, 178-9, 181, 247 and fig.
Weir 1980, 156 and fig. 39 on p. 47
Fanning 1981, 171
Cuppage *et al.* 1986, 289, fig. 178b and pl. XIV
Killanin and Duignan 1989, 62
Windele MSS 12.C.11, p. 199 and fig., p. 278 and fig.

EXAMINED

June 1996 (KF, EO); September 1999 (EO)

SITE

The ecclesiastical site is delineated by the partial remains of a large dry-stone-walled sub-circular enclosure which contains the well-known oratory, the only perfectly preserved example of a 'boat-shaped' dry-stone oratory. The structure and its date were discussed in detail by Harbison (1970, 34-59) and more recently by O'Keeffe (1998, 114). Immediately to the east of the oratory is a *leacht* consisting of a low rectangular mound of stones (9 m long and 5 m wide) including a quantity of quartz. The inscribed pillar stands at its eastern end although this may be a secondary position. No other remains are known from the site and nothing is known of its early history (for a detailed discussion see Cuppage *et al.* 1986, 286-9).

ILLAUNTANNIG (MAGHAREE ISLANDS): OILEÁN tSEANAIGH

SITE NAME Illauntannig
Townland Illauntannig
NGR 06234, 12127
SMR site no. KE019-00206

The three fragments of an inscribed pillar came from the eremitical monastic site on this off-shore island.

CURRENT LOCATION
The stone is now lost.

Pieces b and c

Pieces a and c

HISTORY

The Dingle survey team whose work was published in 1986 (Cuppage *et al.* 1986) recorded the stone in three pieces around 1982 (Isabel Bennett, pers.

com.). A slide taken by the survey team is on file in Músaem Chorca Dhuibhne, Ballyferriter; it shows two pieces of the stone, a and c, both with the texts chalked in (see illustration above). Also in the Museum is a print of a photograph taken by Grellan Rourke of Dúchas showing two pieces of the stone, b and c (see illustration above). According to Cuppage, the original locations of the two uninscribed cross-slabs, as well as that of the inscribed stone, were then 'not known' but the stones had all 'been placed in the main oratory for safe-keeping' (Cuppage *et al.*1986, 295). The entry in the site archive kept in the Museum at Ballyferriter records that in September 1984 two of the three pieces were on the island but one was missing and a return visit was required. It continues: 'Unfortunately I was unable to find one of the fragments and an OPW photo does not include 1 recorded by us ...'. It is not clear which of the three fragments disappeared first but all three have been lost for some time. We are most grateful to Isabel Bennett of Oidhreacht Chorca Dhuibhne, Ballyferriter, for her help in tracing the history of the stone and for permission to quote from the site archive.

DESCRIPTION
The description is taken from the two existing photographs. The slide, which illustrates pieces a and c, was taken with a metre-scale from which the height and width can be gauged. Since the Dúchas photograph shows pieces b and c, the height and width of piece b can therefore be estimated.
The dimensions of the pieces of stone were:
a: H. *c.* 33 cm, W. *c.* 18 cm
b: H. *c.* 14 cm, W. *c.* 9 cm
c: H. *c.* 39 cm, W. *c.* 12 cm.
The three pieces appear to have fitted well together with a triangular piece, containing part of the upper line of text, lacking between pieces b and c. When fitted together, the three fragments formed a thin, pillar-shaped slab with a total length of about 80 cm and a width tapering from more than 18 cm to less than 12 cm. The upper and lower edges of pieces a and b, and the lower edge of piece b, appear to have been intact. The slide shows piece c ending in a point which also appears to be original. It is not clear whether or not the left edge of piece a is original. The broken left edge of piece c appears weathered, suggesting that the fracture was not recent, but the edges of piece b look sharp and fresh. Pieces a and b match closely, and the taper of the slab is a guide to suggest that the lower part of the right edge of piece b fitted directly on to piece c. The visible face contains no carving other than the lettering which appears to have been rather shallowly pecked. The text, which reads from broad to narrow end, runs along the long axis of the slab in two lines which occupy its full width. The original orientation of the slab is not known but if it stood with its pointed end in the ground then the text would have read vertically down with the bottoms of the letters to the reader's left. Both lines of text are visible on pieces b and c, although only a corner of one or two letters can be seen at the point of piece b. No letters are chalked on piece a in the area corresponding to the lower line, but the surface is obscured here so it is not certain that there was only the upper line on this piece.

LETTERING

The text used half-uncial script and appears to have been slightly deteriorated.'
The letters appear well-formed but are simply cut with the peck marks visible
in the photograph.

TEXT

Piece a: [–]UIN F[.]
Piece b: [D]A–
Piece c: [T]H[–] | ..–]

INTERPRETATION

A text can be tentatively reconstructed: the upper line seems to have read *uin
f[–]th* with a deliberate space between the N and the F. The lower line seems to
have read *[-d]a[..]*, where the last letter was either N or H. It is not clear how
much text, if any, was lost from the beginning of each line. The text was
probably in Irish but cannot now be interpreted further.

DISCUSSION

It is possible that the Illauntannig pillar was like the Kilfountan stone with text
to the side of an incised cross. Perhaps the head of an incised cross has been lost
at the broader end, and a simple shaft overlooked in the area below the letters
UIN. This is pure speculation, and a more appropriate comparison may be with
the much later lost slab from Inishvickillane which had no cross other than a
small initial one. As a clue towards orientation, it should be noted that the
texts on pillars like Kilfountan and Kilmalkedar read vertically downwards. The
text seems to be rather long for a single personal name but there is no trace of
any of the familiar formulae requesting prayers or blessings.

BIBLIOGRAPHY

Cuppage *et al.* 1986, 293, 295-7

SITE

The island, the largest of the Magharees, is named after St Senach who
reputedly founded the early Christian monastery on the island. The visible
remains are substantial and consist of two oratories, three circular huts (one
with a souterrain), three examples of a *leacht* (one with a plain stone cross
beside it) and a burial ground, all within an enclosing wall (Cuppage *et al.*

1986, 293-7). The date of the buildings is uncertain. Harbison argued for a twelfth-century date for one of the oratories (1970, 58) and the cross may be of a similar date. A bronze-coated iron hand-bell, now in the NMI, came from a recess in one of the walls; it may date from the period 600-900 (Cuppage *et al.* 1986, 297). Until 1998 two small cross-incised stones were preserved in the oratory with the lost fragments. These have now been removed and are in Killarney, in the care of Dúchas.

INISHVICKILLANE (BLASKET ISLANDS): INIS MHIC AOIBHLEÁIN

Site name Inishvickillane
Townland Inishvickillane
NGR 02124, 09114
SMR site no. KE061-00603-

The stone, which may have dated from the tenth century or later, was found at the eremitic monastic site on the most southerly of the Blasket Islands.

CURRENT LOCATION

The stone is now lost.

HISTORY

In 1856 du Noyer visited Inisvickillane and noted 'some ancient ecclesiastical remains, but so ruinous as not to afford a subject for a sketch' (du Noyer 1861-64, 430). The stone was first recorded in June 1901 'built into the wall of the *cella*', that is, of the oratory on Inisvickillane (Macalister 1902, 46). However, in his full publication of the stone published in 1903, Macalister described it as 'lying on the south wall of the little ruined oratory' (Macalister 1903, 279). In view of Macalister's comment about the inaccessibility of the island (Macalister 1902, 44), it seems unlikely that he visited it a second time between 1901 and 1903. There are at least three possibilities: the stone may never have been built into the wall and Macalister was silently correcting his own error; the stone was built into the wall and Macalister made an error in his second account of it; Macalister had been told that, after his visit in 1901, the stone had been taken from the wall and was lying loose. The stone has been noticed several times in print between its finding and 1986, but all these reports are traceable to one of Macalister's accounts and do not seem to have been based on first-hand knowledge. Cuppage *et al.*, whose work was based on an actual visit to Inisvickillane, looked for the stone on the south wall of the oratory and when they could not find it, recorded it as missing (Cuppage *et al.* 1986, 301).

DESCRIPTION

The description and text are taken from Macalister 1903, 279, illustrated below. The length of the stone is given as corresponding to *c.* 135 cm. No description of the stone itself exists since Macalister concentrated on the text, although it may be significant that he described it as a 'stone' rather than a slab. He mentioned no carving other than the inscription with its initial cross, and did not indicate the size of the letters nor their orientation on the stone. He said only that the text, incised in one line, was 'on the present underside' of the stone and was cut through by a scratch on the stone which he took to be a 'guide line to the carver'. The text appears to have been complete.

LETTERING

The text was in half-uncial script and appears legible on the illustration; Macalister, however, described the letters as 'of strange form and the execution careless'. Certainly the letters seem to have been uneven in size, although Macalister's drawing shows serifs on several of them. He described the lettering as 'scratched rather than cut', implying a shallow incision, although he noted that the initial letter O was 'in a quite different style of carving from the rest' and his illustration suggests that it may have been more deeply cut.

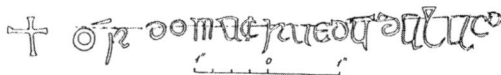

TEXT

+ŌR̄DOMACRUEDUDALAC[.]

INTERPRETATION

From Macalister's illustration, the text appears to read +ōr̄ *domacruedudalac[.]* for + *or(óit) do Mac Rued ú Dalac[h].* The initial cross and the first two words seem clear. Macalister saw an I cut through the C of *mac* which he took to be an error. In his drawing Macalister distinguishes between Us, with straight right-verticals, and As, which have right-verticals terminating at the bottom in a little hook. It therefore seems likely that he meant the letter between the two Ds as U with an acute accent (see the **Introduction §4.3** for a discussion of the marking of vowel length). Following the final C there was a further character, a 'little figure like a D', about which Macalister was dismissive: 'I took [it] to be a mere flourish, as it did not seem to have any phonetic significance: it is hardly a mark of lenition.' (Macalister 1949a, 96). The text can be interpreted as 'a prayer for Mac-Ruaid, grandson of Dálach' or 'a prayer for Mac-Ruaid Ó Dálaigh'.

DISCUSSION

The Inishvickillane stone seems to have been unlike the inscribed pillars on the neighbouring mainland, and was probably considerably later than most of them. It is one of only two examples of the *oróit do* formula in County Kerry, the other being the slightly doubtful example on the lost stone from Ballymorereagh. It is unusual too, in identifying the person for whom prayers are requested by more than a simple personal name. Mac-Ruaid Ua Dálaich cannot be identified. While it is possible that Mac-Ruaid may have been the grandson of an unidentified Dálach, it is more likely that *Ua Dálaich* was used here as the surname Ó Dálaigh (O'Daly), which belonged to one of the prominent learned families of medieval Ireland. This would date the Inishvickillane text to the tenth century or later since, according to Ó Murchadha, the eponymous Dálach died *c.*973 (1999, 43). Four other Munster inscriptions, all of them comparatively late, incorporate or incorporated the word *Ua* 'grandson' or 'descendant': Ardfert, Church Island 2, Monaincha 1 and Roscrea 2. The last two were, like Inishvickillane, sizeable monuments lacking any carving other than the text.

BIBLIOGRAPHY

Macalister 1902, 46
Macalister 1903, 279 and fig.
Crawford 1912, 237
Macalister 1949a, no. 911, p. 96 and pl. XXXVI, fig. 911
Lionard 1961, fig. 2.3
Barrington 1976, 181-2
Cuppage *et al.* 1986, 301

SITE

Inishvickillane lies *c.* 4 km south-west of Slea Head, and since at least the eighteenth century has been inhabited only intermittently. At the south-east end of the island are the remains of an early monastic settlement. The site, although apparently lacking formal enclosure, comprises the ruins of a dry-stone oratory, a graveyard, a *leacht*, a possible beehive hut-site, and a holy well dedicated to St Brendan (see Cuppage *et al.*1986, 298-301). In front of the oratory into which the inscribed stone may have been built, Windele discovered, in or before 1849, a cross-inscribed ogham stone (Brash 1879, 226). By 1901 it was acting as a lintel (Macalister 1902, 44), and in 1902 it was removed to Trinity College, Dublin where it remains. The ogham stone is a tall slim pillar with a cross on each face and the ogham text on one arris (Macalister 1945, no. 185, pp. 178-9 and figs). Macalister also recorded another stone incised with a 'plain cross of two lines' (1902, 46) but it is no longer in evidence. Cuppage's team noted only 'a few low orthostats' in what was probably the graveyard (1986, 300) and a cross-incised portion of a stone font formerly kept in the oratory (1986, 301).

INNISFALLEN (LOUGH LEANE): INIS FAITHLENN

Site name Abbey Church, Innisfallen Island
Townland Innisfallen
NGR 09338, 08937
SMR site no. KE066-07201-

This fragment of a small cross-slab is from the important island monastery of Innisfallen.

CURRENT LOCATION

The carved stone is built into the Abbey church of the ruined Augustinian Monastery on Innisfallen Island, Lough Leane. It is in the north splay of the central baulk of the interior face of the east window.

HISTORY

The stone was first noticed by John Sheehan of University College Cork, and is discussed and illustrated in an unpublished MA thesis by Weaver (unpublished 1995, Appendix 1 and fig. 22). It is not mentioned in any previous written sources and was not recorded by the OPW during the course of its work on the island between 1929 and 1931.

DESCRIPTION

The stone is a small fragment of a sandstone cross-slab. It has suffered severe damage and is broken on all four edges. A large area of the surface has broken off along the right side. The maximum dimensions of the surviving portion are: H. 25 cm, W. 15 cm, T. 3 cm visible.

As the slab is built into the wall, its total thickness cannot be ascertained. The upper half of the fragment is occupied by the remains of an incised linear cross, enclosed in a circular frame of diameter 15.5 cm. The cross is equal-armed with a short perpendicular bar at each terminal. In the bottom right corner of the fragment, below the cross, are the remains of further carving. The incision is identical in character to that of the cross and the figure is clearly part of the original scheme. The carving is of F-shaped form with the right tips of its two horizontal strokes and the bottom of its vertical stroke lost at the broken edges of the stone. Weaver identified this as a letter. In comparison with the cross, the letter is not perpendicular but leans slightly backwards. If this is part of an inscription then the text appears to have been arranged in a curve round the cross, as on the similar monument from Cloghinch. The large gap to the left of the letter indicates that it is either the first or last letter of the text. If the slab were turned 90 degrees then the text would run round the top or bottom of the slab. The latter compares with the layout of the Cloghinch text.

An alternative, but less likely, explanation could be that the lower carving is not a letter but the remains of some geometric embellishment of the cross. The vertical stroke could be interpreted as one edge of a splaying shaft supporting the encircled cross, with the upper horizontal stroke part of an outer circular frame and the lower horizontal stroke perhaps a third framing line. Such an arrangement would be comparable with other cross-in-circle motifs with elaborate handles which are persuasively interpreted as representations of flabellae or liturgical fans (Lionard 1961, 111, 137; see also Richardson 1993, 30-1).

LETTERING

The script used is probably half-uncial and the letter H. is 8 cm.

TEXT

Depending on which way up the slab is orientated, the text reads

F—

or

—D

INTERPRETATION

The text reads either *f–* or *–d*. Comparison with other stones suggests that the text probably contained a personal name. Depending on how the slab was orientated, the text may therefore have been a name beginning with *f* or one ending in *d*.

DISCUSSION

The slab's distinctive features are its diminutive scale and the relative prominence given to the lettering. The simple cross-in-circle motif is very common on early Christian monuments in Ireland, being found predominantly on upright cross-slabs. Kelly described a seventh-century sub-group of monuments as 'distinguished by the use of particularly small, compact stones, ornament of cross-in-circle motif and the rare inclusion of inscriptions, restricted to the name of an individual where these occur' (Kelly, D. 1988, 98). The Innisfallen fragment has been reused in a structure dating from the thirteenth century but is clearly considerably older. Although Kelly's group is distinctive, the form is simple and dating remains tentative. Kelly nevertheless argued cogently that this sub-group is of early date, most likely seventh century, but belonging to 'an ornamental tradition which extends back to the sixth century' (Kelly, D. 1988, 100). If Kelly's dating is correct then the Innisfallen stone would date from the earliest days of St Finian's foundation, and be the sole relic of the initial phase of ecclesiastical activity on the island.

Emphasizing the distinction between such stones and larger recumbent slabs, which were intended to lie over the grave, Kelly concluded that the smaller monuments differed in function and may have been intended to be placed within the grave (Kelly, D. 1988, 98). Kelly characterized the distribution of this type of monument as a dense cluster in the Midlands (counties Tipperary and Offaly) with an extension along the Shannon to Inishcaltra. On the basis of outliers in Donegal, Galway and Wexford and the widespread distribution of the cross-in-circle motif, she suggested that 'the original occurrence of this type of slab may have been more widespread' (Kelly, D. 1988, 99). The Innisfallen discovery appears to bear out her conjecture.

As Weaver noted, the similarity between this piece and the Cloghinch slab is striking; they differ only in that the latter has a double circle. The original surface of the Innisfallen stone is a striking pinky-orange colour but the underlying stone, visible in the carved incisions and the broken portions, is a pale grey. As at Lismore and Toureen Peacaun, it is possible that this feature was used to deliberate effect to heighten the contrast of the incised carving.

BIBLIOGRAPHY

Weaver unpublished 1995, Appendix 1 (unpaginated), slab 2 and fig. 22

EXAMINED

July 1998 (KF)

SITE

Innisfallen is the largest of several islands in Lough Leane. In the seventh century the island was at the heart of the territory of Munster's dominant political group, the Eóganacht Locha Léine. According to tradition the monastery of Innisfallen was founded in the seventh century by Finian the Leper. It is mentioned several times in the Annals, being twice plundered by Vikings, and was renowned as a centre of learning into the fourteenth century. The Annals of Inisfallen (Oxford, Bodleian Ms. Rawl. B503; Mac Airt 1951), the oldest major collection of Irish annals, which was begun at Emly around 1092, was still being continued on the island around 1215.

The oldest surviving structure on Innisfallen is the remains of an early church incorporated as the western two-thirds of the later Abbey church. The *antae* and the (restored) flat-headed doorway, indicate a tenth-century date for this building. The rest of the church and domestic buildings were added in the thirteenth century. A twelfth-century oratory by the shore features Romanesque carving.

In addition to the inscribed slab there are seven other pieces of early sculpture, all large recumbent slabs. Six are similar, of trapezoidal form, varying in length from 2.1 m to 1.6 m, and in width from 0.7 m to 0.5 m and all with chamfered edges. Four of these are too heavily weathered to determine whether or not they ever bore carving but the other two have incised crosses. They are likely to date from the twelfth century or later (Weaver unpublished 1995, Appendix 2). The seventh slab is likely to be earlier; it was discovered beneath the cloister wall and may relate to the tenth-century phase of building. It is a little smaller than the others, lacks the chamfered edges, and is incised with a Latin cross with semi-circular expansions at the terminals and a circle at the intersection of the arms (Weaver unpublished 1995, fig. 24). Such slabs are usually dated to the ninth or tenth century (Lionard 1961, 131). Much of the lower right quadrant of the surface of the Innisfallen slab has broken away and there are no traces of any lettering.

KILFOUNTAN: CILL FHIONNTAIN

Site name Kilfountan
Townland Kilfountan
NGR 04255,10330
SMR site no. KE043-136---

This cross-incised pillar probably dates from the seventh century.

CURRENT LOCATION
The stone is standing in a pile of quartz rubble to the east of the ruined oratory.

HISTORY
The stone was first recorded by Windele in September 1848 when it was standing in the graveyard. Windele described the stone as 'Near its S E angle but a few feet from it' (Windele MSS 12.C.11, p. 416). It is not clear, however, if Windele was referring to the south-east angle of the oratory or of the graveyard. Petrie recorded the stone both 'about ten feet from the north-east corner of the church' and 'near the side of a road' (Petrie 1878, 5). It is not clear whether these descriptions refer to the same location or whether the stone was moved. Macalister's photograph (1937, pl. XXIII) suggests that the stone was then in roughly the position it occupies today. Petrie said that an illustration of the stone had 'been already published' by Windele (Petrie 1878, 5) but we have failed to trace this publication.

DESCRIPTION

The current dimensions of the stone as it stands in the ground are:
H. 150 cm, W. 25 cm (maximum), T. *c.* 9 cm.

The stone is a tall, slender pillar, roughly square in section, and tapering towards the base. Only the west face, which Cuppage described as 'peculiarly spatulate' in form, is decorated (Cuppage *et al.* 1986, 304). The upper part of this face contains an equal-armed cross set inside a circle; the cross has expanded terminals with the lower one joining on to the circle. Above the circle and joined to it by a small stem is a scrolled crest. Beneath the circle and separate from it is an elaborate design ending in a pelta motif. The design comprises a sunken field of inverted triangular shape with a concave upper edge. A short stem issues from its lower apex. At the left and right apices is a large incised oval with a pendant 'string' looping to the outer edge of the stone. Also pendant from each apex is a line which runs down to form the pelta. In addition, two short lines curve upwards and outwards from the right oval towards the edge of the stone. The text is incised in one line beneath the design and reads vertically upwards with the bottoms of the letters to the viewer's right. Macalister (1937, 224) read a preceding line of text, parallel to the existing line and reading in the opposite direction, that is, downwards with the bottoms of the letters to the viewer's left. There are traces of what was possibly lettering here but nothing is now legible and the orientation cannot be determined. A short ogham text is incised on the lower part of the south-east angle of the stone, reading upwards.

LETTERING

The text uses half-uncial script and, although slightly worn, is legible. Apart from the first letter, the letters are deeply incised. They vary quite considerably in size, the maximum letter H. being 7.5 cm.

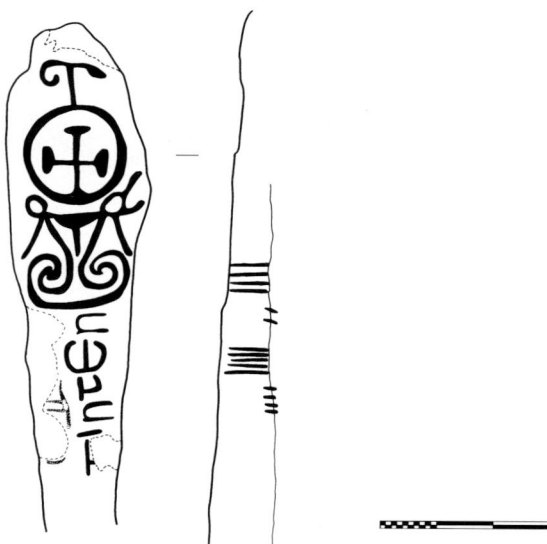

TEXT

[–]
[F̱]INTEN

INTERPRETATION

As suggested by Macalister, the first letter is most plausibly read as ƒ (Macalister 1937, 223) and thus the second line of text reads –[F]inten, the male personal name Fintan. Macalister thought the F was set at right angles to the other letters, that is, with the bottom of the letter towards the base of the stone; while this is possible, it is also possible to read the F set the same way as the rest of the text. Macalister read a preceding line of text as a *chi-rho* followed by *sci* (Macalister 1937, 224) but there is no legible text there now. Hamlin looked for the *chi-rho* but reported 'I could not see this to my satisfaction' (Hamlin 1972, 26). The ogham text reads *eqodd–*. The letters are reasonably clear but any trace of the final I read by Macalister has gone (McManus 1991, 61, 67). There are traces of what may be further letters before the E and at the top of the pillar but these are highly uncertain. Macalister noted the lower marks but dismissed them as 'illusory' (1945, 179).

DISCUSSION

The ogham and roman alphabet inscriptions appear to be unrelated to one another, that is, an existing ogham stone seems to have been re-used as a cross-slab. The stone was not inverted; since the two sets of carving do not impinge on one another, it is impossible to test the assumption that the ogham is the earlier. The form of the cross design may be paralleled on numerous cross-slabs from the Dingle and Iveragh peninsulas assigned by Henry to the sixth and seventh centuries (1937a, 279). The lower part of this design, with its opposed inward-turning spirals and flattish bottom, is reminiscent of the lower part of the cross-shaft on Reask 1, although here the 'stem' is truncated. The ovals with pendant lines are reminiscent of the 'ribbon-bow' shapes in the cross-head on Reask 1. The crest above the encircled cross is an unusual feature, perhaps intended for the *titulus*. It may be compared with horizontal bars above crosses on cross-slabs from Reask, stones B, C and G, and from Lateevemore, stone 2 (Cuppage *et al.* 1986, pp. 341-4 and fig. 205; pp. 330-32 and fig. 199). The comparison with Reask G is strengthened by the presence of a triangular field on a stem with scrolls at the upper corners. Fanning dismissed the design on the Kilfountan stone as 'crude' and 'poorly executed' and saw it as 'possibly a poor copy' of Reask 1 (1981, 140). However, with allowance made for damage and for the uneven surface of the stone, the Kilfountan stone may be considered as successfully combining a number of disparate elements into an unusual design.

The tentative art-historical dating of the Kilfountan cross-pillar to the seventh century appears to be corroborated by the text. The spelling *Finten* for the later *Fintan* is conservative and implies a comparatively early date, perhaps seventh- or early eighth-century. The name appears in the form *Finten(us)* in Adomnán's *Vita Columbae* written probably in the late 690s (Anderson, A. O.

and Anderson, M. O. 1991) while *Fintan* is found in the *Notulae* in the Book of Armagh written in 807 (Bieler 1979, 181 (35)). *Fintan* was a popular male personal name borne both by clerics and secular figures (Uhlich 1993, 255; Ó Corráin and Maguire 1990, 104). While it is possible that a later reading of the text may have inspired the dedication of Kilfountan/*Cill Fionntain*, it is more likely that the text is a dedicatory one, recording the donation or dedication of the site to the eponymous saint, although to which of the many St Fintans is not known. A parallel is provided by the cross-incised pillar from Kilnasaggart, Co. Armagh which records a probably early eighth-century donation of *in loc so*, 'this place', to the Apostle Peter (Macalister 1949a, no. 946, pp. 114-15 and pl. XLVI, fig. 946). Epigraphic dedications to eponymous saints are known from Ireland, for example the stone which was probably inscribed *S(an)c(t)i Brecani* at Kilbrecan, Aran Mór (Macalister 1949a, no. 531, p. 5 and pl. II, fig. 531).

BIBLIOGRAPHY

Petrie 1878, 5 and pl. III, fig. 5
Brash 1879, 226-7, 373 and pl. XXX
Ferguson 1879, 39
Allen 1887, 104
Ferguson 1887, 37
Allen 1889, 79
Wakeman 1890-91b, 358 and pl. III, fig. 44
Macalister 1897, 61-2
Crawford 1912, 234 and pl.
Henry 1933, vol. 2, pl. 5.7
Macalister 1937, 221-6, pl. XXIII and figs
Macalister 1945, no. 186, pp. 179-80 and figs
Henry 1965, 57 and pl. 15
Evans 1966, 130-1
Hamlin 1972, 26
Barrington 1976, 179, 246
Weir 1980, 157 and fig.
Fanning 1981, 140, 171
Cuppage *et al.* 1986, 302-4, fig. 178a and pl. XVIb
Killanin and Duignan 1989, 129
Herity 1990, 208
Sheehan 1990, 160
McManus 1991, 61, 67
Herity 1995, 239
Swift 1997, 41, 57-60 and fig.
Windele MSS 12.C.11, pp. 416-8

EXAMINED
June 1996 (KF)

SITE

The remains at Kilfountan are typical of the early ecclesiastical sites of the south-west. Within the sub-oval enclosure there are the remains of a dry-stone oratory and a rectangular building. As well as the inscribed stone, a *bullaun* stone and a quernstone of Disc A type were discovered here. The mound of quartz in which the inscribed pillar is loosely set merges with the rubble of the collapsed corner of the oratory. There is a further area of stone collapse, an arc extending westwards from the northern edge of the quartz. It is possible that the quartz was once part of a *leacht* but this is far from certain. The site was in use as a *ceallúrach* until the nineteenth century but nothing is known of its early history. For a detailed discussion, see Cuppage *et al.* 1986, 302-4.

KILMALKEDAR: CILL MAOLCHÉDAIR

Site name Kilmalkedar Church
Townland Kilmalkedar
NGR 04027, 10617
SMR site no. KE042-02608-

Two inscribed stones are known from this important early Christian and medieval ecclesiastical site, a large cross-incised slab and a fragment of a second cross-incised slab.

Kilmalkedar 1: cross-incised pillar

CURRENT LOCATION

The stone is cemented into a modern base beside the chancel arch, inside the ruins of the Romanesque church.

HISTORY

The stone was recorded and drawn by Pelham in 1804 and by Chatterton and Windele in 1838. Pelham described it as standing in the churchyard, 'about five yards from the church door' (Pelham 1804, 183). Chatterton recorded it as 'near the entrance of the church' (Chatterton 1839, 156) but Windele gave more detail. It was then standing 'Facing the West door of the Church' and '8 feet to the West of the door' (Windele MSS 12.C.11, p. 84), with the inscribed face of the stone described as the 'Western face of the Stone facing the door' (Windele MSS 12.C.11, p. 187). This seems to indicate that the stone was then inside the west door of the church. Windele noted that it was described as five yards from the door in 1804 but said that this was 'wrong' (Windele MSS 12.C.11, p. 84). It seems, however, that the stone had been moved: Chatterton's and Windele's drawings show the stone buried quite deeply in the earth so that none of text b below/to the right of text a was then visible; Pelham's drawing, however, shows that most, if not all, of text a was visible in 1804.

By 1877 the stone was certainly in the churchyard: Quin illustrated the stone with two photographs, both showing the full length of the stone as it is today, but with it in slightly different places. In one photograph (pl. XCIII), the stone is shown in a corner, outside and to the right of the west door, and a metre or more from it. In the other (pl. XCV) the stone is shown outside the door and immediately to its right. The latter photograph accords with Quin's description of the stone as standing 'at the side of the west door' (Quin, E. R. W. 1877, 54). By 1892 the stone was 'lying about in the church-yard at Kilmalkedar utterly uncared for' ((-) 1892, 145), which may or may not indicate that it had been moved again. It remained in the churchyard for many years but by 1975 was again inside the church (Harbison 1975, 109). By 1982 it was in its present position as Hamlin's photograph shows (Hamlin 1982, pl. 17.1 C).

DESCRIPTION

The current dimensions of the stone as it stands in its base are:
H. *c.* 121 cm, W. *c.* 32 cm, T. *c.* 15 cm (maximum).
The stone is a worked pillar of rectangular cross-section. It is neatly broken at the top and the extant design indicates that a sizeable portion is missing. Both broad faces are incised with crosses. On one face there is a linear Latin cross with inwardly disposed 'C' scrolls at each terminal. Above this is the lower arc of a circle inside which is what appears to be part of a cross-arm, also with a scrolled terminal. On the other face is the long shaft of a cross terminating in

an inward turning 'C' scroll. The texts are incised on the left side of the stone, set vertically downwards with the bottoms of the letters to the viewer's left. Text a is complete but text b is incomplete at the beginning and there are traces of further lettering at the end. Text b is set in four portions, on both sides, above and below text a. Text a was obviously inscribed first, in rather large letters; text b, in rather smaller letters, was then fitted in around it.

LETTERING
Text a is clearly legible; some letters of text b are damaged but this text is also mostly legible. Both texts are in half-uncial script with a maximum letter H. of 8 cm.

TEXT

a DN̄I

b –BCDEFGHIKLMN
  OPQRS ‖ TUX[..]E/T

INTERPRETATION
Text a reads *dn̄i* for *D(omi)ni* 'of the Lord'. (See the **Introduction §5.3.3** for a discussion of the *nomen sacrum*). Text b is a Latin alphabet, incomplete at the beginning. It reads *–bcdefghiklmn opqrs tux[–]et* for *[a]bcdefghiklmnopqrstux[yzet]*. The last letter appears to be the manuscript ligature of E and T for Latin *et* 'and'. The preceding two letters appear to be a Y of rather unusual form and a Z.

DISCUSSION
The form of cross used, with inwardly disposed scrolled terminals, is widely paralleled elsewhere on the Dingle Peninsula, for instance on slabs from Glin North, Kilduff and Kilshannig (Sheehan 1990, 160; Cuppage *et al.* 1986,

pp. 291-3, 301-2, fig. 177; p. 324, fig.171), and also on Reask 1. The Kilmalkedar stone is more regular in shape than most of these other examples.

Contracted forms of *Dominus* are also found on Kilmalkedar 2 and on Reask 1 and 2, though Kilmalkedar 1a is the only example of the genitive case. Text b, the Latin alphabet, is not paralleled on any other Irish stone. However a piece of leather with a partial alphatet, A – F, was found in Dublin in 1978 and is now in the NMI (Okasha 1992, no. 190, pp 44-5 and fig. III a). As first suggested by Petrie (1845, 132), text b may have been cut as a teaching aid for the Latin language. Alternatively, it may have had a more symbolic meaning. The alphabet comprised the *elementa fidei*, 'the elements of faith' and the Latin alphabet could stand for the whole of scripture. As Márkus discussed, alphabets were used in church consecration rituals and could also stand metaphorically for (monastic) rules of life (Márkus 1996). Henry's art-historical dating of similar cross-slabs to the sixth or seventh century (1937a, 279) is corroborated by the palaeographical evidence. Bieler dated the form of half-uncial used to the sixth-century (1949, 271) although, as Higgitt suggested, this date is probably rather early and a seventh-century date may be more likely (Higgitt 1990, 154).

BIBLIOGRAPHY

Pelham 1804, 183-4 and pl. II, fig. 1
Chatterton 1839, 156-7 and figs
Petrie 1845, 131-3 and fig.
Quin, E. R. W. 1877, 54-5, pls XCIII, XCV and fig. on p.190
Petrie 1878, 7-8 and pl. V, fig. 9
Ferguson 1879, 39, 43-4
Allen 1887, 104-5
Ferguson 1887, 55
Stokes 1887, 119-20 and fig. 53
Allen 1889, 113
Wakeman 1890-91b, 356 and pl. II, fig. 9
(-) 1890-91, 616 and fig.
Allen 1892, 267 and figs on p. 268
(-) 1892, 139-40, 145-6 and figs
Westropp 1897b, 294, 296 and fig.
Macalister 1902, 42, 60n
Crawford 1912, 232
Macalister 1928, 230-1 and fig. 13
Bieler 1949, 271
Macalister 1949a, no. 913, pp. 96-7 and pl. IX, figs 913
Lionard 1961, 106n, 108 and figs 8.7
Ó hÉailidhe 1967, 121
Harbison 1975, 109
Barrington 1976, 248
Weir 1980, 157

Fanning 1981, 141, 171
Hamlin 1982, 286, 291 and pl. 17.1 C
Cuppage *et al.* 1986, 311, fig. 184 and pl. 30
Killanin and Duignan 1989, 62
Higgitt 1990, 153-4
Sheehan 1990, 160
Harbison 1997, 37
Hughes and Hamlin 1997, 84, 124 and fig. 17
Swift 1997, 57-8 and fig.
Thomas 1998, 56
Windele MSS 12.C.11, p. 84 and figs, pp. 186-7 and figs

EXAMINED

June 1996 (EO); July 1996 (KF)

Kilmalkedar 2: probably a cross-incised pillar

CURRENT LOCATION

The stone is now lost.

HISTORY

The stone was first mentioned in 1889 as 'At Kilmalkedar' (Allen 1889, 120). In 1892 it was described as 'lying about in the church-yard at Kilmalkedar utterly uncared for' ((-) 1892, 145). In 1986 Cuppage reported that it was then missing but had still been at the site in 1965 when 'two freshly-broken fragments of it lay on a large tomb in the chancel of the church' (Cuppage *et al.* 1986, 311).

DESCRIPTION

The dimensions, description and text are taken from the anonymous 1892 account of the stone ((-) 1892, 145-7 and fig.; see illustration below):
H. *c.* 45 cm, W. *c.* 30 cm, T. *c.* 10.5 cm.
The stone was described as 'the fragment of a slab' ((-) 1892, 146). From the published drawing, one end and the two long edges appear straight and may have been original. The other end is irregular and was clearly broken. At the straight end, which may have been the original top of the stone, was an equal-armed cross in a circle. The right, left, and lower arms had slightly expanded terminals and the upper arm ended in a horizontal B-shaped terminal. Below this was the remains of a cross with slightly expanded terminals. Beneath this cross was a one-line text, which may or may not have been complete. Since it is not clear which way up the stone originally was, it is not clear how the text was orientated on the stone.

LETTERING

The text was legible and used half-uncial script.

TEXT

DNE—

INTERPRETATION

The text appears to have read *dne*– for *D(omi)ne* –. This was presumably the Latin vocative *domine* 'O Lord'. (See the **Introduction §5.3.3** for a discussion of the *nomen sacrum*).

DISCUSSION

The fragment was of similar width and thickness to Kilmalkedar 1, although the design suggests that it is unlikely to be the missing portion of that stone. It is more likely to have been the remains of a similar monument. The B-shaped terminal is unusual, but resembles the scroll terminals on the cross-slabs at Kilshannig (Cuppage *et al.* 1986, 324 and fig. 171) and at Reask, stone F (Cuppage *et al.* 1986, 342-3 and fig. 206). The contracted form of *Dominus* links Kilmalkedar 2 with Kilmalkedar 1 and with Reask 1 and 2. Like the Reask texts, and unlike that of Kilmalkedar 1, this text does not appear to have had a horizontal mark of contraction. The fragment is likely to have been contemporary with these other monuments and thus dated to the seventh century.

BIBLIOGRAPHY

Allen 1889, 120
Allen 1892, 267-8 and figs
(-) 1892, 139-40, 145-7 and fig.
Crawford 1912, 232
Macalister 1949a, no. 912, p. 96 and pl. XLI, fig. 912
Macalister 1949b, 337-8
Lionard 1961, fig. 28.2
Fanning 1981, 141
Cuppage *et al.* 1986, 311-12 and fig. 185

SITE

The early Christian and medieval site at Kilmalkedar covers a large area (see Cuppage *et al.* 1986, 308-23). Although reputedly founded by Maolcethair in the seventh century, the site is associated with St Brendan. The church was probably built in the mid twelfth century and remained important throughout the medieval period. Existing remains from the early Christian period include a corbelled building, perhaps a cell, some 50 m from the church, an ogham stone, the sundial stone, a plain stone cross and some *bullaun* stones. There is also St Brendan's oratory, situated some 400 m from the church. Existing buildings dating from medieval times include the Romanesque church with some fine architectural sculpture, St Brendan's House and the Chancellor's House. There are also two wells and a number of cross-inscribed stones in the graveyard.

LOHER: AN LÓTHAR

Site name Kildreenagh burial ground
Townland Loher
NGR 05091, 06158
SMR site no. KE106-00701-

A cross-incised pillar, of possibly seventh-century date, was found at this early ecclesiastical site.

CURRENT LOCATION
The stone stands at the north-west corner of the *leacht* inside the ecclesiastical site.

HISTORY

The stone was found by Henry in 'the course of field-work in Kerry in 1946 and 1947' and she recorded her indebtedness for its discovery to Kevin Danaher, and to T. Murphy of Waterville (Henry 1948, 175). The stone was then on the *leacht* at the site, presumably in its present position.

DESCRIPTION

The current dimensions of the stone as it stands in the ground are:
H. *c.* 129 cm, W. *c.* 23 cm, T. *c.* 15 cm.
The square pillar is roughly worked but its carved (west) face has been dressed slightly smooth. The incised design consists of an outline Latin cross 37.5 cm high with expanded horizontal and upper arms. Except for the bottom of the shaft, the whole cross is outlined by a parallel contour, at a distance of *c.* 6 mm. Henry commented on the 'very fine quality' of the carving (1956-57, 159). Immediately below the bottom of the shaft are two 'conical drilled holes' (Herity 1995, 240). Herity stated that the 'outer line at the right-hand corner of the upper limb is drawn out in a slightly more marked curve to the right and terminates in a short oblique stroke immediately right of a vertical crack in the stone'; he considered that this feature 'subtly but clearly defines the cross as a Chi-rho' (Herity 1995, 240). However, the present authors were unable to verify the existence of this feature. The two letters are incised in the lower quadrants of the cross; they are not joined to the cross but float free.

LETTERING

The text is legible and the maximum letter H. is *c.* 7 cm. The *alpha* is an angular and elegant capital A which may be compared with the display capitals of insular manuscripts (Herity 1995, 240). It has an x-shaped bar, with the free ends joined by a small horizontal line to create a triangular wedge. A mirror image of this triangle is formed in a similar way at the apex of the A. The *omega* is formed from three straight lines 'fanning outwards from a single point at the lower end and terminating in triangular expansions similar in size and similarly placed to those of the Alpha at the upper ends' (Herity 1995, 240).

TEXT

A ‖ ω

INTERPRETATION

The text reads A ω, the first and last letters of the Greek alphabet, which constitute a *nomen sacrum* of Christ. The reference is to the book of Revelations, for example Revelations 22:13. *Alpha* and *omega* are also found on Church Island 1 (see the discussion in the **Introduction §5.3.3**).

DISCUSSION

The inscribed pillar is one of three which mark a poorly preserved *leacht* at the south end of the sub-rectangular raised area situated at the northern edge of the enclosure. The other two are smaller, rough pillars each incised with a linear Latin cross. Henry placed the inscribed stone from Loher with three other examples of plain Latin crosses from the area (Inchfarrannaglerach and Dromkeare, both in the vicinity of Lough Currane, Waterville, and Skellig Michael) (Henry 1948, 175-7). These she contrasted with the more elaborate cross forms found more generally on slabs on the Iveragh and Dingle peninsulas. A slab from Shronahiree More may also be considered part of this smaller group, particularly as the square panel at its crossing recalls the three-line arrangement in the similar position on the Loher slab (O'Sullivan and Sheehan 1996, 312, fig. 204b).

Henry compared the Loher design to a manuscript illustration from the seventh-century *Codex Usserianus* of a cross-like *chi-rho* with *alpha* and *omega* in its lower quadrants (Henry 1948, 177 and pl. XXXV, fig. 5; *Codex Usserianus Primus*, Trinity College Dublin, MS A.4.15 (55), folio 149v: see Alexander 1978, no. 1, p. 27 and pl. 1). While the general similarity is striking, the manuscript cross differs from Loher in several respects: it has an expanding shaft; all four of its terminals have concave ends; its transom is lower; its upper arm has a *chi-rho* hook (although see Herity's identification above), and the letter-forms are different. As Sheehan pointed out the form of cross with pendant *alpha* and *omega* is ultimately derived from bronze altar-crosses of Coptic type and is found copied in stone on Merovingian grave-slabs (see for example Le Blant 1856, pl. 40, no. 238). Sheehan argued for a metalwork, rather than manuscript, model for Loher on the basis of the 'carefully disposed basal dots' which he considered 'suggestive of rivets serving to join a metal cross to a stand' (Sheehan 1990, 164).

Sheehan considered the Loher text to be 'the finest and in all likelihood ... the earliest representation of *alpha* and *omega* on an Irish slab' (Sheehan 1990, 164). It may have been a model for the epigraphic use of *alpha* and *omega* in the local area, for example on the nearby slab Church Island 1. Two slabs on Skellig Michael may be debased examples of the same motif, although having saltires in place of the letters (O'Sullivan and Sheehan 1996, 280, fig.180).

BIBLIOGRAPHY

Henry 1948, 175-7 and pl. XXXV, fig. 2
Henry 1956-57, 158-9 and pl. XXIX, a

Lionard 1961, 139
Henry 1965, 54-6 and pl. 16
Evans 1966, 131 and fig. 10
Thomas 1971, 115 and fig. 54
Hamlin 1972, 28n
Barrington 1976, 178, 284 and fig. on p. 177
Weir 1980, 53, 162 and pls on pp. 88, 122
Killanin and Duignan 1989, 304
Edwards 1990, 162 and fig. 83b
Sheehan 1990, 164 and fig. 3a
Herity 1995, 239-40 and pl. 5, fig. 1
O'Sullivan and Sheehan 1996, 307, fig. 199 and pl. XVIIb
Hughes and Hamlin 1997, 84, 86 and fig. 17
Swift 1997, 74

EXAMINED

May 1998 (EO); July 1998 (KF)

SITE

The site, known as *Cill Draighneach* (Kildreenagh) and as *Ceallúnach an Lóthair*, lies in rough pasture to the west of the old road between Waterville and Derrynane. The early Christian site includes the remains of an oratory and of a circular hut, a *leacht* and a burial ground, all set within a sub-circular enclosure defined by a poorly preserved stone wall. There is also a large number of modern plain grave-markers. Nothing is known of the early history of the site; see further O'Sullivan and Sheehan 1996, 305-7.

REASK: AN RIASC

Site name Calluragh burial ground (An Cheallúnach)
Townland Reask
NGR 03669,10433
SMR site no. KE042-06001-

Two inscribed and cross-incised pillars, of late sixth- or early seventh-century date, are part of a collection of ten cross-slabs from this early monastic site.

Reask 1: cross-inscribed pillar

CURRENT LOCATION

The stone stands, possibly *in situ*, at the eastern edge of the enclosure, north of the internal dividing wall of the early ecclesiastical site.

HISTORY

The stone has been at Reask since at least June 1838 when Windele drew and examined it, describing it as at 'Riesk about a quarter of a Mile SE of Ballinrannig' (Windele MSS 12.C.11, p. 149). He returned there in September

1848, describing the site as 'a Cealuragh or ancient and now neglected burial place' (Windele MSS 12.C.11, p. 435). When du Noyer examined and drew the stone in 1866, he described it at 'Calluragh Burial Ground 1 mile East of Ballyferriter Dingle' and 'on Dingle Road' (du Noyer unpublished, vol. I, p. 61; the drawing is dated 1866). These descriptions presumably all refer to the early Christian site at Reask although Crawford introduced a note of caution in describing the six stones he knew as 'In or near the old graveyard' (Crawford 1912, 232). Macalister stated that the stone had been moved to University College Cork (Macalister 1949a, 97) but, as Fanning pointed out, Macalister had confused this stone with one of the other, uninscribed, stones from Reask (Fanning 1981, 140).

DESCRIPTION

The current dimensions of the stone as it now stands in the ground are:
H. *c.* 188 cm, W. *c.* 57 cm, T. *c.* 10 cm.
The stone is a tall, thin sandstone slab; it is intact but of an irregular natural shape. The back and sides are plain but the face is decorated with a full-length cross. This takes the form of a cross-of-arcs enclosed in a circle. In each angle of the arms a stem terminates in a double loop and tails, like a stylised ribbon bow. The cross stands on a linear shaft joined to the lower arm with a pair of inwardly disposed scrolls. The shaft terminates in a pelta and is further embellished by an irregularly shaped frame which incorporates three pairs of inwardly disposed scrolls. The text is complete and is incised low down and to the left of the cross shaft. It reads vertically downwards in one line with the bottom of the letters to the viewer's left.

LETTERING

The text is legible and uses half-uncial script. The maximum letter H. is 8 cm.

TEXT
DNE

INTERPRETATION

The text reads *dne* for *D(omi)ne*, an abbreviated form of the Latin vocative *domine*, 'O Lord'. (See the **Introduction §5.3.3** for a discussion of the *nomen sacrum*).

DISCUSSION

The pillar's position marks the northern extremity of an inhumation cemetery which has been dated between the late fourth and late seventh centuries. The excavator considered this boundary position to be original (Fanning 1981, 152). The cross design is similar to that on the Kilfountan stone and on other cross-slabs from the Dingle and Iveragh peninsulas, although Fanning considered Kilfountan a 'poor copy' of the Reask stone (Fanning 1981, 140). Fanning's proposed dating of the slab to the sixth or seventh century (1981, 152) concurs with Henry's art-historical dating of related cross-inscribed monuments to the late sixth or seventh century (1937a, 279). Swift compared Reask 1 to other examples of single cross-incised monoliths marking a cemetery of inhumation graves (1997, 40), including the inscribed pillar from Kilnasaggart, Co. Armagh (Macalister 1949a, no. 946, pp. 114-15 and pl. XLVI, fig. 946). The text on this latter stone suggests a date before the second decade of the eighth century and makes explicit the role of the stone as an estate marker. The use of contracted forms of the *nomen sacrum 'Dominus'* on Reask 1 is paralleled on Reask 2, Kilmalkedar 1 and, apparently, on the lost Kilmalkedar 2, the only other example of the vocative *D(omi)ne*. As on Reask 2 and Kilmalkedar 2, there is no horizontal mark of abbreviation.

BIBLIOGRAPHY

du Noyer 1857-61, 253
Petrie 1878, 5-6 and pl. IV, fig. 8
Allen 1887, 104 and fig. 16.1
Allen 1889, 115, 120
Wakeman 1890-91b, 358 and pl. III, fig. 45
Allen 1892, 268 and fig. on p. 274
(-) 1892, 147 and fig.
Macalister 1902, 42
Allen 1904, 165-6
Crawford 1912, 232
Crawford 1926a, 8 and pl. XI
Henry 1933, vol. 1, pp. 42-3, 50; vol. 2, pl. 7.1
Henry 1937a, 278-9 and pl. XXXII, fig. 1
Macalister 1949a, no. 914, p. 97 and pl. XLI, fig. 914
Macalister 1949b, 337-8
Lionard 1961, 137 and fig. 28.3
Henry 1965, 57, 128, 204 and pl. 15
Evans 1966, 127, 131-2 and fig. 60
Fanning 1971, 25, 27-8

Fanning 1975, 7
Harbison 1975, 114 and fig. 36
Barrington 1976, 179, 246 and fig.
Harbison 1976, 68 and fig.
Weir 1980, 159
Fanning 1981, 139-41 and fig. 29 A
Hamlin 1982, 286, 289, 291 and pl. 17.3A
Cuppage *et al.* 1986, 342, fig. 205a and pl. 44
Killanin and Duignan 1989, 61-2
Edwards 1990, 117, 162 and fig. 83c
Sheehan 1990, 160
Manning 1995, 9-10, 20 and pl. 6
Hughes and Hamlin 1997, 86, 125 and fig. 17
Swift 1997, 38, 40-1, 71, 83 and fig. on p. 81
du Noyer unpublished, vol. I, p. 61 and fig.
Windele MSS 12.C.11, pp. 149, 435 and fig. on p. 149

EXAMINED

July 1996 (KF); June 1996, September 1999 (EO)

Reask 2: cross-inscribed pillar

CURRENT LOCATION

The stone stands in the early ecclesiastical site, a little to the east of Reask 1.

HISTORY

The stone was at Reask in September 1848 when Windele revisited Reask and drew 'Those omitted by me on my former inspection' (Windele MSS 12.C.11, p. 435). A sketch made by du Noyer is from a drawing by Graves, made when the stone was still at Reask (du Noyer unpublished, vol. I, p. 41). Quin stated that the stone, with others, was 'brought to Adare about ten years ago', that is, around 1855 (Quin, C. W. 1865, 153). According to Petrie, the stone 'came originally from the burying-place of Reask, but was found by Lord Dunraven, not *in situ*, but lying in an open field in the neighbourhood' (Petrie 1878, 5). Fanning notes an OS Memorandum which substantiates this provenance (Fanning 1971, 27). In 1971, the stone was standing 'in a grove of trees in the manor grounds' (Fanning 1971, 25) but by 1975 it had been returned to Reask (Fanning 1975, 10).

DESCRIPTION

The current dimensions of the stone as it stands in the ground are:
H. *c.* 76 cm, W. *c.* 7 to *c.* 18 cm, T. *c.* 14 cm.
Fanning gives the length of the stone as 114 cm, although this does not tally well with his scaled illustration (Fanning 1971, 25 and fig. 1). The figure of 114 cm was, however, repeated by Cuppage *et al.* (1986, 342) and this may be the length of the whole stone.

The stone is a small, slender pillar of sandstone, probably roughly shaped and dressed. The two sides are plain except for a substantial rectangular slot on the north face which bears signs of wear (Fanning 1971, 27). The west and east faces are both carved with similar linear Latin crosses whose arms and head extend to the edge of the stone. The grooving of the crosses is deeper and wider than that of the texts.

The cross on the east face measures 41 cm by 13 cm and has a shaft which merges with the last letter of the text. There is a small dot in each angle of the cross and two others, one on either side of the top of the upper arm. Text a is incised beneath the cross and following the line of the cross shaft. The text is complete and reads vertically upwards in one line with the bottom of the letters to the viewer's right. On the west face the cross measures 46 cm by 13 cm, and has a shaft with a slightly expanded terminal. Text b is incised beneath the cross on this face and following the line of the cross shaft. The text is complete and reads vertically downwards in one line with the bottoms of the letters to the viewer's left.

LETTERING

Both texts are in half-uncial script and both are clearly legible although the D in text a is of an unusual shape. The maximum letter H. is 8.5 cm.

TEXT

a   DNO
b   DNS

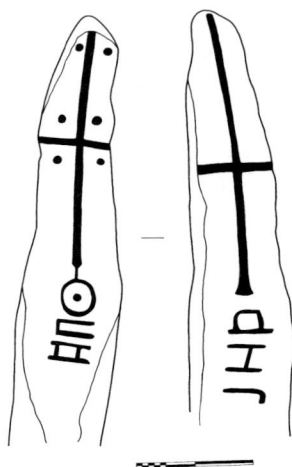

INTERPRETATION

Text a reads *dno* for *D(omi)no*. The text is an abbreviated form of the Latin dative or ablative *Domino*, 'to/from the Lord'. The final letter, O, has a dot at its centre which Fanning interpreted as the trace of a compass used in its execution (1971, 27). Text b reads *dns* for the Latin *D(omi)n(u)s*, 'Lord'. (See the **Introduction §5.3.3** for a discussion of the *nomen sacrum*).

DISCUSSION

The use of forms of the *nomen sacrum* 'Dominus' is paralleled on Reask 1 and Kilmalkedar 1, although the use here of the nominative and dative/ablative cases is unique. As on Reask 1 there is no horizontal bar to mark the abbreviation. Fanning offered a tentative date for Reask 2 of the late sixth or early seventh century (1971, 27-8) by analogy with related monuments bearing contracted forms of the *nomina sacra* dated by Henry to this period (1965, 57).

Dots in the angles of a cross are found on other early cross-slabs from the Dingle and Iveragh peninsulas, for example Reask stone F (Cuppage *et al.* 1986, 342-3 and fig. 206), a stone from Kilvickadownig (Cuppage *et al.* 1986, 327 and fig. 196a) and Shronahiree More stone 1 (O'Sullivan and Sheehan 1996, 312 and fig. 204a). The purpose of the slot, however, remains uncertain. It could have been a mortice to receive the tenon of another element, for instance in a composite structure such as a stone shrine or tomb (Fanning 1981, 143). The presence of wear indicates movement of some sort, perhaps the periodic removal of a component to gain access. A further possibility is that the slot housed a small reliquary which would have been removed and reinserted periodically. Alternatively the slot may reflect a later re-use of the stone.

The relationship between the two inscribed pillars from Reask recalls the arrangement of pillars at the *leacht* at Loher, where a larger and more elaborately carved stone stands in front of a smaller pillar incised with a linear

Latin cross. The Reask pillars are, however, only two out of a total of ten cross-incised slabs extant from the site and the original location of Reask 2 is not known, so the parallels may be coincidental.

BIBLIOGRAPHY

Quin, C. W. 1865, 153-4 and figs
Petrie 1878, 5 and pl. III, figs 6, 7
Brash 1879, 373 and pl. XXX
Allen 1889, 120
Crawford 1912, 232
Macalister 1949a, no. 915, p. 97 and pl. XLI, figs 915
Fanning 1971, 25-8 fig. IA and pl. I
Fanning 1975, 7, 10
Killanin and Duignan 1989, 61-2
Weir 1980, 159
Fanning 1981, 141-3 and fig. 30 D
Cuppage *et al.* 1986, 342, fig. 205d and pl. 43
du Noyer unpublished, vol. I, p. 41 and fig.
Windele MSS 12.C.11, p. 435 and figs

EXAMINED

July 1996 (KF); June 1996, September 1999 (EO)

SITE

The early Christian site at Reask is located about 1 km east of Ballyferriter on high ground overlooking Smerwick harbour. As with the majority of such sites in the south-west little is known of its early history, not even the name of its patron saint. The site at Reask is, however, exceptional in having been fully excavated in modern times. The excavations were undertaken between 1972 and 1975 by the OPW under the direction of Thomas Fanning, in advance of a programme of conservation (Fanning 1981, 68). Prior to excavation the only visible remains were Reask 1, another cross-slab and some traces of dry-stone huts. Excavation of the extensive site revealed three broad phases of use. The earliest occupation level was assigned on the basis of a radio-carbon date of 385 ± 90 a.d. to a 'broad fourth- to seventh-century' bracket, the upper limit being furnished by sherds of Bii ware (Fanning 1981, 155). The main feature of this phase was an inhumation cemetry of 42 lintel and dug graves oriented east-west and aligned in rows which respected the line of the enclosing wall. The northern extremity of the burial ground was marked by Reask 1, the western extremity by a slab-shrine. None of these graves had a marker *in situ* although most of the remarkable collection of cross-slabs from the site were discovered loose in the immediate vicinity. During the second phase of occupation, an oratory and dividing wall were built across the cemetery leaving Reask 1 outside the inner enclosure to the north. Contemporary with this phase are a number of dry-stone huts and evidence for iron-, bronze- and possibly glass-working.

This main phase of development, 'incorporating elements of worship, burial and a range of domestic activity and craftsmanship of a broadly "monastic" character', is loosely dated to between the eighth and twelfth century (Cuppage *et al.* 1986, 338). In the final phase, following the abandonment of the oratory, the site became a *ceallúnach* and continued in use for clandestine burial until modern times (for a full discussion see Fanning 1981, 67-172; for a detailed illustrated summary see Cuppage *et al.* 1986, 336-45).

COUNTY LIMERICK

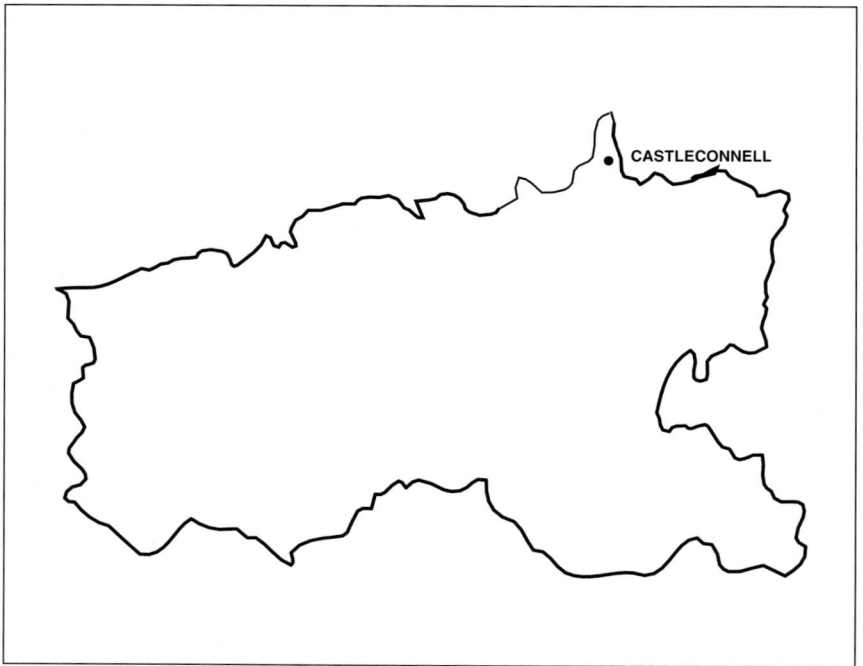

Early Christian inscribed stones of County Limerick

CASTLECONNELL: CAISLEÁN UÍ CHONAILL

Site name Cloon Island
Townland Cloon and Commons
NGR 16604, 16274
SMR site no. LI001-00401-

This small cross-slab comes from an apparently early ecclesiastical site at Cloon Island.

CURRENT LOCATION

The stone is built into the exterior face of the west wall of Cloon church. This ruined medieval church is in the grounds of a private house at Cloon Island, Castleconnell. The stone is set 81 cm from the ground and 69 cm to the right (that is, the south) of the doorway and is obscured from view by a large shrub.

HISTORY

The stone has been known since 1840 when W. F. Wakeman drew it for Petrie (Petrie 1878, 13 and pl. VIII, fig. 15). Petrie stated that this stone was 'built into the interior face of the north wall of a very ancient church upon an island in the Shannon, near Doonass' (1878, 13). Petrie may have made an error in describing which wall it was built into, an easy mistake if he had not himself seen the stone. Alternatively, the stone might have been moved from the north to the west wall at some time between 1840 and 1912 when Crawford described it in its present position (Crawford 1912, 240).

DESCRIPTION

The current dimensions of the stone are:
H. 34 cm, W. 35 cm.
The stone is an irregular slab of sub-circular shape. Its edges are rough and rather damaged but it appears to be substantially intact. Since it is built into the wall, the thickness of the stone cannot be measured. The carving is pecked and both the stone and the carving are badly weathered. The face of the stone contains an outline equal-armed cross set inside two concentric circles. The arms of the cross open into the circular frame formed by these two circles. As currently set in the wall, the cross is positioned vertically and horizontally. The text fills the available space and may be complete. It is incised in two curved lines around the perimeter of the circle with the bottoms of the letters to the circle. The inner line begins at about the ten o'clock position and continues to the five o'clock position. The outer line begins at the two o'clock position and continues until the three o'clock position.

LETTERING

The text probably uses half-uncial script with a maximum letter H. of 3 cm. However the face of the stone is damaged and the letters are highly deteriorated.

TEXT

[.–B̲.N̲D̲–L̲]
A̲[.–]A̲

INTERPRETATION

The text is now very worn and too indistinct to read with any confidence. Macalister interpreted the first character as an initial cross. There are indentations to the right of this character which could be letters or casual damage. Above the upper arm of the cross is the circular bowl of a letter which could be a B. The next letter is obscure but following it is what appears to be an N. Next is a B or D with the lower part of the bowl damaged. It is possible that the text continues with the A of the outer line, but this would give a disjointed layout. It may instead have continued round the perimeter of the circle. The next letter of the lower line is obscure. What follows may be an A and then a G (or B). In the space before the final letter there is what may be the remains of an A or parts of two letters. The last letter could possibly be an L. The outer line begins with an A, followed by what could be an L or T. After a worn area with space for two or three letters is another A. The text might begin *[–b.nd]–*. If this is the correct reading, it could be the beginning of Irish *bendacht*, 'blessing' but the continuation -AC(H)T cannot be made out. We would then expect *ar* and a personal name, but these cannot be read. Macalister described the letters as 'difficult to make out' but suggested that the text read + *lobed fecet cruce(m)* (Macalister 1949a, 100). The present authors could find no evidence on the stone to justify this reading and, indeed, the extant remains seem to rule it out.

DISCUSSION

This is a small, irregular slab, unusual for being more circular than rectangular in outline. A similar cross-form is found on Lismore 1 and on an uninscribed slab from Gallen (Lionard 1961, fig. 12.2), although in both cases with different terminals. The Castleconnell text is placed outside the encircled cross, as it sometimes is on other slabs, for example two from Clonmacnoise (Macalister 1949a, nos 652, 653, p. 48 and pl. XVII, figs 652, 653). Despite the difficulties in interpreting the text, it is clear that it is not an example of the *oróit do* formula. It might have opened with *bendacht ar* but, whatever the reading, it is clearly longer than a single personal name. This marks it out from other small slabs with text outside a framed cross, for example Inishcaltra 21 and the 'Type A' slabs from Clonmacnoise (Ó Floinn 1995, 252-3), which typically are inscribed with only a personal name. This class of slabs is tentatively dated to the eighth century and usually has crosses within a rectilinear frame, not a circle. Those in a circular frame are almost all from Gallen (Lionard 1961, 117).

BIBLIOGRAPHY

Petrie 1878, 13 and pl. VIII, fig. 15
Crawford 1912, 240
Macalister 1949a, no. 918, pp. 98, 100 and pl. XXXV, fig. 918
Lionard 1961, fig. 12.7

EXAMINED

July 1998 (KF)

SITE

Cloon Island is a former island in the channels of the river Shannon, 7 km downstream of Killaloe. The site now covers approximately nine acres but the water is considerably lower than previously, due to a hydro-electric scheme extraction. The ruined church may date from the twelfth century. The later medieval affiliations of the foundation are uncertain. It is stated locally to have been a Franciscan foundation, and was claimed in the seventeenth century to have belonged to the Augustinian Friars (Gwynn and Hadcock 1970, 303, 364). In addition to the inscribed stone, evidence of an early medieval foundation is provided by an uninscribed cross-slab (H. 65 cm, W. 80 cm) incised with a Latin cross with expanded terminals, enclosed in a rectangular frame. It is built into the west exterior wall of the church to the north of the doorway opposite the inscribed slab (Macalister 1949a, 98, 100). Between the church and the house there is a cross-base, with a T-shaped slot, of unknown date.

COUNTY TIPPERARY

Early Christian inscribed stones of County Tipperary

CLOGHINCH: CLOCH hINISE

Site name Cloghinch
Townland Cloghinch
NGR 19592, 16923
SMR site no. TN027-16602-

This small cross-incised stone, of possibly seventh-century date, comes from a site which has also produced a *bullaun* stone and some other cross-incised stones.

CURRENT LOCATION

The stone is in the National Museum of Ireland, reg. no. 1967:138.

HISTORY

The discovery of the stone was recorded by Raftery and described by him as 'Recently' (1966-67, 219). The stone was found lying face downwards in a field about 100 m from the River Nenagh with a limestone *bullaun* stone beside it. In June 1967 the land-owner, Patrick Harrington, presented it to the NMI.

DESCRIPTION

The current dimensions of the stone are:

H. 35 cm, W. 22 cm, T. 21 cm.

The stone is of irregular, sub-rectangular shape. The front and right faces are perpendicular and the back face slopes to give a roughly triangular cross-section. Damage has been sustained along the left edge and it is possible that a wedge has been broken off the back. The long edges of the face, although damaged, are straight. The upper and lower edges are irregular but may be original. It seems likely that this is a carefully selected natural boulder rather than a deliberately shaped stone. The flat carved surface is, however, 'apparently prepared' (Raftery 1966-67, 219). The design, which has been pecked, consists of an equal-armed cross with expanded terminals set inside two concentric circles, *c*. 16 cm and *c*. 19.5 cm in diameter. The cross occupies the full width of the face. The text is set in one curving line beneath the encircled cross. Some text is lost at the left side where the stone's surface is damaged. If the lower edge is not original it is possible that further lines of text could have been lost from beneath the existing one. The stone has been identified as 'medium grained ferruginous micaceous sandstone', perhaps from the immediately local area (NMI file, 1967: 138, analysis by Dr J. S. Jackson).

LETTERING

The text is in half-uncial script and is legible. The maximum letter H. is *c*. 4 cm.

TEXT

−ANLAD

INTERPRETATION

The text reads *-anlad* with one or two letters lost before the first *a*. Comparison with other similar stones suggests that the text is likely to have contained a simple personal name, but its form is not now certain.

DISCUSSION

Kelly noted the similarities, in both cross-design and form of monument, between this stone and a group of uninscribed cross-carved stones from the early monastic site of Latteragh, less than three miles to the north-east. She argued that the stones are all 'closely related, probably contemporaneous, possibly even the work of the same hands' (Kelly, D. 1988, 96). The Cloghinch and Latteragh monuments are examples of a group 'distinguished by the use of particularly small, compact stones, ornament of cross-in-circle motif and the rare inclusion of inscriptions, restricted to the name of an individual where these occur' (Kelly, D. 1988, 98). Although the group is distinctive, the form is simple and dating remains tentative. Kelly nevertheless argued cogently that this subgroup is of early date, probably seventh-century, but belonging to 'an ornamental tradition which extends back to the sixth century' (Kelly, D. 1988, 100). She characterized the distribution of this type of monument as a dense cluster in the Midlands (counties Tipperary and Offaly) with an extension along the Shannon to Inishcaltra. Outliers in Donegal, Galway and Wexford and the widespread distribution of the cross-in-circle motif suggested, however, that 'the original occurrence of this type of slab may have been more widespread' (Kelly, D. 1988, 99). It is argued above that the fragment from Innisfallen, Co. Kerry, may be another example of this class.

BIBLIOGRAPHY

Raftery 1966-67, 219-21 and fig.
Kelly, D. 1988, 96-100 and fig. 30E

EXAMINED

July 1996 (KF)

SITE

The stone was found lying 'on a slight rise in a field about one hundred yards from the right bank of the Nenagh River' (Raftery 1966-67, 219). As pointed out by Raftery (1966-67, 221), there is now no evidence of any human activity at the site, nor any historical evidence that there ever was any. The site is not mentioned in any written sources. Raftery recorded the local information that other cross-incised stones had been found there but had been 'rolled into the river by local children' (Raftery 1966-67, 221). The former presence of these cross-marked stones, along with the existing *bullaun* stone, suggests that this may have been an early ecclesiastical site.

DERRYNAFLAN: DOIRE NA bhFLANN

Site name Derrynaflan
Townland Lurgoe
NGR 21805, 14959
SMR site no. -

A large plain recumbent slab was found at this important island monastery.

CURRENT LOCATION
The stone is in the store of the National Museum of Ireland.

HISTORY
The stone appears to have come to the NMI in 1980 at the time of the discovery of the famous Derrynaflan hoard, but the relevant file contains no record of how or when the slab was discovered (NMI file, DNF IA/19/80).

DESCRIPTION
The current dimensions of the stone are:
H. 91 cm, W. 37 cm, T. 4 cm.
The stone is a complete slab of smooth and fine-grained grey sandstone. The slab is squarely cut and is undecorated except for the single line of text lightly incised along its long axis. The text is complete and well preserved. The original orientation of the slab is not known but if the text read vertically down, the bottoms of the letters would be to the viewer's left. The letters are set close to the right edge of the slab, straddling the middle third of its length. The slim carved line is very shallow and may have been cut rather than pecked. The incisions have been filled with white paint, more-or-less accurately, although with a few minor details overlooked.

LETTERING

The text uses half-uncial script with rather round, unseriffed letters and is legible. There has been some loss to the second A and the interior of the final letter has de-laminated, but otherwise the lettering is undamaged. The form of A is flat-topped and open at the base. A curious feature of this inscription is the marked differences in scale between some of the letters: the letter H. varies between 0.8 cm and 2.5 cm. The letters of the personal name are even and well-spaced. The first four letters are on the same scale, as is the A of *anmain*. However the N is smaller and the M smaller still, with the last three letters continuing at this reduced scale.

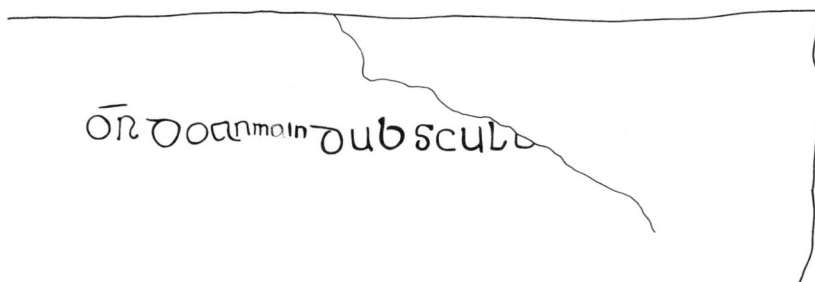

TEXT

OR̄ DOANM<u>A</u>IN DUBSCUL[<u>E</u>]

INTERPRETATION

The text reads ō*r doanmain dubscul[e]* for *or(óit) do anmain Dubscul[e]*, 'a prayer for the soul of Dub-scuile'. Requests for prayers on behalf of the soul of a deceased person, using the formula *or(óit) ar anmain N.*, are unusual, and Macalister lists only seven examples from Ireland (Macalister 1949a). The Derrynaflan slab is unique in using the preposition *do* rather than *ar* to govern *ainim* (see the **Introduction §5.3.4** for discussion of this formula).

DISCUSSION

The Derrynaflan slab is similar to Monaincha 1, 2 and Inishcaltra 5 in bearing text along the long axis of a large flat face but being otherwise undecorated. At Monaincha the lettering is substantial, in size and depth, and dominates the two slabs. On Inishcaltra 5 the proportions are closer to those at Derrynaflan although the inscription is more deeply cut. The Derrynaflan lettering is slight in both incision profile and in scale. The curious variation in scale within the Derrynaflan text may betray a lack of planning by the carver. The use of successively smaller letters in a word (known as 'diminuendo') occurs as a decorative feature in early manuscripts, for example in the late sixth-century

Cathach, RIA MS 12 R 33; O'Neill 1984, 2). However, this is usually restricted to opening words and can scarcely be the reason here. A possible explanation may be that the words were not carved in sequence. It may be that DUBSCULE was carved first and ŌR DO ANMAIN added later, either immediately by the same hand or at a later date. The carver may have moved to the left and begun boldly on the same scale as the personal name, realising only when the A of *anmain* was reached that insufficient room had been left for the rest of the word. It is unclear whether the departure from the more frequent *or(óit) do* formula is merely a stylistic variation, or has some chronological or theological significance.

The male personal name *Dub-scuile* is very uncommon and we know of only two attestations. One is Dub-scuile mac Cinaeda, who, at his death recorded *s.a.* 964 was designated *comarba Coluim Cille*, that is, head of the Columban *paruchia* (Mac Airt and Mac Niocaill 1983, 404-5). Nothing is known of his pedigree. At the time of his abbacy the paruchia's seat was at Kells (Herbert 1988, 82) and there is no obvious link with Derrynaflan. Somewhat closer is Dub-scuile of Clonfert whose death is recorded *s.a.* 946 (Annals of Inisfallen: Mac Airt 1951, 152-3) but again, there is no specific link with Derrynaflan. Dub-scuile remains, therefore, unidentified.

BIBLIOGRAPHY

The stone is unpublished.

EXAMINED

July 1996 (KF)

SITE

Derrynaflan is a virtual island, *c.* 30 hectares in extent, in the extensive bog of Littleton. It is mentioned as *Daire na Fland*, 'oak-grove of the Flanns', and under its earlier name of *Daire Eidnech*, 'ivied oak-grove', in several hagiographical sources (Ó Muraíle 1983). It is not mentioned in the Annals, Byrne having disposed of the supposed reference in the Annals of Ulster and Inisfallen *s.a.* 800 (Byrne 1980, 116-17). Situated on the border of Éile and Éoganacht (Byrne 1980, 117), Derrynaflan appears to have flourished between the early eighth century and the early-to-mid ninth century when it was one of the most important centres of the *céli Dé* reform movement (Ó Muraíle 1983, 58). After the death in 847 of its patron Feidlimid mac Crimthainn, King-Bishop of Cashel, the monastery appears to have declined although there are ruins of ecclesiastical buildings of possibly thirteenth-century date (Ó Muraíle 1983, 59; Ó Floinn 1983, 50-51). The famous hoard of ecclesiastical silver was discovered in 1980 as a result of unlicensed digging. It was concealed near the pre-Romanesque church within the monastic enclosure and had probably been buried there in the later ninth or tenth century. The objects were made at different periods through the eighth and early ninth centuries, that is, during the site's hey-day (Ryan, M. 1983, 40). The standing remains at Derrynaflan include a pre-Norman single-celled church without *antae* (Ó Floinn 1983, 50) and to the north-east a trapezoidal enclosure, open on one side. The presence of some carved medieval slabs indicate that this was a graveyard (Kelly, E. P. 1983, 46. See also Harbison 1975, 226; Killanin and Duignan 1989, 292-3).

MONAINCHA: MÓIN NA hINSE

Site name Holy Island
Townland Monaincha
NGR 21650, 18844
SMR site no. TN017-01901-

Six inscribed stones are known from the well-documented monastery dependent on nearby Roscrea. These were carved on: two large, plain slabs (nos 1, 2) and two sets of fragments which may be from similar stones (nos 5, 6), all of which have been removed from the site; a tenoned block (no. 3), which is now lost; and (no. 4) some of the pilasters of the door of the twelfth century church which are *in situ*.

Monaincha 1: large plain slab

CURRENT LOCATION

Part of the stone is in the basement store of the British Museum, London, reg. no. 86/5-10.1; the additional parts, recorded in the nineteenth century, are now lost.

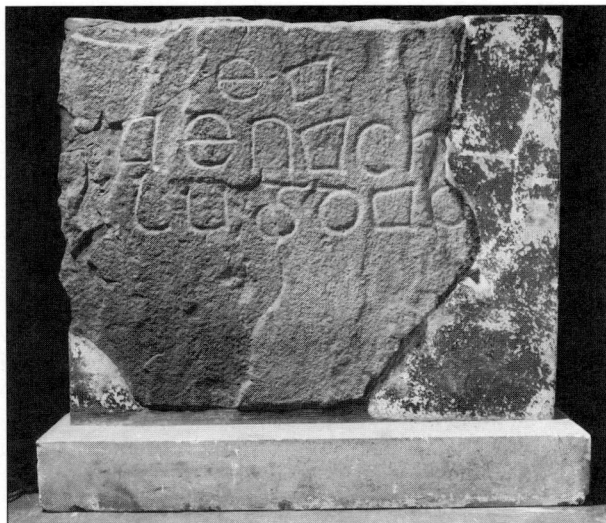

HISTORY

In 1790 Ledwich, illustrating the inscribed doorway (Monaincha 4), noted in addition that he had 'been favoured with some antient inscriptions, which I shall not transcribe, as they do not at present appear, nor am I certain of their authenticity' (Ledwich 1790, 73). This statement is rather obscure but might mean that Ledwich had been shown drawings of some inscribed stones but not the actual stones. It is possible, but by no means certain, that Ledwich saw one or more of the other five Monaincha stones. However, according to Cooke, stone no. 1 was found 'lately' (Cooke 1852-53, 56). Petrie stated that stones nos 1, 2 and 3 were all found 'in the church' (Petrie 1878, 35) but this presumably refers to the church site since Petrie also stated that Monaincha 1 had been found in 1851 'in the churchyard' (Petrie 1878, 36). In 1851 this stone was drawn by a Mr Waters, a police constable from Roscrea, who sent the drawing to Petrie (Petrie 1878, 36). When it was found, the stone was taken to the house of the landowner and was there in 1869 when it was drawn by Stokes (Petrie 1878, 36). At some time after this, the middle and left portions went missing. In 1886 William Birch presented the right portion to the British Museum. Crawford was therefore presumably in error in stating in 1912 that the stone was still in the possession of the land-owner (Crawford 1912, 240). Macalister was unaware of where the stone was (Macalister 1949a, 102). The right piece of stone, now in two pieces, was seen and recognised by KF in the British Museum store in 1996.

DESCRIPTION

When the sandstone slab was recorded by Cooke, it was already broken (Cooke 1852-53, 56) and Petrie's drawing shows it in three pieces (Petrie 1878, pl. XXIII, fig. 49: see illustration below, p. 200). Cooke gave the measurements of the complete slab in inches, corresponding to:
H. 57 cm, W. 124.5 cm, T. 5 cm.
The right-hand pieces of stone, in the British Museum, are mounted in a plaster slab and the thickness given is therefore the maximum visible. The stone's measurements are:
H. 59 cm, W. 62 cm, T. c 8.5 cm.
The apparent disparity in height and thickness is probably due to the difficulty of obtaining accurate measurements of irregularly shaped stones. The two horizontal edges appear to be original but the two ends are broken. The surface is friable and large patches of varying depth have laminated away taking with them parts of letters. The stone contains no carving or other decoration. The text is incised in three horizontal lines along the long axis of the stone. No lettering is lost from the bottom and probably none from the top. The text is set closer to the top edge of the stone than to the bottom. This could suggest that the stone was intended to be sunk into the ground with the letters set horizontally, but a similar layout is found on Inishcaltra 5 which is in its original, recumbent, position. The letters are large and dominate the slab.

From Petrie's description and drawing it appears that the two lost pieces of stone fitted together and also fitted on to the left side of the existing stone. Both the lost pieces of stone were apparently broken on all sides. Traces of a top line of text were visible, followed by two incomplete lines set along the long axis of the stone.

LETTERING
The lettering on the surviving piece of stone is crisply carved and legible. The script is half-uncial with a maximum letter H. 8.5 cm. The lettering is rather square, especially the four-sided form of A.

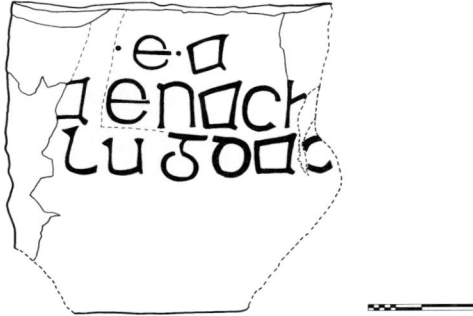

TEXT

–E A
–AENACH–
–LUGDAC–

INTERPRETATION
The text on the existing pieces of stone reads *–ea[–] [–]aenach [–]lugdac–*. The letter lost after the final A could have been O or C, less likely D. This reading is in accordance with Petrie's drawing of the complete stone, although he showed further lettering at the end of the third line (Petrie 1878, pl. XXIII, fig. 49: see illustration below). This suggests that Petrie's reading of the text on the part of the stone now lost may be accepted with some confidence. He showed part of a letter, perhaps an O, on the first line but too much was missing for this line to be reconstructed. It could have contained a personal name. The second line can be reconstructed as *–[rarm]aenach* for *–[or(óit) ar M]áenach*. The third line can be reconstructed as *[uamae–] lugdac[h]*.

The reconstructed text would then read *–[or(óit) ar M]áenach [úa Máel–] Lugdac[h]*, '– a prayer for Máenach úa Máe[l]-Lugdach'. (See the **Introduction §5.3.4** for discussion of the *or(óit) ar* formula).

DISCUSSION
This is one of at least two large slabs from Monainacha which bore an inscription but no further carving. The other is Monaincha 2 and the fragments Monaincha 5 and 6 might be the remains of further examples. The large cross-less slab is comparatively unusual in Ireland. There are a few examples at

Clonmacnoise (for example Macalister 1949a, no. 604, p. 43 and pl. X, fig. 604), one at Duleek (Macalister 1949a, no. 583, p. 33 and pl. VIII, fig. 583), and those at Derrynaflan and Inishcaltra (no. 5).

The name *Máenach*, also spelt *Móenach* and *Moínach* (as on the Scattery Island slab) was a popular and widespread male personal name (O'Brien 1976, 701-2; Ó Corráin and Maguire 1990, 131-2). Although apparently not otherwise attested, *Máel-Lugdach* 'devotee of *Lugaid*' conforms to the well-known type of 'patronal' names which reflect devotion to the cults of particular saints (O'Brien 1973, 229).

The use of the formula *or(óit) ar* rather than *or(óit) do* is unusual but not unprecedented (see the **Introduction §5.3.4**). The Derrynaflan inscription also has *ar* rather than *do* but with *or(óit) ar anmain*. Another unusual feature of the Monaincha text is that, although the first line of the text cannot be reconstructed, the request for a prayer for Máenach was obviously preceded by something. A third unusual feature is the recording of a patronymic, something found on slabs only in 'extremely rare' cases (Swift 1999, 111). In the narrow sense *úa* means 'grandchild', and so *úa Máel-Lugdach* could mean simply 'grandson of Máel-Lugdach'. More broadly, *Úa* denotes a descendent in a general sense, and from the tenth century it comes to be used to form surnames. In tenth and eleventh century sources it is 'notoriously difficult to distinguish' between these two usages (Ó Murchadha 1999, 33), and no such distinction can be made here.

The name Máel-Lugdach means 'devotee of Lugaid'. There are several saints named Lugaid, one of the more popular being the seventh-century Lugaid moccu Ócchae, more commonly known as Mo-Lúa of Clonfertmulloe (Kenney 1979, 397-8). This Mo-Lúa was traditionally associated with Monaincha and the name Máe[l]-Lugdach may provide additional evidence of a local cult. The name Máel-Lugdach does not appear to be attested as a surname in exactly this form but a hypocoristic form of Lugaid (Lúóg/Lúag) underlies the surname Úi Máel-Lúaig (Hogan 1910, 675). Close to Monaincha were the Úi Lugdech Elí whose name is preserved in the barony of Ileagh (hence Borrisoleigh) now part of the barony of Eliogarty (Hogan 1910, 674). As noted by Petrie (1878, 36), the death is recorded *s.a.* 862 in the Annals of the Four Masters of one Máenach, son of Conmhach, abbot of Roscrea (O'Donovan 1851, 498-9). The localisation to Roscrea is suggestive and the son of Conmhach could have been the grandson of a Máel-Lugdach, this being too early for the name to be a surname. However Máenach is not an uncommon name and Máenach úa Máe[l]-Lugdach remains unidentified

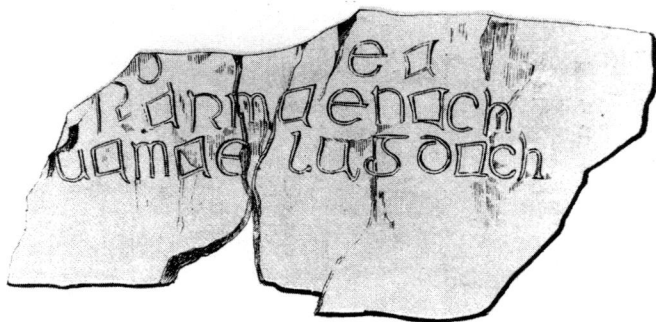

BIBLIOGRAPHY

Cooke 1852-53, 56-7
Petrie 1878, 35-6 and pl. XXIII, fig. 49
Crawford 1912, 240-1
McNeill and Leask 1920, 24
Macalister 1949a, no. 926, p. 102
Stout 1984, 96

EXAMINED

July 1996 (KF)

Monaincha 2: large plain slab

CURRENT LOCATION

Part of the stone is in the store of the National Museum of Ireland, reg. no. W 17, and part is now lost.

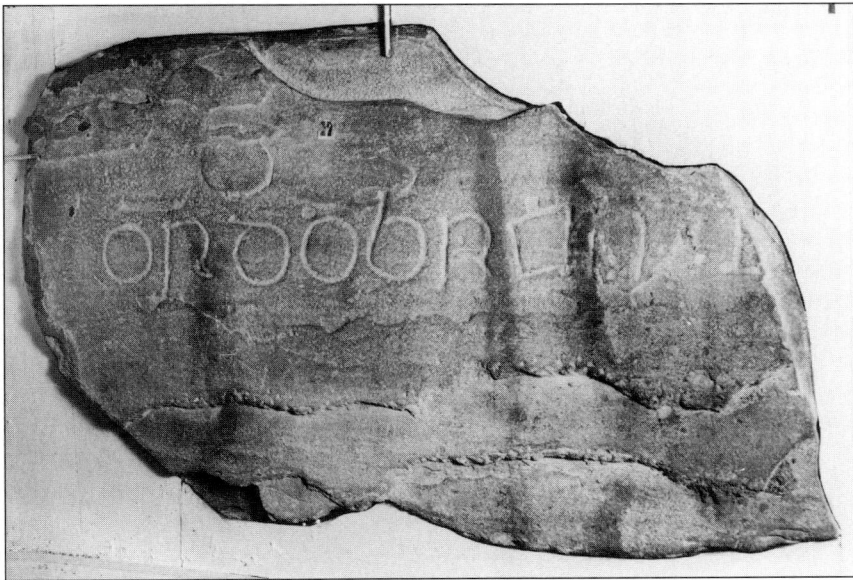

HISTORY

It is possible that this stone was seen by Ledwich in 1790 (see Monaincha 1: History) but, if it was not, then it was first recorded by Petrie who drew it in 1837 (Petrie 1878, 37 and pl. XXIV, fig. 50). Petrie recorded that stones nos 1, 2 and 3 had been found 'in the church' (Petrie 1878, 35). This may, however, merely indicate that they were found around the church site, as seems to have been the case with Monaincha 1 (see above). Monaincha 2 was broken before 1853 when the portion still in existence was exhibited at the Great Exhibition by the Royal

Irish Academy (Hitchcock 1852-53, 284). It may by then have been presented to
the Academy by a Mr Birch and certainly had been so by 1857 (Wilde 1857, 141).
This portion of the stone was transferred with the rest of the Academy collection
to the NMI in 1890. The portion of the stone now lost is known only from Petrie's
account and drawing (Petrie 1878, 37 and pl. XXIV, fig. 50).

DESCRIPTION

The current dimensions of the stone are:
H. 59 cm (maximum), W. 93 cm, T. 7 cm.
The stone is complete except for the right-hand edge which is now broken, the
break coming in the middle of the second letter D. Petrie's drawing shows the
slab complete and his scale drawing indicates that the stone was then about 156
cm in width (Petrie 1878, pl. XXIV, fig. 50). This indicates that a sizeable piece
of the stone is now lost. The stone contains no carving and Petrie's drawing
confirms that the portion now lost did not contain any either. The text is
incised in a single horizontal line along the long axis of the stone, roughly
equidistant from both upper and lower edges. The letters are large and
dominate the slab.

LETTERING

The script used is half-uncial except for the second D which in Petrie's drawing was
clearly a capital. The lettering is rather square, especially the four-sided form of A.
The first eight letters are undamaged and legible and of maximum H. 10 cm.

TEXT

ŌR DOBRAN [D̲]–

INTERPRETATION

The text reads o̅r̅ *dobran[d]–* for *or(óit) do Bran [d]–* 'a prayer for Bran –'. Petrie's drawing shows the slab complete, with the final word apparently *dub* (Petrie 1878, pl. XXIV, fig. 50). The personal name could be *Brandub*, literally 'raven-black', a name attested in both Annals and Martyrologies (Uhlich 1993, 185; Ó Corráin and Maguire 1990, 33). Petrie's drawing does, however, show what appears to be a deliberate space between the N of *Bran* and the D of *dub* and he took *dub* as a separate word. The adjective *dub* can mean 'black; dark (morally or metaphorically); great' (*DIL* s.v.). Although doubtless ubiquitous in everyday usage, personal epithets are rarely recorded in memorial inscriptions. The instance given by Petrie (1878, 37) of Bran *ailither* from Kilbrecan (Macalister 1949a, no. 532, p. 6) is more probably a vocational title. A more appropriate comparison is the word *bic* 'little' found, for example, on the stone from Kilnasaggart (Macalister 1949a, no. 946, pp. 114-15 and pl. XLVI, fig. 946). (See the **Introduction §5.3.4** for discussion of the *or(óit) do* formula).

DISCUSSION

An abbot of Roscrea, Bran son of Colmán, is recorded in the Annals of the Four Masters as having been killed during the Scandinavian invasion of Munster *s.a.* 929 (O'Donovan 1851, 624-5). Although it is possible that the person commemorated in the text was this Bran, the name is a common one; moreover, the reading of the name could also be Brandub (see above). It seems more likely that Bran, or Brandub, cannot now be identified.

Although not identical, this stone and Monaincha 1 are similar in several respects. Both are short wide slabs with lettering set along their long axis. Neither has any carving other than the lettering and, in both cases (unlike, for example, Derrynaflan), the lettering is large and dominates the surface of the stone. In height and thickness the two slabs are virtually identical although Monaincha 1 was rather wider. Where they can be compared, the letter-forms of both are similar, especially the distinctive four-sided A. There are, however, differences between the two stones. The script of Monaincha 1 is more angular than that of Monaincha 2 and the formula used is slightly different, *or(óit) ar* instead of *or(óit) do*.

BIBLIOGRAPHY

Hitchcock 1852-53, 284
Wilde 1857, 141, no. 17
Petrie 1878, 37 and pl. XXIV, fig. 50
Allen 1889, 119
Crawford 1912, 241
Macalister 1949a, no. 927, p. 102 and pl. XLI, fig. 927
Stout 1984, 96

EXAMINED

July 1996 (KF)

Monaincha 3: tenoned block, possibly part of a cross

CURRENT LOCATION

The stone is now lost.

HISTORY

It is possible that this stone was seen by Ledwich in 1790 (see Monaincha 1: History) but, if it was not, then it was first recorded by Petrie who made a drawing of it (Petrie 1878, pl. XXIV, fig. 51). Petrie's drawing is initialled but not dated, but it must pre-date his death in 1866. Petrie recorded that stones nos 1, 2 and 3 had been found 'in the church' (Petrie 1878, 35). This may, however, merely indicate that they were found around the church site, as was certainly the case with Monaincha 1 (see above). Monaincha 3 was lost before 1878 (Petrie 1878, 37).

DESCRIPTION

The description is based on Petrie's description and drawing of the stone (Petrie 1878, 37 and pl. XXIV, fig. 51: see illustration below). On the basis of this scale drawing, the dimensions were:
H. c. 78 cm, W. c. 48 cm.
Petrie described the stone as 'a portion of a cross' (Petrie 1878, 37). His drawing shows what appears to be a semi-circular tenon projecting from one of the narrow sides of the stone: the stone is thus most readily explained as a component of a larger structure, for example the tenoned arm of a free-standing cross. From Petrie's drawing, most of the visible surface of the stone contains a large curved heart-shape with four short lines projecting from its perimeter, as if the heart-shape had been superimposed on a saltire. Taken at face value, such a design cannot be of early medieval date, but it could possibly represent the misunderstood remains of a panel of interlace. Alternatively, if Petrie drew it accurately, the design might indicate that the stone had been re-used as a grave-marker in modern times. The text was incised in one line across the full width of the lower, untenoned, edge of the stone. It was incomplete at the end where part of the stone was broken off.

LETTERING

The script used was half-uncial with a maximum letter H. of c. 6 cm. Petrie's drawing shows the text as legible except for the last letter which appears to be damaged.

TEXT

In Petrie's drawing the first six letters are legible but the seventh appears to be damaged. There might have been room for two or three more letters at the end. The text appears to have read:
OR̄ AR DO[.]–

INTERPRETATION

The text apparently read o͞r *ar do[.]–* for *or(óit) ar Do[.]–*. Petrie read the next letter as a damaged M but N appears equally possible. The popular male personal name Domnall might fit into the available space but equally possible would be a name formed from *donn* 'dark; brown', for example Donnán. (See the **Introduction §5.3.4** for discussion of the *or(óit) ar* formula).

DISCUSSION

If this stone was the top arm of a cross, then the text would have been upside-down; if the stone was one of the cross-arms, then the text would have been vertical. There are no parallels for an inscribed text set in such a position on a cross. It may be, therefore, that the stone was originally part of a cross and that the text refers to an early medieval re-use of part of this broken cross as a grave-marker. As suggested above, the stone might then have had yet another re-use, as a grave-marker in modern times. A ninth-century cross base, carved with a hunting scene, survives at Monaincha but the cross from the base has disappeared. Petrie, however, recorded at the site 'a portion of the shaft of a cross covered with Celtic ornamental design' (Petrie 1878, 35). If the inscribed stone was originally part of a cross, it might have been associated with either the existing base, or with the now lost cross-shaft, or with both. The person commemorated on the inscribed stone cannot now be identified.

BIBLIOGRAPHY

Petrie 1878, 37 and pl. XXIV, fig. 51
Crawford 1912, 241
Macalister 1949a, no. 928, p. 102
Stout 1984, 96

Monaincha 4: architectural feature

CURRENT LOCATION

The inscribed blocks are *in situ*, built into the external face of the western doorway of the church. The doorway consists of three recessed orders framed by pilasters; the inscription is on the pilaster of the southern jamb.

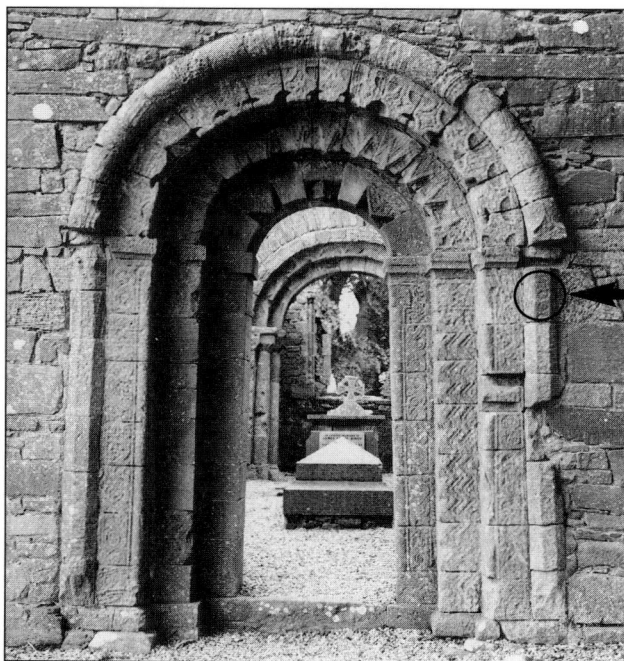

HISTORY

The inscribed doorway was first recorded by Ledwich in 1790 (Ledwich 1790, pl. V). Although Ledwich did not give a transliteration, his drawing suggests that he read the text substantially as Petrie did (Petrie 1878, 35, note b). In his earlier survey of Monaincha, Leask overlooked the text (McNeill and Leask 1920, 27) but he later recorded it (Leask 1955, 131).

DESCRIPTION

The pilaster of the northern jamb is in reasonably good condition and it is clear that it never contained any lettering. The pilaster of the southern jamb is now badly weathered. It consists of seven shaped stones, one above the other, and the text appears to have run the entire length of the pilaster, just under 200 cm. The uppermost stone is the best-preserved and its measurements are:

H. 29.5 cm, W. 40 cm, T. *c.* 19 cm. (The full thickness of this stone cannot be determined because of its position, and the figure given refers to the next stone down).

The uppermost stone is a noticeably different colour to the others and it may be that a slight difference in geological composition accounts for its better state of preservation. Only on this stone can letters be discerned with any confidence. The second, fifth and sixth stones down bear traces of letters but these are not now legible. The third stone is partially broken, the fourth is almost entirely broken away and the seventh has lost almost all its original surface. The text is set in one line and reads vertically downwards with the bottoms of the letters to the viewer's left, that is, to the interior of the doorway. There is no decoration or other carving on the inscribed stones.

LETTERING

The script used is probably half-uncial with the letters well-shaped although rather roughly pocked and now highly deteriorated. The maximum letter H. is 6 cm.

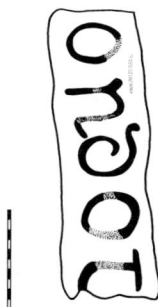

TEXT

ŌR̄DO[T]–

INTERPRETATION

The text on the top stone reads o̅ r̅ do[t]– for or(óit) do [T]–. The fifth letter is probably c. or, less likely, c. Ledwich's drawing suggests that the text could have begun or do c- or or do t- (Ledwich 1790, pl. V) and Petrie read it as o̅ r̅ do c- (Petrie 1878, 35). Leask read the text as or do t... (Leask 1955, 131). The text is likely to have continued with a personal name beginning with T. (See the **Introduction §5.3.4** for discussion of the or(óit) ar formula). On one of the lower stones Ledwich read a c and on the lowest stone a line that could have been F or s or part of a different letter (Ledwich 1790, pl. V). Petrie read these letters as cs and Leask read o.. ʄ (Petrie 1878, 35; Leask 1955, 131). However, none of these letters is legible today.

DISCUSSION

There are two other inscribed doorways, of roughly contemporary date, from nearby, although they are outside Munster. One is at Freshford, Co Kilkenny, a little over 30 km away (Macalister 1949a, no. 569, p. 24 and fig.); the other is at Killeshin, Co. Laois, about 48 km away (Macalister 1949a, no. 574, pp. 26-

8 and pl. VI). From further afield, although inside Munster, is the inscribed doorway from Ardfert, Co. Kerry. The best-preserved of these texts is that at Freshford which Macalister, following Petrie, translated as: 'A prayer for Gilla-Mocholmoc o Cenncucain who made. A prayer for Niam daughter of Corc and for Mathgamain o Chiarmeic under whose auspices this church was built' (Macalister 1949a, no. 569, p. 24). In the light of this, it may be that the 'T-' of the Monaincha text was the master-builder or patron of the church. The inscription is primary and its date is therefore the date of the doorway of the church. Leask dated the building to the twelfth century (Leask 1955, 130) and O'Keeffe suggested a date in the 1160s (O'Keeffe 1994, 123).

BIBLIOGRAPHY

Ledwich 1790, pl. V
Petrie 1878, 35, note b
Leask 1955, 131 and fig. 73
Killanin and Duignan 1989, 275
Stout 1984, 93
O'Keeffe 1994, 123

EXAMINED

July 1996, July 1998 (KF)

Monaincha 5: fragments of a (?plain) slab

CURRENT LOCATION

The fragments are now in the Dúchas depot at Kilkenny.

HISTORY

It is possible that this stone was seen by Ledwich in 1790 (see Monaincha 1: History) but, if it was not, then it was first recorded in 1964 when it was in the NMI. A file record sheet, File IA/192/64 was then made by the Museum, and the three fragments were photographed. The file record states that the fragments had been found 'in various places in the early church site of … Monaincha' and were mounted on the wall of the church at Monaincha. In October 1964 the fragments were removed from the Museum by the OPW and by 1983 were in the depot in Kilkenny, where they remain.

DESCRIPTION

When fitted together, the current dimensions of the fragments are:
H. 44.5 cm, W. 58 cm, T. 4 cm.
What survives of the stone are three contiguous fragments of a large slab, two of which have been stuck together. The upper edge of the largest fragment may be original, but none of the others is. The file record states that the stone is of 'Old Red Sandstone', an identification attributed to Dr J. S. Jackson. There is no carving apart from the text. The incomplete text is incised in one horizontal line across the fragments of stone. The large space above the text suggests that no line of text is lost from there. It is not clear how much text was lost from each end, nor whether there were originally further lines of text below the existing line.

LETTERING

The script used is half-uncial with a four-sided form of A. The maximum letter H. is 13 cm. The lettering on all three pieces is damaged but legible.

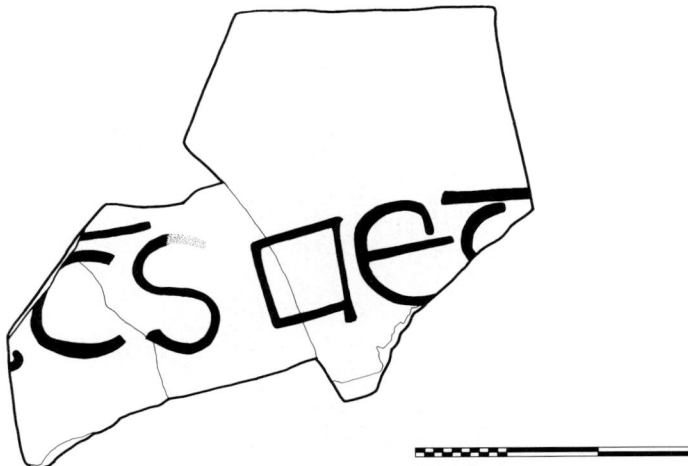

TEXT

–[.]C̄S̄ AE[.̄]

INTERPRETATION

The text reads –[.]c̄s̄ ae[.̄]–. Before the damaged C there is part of the curving lower part of the preceding letter, possibly an S, alternatively a D or O. The letters CS are an abbreviation, or part of an abbreviation, perhaps [s]c̄s̄, the standard abbreviation of s(an)c(tu)s 'saint', found in the genitive case s̄c̄ī on a slab from Kilbrecan, Aran Mór, (Macalister 1949a, no. 531, p. 5 and pl. II, fig. 531). The final, damaged, letter looks like part of a C with an abbreviation mark above; alternatively it could be a damaged D. If the text starts with s(an)c(tu)s, then the personal name of the saint, beginning ae–, would be expected to follow.

DISCUSSION

This stone appears to have resembled Monaincha 1 and 2 in being a large uncarved slab dominated by its text. The form of lettering used is also similar but the letters are larger than those on Monaincha 1 and 2.

BIBLIOGRAPHY

The stone is unpublished.

EXAMINED

November 1999 (EO)

Monaincha 6: fragments of a (?plain) slab

CURRENT LOCATION

The fragments are now in the Dúchas depot at Kilkenny.

HISTORY

It is possible that this stone was seen by Ledwich in 1790 (see Monaincha 1: History) but, if it was not, then it was first recorded in 1964 when it was in the NMI. A file record sheet, File IA/192/64 was then made by the Museum, and the fragments were photographed. The file record states that the fragments of stone had been found 'in various places in the early church site of ... Monaincha' and were mounted on the wall of the church at Monaincha. In October 1964 the fragments were removed from the Museum by the OPW and by 1983 were in the depot in Kilkenny, where they remain.

DESCRIPTION

When fitted together, the current dimensions of the fragments are:
H. 33 cm, W. 33.5 cm, T. 4.5 cm (maximum).
What survives of the stone are three contiguous fragments of a large slab which have been stuck together. None of the edges is original and there is no carving other than the text. The file record states that the stone is of 'Old Red Sandstone', an identification attributed to Dr J. S. Jackson. The incomplete text is incised in one horizontal line on one face of the stone. It is not clear how much text was lost from each end, nor whether there were originally further lines of text above or below the existing line.

LETTERING

The script used is half-uncial with a maximum letter H. of *c.* 12 cm. The lettering on all three pieces is damaged.

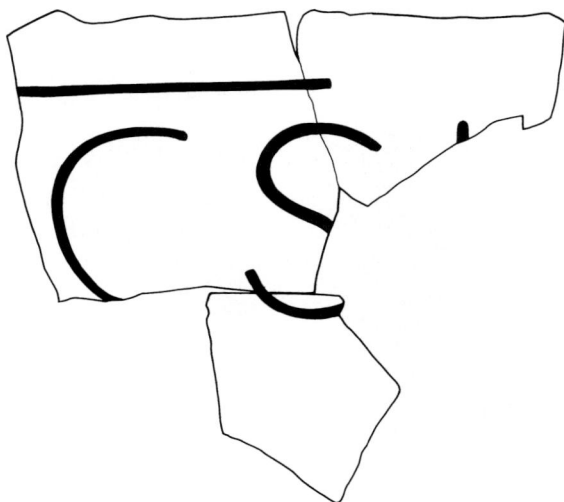

TEXT
–C̄[S̄.]–

INTERPRETATION

The text reads –c̄[s̄.]–. The horizontal bar of abbreviation began before the C suggesting that the abbreviation was of at least three letters. The close similarity with the lettering on Monaincha 5 suggests that this might also have read [s]c̄[s] for s(an)c(tu)s 'saint'.

DISCUSSION

The similarities of scale, lettering and text suggest that the fragments that make up Monaincha 6 are part of a very similar monument to Monaincha 5, or possibly even the same monument. The two sets of fragments do not now fit together but it is possible that, with intervening pieces, they might have done so originally.

BIBLIOGRAPHY

The stone is unpublished.

EXAMINED

November 1999 (EO)

SITE

Monaincha was once an island in a bog but is now a mound in marshy pasture land. Traditionally it was founded by St Cainnech of Aghaboe in the seventh century and served as a hermit retreat (McNeill and Leask 1920, 20-22). It is also associated in the hagiographic sources with St Cronán of Roscrea

(Gleeson, J. 1915, 328-30). The earliest annalistic reference to the site is the death of Elarius 'anchorite and scibe of Loch Cré' *s.a.* 806 (Annals of Ulster: Mac Airt and Mac Niocaill 1983, 262-3). The earliest building now on Monaincha is the ruined but highly ornate Romanesque church; built in the twelfth century, the church had alterations and additions made to it in the thirteenth and fifteenth centuries (Leask 1955, 130-1). Petrie recorded the existence of 'a portion of the shaft of a cross covered with Celtic ornamental design' (Petrie 1878, 35). This may refer to the twelfth-century cross now re-erected to the west of the church (Harbison 1975, 232-3). Crawford also recorded an uninscribed cross-slab then lying north-east of the chancel (Crawford 1912, 240).

ROSCREA: ROS CRÉ

Site name St Crónán's Monastery
Townland Town Parks
NGR 21382,18941
SMR site no. TN0012-01002-

This important monastery has produced two inscribed stones: a cross-slab of possibly ninth-century date, and a plain slab of possibly eleventh- or twelfth-century date.

Roscrea 1: medium-sized cross-slab

CURRENT LOCATION

The stone is in the National Museum of Ireland, reg. no. x2903 (in the store).

HISTORY

The stone was found 'in the churchyard of Roscrea' and was known in 1870 when it was drawn by a Miss Boxwell (Petrie 1878, 39). No further details of the circumstances of its discovery are recorded. In 1878 it was in the possession of Stokes. It later formed part of the Royal Irish Academy's collection, which was transferred to the NMI in 1890.

DESCRIPTION

The current dimensions of the stone are:

H. c. 55 cm, W. 41.5 cm, T. 5 cm.

The stone is the middle portion of a recumbent cross-slab with side edges intact but broken at top and bottom. The slab is a well-dressed piece of medium-grained sandstone, the carved surface being smooth and even. The intact edges bear the remains of a two-line frame running round the perimeter of the carved surface. The interior is filled with a ringed cross cut in false relief. The cross has squared terminals, and a circular ring at the edge of the curved armpits. Within the ring the armpits are sunk deeper than the surrounding surface. The remains of an oblique bar, joining frame and cross-shaft, are visible in the lower left quadrant of the cross.

The text is incised in three horizontal lines across the two quadrants below the cross-arms, between the ring and the bar. The letters are substantial and deeply cut and fill the available space. The portion of text in the left quadrant appears to be complete. The portion in the right quadrant is damaged; in the second line, the fracture has taken part of the first letter and much of the second. If there was a third line in this quadrant, it has now disappeared. Enough of the upper quadrants survive to indicate that they were not inscribed.

LETTERING

The text uses half-uncial script of maximum letter H. 4.5 cm. That part of the text in the left quadrant is legible but that in the right quadrant is damaged.

TEXT

R ‖ E
CHT ‖ A̠[.]
RA ‖ −

INTERPRETATION

The text reads *r e cht a[.] ra* − , probably for *Rechta[b]ra–*. The lost letter has the top of an upright clearly visible but the rest of the surface has been lost. The letter could have been B, H or L but the rest of the text suggests that it should be read as *b.* The Irish male personal name Rechtabra is well-attested (O'Brien 1976, 722-3). It is a compound of *recht* 'straight' and *abra* 'eye-lash', perhaps meaning 'straight-browed' (Uhlich 1993, 291). If the text is complete as it stands then the name is in the nominative. If, however, further letters have been lost from the third line of the right quadrant, the name could have been in an oblique case.

DISCUSSION

The slab contrasts in several respects with the kinds typical at Clonmacnoise and related sites: it has, for example, a frame around the cross with the text laid out horizontally in its lower quadrants, while the text does not contain the *or(óit) do* formula. Petrie pointed out the death notice in the Annals of the Four Masters *s.a.* 898 of a *Reachtabhra* of Roscrea (O'Donovan 1851, 556-7). Although the name is not uncommon, the explicit identification with Roscrea makes it possible that this is the individual commemorated here.

BIBLIOGRAPHY

Petrie 1878, 39 and pl. XXV, fig. 52
Crawford 1912, 240
Macalister 1949a, no. 929, p. 103 and pl. IX, fig. 929
Lionard 1961, 127, 162 and fig. 16.5
Gwynn and Gleeson, D. F. 1962, 63
Stout 1984, 98

EXAMINED

July 1996 (KF)

Roscrea 2: large plain slab

CURRENT LOCATION

The stone is now lost.

HISTORY

Most of the twelfth-century church was demolished in 1812 to make way for the present church (Harbison 1975, 235). The stone was found in pieces in 1812 'When removing the foundation stones' (Gleeson, J. 1915, 371), but it was already lost in 1878 (Petrie 1878, 39). It was drawn by Richard Molloy of Roscrea at some time between 1813 and 1815; this drawing is preserved in the RIA (Molloy unpublished, 119 (= 61)). Apparently Molloy was then only a boy (OS Letters unpublished 1930, 127). Molloy's drawing was reproduced by Macalister who, however, wrongly attributed it to Windele (Macalister 1949, 103). Another drawing of the stone, made by a local police-sergeant, Mr Waters, and dating from about the 1850s, was found among Petrie's papers on his death in 1866 and published in 1878 (Petrie 1878, 39-40 and pl. XXV, fig. 53: see illustration below).

DESCRIPTION

The stone appears to have been a plain rectangular slab with no carving other than the two lines of text. Neither drawing is to scale and no dimensions are given. The upper and right-hand edges of the stone, although abraded, may have been intact at the time of the drawings, but the lower and left-hand edges were clearly broken. The surviving portion was broken into three unequal pieces. The text was set in two lines along the long axis of the stone. It is not clear how much text was lost where the stone was broken. The clear space above the upper line of text suggests that it is the first line. The slab is fractured below the lower line and further lines of text could have been lost from here. Some letters could have been lost at the beginnings of both upper and lower lines; a meaningful text can, however, be made out if the existing first letters were the start of the lines. Two oblique fractures run through both lines of text but no letters appear to be lost here.

The two drawings are in substantial agreement on the reading of the text. The main point of difference is with what immediately follows the letters OR at the beginning of the lower line. The earlier drawing seems to show three letters, the middle one damaged by the fracture and flanked by two letters O. Macalister interpreted this as ŌRO, a non-standard abbreviation for *oróit*. The later drawing merely indicates wear at this point with a hint of a circular letter in the middle. Although the spacing suggests there were three letters here, the context suggests the reading DO.

LETTERING

The text used half-uncial script and was mostly legible.

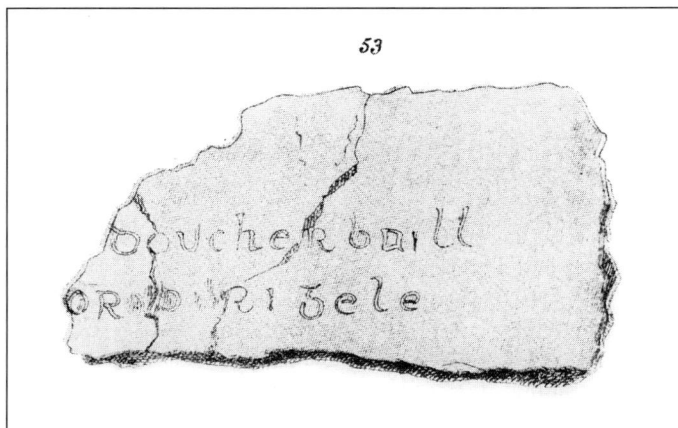

53

TEXT

A text can be reconstructed from the two drawings:
    –DOUCHERBAILL
    O͞R[DO]RIGELE

INTERPRETATION

The text appears to read – *doucherbaill* *o͞r[do]rigele* and can be reconstructed as
– *[oróit] do u Cherbaill or(óit) [do] rig Ele*, '[a prayer] for Ua Cherbaill, a prayer for
the king of Éile'. This conforms to the familiar Irish *or(óit) do N* formula with
the dative singular forms *U* (*úa*) and *ríg* (*rí*) following *do*. The lenition of *C*
following the dative *U* is indicated by the insertion of *h* (see the **Introduction
§§5.3.4, 5.3.8** for discussion of both the *or(óit) do* formula and the indication
of lenition). Éile was the name of the petty kingdom in which Roscrea was
situated (Hogan 1910, 395-6).

DISCUSSION

Although the scale of this slab is not known, its general appearance is similar
to two slabs from nearby Monaincha: Monaincha 1 and 2 are inscribed with
large letters set along the long axis of the slab and have no carving other than
the text. This Roscrea slab is quite unlike the other slab from Roscrea and is
likely to be considerably later in date. It commemorates, not a member of the
monastic community, but the local secular ruler. In a narrow sense *úa* means
grandchild, but came to be used in the sense 'descendent' to form surnames
(Ó Murchadha 1999). The Uí Cerbaill (O'Carroll) family took their name
from the eponymous Cerball who died *c.* 978 (Ó Murchadha 1999, 43). The
dynasty achieved dominance in Éile in the eleventh and, especially, the
twelfth century. In the Annals of the Four Masters they are described as lords
of the area on several occasions between 1033 and 1168 (O'Donovan 1851,
826-7, 1170-1). The anonymous Ua Cherbaill mentioned here cannot be

identified but the history of the family suggests the slab cannot be much earlier than the middle decades of the eleventh century. Patronage by the Ua Cherbaill as king of Éile is recorded in the post-twelfth century Latin inscription on the shrine of Roscrea's Book of Dimma where it is stated that the book was gilded by *Tatheus O Kearbull rex de Elu* (Macalister 1949a, no. 931, pp. 103-4).

If the reading O̅R̅O DO, for *oró(it) do*, is correct then this is an apparently unique variant of the standard O̅R̅ DO. Unfortunately neither drawing is sufficiently clear to be certain. This slab is one of only two from Ireland to explicitly identify the commemorated person as a king (Swift 1999, 112). The other, from Clonmacnoise, is also lost but apparently commemorated the king of Uí Maine: *or(óit) do Aed ...hUi Cellaich rig hU Mane* (Macalister 1949a, no. 798, p. 64).

Gleeson stated that: 'During the summer of the year 1826, when digging the foundation of a new church at Roscrea, the covering stone of St. Cronan's grave was found, bearing the simple inscription "Cronan."' (Gleeson, J. 1915, 361-2). No other source refers to this discovery and there must be doubt as to its authenticity. The foundations of the new church were built in 1812 not 1826 and it is possible that Gleeson had picked up a garbled local tradition of the discovery of the, by then lost, Roscrea 2.

BIBLIOGRAPHY

Petrie 1878, 39-40 and pl. XXV, fig. 53
Crawford 1912, 240
Gleeson, J. 1915, 371
Macalister 1949a, no. 930, p. 103 and fig.
Gwynn and Gleeson, D. F. 1962, 63
Stout 1984, 98
Swift 1999, 112-13
Molloy unpublished, 119 (61)
OS Letters unpublished 1930, 127

SITE

Roscrea was one of the principal churches of Éile, occupying a pivotal position on the northern borders of Munster. According to tradition, its founder was Crónán son of Silne whose death is recorded s.a. 665 (Annals of Ulster: Mac Airt and Mac Niocaill 1983, 136-7), but little is known of the church's early history. The famous mid-eighth-century gospel-book known as the Book of Dimma, TCD MS 59 (A.4.23), was held to have been written there and was regarded as a relic of Crónán when it was enshrined at Roscrea in the twelfth century (O'Neill 1984, 14; Kenney 1979, 633, 703-4). The Annals of Ulster and the Annals of the Four Masters record the succession of abbots at Roscrea from about 800 to 1154. From 1152 to 1161 the site enjoyed a brief period as the seat of the independent bishopric of Éile and

Roscrea, before returning to the Diocese of Killaloe. To this mid-twelfth-century period are attributed a number of cultural achievements at Roscrea, including the composition of a Latin Life of Crónán, the enshrining of the Book of Dimma and the building of an impressive Romanesque church on the site of the earlier monastery. All that remains of the latter are the west gable and a portion of the nave which now form the entrance to the churchyard. There is also a twelfth-century cross to the north of the church and a round tower nearby (Harbison 1975, 235). Other relics of the early Christian period from the area are the late eighth-century 'Roscrea pillar' (Stout 1984, 91-2) and the mid-to-late ninth-century 'Roscrea brooch' now in the NMI (Ó Floinn 1989, 98-9 and pl. on p. 84). The anchoritic community of nearby Monaincha appears to have been subsidiary to Roscrea. For discussions of the historical record and physical remains see Kenney 1979, 460; Gwynn and Hadcock 1970, 43; Stout 1984, 96-99.

ST BERRIHERT'S KYLE:
CILL NAOIMH BHEIRCHEIRT

Site name St Berrihert's Kyle
Townland Ardane
NGR 19478, 12870
SMR site no. TI074-01001-

The ony inscription among the large collection of carved stones from this enclosed burial site is on an otherwise undecorated stone.

CURRENT LOCATION

The stone is built face inwards into the oval structure at the southern end of the enclosure; it is cemented to the top of the wall, to the right of the large cross-head.

HISTORY

The stones at St Berrihert's Kyle were first described by Crawford (1909, 60-2; 1912, 241-2). Crawford described over twenty stones at the site (his figures varying between 20 and 27), but none of them was inscribed. In 1946 the OPW cleared the site, discovered the rest of the stones and built the wall on which most of the stones are now fastened (Ó hÉailidhe 1967, 102-3). Although Ó hÉailidhe did not actually state this, his account suggests that the inscribed stone was found in 1946. However, Lionard reported seeing no inscribed stones at the site (Lionard 1961, 154). In 1967 the inscribed stone was lying loose inside the enclosure (Ó hÉailidhe 1967, 106, 108) and must subsequently have been cemented on to the wall.

DESCRIPTION

The current dimensions of the stone are:

H. 23 cm, W. 26 cm, T. 6.5 cm.

The stone is a natural slab of irregular shape, broken across its short axis and missing the left portion. The inscribed surface is flat and smooth while the reverse face is blank. There is no trace on the surviving portion of any carving other than the text. As the stone is now set on end on top of the wall, the text reads up the stone, with the bottoms of the letters to the viewer's right.

LETTERING

The text uses insular minuscule script and the lettering is pecked. The text is slightly deteriorated, with a maximum letter H. of 8 cm.

TEXT

–GU/SS/AN

[–] DO

INTERPRETATION

The text reads *–gussan [–]do*. Some letters are lost at the beginnings of both lines where the stone is broken; letters are also lost from the second line of text where the surface is damaged. Cement now obscures the area immediately after the fracture. This area was apparently visible to Ó hÉailidhe and in his drawing he shows an R in the first line and AIT at the beginning of the second. He read the text as *[-]rgussan* and *[-]ait do*, for *[Fe]rgussan [or]ait do*, 'a prayer for Fergussán' (Ó hÉailidhe 1967, 108, 120-2). The reconstruction of the personal name is plausible but the lower line is less clear. The lower letters are slightly smaller than those in the upper line and seem less well carved and laid out. It is possible that they are a secondary addition. If Ó hÉailidhe's reading of -AIT is correct, *orait* could not be early.

DISCUSSION

The small size of the stone and the prominence of its lettering is similar to many of the large collection of small slabs at Toureen Peacaun, only 5.5 km to the east along the Glen of Aherlow. In contrast to the Toureen Peacaun slabs, however, this one does not appear to have had a cross. Another difference is the possible use of the *oróit do* formula: the Toureen Peacaun slabs have personal names only and there is only one, somewhat doubtful, example of *or(óit) do*, on the lost slab no. *56. If the second line of the St Berrihert's Kyle text were a later addition, then its original form would have been closer to the Toureen Peacaun monuments. The lettering of the first line has been well laid-out in the middle of the slab with the letters reaching right into the corner, while the lower line has been squeezed in below, with the DO tilted to fit. The lettering of the upper line is elegant. Its calligraphic quality is apparent in the sweep of the G and, particularly, in the overlapping arrangement of the tall insular letters S, the first ligatured with the U. As Ó hÉailidhe observed, the influence of manuscript writing is obvious and 'the easy flow of the long curves is indicative of ... brush-work' (1967, 122). Other features of note are the large triangular serifs carved in outline and the pointed-top minuscule A (see Bieler's detailed comments in Ó hÉailidhe 1967, 121-122).

Ó hÉailidhe discussed parallels with monuments dating from the sixth to the eighth and early ninth centuries and concluded that both script, text and monument form point to an 'early date' (Ó hÉailidhe 1967, 122). Fanning tentatively suggested a ninth-century date for the stone (1976, 36).

Fergussán has not been identified and it is curious that there should be only one inscription among such a large number of slabs. This is even more noteworthy since virtually all the large number of slabs at nearby Toureen Peacaun are inscribed. It is difficult to account for this discrepancy. The relationship between the two sites is not, however, clearly understood. We do not know whether or not they were contemporary nor whether St Berrihert's Kyle was a dependency of Toureen Peacaun. We do not even know if there was ever a monastery at St Berrihert's Kyle.

BIBLIOGRAPHY
Ó hÉailidhe 1967, 106, 108, 120-2 fig. 2,1 and pl. IX, 2
Fanning 1976, 36

EXAMINED
May 1996, March 1998 (EO); May 1996, June 1996 (KF)

SITE
There is no reference to the site in the historical record. The Kyle is an oval enclosure, approximately 36 m x 27 m, defined by a stone and earth bank 1-2 m high. In 1909 Crawford described the site as a circular enclosure, overgrown with bushes. No remains of any buildings were visible but the stones had been 'built up into a station' (Crawford 1909, 61). In 1946 the OPW cleared the site and constructed a small oval stone structure at the southern end of the enclosure. Most of the carved stones were gathered into this structure and many were built into or on top of the wall (Ó hÉailidhe 1967, 102-3, 106). All the stones were subsequently secured in or on to the wall. A number of small undecorated stones in the centre of the enclosure relate to the site's use as a calluragh burial ground (Ó hÉailidhe 1967, 103). The carved stones consist of the remains of two free-standing crosses, and seventy-two small upright cross-slabs, of which twenty-eight have crosses on both faces. The cross-slabs are probably grave-markers, although Harbison suggested that they might have been votive rather than commemorative (1975, 219). There is also a *bullaun* stone. For a detailed description of the site and its stones see Ó hÉailidhe 1967. About 170 m to the east of the Kyle is a pond formed from a strong spring, known as 'St Berrihert's Well'. Both the Kyle and the Well are still the focus for popular devotion. On the cult of St Berichter, apparently also the patron of Tullylease and other sites in Co. Cork and Co. Kerry, see Henderson and Okasha 1992, 10-12.

TOUREEN PEACAUN: TUAIRÍN PHÉACÁIN

Site name Peacaun
Townland Toureen
NGR 20051, 12857
SMR site no. TI075-02301-

The documented monastic site at Toureen Peacaun has produced a large number of inscribed stones. These include a free-standing cross, a small cross-carved pillar, forty-one small slabs or fragments of slabs incised with personal names and simple crosses (or the remains thereof), and a further fifteen small fragments which are probably the remains of such slabs. There are also four small slabs which were probably not inscribed but which are included for the reasons outlined below. Thirty-one of the slabs are on the site, built into walls, as is the small cross-pillar. The shaft of the free-standing cross has been re-erected in its original position on site. Three slabs are in the care of Dúchas, Dublin. The remainder are lost but are documented by photographs, drawings, rubbings or descriptions.

The exceptional nature of the collection of stones at Toureen Peacaun has entailed a departure from the format used in the other entries. The structure adopted is as follows:

I.   Discovery of the slabs (summary)

II.   Note on numbering

III. Entries for individual stones, 1-62

IV.   Discussion of small slabs

V.   Site

VI.   Concordance

Discussions of the free-standing cross (no. 40) and the inscribed cross-pillar (39) appear at the appropriate point in their individual entries. Some specific comments appear under Discussion in the entries for slabs 15, 16, 28, 29, 35, *41, *42 and *61, but discussion of the other slabs is deferred until section IV.

Most of the extant slabs are now built into the wall, flush or with only a small portion proud. Thus, with only a few exceptions (34, 36, 37, 38), the thickness of the individual slabs is not known. While the stones were still loose, Duignan recorded that the thicknesses varied from 2.5 cm to 7 cm (Waddell and Holland 1990, 169), while Macalister gave the average thickness as equivalent to about 6 cm (Macalister 1949a, 213).

Panoramic view, showing position of stones in wall

I. DISCOVERY OF SLABS (SUMMARY)

The first record of inscribed slabs at Toureen Peacaun dates from the 1840 visit of O'Keeffe and du Noyer on behalf of the Ordnance Survey. O'Keeffe's brief report on the remains is contained in the Ordnance Survey letters (OS Letters unpublished 1930, 64-6); du Noyer's full-size sketches (du Noyer, unpublished) were presented to the Royal Irish Academy in 1860 (du Noyer 1857–61, 249, 256). These sketches recorded slabs nos 2, 5, *60 and *61 (du Noyer unpublished, vol. III, pp. 1–4 and figs), described as 'from the old church-yard of Peccaun' (du Noyer 1857-61, 256). Slab no. *61 has not been recorded subsequently. Petrie visited the site and published scale drawings of slabs nos 2 and 5 and *60, and of two slabs, *58 and *59, not previously noted (Petrie 1878, 33–4 and fig., and pl. XXII, figs 44–8). Slab *59 was at that time 'in a small recess in the south side-wall within the church' (Petrie 1878, 34). It has not been recorded subsequently. The other slabs were then 'heaped up in the north-west corner of the church' (Petrie 1878, 33). Petrie also recorded the shaft of the East Cross (no. 40) and one of the cross-pillars but appears not to have recognised texts on them (Petrie 1878, 33–4 and fig.).

In February 1909, Crawford reported on a visit he had made to the site and recorded two of the stones seen by Petrie (2, 5) and three new ones (14, 34, *51); he failed to locate nos *58, *59, *60 (Crawford 1909, 59–66). He published scaled rubbings of nos 2, 5, and 14 and photographs of 34 and *51. At the time of Crawford's visit, no. 34 was lying loose on top of the wall of the small enclosure (Crawford 1909, 63, 65). No. *51 was lying loose on top of the 'station' or 'altar' in the north-west corner of the church, 'into the back of which a small erect slab, with a ringed cross in relief, and three inscribed fragments have been built' (Crawford 1909, 65). A photograph taken in the early 1930s (Holland and Waddell 1990, pl.1) shows slabs 2, 5, 14, and *51 as Crawford described them, as part of a 'station' at the west end of the church, together with the inscribed cross-pillar (39) and the middle portion of the uninscribed small cross-pillar. It seems likely that this station grew out of the heap referred to by Petrie. Waddell and Holland (1990, 169) asserted that a photograph published by McCraith in 1912 (McCraith 1912, 28, not p. 17 as Waddell and Holland stated) shows the west end of the church without the station and that, therefore, the station was built between this date and the 1930s. However, the photograph clearly shows the well and not the church and therefore has no bearing on the date of the 'station'. Crawford sent Macalister drawings, rubbings and descriptions of the then extant slabs, on which Macalister was able to comment (Macalister 1909, 67-9). Macalister subsequently visited the site and recognised for the first time that there was an inscription on the East Cross (Macalister 1949a, 101).

The ruined church at Toureen Peacaun and the cross were taken into state care in 1935 (Manning 1991, 209). In the autumn of 1944 the Office of Public Works tidied up the site and consolidated the ruins. As part of this operation Duignan, with the financial assistance of the Royal Irish Academy, undertook a small excavation. Except for a brief note (Duignan 1944), Duignan did not publish an account of the excavation. This was done only posthumously from notes, rubbings and drawings made at the time (Waddell and Holland 1990). Duignan reported that as a result of his excavation the number of known grave slabs at Toureen Peacaun was raised to thirty (1944, 227), implying the discovery of an additional twenty-five slabs. In fact, once all the miscellaneous fragments are included, the OPW interventions produced thirty-eight new pieces, most of them from around the East Cross.

At the time of this excavation, Macalister's *Corpus* (Macalister 1949a) was passing through the press. In the main body of the text, Macalister gave entries for the five slabs noted by Crawford, plus a further slab, no. *56, which he did not illustrate. This slab had not been previously recorded, was not noted among those on site in 1944 and has not been recorded subsequently. Duignan's timely discoveries meant that Macalister was able to insert into his *Corpus* a list of nineteen additional slabs found during the excavation (Macalister 1949a, 213). These are nos 1, 3, 4, 6, 7, 10, 13, 15, 16, 18, 19, 25, 26, 31, 33, *47, *48, *52, *57, plus four 'insignificant fragments' (which are probably nos 8, 11, 22, 27 noted among Duignan's finds by Waddell and Holland). Fragment no. 32 was omitted by Macalister, presumably because it had not been recognised as containing part of a letter. Duignan also discovered a further fourteen fragments containing only crosses or parts of crosses (nos 9, 17, 20, 23, 29, 30, *41, *42, *44, *45, *50, *53, *54, *55).

Between September and December 1944 the OPW cleared, consolidated and partially rebuilt the collapsed wall of the ruined church. The opportunity was taken to incorporate into the rebuilt east wall the majority of the carved stones then extant. The two small cross-pillars were built into the exterior east wall and the extant slabs (1-33, *43-*50) were set into the interior east wall. The various pieces of the East Cross (no. 40) were excavated and the shaft was re-erected in its original position to the south-east of the church. The fixing of slab 34 to the wall of the small enclosure was presumably done at this time also.

A series of OPW photographs, preserved in the Dúchas archive and probably taken in the 1960s, shows in detail the slabs set into the interior east wall. Most are still in these positions today. A number, however, have been moved or become lost. These come from two areas, the north (left) end of the upper register and the area to the south (right) of the plain free-standing cross. The OPW photographs show the upper register of slabs in the following sequence (lost stones marked *, stones still in position underlined): in sequence 1, *43, *44, uninscribed, *45, 33, uninscribed, 8, uninscribed, 3, *46. The area to the right of the cross is shown full of slabs: 31, 32, *47, *48, *49, *50. In addition, *62 is shown between 11 and 14, in the place now occupied by 12. The photographs show the wall in a sound condition but it subsequently fell into disrepair. By the time the wall was rebuilt by the OPW in the winter of 1986 and spring of 1987 a number of pieces, mainly from the vulnerable upper register, had fallen out. Slab 3 was reinserted where *43 had been, and 32 and 33 were built into the north interior wall. The remaining nine slabs had, however, disappeared. In November 1987 a small excavation was conducted by the OPW around the East Cross in advance of the installation of a cattle-grid. Three more slabs came to light in the trenches, nos 36, 37 38 (Manning 1991, 221-2).

During their visits to the site in 1996 the authors recognised a further four inscribed fragments in the interior east wall which had not been previously noted: nos 12, 21, 24, 28. Examination of the OPW photographs of the wall revealed four further lost fragments, three of them with lettering, which had not been noted previously (nos *43, *46, *49, *62). The cross-incised slab no. 35 is also noted here for the first time.

II. NOTE ON NUMBERING

The large number of slabs, extant and lost, and their small and often highly fragmentary nature means that it is not always easy to correlate the various descriptions of the individual stones with what is visible today. Rather than continue earlier, necessarily incomplete, sequences, the present authors have generated a new numbering system, based on the following principles: extant stones are listed before lost stones and photographed lost stones before others; extant stones are numbered according to their present position, slabs first. Thus:

1-31	on site, built into the interior east wall of the church (numbered top to bottom and left to right across the wall)
32-33	on site, built into the interior north wall of the church
34	on site, set on to the wall of the small enclosure to the south-east of the church (the 'cell')
35	on site, set on to the wall of the well
36-38	in Dúchas store, Dublin
39	on site, built into the exterior east wall of the church
40	on site, freestanding
*41-*42	lost; allegedly in the NMI, illustrated by Waddell and Holland
*43-*50, *62	lost; shown in the OPW photograph built into the east interior wall of the church
*51-*55	lost; illustrated by Waddell and Holland, but not visible in the OPW photograph
*56-*57	lost; described although not illustrated by Macalister, but not otherwise recorded
*58-*60	illustrated by Petrie, but not otherwise recorded
*61	illustrated by du Noyer, but not otherwise recorded

All the small slabs have been numbered, regardless of whether they exhibit traces of lettering. This has been done to minimize confusion, aid identification, and because a high proportion of the now uninscribed slabs are likely to be part of slabs which were originally inscribed. One slab (29) is a fragment of an altar slab and would not have been inscribed; three others (35, *41, *42) are somewhat different in character to the others and may not have been inscribed. Macalister (1949a, 110) mentions four 'insignificant fragments' but gives no further details. These pieces cannot be identified and have not been numbered separately. They are probably included in the above sequence, perhaps nos 8, 11, 22, 27. In section VI below, a concordance is given which tabulates the new numbering sequence with the sequences used by Waddell and Holland 1990, Moloney 1964, Lionard 1961, Macalister 1949a, Petrie 1878 and du Noyer unpublished.

Other pieces of worked stone extant on the site do not appear to be inscribed and are not included in the numbered sequence. These comprise: some architectural fragments; two plain water stoups; parts of three rotary querns; two plain free-standing granite crosses (propped against the interior and exterior east wall); a sundial; the West Cross; the two large cross-pillars (standing by the East Cross); the uninscribed small cross pillar (built into the exterior east wall of the church). For these see Waddell and Holland 1990, 169, 175-181.

Key to numbering, showing position of stones in wall

III. ENTRIES FOR INDIVIDUAL STONES

Toureen Peacaun 1: small slab

CURRENT LOCATION

The stone is built into the interior east wall of the ruined church.

HISTORY

The stone was found in the summer of 1944 during excavation at the site (Duignan 1944, 227; Macalister 1949a, 213). It was a stray find from the vicinity of the ruined church (Waddell and Holland 1990, 169, 171). During September to December 1944 the east wall of the church was rebuilt, incorporating many of the inscribed stones, including this one. The stone has remained there since.

DESCRIPTION

The current dimensions of the stone are:
H. *c.* 6 cm, W. *c.* 23.5 cm, T. *c.* 4 cm visible.
The stone is a fragment of a slab of unknown form. In its present condition, the visible face of the stone contains parts of four characters incised in one line. Only a small portion of the fourth character survives but it appears to be the bottom left-hand corner of an outline cross. The space preceding the D suggests that it was the first letter in that line, and presumably the second syllable of the name was on the opposite side of the cross. There is no way of knowing if other lines of text are lost from above or below.

LETTERING

The text is in half-uncial script and is slightly deteriorated. The maximum letter H. is *c.* 4 cm.

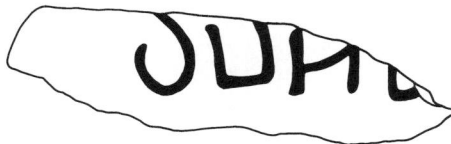

TEXT

DUN || –

INTERPRETATION

The text reads *dun–*, presumably the first syllable of a personal name such as *Dúnchad* or *Dúngall*.

BIBLIOGRAPHY

Macalister 1949a, no. 13, p. 213
Waddell and Holland 1990, no. 20, pp. 165-86 and fig. 5.20

EXAMINED

May 1996 (KF, EO); July 1996 (KF)

Toureen Peacaun 2: small slab

CURRENT LOCATION

The stone is built into the interior east wall of the ruined church.

HISTORY

In 1860 a full-size drawing of this stone by du Noyer was presented by him to the Royal Irish Academy where it is still preserved (du Noyer unpublished, vol. III, p. 3; see du Noyer 1857-61, 249-50, 256). The stone was then described as in the graveyard (du Noyer unpublished, vol. III, p. 3). In 1878 this stone was one of several fragments 'heaped up in the north-west corner of the church' (Petrie 1878, 33). In 1909 this stone was built into the 'north-west corner of the church' which had been 'formed into a kind of station' (Crawford 1909, 65). In the early 1930s it was photographed lying loose as part of a 'crude pilgrim's "station'" which had been built to the west of the church some time before (Waddell and Holland 1990, 169 and pl. 1, p. 183). During September to December 1944 the east wall of the church was rebuilt, incorporating many of the inscribed stones, including this one. The stone has remained there since.

DESCRIPTION

The current dimensions of the stone are:
H. *c.* 20 cm, W. *c.* 41 cm, T. *c.* 2 cm visible.
The stone is an apparently complete rectangular slab. Incised on the visible face of the stone are an outline equal-armed cross and a text in one horizontal line. The text is set in two parts, one on either side of the lower cross-arm. There is a small incised line, an acute accent, above the ligatured A and E. The text is likely to be complete.

LETTERING

The text is in half-uncial script and is slightly deteriorated. The maximum letter H. is *c.* 7 cm.

TEXT

FID ‖ LÁ/ER

INTERPRETATION

The text reads *Fidláer*, a male personal name in the nominative case.

BIBLIOGRAPHY

du Noyer 1857-61, 256
Petrie 1878, 33-4 and pl. XXII, fig. 46
Wakeman 1890-91b, 354 and pl. I, fig. 34 (unless this is Toureen Peacaun 5)
Crawford 1909, 65 and fig. 15
Macalister 1909, 67

Crawford 1912, 242
Macalister 1949a, no. 920, p. 100 and pl. XLIV, fig. 920
Lionard 1961, 105, 154 and fig. 5.2
Waddell and Holland 1990, no. 7, pp. 165-86, fig. 4.7 and pl. 1
du Noyer unpublished, vol. III, p. 3 and fig.

EXAMINED

May 1996 (KF, EO); July 1996 (KF)

Toureen Peacaun 3: small slab

CURRENT LOCATION

The stone is built sideways into the interior east wall of the ruined church.

HISTORY

The stone was found in the summer of 1944 during excavation at the site (Duignan 1944, 227; Macalister 1949a, 213). It was a stray find from the rubble around stone no. 40 (the East Cross) (Waddell and Holland 1990, 169, 171). During September to December 1944 the east wall of the church was rebuilt, incorporating many of the inscribed stones, including this one. In photographs possibly dating from the 1960s, preserved in Dúchas (negative nos 75, 76), the stone is shown built into the east interior wall of the church but in a different place in the wall, above stone no. 9, and the right way up. The stone presumably became loose before 1986-87 and was then rebuilt into the wall in its present position.

DESCRIPTION

The current dimensions of the stone are:
H. c. 16 cm, W. c. 26.5 cm, T. c. 2 cm visible.
The stone is a fragment of a slab of unknown form. In its present condition, the visible face of the stone contains one complete letter and fragments of two

others, one on each side, but nothing else. The space below the text suggests that no further lines of text are lost here. There is no way of knowing if other lines of text are lost above, nor if the stone originally contained a cross.

LETTERING

The text is in half-uncial script and is slightly deteriorated. The maximum letter H. is *c.* 4.5 cm.

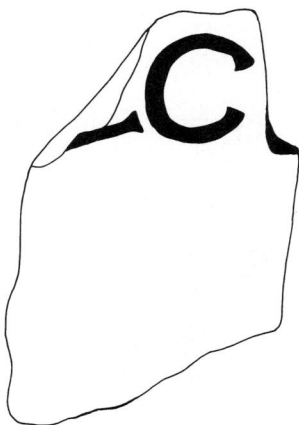

TEXT

–c–

INTERPRETATION

The text reads –c– but is too fragmentary to be interpreted.

BIBLIOGRAPHY

Macalister 1949a, no. 2, p. 213
Waddell and Holland 1990, no. 22, pp. 165-86 and fig. 5.22

EXAMINED

May 1996 (KF, EO); July 1996 (KF)

Toureen Peacaun 4: small slab

CURRENT LOCATION

The stone is built into the interior east wall of the ruined church.

HISTORY

The stone was found in the summer of 1944 during excavation at the site (Duignan 1944, 227; Macalister 1949a, 213). It was a stray find from the vicinity of the ruined church (Waddell and Holland 1990, 169, 171). During September to December 1944 the east wall of the church was rebuilt, incorporating many of the inscribed stones, including this one. The stone has remained there since.

DESCRIPTION

The current dimensions of the stone are:
H. *c.* 19 cm, W. *c.* 36 cm, T. *c.* 5.5 cm visible.
The stone is an apparently complete slab of irregular rectangular shape. Incised on the visible face of the stone are an outline equal-armed cross and a text in one line. The text, which is complete, is set in a single horizontal line, interrupted by the lower cross-arm.

LETTERING

The text is in half-uncial script and is slightly deteriorated. The maximum letter H. is *c.* 4 cm.

TEXT

ᴅᴏɴ ‖ ɢᴜs

INTERPRETATION

The text reads *dongus*. This is the male personal name *Donngus*, in the nominative case (for early forms see Uhlich 1993, 231).

BIBLIOGRAPHY

Macalister 1949a, no. 18, p. 213
Killanin and Duignan 1989, 87
Waddell and Holland 1990, no. 13, pp. 165-86 and fig. 4.13

EXAMINED

May 1996 (KF, EO); July 1996 (KF)

Toureen Peacaun 5: small slab

CURRENT LOCATION

The stone is built into the interior east wall of the ruined church.

HISTORY

In 1860 a full-size drawing of this stone by du Noyer was presented by him to the Royal Irish Academy where it is still preserved (du Noyer unpublished, vol. III, p. 2; see du Noyer 1857-61, 249-50, 256). The stone was then described as in the graveyard (du Noyer unpublished, vol. III, p. 2). In 1878 this stone was one of several fragments 'heaped up in the north-west corner of the church' (Petrie 1878, 33). In 1909 the stone was built into the 'north-west corner of the church' which had been 'formed into a kind of station' (Crawford 1909, 65). In the early 1930s it was photographed lying loose as part of a 'crude pilgrim's "station"' which had been built to the west of the church some time before (Waddell and Holland 1990, 169 and pl. 1, p. 183). During September to December 1944 the east wall of the church was rebuilt, incorporating many of the inscribed stones, including this one. The stone has remained there since.

DESCRIPTION
The current dimensions of the stone are:
H. *c.* 23 cm, W. *c.* 28 cm, T. *c.* 4.5 cm visible.
The stone is part of a rectangular slab which lacks its bottom left corner and the whole of the right side. An outline equal-armed cross is incised on the visible face and below it the text, set in one horizontal line. Comparison with stones nos 2, 4 and 7 suggests that this stone contained only the one line of text and is missing only a few letters at the end.

LETTERING
The text is in half-uncial script and is rather deteriorated. The maximum letter H. is *c.* 6 cm.

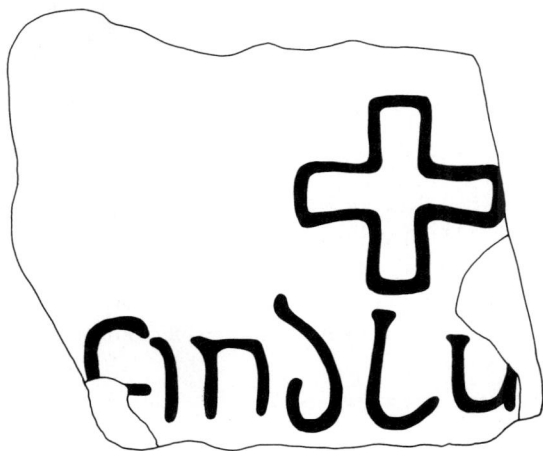

TEXT
FINDLU–

INTERPRETATION
The text reads *findlu–*, possibly for the male personal name *Findlug*.

BIBLIOGRAPHY
du Noyer 1857-61, 256
Petrie 1878, 33-4 and pl. XXII, fig. 44
Crawford 1909, 65 and fig. 14
Macalister 1909, 67

Crawford 1912, 242
Macalister 1949a, no. 921, p. 100 and pl. XLIV, fig. 921
Lionard 1961, 105, 154 and fig. 5.6
Waddell and Holland 1990, no. 8, pp. 165-86, fig. 4.8 and pl. 1
du Noyer unpublished, vol. III, p. 2 and fig.

EXAMINED

May 1996 (KF, EO); July 1996 (KF)

Toureen Peacaun 6: small slab

CURRENT LOCATION

The stone is built into the interior east wall of the ruined church, in an inverted position.

HISTORY

The stone was found in the summer of 1944 during excavation at the site (Duignan 1944, 227; Macalister 1949a, 213). It was found 'in the packing in front of the East Cross' (stone no. 40) (Waddell and Holland 1990, 171). During September to December 1944 the east wall of the church was rebuilt, incorporating many of the inscribed stones, including this one. The stone has remained there since.

DESCRIPTION

The current dimensions of the stone are:
H. *c*. 8 cm, W. *c*. 19.5 cm, T. 0 cm visible.
The stone is a fragment of a slab of unknown form broken on all four sides. On the visible face of the stone is a pair of parallel horizontal lines which may have been guide-lines. Pendant from the lower line is a straight vertical line and, a short distance to the right, a curved line, both of which run to the broken bottom edge. These may have been part of a cross or some other design, but the stone is now too fragmentary and too deteriorated to be certain. Set between the parallel lines is a one-line text. The space preceding the C might indicate that this was the first letter of the line but it is quite uncertain how much else has been lost from this stone.

LETTERING

The text is probably in half-uncial script and is highly deteriorated. The maximum letter H. is *c.* 3 cm.

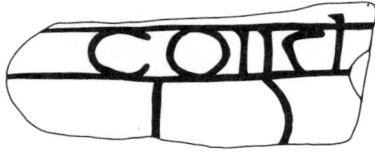

TEXT

COND–

INTERPRETATION

The text reads *cond–*, possibly the beginning of a personal name such as *Condolb*, *Condla* or *Condmach*.

BIBLIOGRAPHY

Macalister 1949a, no. 17, p. 213
Waddell and Holland 1990, no. 24, pp. 165-86 and fig. 5.24

EXAMINED

May 1996 (KF, EO); July 1996 (KF)

Toureen Peacaun 7: small slab

CURRENT LOCATION

The stone is built into the interior east wall of the ruined church.

HISTORY

The stone was found in the summer of 1944 during excavation at the site (Duignan 1944, 227; Macalister 1949a, 213). It was a stray find from the rubble around stone no. 40 (the East Cross) (Waddell and Holland 1990, 169, 171). During September to December 1944 the east wall of the church was rebuilt, incorporating many of the inscribed stones, including this one. The stone has remained there since.

DESCRIPTION

The current dimensions of the stone are:
H. *c.* 26.5 cm, W. *c.* 25 cm, T. *c.* 3.5 cm visible.
The stone is part of a slab of unknown form; comparison with stone nos 2, 4 and 5 suggests, however, that if these stones are largely complete then this one might also have contained only one line of text. Incised on the visible face of the stone are an outline equal-armed cross with slightly expanded arms and the remains of a single horizontal line of text interrupted by the lower cross-arm.

LETTERING

The text is in half-uncial script and is slightly deteriorated. The maximum letter H. is *c.* 4.5 cm.

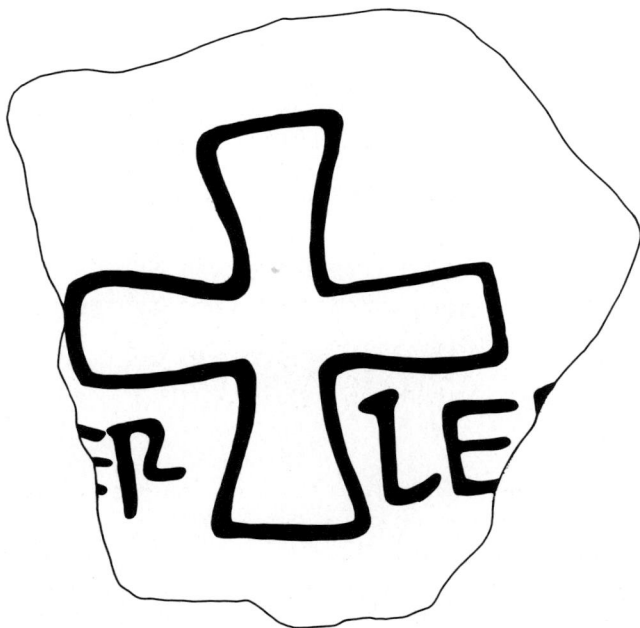

TEXT

−ER ‖ LE−

INTERPRETATION

The text reads −*er le*−. Comparison with stones nos 2 and 4 suggests that the text is likely to have been a single personal name and to be lacking only a few letters from beginning and end. These same stones suggest that the break in the text might have been made to coincide with a syllable break. The name could have been something like the *Soerlech* of slab 26 but cannot now be recovered.

BIBLIOGRAPHY

Macalister 1949a, no. 9, p. 213
Waddell and Holland 1990, no. 10, pp. 165-86 and fig. 4.10

EXAMINED

May 1996 (KF, EO); July 1996 (KF)

Toureen Peacaun 8: small slab

CURRENT LOCATION

The stone is built into the interior east wall of the ruined church.

HISTORY

The stone was found in the summer of 1944 during excavation at the site (Duignan 1944, 227). It was a stray find from the rubble around stone no. 40 (the East Cross) (Waddell and Holland 1990, 169, 175). During September to December 1944 the east wall of the church was rebuilt, incorporating many of the inscribed stones, including this one. The stone has remained there since.

DESCRIPTION

The current dimensions of the stone are:
H. *c.* 11.5 cm, W. *c.* 10 cm, T. 0 cm visible.

The stone is a fragment of a slab of unknown form. On the visible face are incised parts of two lines, each with a right angle; they appear to have formed part of the underside of a transom and the shaft of a cross. One letter remains in each of the two lower quadrants so formed. The space below the letters suggests that no further line of text is lost but presumably text is lost from each side of the existing letters.

LETTERING

The text is in capitals and is rather deteriorated. The maximum letter H. is c. 2.5 cm.

TEXT

–A ‖ R–

INTERPRETATION

The text reads –a r– but is too fragmentary to be interpreted.

BIBLIOGRAPHY

Waddell and Holland 1990, no. 39, pp. 165-86 and figs 6.39

EXAMINED

May 1996 (KF, EO); July 1996 (KF)

Toureen Peacaun 9: small slab

CURRENT LOCATION

The stone is built into the interior east wall of the ruined church.

HISTORY

The stone was found in the summer of 1944 during excavation at the site (Duignan 1944, 227). It was a stray find from the rubble around stone no. 40 (the East Cross) (Waddell and Holland 1990, 169, 171). During September to December 1944 the east wall of the church was rebuilt, incorporating many of the inscribed stones, including this one. The stone has remained there since.

DESCRIPTION

The current dimensions of the stone are:

H. *c.* 21 cm, W. *c.* 21 cm, T. 0 cm visible.

The stone is part of a slab of unknown form, broken on all four sides. On its visible face there is incised an outline equal-armed cross with expanded terminals. There is no trace of any lettering but since the slab has been trimmed so tightly round the cross, if there had been a line of text underneath or above the cross it would have been on the missing piece.

LETTERING AND TEXT

There is no visible text on this stone.

BIBLIOGRAPHY

Waddell and Holland 1990, no. 28, pp. 165-86 and fig. 6.28

EXAMINED

May 1996 (KF, EO); July 1996 (KF)

Toureen Peacaun 10: small slab

CURRENT LOCATION

The stone is built into the interior east wall of the ruined church.

HISTORY

The stone was found in the summer of 1944 during excavation at the site (Duignan 1944, 227; Macalister 1949a, 213). It was a stray find from the rubble around stone no. 40 (the East Cross) (Waddell and Holland 1990, 169). During September to December 1944 the east wall of the church was rebuilt, incorporating many of the inscribed stones, including this one. The stone has remained there since.

DESCRIPTION

The current dimensions of the stone are:
H. *c.* 30 cm, W. *c.* 38.5 cm, T. *c.* 8 cm visible.
The stone is an irregular rectangular slab missing its bottom left corner. On the lower half of its visible face is incised a linear cross with expanded terminals. Above it is a single complete horizontal line of text. The surface of the slab is 'split-level' due to spalling at an ancient date. The upper area, where the text is incised, is therefore recessed relative to the area with the cross.

LETTERING

The text is in half-uncial script and is legible. The maximum letter H. is *c.* 5 cm.

TEXT

FLAND

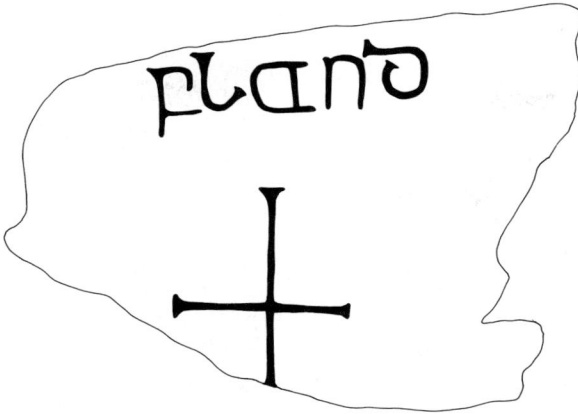

INTERPRETATION

The text reads *fland*. The personal name Fland, later Flann, here in the nominative case, was borne by both men and women (Ó Corráin and Macguire 1981, 105). Since there is not a single example of a woman commemorated on a slab anywhere else in Munster, it may be assumed that the Fland commemorated here was male.

BIBLIOGRAPHY

Macalister 1949a, no. 16, p. 213
Moloney 1964, 106
Killanin and Duignan 1989, 87
Waddell and Holland 1990, no. 4, pp. 165-86 and fig. 3.4

EXAMINED

May 1996 (KF, EO); July 1996 (KF)

Toureen Peacaun 11: small slab

CURRENT LOCATION

The stone is built into the interior east wall of the ruined church.

HISTORY

The stone was found in the summer of 1944 during excavation at the site (Duignan 1944, 227). It was a stray find but Waddell and Holland do not record exactly where it was found (Waddell and Holland 1990, 171). During September to December 1944 the east wall of the church was rebuilt, incorporating many of the inscribed stones, including this one. The stone has remained there since.

DESCRIPTION

The current dimensions of the stone are:
H. *c.* 9 cm, W. *c.* 13 cm, T. *c.* 0.5 cm visible.
The stone is a fragment of a slab of unknown form. A fragmentary text is incised on the visible face, taking up most of the existing piece of stone. There is no way of knowing how much other text there was originally, nor if the stone contained a cross.

LETTERING

The text is in half-uncial script and is slightly deteriorated. The maximum letter H. is *c.* 6 cm.

TEXT

FIN—

INTERPRETATION

The text reads *fin–* and is likely to be the beginning of a personal name.

BIBLIOGRAPHY

Waddell and Holland 1990, no. 26, pp. 165-86 and fig. 5.26

EXAMINED

May 1996 (KF, EO); July 1996 (KF)

Toureen Peacaun 12: small slab

CURRENT LOCATION

The stone is built upside down into the interior east wall of the ruined church.

HISTORY

This stone is not mentioned in any work on the stones. It is likely to have been found in 1944 and built into the east wall when the other stones were built in between September and December 1944. In a photograph possibly dating from the 1960s, preserved in the Dúchas archive (negative no. 79), the stone is shown built into the east interior wall of the church but in a different place in the wall from where it now is. The stone presumably became loose before 1986-87 and was then rebuilt into the wall in its present position.

DESCRIPTION

The current dimensions of the stone are:
H. *c.* 9 cm, W. *c.* 13 cm, T. *c.* 0.2 cm visible.
The stone is a fragment of a slab of unknown form. The visible face contains a fragment of an outline cross, the corner of a top or right cross-arm, and a single letter above it. There is no way of knowing how much text was originally contained on this stone.

LETTERING

The text is in capital script and is slightly deteriorated. The maximum letter H. is *c.* 7.6 cm.

TEXT

—N—

INTERPRETATION
The text reads –n– but is too fragmentary to be interpreted.

BIBLIOGRAPHY
The stone is unpublished.

EXAMINED
May 1996 (KF, EO); July 1996 (KF)

Toureen Peacaun 13: small slab

CURRENT LOCATION
The stone is built into the interior east wall of the ruined church.

HISTORY
The stone was found in the summer of 1944 during excavation at the site (Duignan 1944, 227; Macalister 1949a, 213); it was 'Noted near West Cross' (Waddell and Holland 1990, 171). During September to December 1944 the east wall of the church was rebuilt, incorporating many of the inscribed stones, including this one. The stone has remained there since.

DESCRIPTION
The current dimensions of the stone are:
H. *c.* 17 cm, W. *c.* 29 cm, T. *c.* 0.5 cm visible.
The stone is part of a rectangular slab which is missing its bottom left-hand corner. A large area of the surface has broken off in this same corner. Incised on its visible face is an outline equal-armed cross with the remains of a single horizontal line of text below. The space after the E suggests that it was the end of this line of text; some three or four letters may have been lost from the earlier part of the line.

LETTERING
The text is in half-uncial script and is slightly deteriorated. The maximum letter H. is *c.* 3.5 cm.

TEXT

—ALE

INTERPRETATION

The text reads –*ale*. Comparison with stones nos 2 and 4 suggests that this text is likely to have been a single personal name but the form of the name cannot now be recovered.

BIBLIOGRAPHY

Macalister 1949a, no. 19, p. 213
Waddell and Holland 1990, no. 14, pp. 165-86 and fig. 4.14

EXAMINED

May 1996 (KF, EO); July 1996 (KF)

Toureen Peacaun 14: small slab

CURRENT LOCATION

The stone is built upside down into the interior east wall of the ruined church.

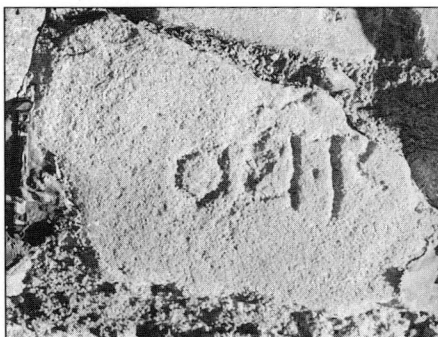

HISTORY

In 1909 this stone was built into the 'north-west corner of the church' which had been 'formed into a kind of station' (Crawford 1909, 65). In the early 1930s it was photographed lying loose as part of a 'crude pilgrim's "station"' which had been built at the west end of the church some time before (Waddell and Holland 1990, 169 and pl. 1, p. 183). Comparison between the photograph of the stone and its present shape suggests that the edges of the stone were trimmed or broken before it was built into the east wall. This was between September and December 1944 when the east wall of the church was rebuilt. The stone has remained there since.

DESCRIPTION

The current dimensions of the stone are:
H. *c.* 14 cm, W. *c.* 25 cm, T. 0 cm visible.
The stone is a fragment of a slab of unknown form which is built upside down into the wall. The visible face contains only a fragmentary incised text. The space preceding the O suggests that this is the beginning of this line of text but it is impossible to say how much text has been lost or if the stone originally contained a cross. An apparently deliberate incised medial dot separates the U and R.

LETTERING

The text is in half-uncial script and is slightly deteriorated. The maximum letter H. is *c.* 6 cm.

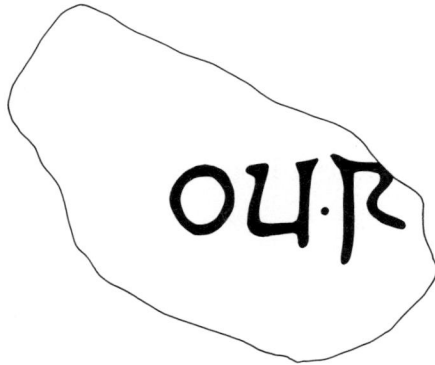

TEXT

OU·R–

INTERPRETATION

The text reads *ou·r–*. The function of the medial point is not clear. A medial point also appears on Toureen Peacaun 16, apparently indicating a syllable break. The text may have been part of a personal name but it is not now possible to reconstruct it.

BIBLIOGRAPHY

Crawford 1909, 65 and fig. 16
Macalister 1909, 67
Crawford 1912, 242
Macalister 1949a, no. 922, p. 100 and pl. XLV, fig. 922
Waddell and Holland 1990, no. 23, pp. 165-86, fig. 5.23 and pl. 1

EXAMINED

May 1996 (KF, EO); July 1996 (KF)

Toureen Peacaun 15: small slab

CURRENT LOCATION

The stone is built into the interior east wall of the ruined church.

HISTORY

The stone was found in the summer of 1944 during excavation at the site (Duignan 1944, 227; Macalister 1949a, 213). It was a stray find from the vicinity of the ruined church (Waddell and Holland 1990, 169). During September to December 1944 the east wall of the church was rebuilt, incorporating many of the inscribed stones, including this one. The stone has remained there since.

DESCRIPTION

The current dimensions of the stone are:
H. *c.* 19 cm, W. *c.* 14 cm, T. 0 cm visible.
The stone is a fragment of a slab of unknown form. Incised on its visible face is a small linear equal-armed cross with expanded terminals. This initial cross is immediately followed by the first letter of a fragmentary text, the letter being only a little smaller than the cross. There is part of a second letter but it is quite uncertain how much further text has been lost.

LETTERING

The text is in half-uncial script and is legible. The maximum letter H. is *c.* 4.5 cm.

TEXT

+c[.]–

INTERPRETATION

The text reads +c[.]–. The lost letter could have been A or O. Comparison with other stones from the site suggests that this might have been the beginning of a personal name but no further interpretation of this fragmentary text is possible.

DISCUSSION

This slab is unique at Toureen Peacaun in having an initial cross aligned with, and the same size as, the lettering. The *Colman 'bocht'* slab from Clonmacnoise has a similar initial cross (Manning and Moore 1991, 10-11 and fig.).

BIBLIOGRAPHY

Macalister 1949a, no. 10, p. 213
Waddell and Holland 1990, no. 3, pp. 165-86 and fig. 3.3

EXAMINED

May 1996 (KF, EO); July 1996 (KF)

Toureen Peacaun 16: small slab

CURRENT LOCATION

The stone is built into the interior east wall of the ruined church.

HISTORY

The stone was found in the summer of 1944 during excavation at the site (Duignan 1944, 227; Macalister 1949a, 213). It was a stray find but Waddell and Holland do not record exactly where it was found (Waddell and Holland 1990, 70-1). During September to December 1944 the east wall of the church was rebuilt, incorporating many of the inscribed stones, including this one. The stone has remained there since.

DESCRIPTION

The current dimensions of the stone are:
H. *c.* 27 cm, W. *c.* 46 cm, T. 0 cm visible.
The stone is a rectangular slab of purplish sandstone. It is substantially complete although damaged on its lower edge and missing its bottom right corner. The visible face of the stone contains two complete horizontal lines of text. Above these are two small incised linear Latin crosses with expanded terminals. The cross on the left is joined to the top of the initial C.

LETTERING

Both lines of text are legible. The upper line is in insular decorative capitals and the lower line is in half-uncial script. An incised medial dot is apparently used to divide the two syllables of the lower line. The maximum letter H. is *c.* 8 cm.

TEXT

CUMMENE
LAD·CEN

INTERPRETATION

The text reads *cummene lad·cen* with a single dot between the D and C of *ladcen*, apparently dividing the syllables. These are the male personal names *Cumméne* (Cuimmíne) and *Laidcenn*.

DISCUSSION

This slab is unique among the Toureen Peacaun slabs in bearing the names of two individuals and in having not one but two crosses, one for each name. The names are presented one above the other, the upper in decorative capitals, the lower in half-uncial script. The hierarchy of scripts traditionally employed in manuscripts is presumably employed to mark the higher status of the upper name.

Cumméne/Cummíne (anglicised Cummian) is a name borne by several prominent churchmen of the seventh and eighth centuries, including an abbot of Iona and a bishop of Bobbio. Laidcen is a more unusual name. It was borne by the famous exegete Laidcend mac Baíth Bandaig, abbot of Clonfert-Mulloe, Kyle, Co. Leix; Laidcen was one of a circle of prominent scholars writing in Latin in the early to mid-seventh century, who were based in the south midlands (Ó Cróinín 1995, 187-8, 202). Another member of this group was Cummian, author of the famous Paschal letter (written c. 633), possibly bishop and scholar of Clonfert Brendan, Co. Galway (Walsh and Ó Cróinín 1988, 7-15). The occurrence on a single stone of the names of two contemporaries known to have been in close intellectual contact is a striking coincidence, especially since, as Moloney pointed out, the Annals of Inisfallen record the deaths of both of them in 661 (Moloney 1964, 103; Mac Airt 1951, 94-5).

It is also worth noting that Cummian addressed his letter on the Easter question, not only to Ségéne, abbot of Iona, but also to a certain Beccán *solitarius* (hermit). That Beccán has been plausibly identified as Beccán mac Luigdech, the author of two Old Irish poems in praise of Colum Cille who has also been equated with the Beccán of Rum who died in 677 (Walsh and

Ó Cróinín 1988, 8-9 n. 26; Clancy and Márkus 1995, 131-3). Moloney suggested instead that the recipient of Cummian's letter might be the Beccán of Toureen (1964, 103-5) but this identification has been dismissed as 'a red herring' (Clancy and Márkus 1995, 248 n. 5). A Peacaun-Columban connection cannot be dismissed entirely, although the Beccán who died in 690 would have been very old if he had been in communication with Cummian in the early 630s. It is also worth noting that the only other cross with the same form as the East Cross is at the Columban site of A'Chill, Canna (see below, no. 40). The identification of Cumméne and Laidcen of the stone with the southern Irish scholars of the same names does not, however, depend on a link with Beccán. See further below, pp. 325–6.

BIBLIOGRAPHY

Macalister 1949a, no. 15, p. 213
Lionard 1961, 103, 154 and fig. 3.2
Moloney 1964, 101-6 and fig. 2
Killanin and Duignan 1989, 87
Higgitt 1990, 156
Waddell and Holland 1990, no. 5, pp. 165-86 and fig. 3.5

EXAMINED

May 1996 (KF, EO); July 1996 (KF)

Toureen Peacaun 17: small slab

CURRENT LOCATION

The stone is built into the interior east wall of the ruined church.

HISTORY

The stone was found in the summer of 1944 during excavation at the site (Duignan 1944, 227). It was found in Trench II, near stone no. 40 (the East Cross) (Waddell and Holland 1990, 171). During September to December 1944 the east wall of the church was rebuilt, incorporating many of the inscribed stones, including this one. The stone has remained there since.

DESCRIPTION

The current dimensions of the stone are:
H. *c.* 13 cm, W. *c.* 13 cm, T. 0 cm visible.
The stone is a fragment of a slab of unknown form. On its visible face there is a small portion of an outline cross with expanded arms, no more than the end of an arm. There is no lettering on the extant portion but there may well have been a text on the missing portion.

LETTERING AND TEXT

There is no visible text on this stone.

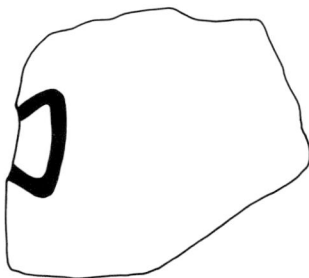

BIBLIOGRAPHY

Waddell and Holland 1990, no. 33, pp. 165-86 and fig. 6.33

EXAMINED

May 1996 (KF, EO); July 1996 (KF)

Toureen Peacaun 18: small slab

CURRENT LOCATION

The stone is built into the interior east wall of the ruined church.

HISTORY

The stone was found in the summer of 1944 during excavation at the site (Duignan 1944, 227; Macalister 1949a, 213). It was a stray find and Waddell and Holland do not record exactly where it was found (Waddell and Holland 1990, 169). During September to December 1944 the east wall of the church was rebuilt, incorporating many of the inscribed stones, including this one. The stone has remained there since.

DESCRIPTION

The current dimensions of the stone are:
H. *c.* 17.5 cm, W. *c.* 21 cm, T. *c.* 1 cm visible.
The stone is part of a slab of unknown form. Incised on its visible face is a linear equal-armed cross with expanded (forked) terminals. Below are the remains of a single horizontal line of text interrupted by the lower arm of the cross. The text is incomplete at both ends and further text could have been lost beneath it.

LETTERING

The text is in half-uncial script and is slightly deteriorated. The maximum letter H. is *c.* 3 cm.

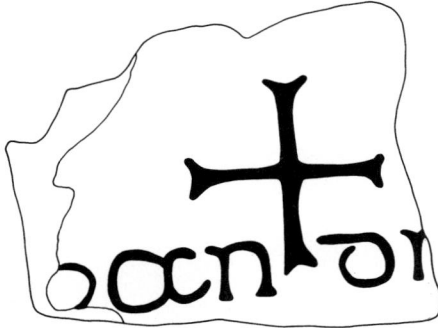

TEXT

[.]AN ‖ D–

INTERPRETATION

The text reads *[.]an d–*. Before the A are the remains of a curved letter, possibly a B, which may be the beginning of the text. Comparison with stones nos 2 and 4 suggests that the text may have been a single personal name containing the letters *–and–* but the form of the name cannot now be recovered.

BIBLIOGRAPHY

Macalister 1949a, no. 12, p. 213
Waddell and Holland 1990, no. 2, pp. 165-86 and fig. 3.2

EXAMINED
May 1996 (KF, EO); July 1996 (KF)

Toureen Peacaun 19: small slab

CURRENT LOCATION
The stone is built into the interior east wall of the ruined church.

HISTORY
The stone was found in the summer of 1944 during excavation at the site (Duignan 1944, 227; Macalister 1949a, 213). It was a stray find from the rubble around stone no. 40 (the East Cross) (Waddell and Holland 1990, 169, 171). During September to December 1944 the east wall of the church was rebuilt, incorporating many of the inscribed stones, including this one. The stone has remained there since.

DESCRIPTION
The current dimensions of the stone are:
H. *c.* 23 cm, W. *c.* 30 cm, T. *c.* 0.5 cm visible.
The stone is an apparently complete slab which has suffered damage to its lower edge. Incised on its visible face is an outline Latin cross with expanded terminals. Below is a single, complete, horizontal line of text.

LETTERING
The text is probably in half-uncial script and is highly deteriorated. The maximum letter H. is *c.* 4 cm.

TEXT

SOADBAR

INTERPRETATION
The text reads *soadbar*, a male personal name in the nominative case. See further below, p. 326.

BIBLIOGRAPHY

Macalister 1949a, no. 5, p. 213
Lionard 1961, 103, 154 and fig. 3.1
Killanin and Duignan 1989, 87
Waddell and Holland 1990, no. 6, pp. 165-86 and fig. 3.6

EXAMINED

May 1996 (KF, EO); July 1996 (KF)

Toureen Peacaun 20: small slab

CURRENT LOCATION

The stone is built into the interior east wall of the ruined church.

HISTORY

The stone was found in the summer of 1944 during excavation at the site (Duignan 1944, 227). It was a stray find from the rubble around stone no. 40 (the East Cross) (Waddell and Holland 1990, 169, 171). During September to December 1944 the east wall of the church was rebuilt, incorporating many of the inscribed stones, including this one. The stone has remained there since.

DESCRIPTION

The current dimensions of the stone are:
H. *c*. 22 cm, W. *c*. 23.5 cm, T. *c*. 1 cm visible.
The stone is part of a slab of unknown form which appears to have been deliberately trimmed to a square shape. Incised on its visible face is an equal-armed linear cross with a square 'ring' at the crossing and matching terminals; the precise form of the terminals is unknown because the slab is incomplete. There is no lettering on the extant portion of the slab but there may well have been a text on the missing portion.

LETTERING AND TEXT

There is no visible text on this stone.

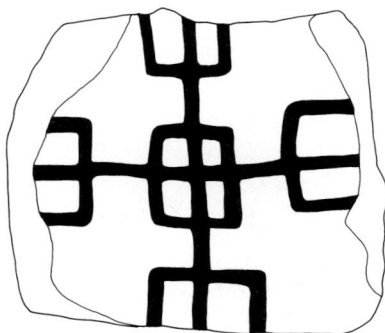

BIBLIOGRAPHY

Waddell and Holland 1990, no. 35, pp. 165-86 and fig. 6.35

EXAMINED

May 1996 (KF, EO); July 1996 (KF)

Toureen Peacaun 21: small slab

CURRENT LOCATION

The stone is built into the interior east wall of the ruined church.

HISTORY

This stone is not mentioned in any work on the stones. It is likely to have been found in 1944 and built into the east wall when the other stones were built in between September and December 1944.

DESCRIPTION

The current dimensions of the stone are:
H. *c*. 8 cm, W. *c*. 12.5 cm, T. *c*. 1 cm visible.
The stone is a fragment of a slab of unknown form. A fragmentary text is incised on the visible face, taking up most of the existing piece of stone. There are traces of either a third letter or, more likely, part of the lower cross-arm of an outline cross. There is no way of knowing how much text has been lost.

LETTERING

The text is in half-uncial script and is slightly deteriorated. The maximum letter H. is *c*. 4 cm.

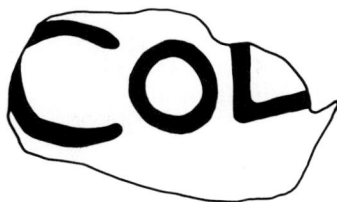

TEXT

–CO || –

INTERPRETATION

The text reads –*co*– but is too fragmentary to be interpreted.

BIBLIOGRAPHY

The stone is unpublished.

EXAMINED

May 1996 (KF, EO); July 1996 (KF)

Toureen Peacaun 22: small slab

CURRENT LOCATION

The stone is built into the interior east wall of the ruined church.

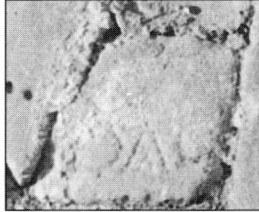

HISTORY

The stone was found in the summer of 1944 during excavation at the site (Duignan 1944, 227). It was a stray find but Waddell and Holland do not record exactly where it was found (Waddell and Holland 1990, 171). During September to December 1944 the east wall of the church was rebuilt, incorporating many of the inscribed stones, including this one. The stone has remained there since.

DESCRIPTION

The current dimensions of the stone are:
H. *c.* 11 cm, W. *c.* 11 cm, T. *c.* 1 cm visible.
The stone is a fragment of a slab of unknown form. A fragmentary text is incised on the visible face, taking up most of the existing piece of stone. The space above the text suggests that there may not have been further text there. However there is no way of knowing how much other text is lost from either end or from below, nor if the stone originally contained a cross.

LETTERING

The text is highly deteriorated and the script uncertain. The maximum letter H. is *c.* 4 cm.

TEXT

–BA[.]–

INTERPRETATION

The text reads –*ba*[.]–. The third letter could be a C, O, or similar rounded letter, but the text is too fragmentary to be interpreted.

BIBLIOGRAPHY
Waddell and Holland 1990, no. 27, pp. 165-86 and fig. 5.27

EXAMINED
May 1996 (KF, EO); July 1996 (KF)

Toureen Peacaun 23: small slab

CURRENT LOCATION
The stone is built into the interior east wall of the ruined church in an inverted position.

HISTORY
The stone was found in the summer of 1944 during excavation at the site (Duignan 1944, 227). It was a stray find but Waddell and Holland do not record exactly where it was found (Waddell and Holland 1990, 171). During September to December 1944 the east wall of the church was rebuilt, incorporating many of the inscribed stones, including this one. The stone has remained there since.

DESCRIPTION
The current dimensions of the stone are:
H. *c.* 13 cm, W. *c.* 13.5 cm, T. *c.* 1 cm visible.
The stone is a fragment of a slab of unknown form. Incised on its visible face is a small portion of two limbs of an outline cross. There is no lettering on the extant portion but there may well have been a text on the missing portion.

LETTERING AND TEXT
There is no visible text on this stone.

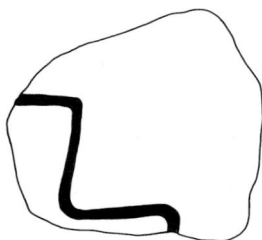

BIBLIOGRAPHY

Waddell and Holland 1990, no. 30, pp. 165-86 and fig. 6.30

EXAMINED

May 1996 (KF, EO); July 1996 (KF)

Toureen Peacaun 24: small slab

CURRENT LOCATION

The stone is built into the interior east wall of the ruined church.

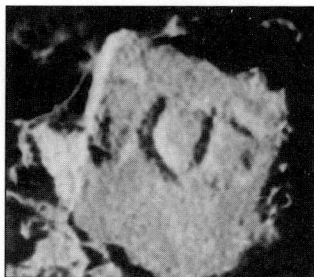

HISTORY

This stone is not mentioned in any work on the stones. It is likely to have been found in 1944 and built into the east wall when the other stones were built in between September and December 1944.

DESCRIPTION

The current dimensions of the stone are:
H. *c.* 10 cm, W. *c.* 7.5 cm, T. *c.* 1.5 cm visible.
The stone is a fragment of a slab of unknown form. A fragmentary text is incised on the visible face, taking up most of the existing piece of stone. There is no way of knowing how much other text there was originally, nor if the stone contained a cross.

LETTERING

The text is in half-uncial script and is legible. The maximum letter H. is c. 3 cm.

TEXT

–[ᴛ]ᴀ–

INTERPRETATION

The text reads –[t]a– but is too fragmentary to be interpreted.

BIBLIOGRAPHY

The stone is unpublished.

EXAMINED

May 1996 (KF, EO); July 1996 (KF)

Toureen Peacaun 25: small slab

CURRENT LOCATION

The stone is built into the interior east wall of the ruined church.

HISTORY

The stone was found in the summer of 1944 during excavation at the site (Duignan 1944, 227; Macalister 1949a, 213). It was a stray find from the rubble around stone no. 40 (the East Cross) (Waddell and Holland 1990, 169, 171). During September to December 1944 the east wall of the church was rebuilt, incorporating many of the inscribed stones, including this one. The stone has remained there since.

DESCRIPTION

The current dimensions of the stone are:
H. *c.* 30 cm, W. *c.* 17 cm, T. *c.* 1 cm visible.
The stone is part of a slab of unknown form. Incised on its visible face is an outline equal-armed cross with rectangular expansions at the terminals and a square expansion at the crossing. A fragmentary text is set in a horizontal line above the cross with the final letter touching the top of the upper cross-arm. The space preceding the H indicates that no text is lost from here but there is no way of knowing how much text is lost from the rest of the stone.

LETTERING

The text is probably in half-uncial script and is highly deteriorated. The maximum letter H. is *c.* 4 cm.

TEXT

HEL–

INTERPRETATION

The text reads *hel–*. Comparison with other stones from the site suggests that the text is likely to have contained a personal name but its form is not now recoverable. The *h* is scribal (see the **Introduction §5.3.7**). On the name, see further below, p. 325–7.

BIBLIOGRAPHY

Macalister 1949a, no. 3, p. 213
Waddell and Holland 1990, no. 16, pp. 165-86 and fig. 5.16

EXAMINED

May 1996 (KF, EO); July 1996 (KF)

Toureen Peacaun 26: small slab

CURRENT LOCATION

The stone is built into the interior east wall of the ruined church.

HISTORY

The stone was found in the summer of 1944 during excavation at the site (Duignan 1944, 227; Macalister 1949a, 213). It was a stray find from the rubble around stone no. 40 (the East Cross) (Waddell and Holland 1990, 169, 171). During September to December 1944 the east wall of the church was rebuilt, incorporating many of the inscribed stones, including this one. The stone has remained there since.

DESCRIPTION

The current dimensions of the stone are:
H. *c.* 17 cm, W. *c.* 50 cm, T. *c.* 0.5 cm visible.
The stone is part of a slab of unknown form. Its visible face contains part of the lower arm of a cross which was formed by incising the outline so as to leave the cross in false relief. The cross is of unusual shape with a rectangular base or expansion to the lower arm and a short cross-arm. No letters seem to be lost beneath the cross and probably not to its right. It is not certain, however, if there was originally further text above and to the left of the existing letters.

LETTERING

The text is in half-uncial script and is slightly deteriorated. The maximum letter H. is *c.* 6 cm.

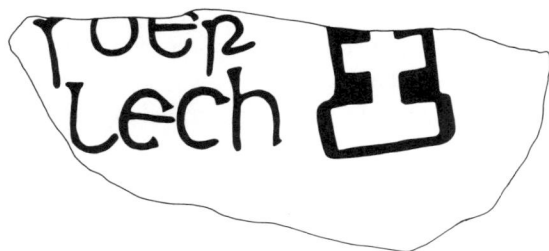

TEXT

SOER || LECH

INTERPRETATION

The text reads *soer lech*, the male personal name *Soerlech*, in the nominative case. See further below, pp 327.

BIBLIOGRAPHY

Macalister 1949a, no. 6, p. 213
Moloney 1964, 106
Killanin and Duignan 1989, 87
Waddell and Holland 1990, no. 17, pp. 165-86 and fig. 5.17

EXAMINED
May 1996 (KF, EO); July 1996 (KF)

Toureen Peacaun 27: small slab

CURRENT LOCATION

The stone is built into the interior east wall of the ruined church.

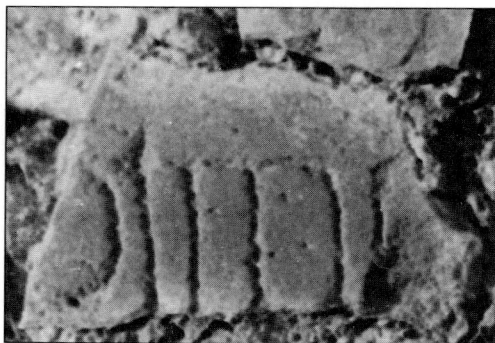

HISTORY

The stone was found in the summer of 1944 during excavation at the site (Duignan 1944, 227). It was a stray find from the rubble around stone no. 40 (the East Cross) (Waddell and Holland 1990, 169, 171). During September to December 1944 the east wall of the church was rebuilt, incorporating many of the inscribed stones, including this one. The stone has remained there since.

DESCRIPTION

The current dimensions of the stone are:
H. *c.* 9.5 cm, W. *c.* 16.5 cm, T. 0 cm visible.

The stone is a fragment of a slab of unknown form. A fragmentary text is incised on the visible face, taking up most of the existing piece of stone. There is no way of knowing how much other text there was originally, nor if the stone contained a cross.

LETTERING

The text is in half-uncial script and is slightly deteriorated. The maximum letter H. is *c.* 6 cm.

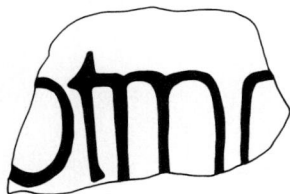

TEXT

–OTM[.]–

INTERPRETATION

The text reads –*otm*– but is too fragmentary to be interpreted.

BIBLIOGRAPHY

Waddell and Holland 1990, no. 25, pp. 165-86 and fig. 5.25

EXAMINED

May 1996 (KF, EO); July 1996 (KF)

Toureen Peacaun 28: small slab

CURRENT LOCATION

The stone is built into the interior east wall of the ruined church.

HISTORY

This stone is not mentioned in any work on the stones. It is likely to have been found in 1944 and built into the east wall when the other stones were built in between September and December 1944.

DESCRIPTION

The current dimensions of the stone are:
H. *c*. 21.5 cm, W. *c*. 23 cm, T. 0 cm visible.
The stone is part of a slab of unknown form. Incised on the visible face are the remains of an encircled cross-of-arcs with a single horizontal line of text below it. No letters appear to be lost at the end of this line nor above it. It is not possible to say if there was originally further text on the portion of stone now lost.

LETTERING

The text is in half-uncial script and is rather deteriorated. The maximum letter H. is *c*. 5 cm.

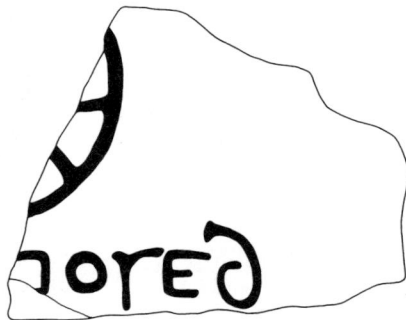

TEXT

–[.]OSED

INTERPRETATION

The text reads –*osed*. Comparison with other stones from the site suggest that this is likely to be the end of a personal name in the nominative but its exact form is not now recoverable.

DISCUSSION

Slab *61 apparently contained a cross-of-arcs although no text was recorded (see below). It is possible that this stone is a fragment of slab *61. Alternatively the two may have been related, or have contained matching designs.

BIBLIOGRAPHY

The stone is unpublished.

EXAMINED

May 1996 (KF, EO); July 1996 (KF)

Toureen Peacaun 29: altar slab (uninscribed)

CURRENT LOCATION

The stone is built into the interior east wall of the ruined church.

HISTORY

The stone was found in the summer of 1944 during excavation at the site (Duignan 1944, 227). It was a stray find but Waddell and Holland do not record exactly where it was found (Waddell and Holland 1990, 171). During

September to December 1944 the east wall of the church was rebuilt, incorporating many of the inscribed stones, including this one. The stone has remained there since.

DESCRIPTION

The current dimensions of the stone are:
H. *c.* 14 cm, W. *c.* 13 cm, T. *c.* 0.8 cm visible.
The stone is part of a slab of unknown form. Incised in the middle of its visible face is a small equal-armed linear cross with expanded terminals. A similar, slightly smaller cross is incised in the bottom left-corner. There is no trace of lettering on the extant portion of the slab which is quite unlike the inscribed slabs from the site: it seems likely that it never contained a text.

LETTERING AND TEXT

There is no text on this stone.

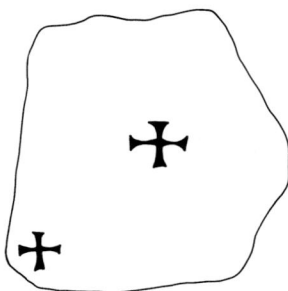

DISCUSSION

Comparison with other slabs incised with five crosses (a central cross and a cross in each of the four corners) suggests that Lionard was correct to identify this as part of an altar slab (Lionard 1961, 136). These were portable, consecrated stones which could be inserted in wooden tables; they were small, just large enough to hold the sacred vessels. Examples from Clonmacnoise and Ardmore, Co. Waterford are particularly close to the Toureen Peacaun slab (Lionard 1961, 136-7 and figs 27.4 and 27.8).

BIBLIOGRAPHY

Lionard 1961, 136 and fig. 27.7
Waddell and Holland 1990, no. 36, pp. 165-86 and fig. 6.36

EXAMINED

May 1996 (KF, EO); July 1996 (KF)

Toureen Peacaun 30: small slab

CURRENT LOCATION

The stone is built into the interior east wall of the ruined church.

HISTORY

The stone was found in the summer of 1944 during excavation at the site (Duignan 1944, 227). It was a stray find from the rubble around stone no. 40 (the East Cross) (Waddell and Holland 1990, 169, 171). During September to December 1944 the east wall of the church was rebuilt, incorporating many of the inscribed stones, including this one. The stone has remained there since.

DESCRIPTION

The current dimensions of the stone are:
H. *c.* 18 cm, W. *c.* 13 cm, T. *c.* 0.5 cm visible.
The stone is a fragment of a slab of unknown form. Incised on its visible face is part of an outline equal-armed cross (a complete limb and parts of two others). There is no lettering on the extant portion but there may well have been a text on the missing portion.

LETTERING AND TEXT

There is no visible text on this stone.

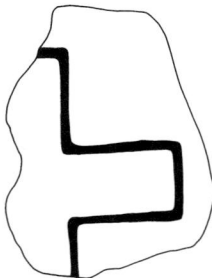

BIBLIOGRAPHY
Waddell and Holland 1990, no. 32, pp. 165-86 and fig. 6.32

EXAMINED
May 1996 (KF, EO); July 1996 (KF)

Toureen Peacaun 31: small slab

CURRENT LOCATION
The stone is built into the interior east wall of the ruined church, to the right of the free-standing cross.

HISTORY
The stone was found in the summer of 1944 during excavation at the site (Duignan 1944, 227; Macalister 1949a, 213). It was a stray find from the rubble around stone no. 40 (the East Cross) (Waddell and Holland 1990, 169). During September to December 1944 the east wall of the church was rebuilt, incorporating many of the inscribed stones, including this one. The stone has remained there since. In a photograph possibly dating from the 1960s, preserved in Dúchas (negative no. 83), slightly more of the stone is shown than is visible today. The whole of this portion of the wall, to the right of the plain, free-standing cross, has been rebuilt since the photograph was taken. Stone no. 31 is still in the same position but the six other fragments shown above and beside it have all now been moved or lost.

DESCRIPTION
The current dimensions of the stone are:
H. *c.* 17 cm, W. *c.* 45 cm, T. 0 cm visible.
The stone is part of a slab of unknown form. Incised on the visible face is the lower half of a linear equal-armed cross with short bar expansions on the right

and left terminals. Beneath this is incised a text in one horizontal line. It is complete at the end and it is unlikely that there was a further line of lettering. Although it is impossible to say if any has been lost from the beginning, the current position of the cross at the mid-point of the six-letter text may indicate that this is unlikely. There is a space between the third and fourth letters corresponding to the lower arm of the cross.

LETTERING

The text is in half-uncial script and is legible. The maximum letter H. is *c.* 4 cm.

TEXT

[D]OM NIC

INTERPRETATION

The text reads *[d]om nic* although further letters could have been lost at the beginning. It looks like a genitive form of *Domnach*, 'Sunday' (Latin *Dominicus*), a word also frequent in place-names meaning 'church' and which occurs as the second element in the male personal name *Ferdomnach* (*DIL s.v.*). Since most of the names on the other small slabs appear to be in the nominative case, the name here could be one with a dependent genitive as second element, for instance, *Cú-Domnaich* (O'Brien 1976, p. 147, §141 b 7). However, as noted above, the position of the cross in the middle of the name may suggest that letters have not been lost from the beginning. The final letter is a C not a T, so the name *Domnit* may be ruled out. On the name *Domnic* see further below, pp 325–7.

BIBLIOGRAPHY
Macalister 1949a, no. 1, p. 213
Lionard 1961, 103, 154 and fig. 3.3
Moloney 1964, 106 and fig. 4
Killanin and Duignan 1989, 87
Waddell and Holland 1990, no. 1, pp. 165-86 and fig. 3.1

EXAMINED

May 1996 (KF, EO); July 1996 (KF)

Toureen Peacaun 32: small slab

CURRENT LOCATION

The stone is built into the interior north wall of the ruined church.

HISTORY

The stone was found in the summer of 1944 during excavation at the site (Duignan 1944, 227). It was a stray find but Waddell and Holland do not record exactly where it was found (Waddell and Holland 1990, 171). During September to December 1944 the east wall of the church was rebuilt, incorporating many of the inscribed stones, including this one. In a photograph, possibly dating from the 1960s, preserved in Dúchas (negative no. 74), the stone is shown in the east interior wall of the church, just above the right end of stone 31. The stone presumably became loose before 1986-87 and was then built into the reconstructed north wall in its present position.

DESCRIPTION

The current dimensions of the stone are:
H. *c.* 18 cm, W. *c.* 16 cm, T. 0 cm visible.
The stone is a fragment of a slab of unknown form built upside down into the wall. Part of an outline cross, including the right cross-arm, is incised on its visible face. There is part of one letter below, with a horizontal line above it. There is no way of knowing how much text has been lost from the stone.

LETTERING

The text contains only one incomplete letter so neither script nor letter H. is certain.

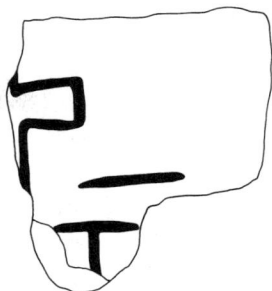

TEXT

−ī−

INTERPRETATION

The text reads −ī− but it is too fragmentary to be interpreted.

BIBLIOGRAPHY

Waddell and Holland 1990, no. 11, pp. 165-86 and fig. 4.11

EXAMINED

May 1996 (KF, EO); July 1996 (KF)

Toureen Peacaun 33: small slab

CURRENT LOCATION

The stone is built into the interior north wall of the ruined church.

HISTORY

The stone was found in the summer of 1944 during excavation at the site (Duignan 1944, 227; Macalister 1949a, 213). It was a stray find from the rubble around the East Cross, that is, stone no. 40 (Waddell and Holland 1990, 169, 171). During September to December 1944 the east wall of the church was rebuilt, incorporating many of the inscribed stones, including this one. In a photograph, possibly dating from the 1960s, preserved in Dúchas (negative no. 74), the stone is shown in the east interior wall of the church, just above stone 5. The stone presumably became loose before 1986-87 and was then built into the reconstructed north wall in its present position.

DESCRIPTION

The current dimensions of the stone are:
H. *c.* 9 cm, W. *c.* 25 cm, T. 0 cm visible.
The stone is a fragment of a slab of unknown form. A fragmentary text is incised on the visible face, taking up most of the existing piece of stone. The space preceding the first letter suggests that nothing has been lost from there but there is no way of knowing how much other text there was originally, nor if the stone contained a cross.

LETTERING

The text is in half-uncial script and is slightly deteriorated. The maximum letter H. is *c.* 4 cm.

TEXT

FO[RF]–

INTERPRETATION

The text reads *fo[rf]–* and could have been the beginning of a personal name.

BIBLIOGRAPHY

Macalister 1949a, no. 4, p. 213
Waddell and Holland 1990, no. 21, pp. 165-86 and fig. 5.21

EXAMINED

May 1996 (KF, EO); July 1996 (KF)

Toureen Peacaun 34: small slab

CURRENT LOCATION

The stone is built sideways on top of the small enclosure, known as the 'cell', in the field to the south-east of the church.

HISTORY

In 1909 this stone was lying 'loose ... on the circular wall', that is, of the 'cell' (Crawford 1909, 65). In 1912 Crawford (1912, 242) described it as being in the same place but he may not have revisited the site. Macalister (1949a, 101) recorded the stone at the 'clochán', that is, the 'cell', and it has now been built on to its wall.

DESCRIPTION

The current dimensions of the stone are:
H. *c.* 43 cm visible, W. *c.* 24 cm, T. *c.* 9 cm.
The stone is part of a slab of unknown form which is now set on to the wall on its side. The back of the stone is plain. Incised on the face of the stone is an outline equal-armed cross with a horizontal line of text above. A drawing shows the whole of the slab when it was lying loose and thus records part of the first letter which is now obscured by mortar (Waddell and Holland 1990, fig. 4.12). It is impossible to know how much text, if any, has been lost from the missing portion of stone.

LETTERING

The text is in half-uncial script and is rather deteriorated. The maximum letter H. is *c.* 4 cm.

TEXT

–[.]AED CU[.]–

INTERPRETATION

The text reads –[.]aed cu[.]–, probably for –[b]aedcu[.]–,. Only a small part of the letter before the A is now visible but the drawing mentioned above suggests that it was a B. Following the U there is the lower part of a vertical stroke which could be part of an I, N, M or similar letter. The gap between it and the U seems rather large in comparison with the spacing of the other letters and this stroke is not shown on the drawing mentioned above. Comparison with other stones from the site suggests the text is likely to have been a personal name in the nominative case. The male personal name *Báethcú* is a possibility if the final vertical is to be disregarded.

BIBLIOGRAPHY

Crawford 1909, 63, 65 and fig. 17
Macalister 1909, 67
Crawford 1912, 242
Macalister 1949a, no. 924, p. 101 and pl. XLIV, fig. 924
Lionard 1961, 105, 154 and fig. 5.4
Waddell and Holland 1990, no. 12, pp. 165-86 and fig. 4.12

EXAMINED

May 1996 (KF, EO); July 1996 (KF)

Toureen Peacaun 35: slab (uninscribed)

CURRENT LOCATION

The stone is built on top of the wall of the well.

HISTORY

This stone is not mentioned in any work on the stones. It was observed by the present authors in 1996.

DESCRIPTION

The current dimensions of the stone are:
H. *c.* 15 cm, W. *c.* 19 cm, T. *c.* 9 cm visible.
The stone is an incomplete slab of irregular shape, broken along its bottom edge. The back of the slab is plain. Incised in the middle of the front face is a linear Latin cross which extends to the broken edge. There is no trace of any lettering.

LETTERING AND TEXT

There is no text on this stone.

DISCUSSION

It is possible that originally there was a text beneath the cross, on the portion of the stone now lost, but it seems more likely that this stone never contained a text.

BIBLIOGRAPHY

The stone is unpublished.

EXAMINED

May 1996 (KF, EO); July 1996 (KF)

Toureen Peacaun 36: small slab

CURRENT LOCATION

The stone is kept in the Dúchas store, Dublin.

HISTORY

The stone was found in November 1987 during excavation at the site. It was found 0.15 m beneath the surface of the ground to the west of the platform on which the crosses (including stone no. 40) are set (Manning 1991, 211-2).

DESCRIPTION

The current dimensions of the stone are:
H. *c.* 27 cm, W. *c.* 23 cm, T. *c.* 4 cm.
The stone is a complete, rectangular slab. The back of the slab is plain. Incised on the face is an outline Latin cross with a single, horizontal line of text below. The text appears to be complete.

LETTERING

The text is in half-uncial script and is legible. The maximum letter H. is *c.* 4 cm.

TEXT

FINÁNPUER

INTERPRETATION

The text reads *finánpuer* for *Finán puer*, 'the boy Finán' where *puer* is in Latin. The use of Latin may indicate that *puer* has a religious significance, meaning perhaps 'oblate'. The line over the A indicates vowel length.

BIBLIOGRAPHY

Manning 1991, 211-3, pl. 2 and fig. 3
Manning 1995, 36 and photo 16

EXAMINED

July 1996 (KF)

Toureen Peacaun 37: small slab

CURRENT LOCATION

The stone is kept in the Dúchas store, Dublin.

HISTORY

The stone was found in November 1987 during excavation at the site. It was found 0.6 m beneath the surface of the ground to the west of the platform on which the crosses (including stone no. 40) are set (Manning 1991, 212).

DESCRIPTION

The current dimensions of the stone are:
H. *c.* 11 cm, W. *c.* 16.2 cm, T. *c.* 3.3 cm.
The stone is a fragment of a slab of unknown form. The back of the stone is plain. A fragmentary text is incised on the face of the stone. The right hand edge of the stone is original and there are no letters lost after the I. However there is no way of knowing how much other text there was originally, nor if the stone contained a cross.

LETTERING

The text is in half-uncial script and is legible. The maximum letter H. is *c.* 4 cm.

TEXT

–CANI

INTERPRETATION

The text reads *–cani*. This looks like the genitive ending of a Latin word, or a name in a Latinised form, but the text is too fragmentary to be interpreted. Manning, however, suggested the reconstruction *[Sancti Bec]cani*, 'of holy Beccán' (Manning, 1991, 213).See further below p. 326.

BIBLIOGRAPHY

Manning 1991, 212-3, pl. 2 and fig. 3

EXAMINED

July 1996 (KF)

Toureen Peacaun 38: small slab

CURRENT LOCATION

The stone is kept in the Dúchas store, Dublin.

HISTORY

The stone was found in November 1987 during excavation at the site. It was found 0.2 m beneath the surface of the ground to the west of the platform on which the crosses (including stone no. 40) are set (Manning 1991, 211-2).

DESCRIPTION

The current dimensions of the stone are:
H. *c.* 21 cm, W. *c.* 34 cm, T. *c.* 5 cm.
The stone is a slab of irregular rectangular shape, possibly complete, although damaged at the left edge. The back is plain. Incised on the face is an outline Latin cross, open at the bottom. Above this is a horizontal line of text with further letters below. The face is badly abraded, especially on the left side, and portions of the cross and letters have delaminated.

LETTERING

The text is probably in half-uncial script and is highly deteriorated. The maximum letter H. is *c.* 5 cm.

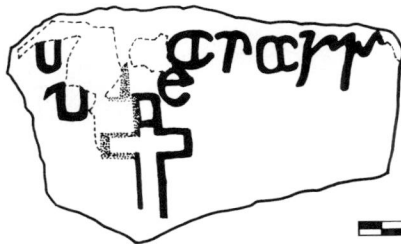

TEXT

– [E]ARASS
[D.E]

INTERPRETATION

The text appears to read –*[e]arass* with *[d.e]* on the lower line. If the delamination of the letters at the beginning of the upper line occurred during carving then it is possible that the letters squeezed on to the lower line were intended to replace them. If this were the case, the reading might be *[d.e]arass* but neither reading nor interpretation is at all certain.

BIBLIOGRAPHY

Manning 1991, 211-3, pl. 2 and fig. 3

EXAMINED

July 1996 (KF)

Toureen Peacaun 39: upright cross-pillar

CURRENT LOCATION

The stone is built into the exterior east wall of the ruined church.

HISTORY

Meagher's photograph, taken in the early 1930s, shows this stone forming part of the 'station' at the west end of the ruined church (Waddell and Holland 1990, pl. 1). It was seen here by Macalister who described the position as 'on a masonry table ... against the West End of the Oratory, beside the entrance-door' (Macalister 1949a, 101). The station was dismantled by the OPW and the stone is shown loose in a photograph taken by them in 1944 (Waddell and Holland 1990, pl. 6: see illustration on p. 289). The stone was probably built into the east wall of the church when this was rebuilt during September to December 1944.

DESCRIPTION

The current dimensions of the stone are:
H. *c.* 77.5 cm, W. *c.* 21 cm, T. *c.* 2.5 cm visible. Macalister measured the stone when it was out of the wall and gives the measurement of the thickness in inches corresponding to *c.* 13 cm (Macalister 1949a, 101).
The stone is a complete pillar-shaped slab. The upper portion is carefully shaped and smoothed. The lower third, in contrast, is irregular and rough, indicating that the stone was intended to be sunk into the ground. On the visible face there is a plain, ringed Latin cross, carved in relief. Its right and left arms extend to the edges of the stone. Running the whole width of the top of this face is a horizontal band joined to the cross. This is mirrored at the bottom of the cross by a horizontal base of similar proportions. When Macalister saw the stone it was not built into the wall but he did not mention any carving on the back (Macalister 1949a, 101). The text is incised on the recessed surface in a single horizontal line interrupted by the upper cross-arm, that is, it is set in the top left and right quadrants of the cross.

LETTERING

The text was probably in half-uncial script, of maximum letter H. *c.* 3 cm, but is now highly deteriorated.

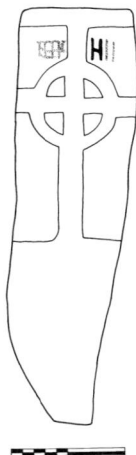

TEXT

– ‖ N̲[..]

INTERPRETATION

The text reads –n– but is now too illegible to be interpreted. There are traces of perhaps three letters in the left quadrant and three in the right, the first of which appears to be a capital N. Macalister read the text as *art uir*, a personal name *Artuir* (Macalister 1949a, 101). Waddell and Holland described this reading as 'questionable' and it is not supported by the, admittedly highly worn, extant traces; Duignan's suggested reading of *c[–]nis* (Waddell and Holland 1990, 179) is closer to what remains today.

DISCUSSION

This stone is one of a pair. Its companion is slightly smaller but the difference lies in the size of the unworked portion and when sunk in the ground the two would have been more or less identical. Two larger pillars (*c.* 140 cm tall) are carved with relief crosses of the same form, although they have a frame all the way round, not just at top and bottom. These larger stones have mortices cut at the top and bottom of one edge, each with a conical peg-hole at the back. They also have hollows low down on the carved face (below current ground level). Clearly they were part of a composite monument. One of them is complete, the other is broken in three. The pieces were found widely scattered across the site, the lowest coming from the platform around the East Cross (stone no. 40). Duignan thought that the East Cross and the two larger pillars 'formed a sort of trinity' (Waddell and Holland 1990, 179) and had them erected in this formation. However, the close similarities between the larger and smaller pairs of crosses suggest that these four may have been part of a composite arrangement, perhaps with one cross in each corner, the taller ones at the back and the smaller ones at the front. There is no trace of lettering on the two larger pillars, nor on the other small one.

BIBLIOGRAPHY

Macalister 1949a, no. 924A, 101
Waddell and Holland 1990, p. 179, fig. 9 and pl. 6

EXAMINED

May 1996 (KF, EO); July 1996 (KF)

Pair of smaller cross pillars, taken in 1944, no. 39 on left

Toureen Peacaun 40: free-standing cross (East Cross)

CURRENT LOCATION

The cross-shaft stands about 7 m to the south-east of the ruined church at the centre of a collection of worked stones which are protected by a cattle grid. The upper limb of the cross is set into the ground immediately behind it. Five large flakes from the top of the west face of the shaft are preserved in the NMI. The inscription is on the west face of the shaft.

HISTORY

Until Duignan's 1944 excavation the cross-shaft stood in its original position in the middle of a sub-rectangular dry-stone platform, about 260 cm by 180 cm (Waddell and Holland 1990, 181 and fig.12). Petrie's figure shows it, and one of the cross-pillars, in this position (Petrie 1878, fig. on p. 34). He described it as a 'pillar-stone about seven feet long' but mentioned no text (Petrie 1878, 33). Crawford described the two stones thus: 'At the south-east corner is the square platform, with two cross-inscribed pillar-stones', as illustrated by Petrie; however he said the larger stone was 'about 5 feet high' (Crawford 1909, 64). Crawford's later description explained that these stones were 'near the S.E. angle of the church' (Crawford 1912, 242). The first to mention the text was Macalister who first thought the letters were runic; later, following a suggestion made by Leask, he came to see them as decorative capitals but 'sadly defaced' (1949a, 101).

In 1944 Duignan opened trenches at the base of the cross-shaft and to the west of the platform. This enabled the construction of the composite cross to be determined (Duignan 1944, 227). Five fragments of the broken west face of the shaft were discovered at the foot of the cross where they had fallen and the separate upper limb was found lying near by (Waddell and Holland 1990, 175, 179, 181, figs 7 and 12, and pls 3 and 4). The shaft was removed from its setting by Duignan and the pieces fitted back together. The shaft was then re-erected in its original position, the upper limb was set in the ground beside it and the fragments were deposited in the NMI. In November 1987 a further small excavation took place around the base of the re-erected cross so that a cattle grid could be installed (Manning 1991, 211-12).

DESCRIPTION

The cross was a composite monument consisting of a monolithic shaft with narrow transom and a separate upper limb. When fitted together by the mortice-and-tenon joint, the two stones had a total length of 406 cm. The rough butt of the shaft would have been sunk into the ground to the depth of the carved shoulder and thus the two stones would have stood 310 cm tall to the top of the massive upper tenon. The finial which presumably sat on this tenon has not been found. The below-ground portion of the shaft has a width of 73.5 cm (Waddell and Holland 1991, 175).
As currently set in the ground the dimensions of the shaft only are:
H. *c.* 200 cm, W. *c.* 52 cm, T. *c.* 23 cm.
Duignan found a dressed sandstone block, about 15 cm square, which he interpreted as a separate right arm of the cross, joined to the shaft by means of a lap-joint and supported by a crutch held in place by a mortice under the transom; no left arm has been found (Waddell and Holland 1990, 175 and pl. 3). Kelly regarded these postulated separate extensions as 'problematic' and omitted them from her reconstruction (Kelly, D. 1991, 111 and fig. 36B). The long edges of the shaft were cut back to give deep rebates. These curve inwards above and below the transom, creating the impression of hollowed armpits. The effect of these rebatements is to leave a 'narrow tongue' of stone *c.* 16 cm thick, standing proud on either side of the shaft (Kelly, D. 1991, 111). A distinction was made between the two broad faces of the shaft, with less stone cut away on the east face than on the inscribed west face (Kelly, D. 1991, 111). The cross is made from 'grey-green micaceous sandstone which is very rich in mica, and therefore both hard to dress and very susceptible to flaking' (Duignan, quoted in Waddell and Holland 1990, 175). As reconstructed, the composite cross would have been top-heavy, which presumably explains why it tilted backwards and the top fell off, fracturing the top of the west face of the shaft (Duignan, quoted in Waddell and Holland 1990, 175).

The cross is plain except for the text and three equal-armed crosses incised on the lower member. There is an outline cross with hollowed armpits at the centre of the crossing on the west face and a similar one in the middle of the shaft on the east face. On the west face, opposite the ends of each arm, are four small circular sockets about 8 cm deep which Duignan suggested were intended to receive the shanks of ornamental bosses (Waddell and Holland 1991, 179). Kelly, however, interpreted these sockets as skeuomorph bolts or rivets (1991, 131). On the west face, near the bottom of the shaft, is incised a third cross which has square expansions at the terminals and crossing. The expansions form five boxes which are internally decorated with one of three simple cruciform patterns.

The text is incised immediately above this cross in six horizontal lines. The letters consist of fine lines shallowly incised. Many of the letters are bounded by head- and foot-lines which give the impression of ruled borders; however it is clear from the feet of the letters in lines 4-6 that these lines were not continuous. The laterally compressed letters form tight horizontal bands which are separated by thin strips of bare stone. The small socket at the top of the shaft appears to be channelling rain-water down the middle of the west face, leading to lichen growth and a deterioration of the surface. As a result the middle portion of the first four lines has almost entirely deteriorated. In addition there are numerous small pockets of delamination where the friable surface of the stone has spalled. The lettering is best preserved at the ends of each line with the lowest two lines being the best preserved of all.

LETTERING

The text is written in a form of insular decorative capitals, the distinctive script used for display purposes in *de luxe* insular manuscripts such as the Lindisfarne Gospels and the Books of Kells, and also on metalwork and some stone sculpture (see Higgitt 1982, 313-15; Higgitt 1994, 216-17). The lettering is highly deteriorated. The maximum letter H. is *c.* 5 cm.

TEXT

O [..–]OR[.]
A[.–]
[.] O [.–R]O[..]
C/ T[.]R[–]
[.]/TTO[–NŪRN̄IN̄Ī]
DERN[A]D[..G]IB

INTERPRETATION

The difficulty in reading and interpreting the text lies not only in its poor state of preservation, although this is a serious problem, but also in the complex layout of the lettering. It is typical of insular display capitals that 'letters overlap and interlock in a dense overall pattern' (Higgitt 1994, 212). Tiny letters are inserted in angular breaks in full-size letters, as in the Book of Kells (see Higgitt 1994, 213, fig. 1), or are slipped into the spaces between tightly-packed letters, as on the Ardagh Chalice (Rynne 1987, pl.1A). Another characteristic of the script is the fluidity of its mix of letters, which typically combines forms from various sources, including both roman capital and half-uncial forms and angular variants and elaborations of these (Higgitt 1982, 310). These three factors combine to mean that legibility is often sacrificed for decorative effect and 'individual letters loose [*recte* lose] their independence in the all-over pattern' (Higgitt 1982, 314). All these features are discernible on the East Cross and even were the inscription perfectly preserved, reading it would still be a challenge. The first character in line 4 appears to be a C with a small T intersecting with its top arm to form a little cross. In the line below there are what look like sideways Ts joined to the tops of both the first and last letters. A small I appears to nestle between the full-size N and A (or N) at the end of line 5. The convoluted arrangement at the end of line 2 is reminiscent of many found in the display sections of the Book of Kells.

The only legible portion of the text is in Irish, and it may well be that originally the whole text was, although too little survives for this to be certain. The first line begins with a large rectangular O which suggests a text opening *or(óit) do / ar* 'a prayer for'. The final two extant letters of this line are also OR. Lozenge-shaped Os can be made out near the beginning and end of the third line. The fifth line, although better preserved, is difficult to untangle. At the end it might read –[URNIAIT] or –[URNINIT] with the T on its side as a head-line for the previous two letters. There appear to be three horizontal marks above the height of the other letters which may be intended as marks of abbreviation.

The only complete word which can be read is, as Duignan saw, the ·dern[a]d at the beginning of the final line (Waddell and Holland 1990, 179). This is the prototonic perfect passive (singular) of *do-gní* 'make, do', a verbal form which indicates that the previous line should end with a particle. The form ·dernad is found epigraphically in two formulae. In the more common one it is preceded by the preposition *la*, 'with, by' (combined with the relative pronoun to give *lasa^n*), to indicate the patron who commissioned a work. Examples of *las(an)* *dernad*, 'for whom [it] was made', are found, for example, on a slab from Clonmacnoise (Macalister 1949a, no. 609, p. 44 and pl. XII, fig. 609) and on a tenth-century cross from Monasterboice (Macalister 1949a, no. 580, pp. 31-2 and fig.). The less common formula incorporates the preposition *oc*, 'at, beside' (combined with the relative pronoun to give *oc(c)-a^n*, *ica^n*) to record the head of the ecclesiastical foundation at which a work was carried out (on the grammatical point see Thurneysen 1946, p. 312, §492). The phrase *ican (d)ernad*, 'at whose house [it] was made', may have occurred on a slab from Clonmacnoise (Macalister 1949a, no. 796, p. 64). Both formulae occur on inscribed metalwork reliquaries of the eleventh and twelfth centuries (Michelli 1996). Although the end of the fifth line has not been interpreted with certainty, it does not appear to read either *lasan* or *ican*. From the parallels noted above, the final line might have been expected to continue *in cros-sa*, 'this cross' but the extant letters do not appear to support this reading. The final characters look instead like *–[g]ib*, or possibly *–[b]i[eu]*, neither reading making immediate sense. Moloney (1964, 101) read them as *in lie* 'the stone', although *lia* usually means a standing stone or a pillar-stone, not a free-standing cross (*DIL lia*). In the form *lec*, the work appears as a label on some of the cross–slabs from Clonmacnoise (for example, Macalister 1949a , no. 857, p. 74 and pl, XXV, fig. 857; no. 858, pp. 74-5 and pl. XXV, fig. 858). Moloney's photograph (Moloney 1964, 100, fig. 1) shows the stone in better condition than it is today, but even so his reading of the final four letters of the fifth line as LAIS is doubtful. Even more so is his tentative reading of the first part of that line as a name in a 'form roughly resembling BIORANAIN' (Moloney 1964, 101).

Related inscriptions, using different parts of the verb *do-gní*, are probably to be found on some ninth-century crosses, for example the South Cross and the Cross of the Scriptures from Clonmacnoise, and the crosses from Castlebernard (Kinnitty) and Durrow (Ó Murchadha 1980; Ó Murchadha and Ó Murchú 1988; see also Harbison 1992, 355-66). Although it can be no more than a conjecture, it seems possible that the Toureen Peacaun text consisted of a request for prayers on behalf of various people involved in the erection of the monument. A longer text on such lines is that on the mid-eleventh-century shrine of the *Cathach* which requests prayers for the patron, craftsman and ecclesiastical sponsor of the shrine (Michelli 1996, 21-2 and pl. VII).

DISCUSSION

Kelly discussed the form of this cross in some detail, linking it with crosses of similar form from A' Chill (Canna), Glendalough and Kilmartin, Argyll (Kelly, D. 1991, 114-16). These, she argued, were constructed in imitation of wooden crosses which had stout central upright elements flanked by thinner elements, the three layers being bolted together (Kelly, D. 1991, 131). The multiple pieces of stone linked by mortice-and-tenon joints had already suggested to Duignan that this was 'in a very real way a joiner's job' (Duignan, quoted in Waddell and Holland 1990, 175). The East Cross is part of a wider tradition of early free-standing stone crosses which are derived from wooden predecessors. These may range in date from the eighth century to the early ninth (Kelly, D.

1991, 142-3). As Kelly conceded, however, the best possibility for dating the cross is the form of the script used. The fashion for insular decorative capitals lasted from the beginning of the eighth century until the early ninth. One of the first fully developed examples is the Lindisfarne Gospels, dated between 698 and 721 (Higgitt 1982, 313). Although too little survives on the East Cross for a thorough comparison, some features appear to link it to examples of insular decorative capitals from the earlier rather than the later part of the eighth century. The lozenge-shaped O with head- and foot-lines is found, for example, in the display script of the Lindisfarne Gospels and on the Ardagh Chalice (dated by Rynne to the first half of the eighth century, 1987, 89). It also occurs on the Tarbat stone (Higgitt 1982, 312) and on a lost eighth-century slab from Hartlepool (Okasha 1971, no. 44, p. 76 and fig.).

Insular decorative capital script may have originated in Northumbria (Higgitt 1994, 218) and epigraphic examples outside north-east England are rare. The script is used in Pictland, both on the Tarbat stone and on one from Lethnot, Angus (Okasha 1985, 53-4 and fig.). It is found once in Wales, on a slab from Ramsey Island (Okasha 1970) which is, as Rynne points out 'the nearest point to Ireland off the south-west coast of Wales ... on the well-known route from Great Britain to Ireland (1987, 85). There is a single example from Brittany, on an inscribed pillar from Lanrivoaré, Finistère (Davies *et al.* forthcoming). The only certain examples in Ireland are the Toureen Peacaun inscription itself and the silver chalice from Ardagh, which was found in Co. Limerick, 80 km from Toureen Peacaun.

The use of insular decorative capitals might imply the presence of a scriptorium at or near Toureen Peacaun, possibly a scriptorium which was in touch with the wider insular world of scholarship and book production. The link with the Ardagh Chalice is suggestive. Ryan argued that it might have been produced in the same (unidentified) north Munster workshop which produced the Derrynaflan paten at about the same time (Ryan, M. 1985, 20). One of several features linking the two communion vessels is that both were assembled using a construction code of half-uncial letters, numbers and related symbols (Brown 1993). Concurring that both items were made in the same eighth-century milieu, or even workshop, Brown commented that the manuscript-like quality of the lettering on the Derrynaflan paten implies that the work was conducted under the supervision of someone who had undergone formal scribal training. The inclusion in the alphabetic sequence used on the paten of the letter K, which is used in Latin but not in Irish, is significant (Brown 1993, 162-3, 165). Although Duignan found evidence of metal-working at Toureen Peacaun (1944, 227), craft-production is a common feature of monasteries of the period and there is no evidence to link the chalice and paten directly with the site.

The East Cross is unusual in several respects. Its structure, although part of a wider tradition of composite crosses, is unique. The presence of an inscription at such an early date is unusual, other inscribed free-standing crosses tending to date from the mid-ninth century or later (see Harbison 1992, 367-84). The length of the inscription is exceptional only in comparison with contemporary cross-slabs which are mostly inscribed with a single name with or without a preceding *or(óit) do*. Inscriptions on upright monuments tend to be longer, for example the stone at Kilnasaggart (Macalister 1949a, no. 946, pp. 114-15 and pl. XLVI, fig. 946). The use of insular decorative capitals for the text marks out the East Cross as an exceptional and ambitious monument. The position of the text at the top of the shaft is in contrast to the majority of inscribed crosses in Ireland, which tend to be inscribed on the base or at the foot of the shaft (Higgitt 1986, 127-9). This, however, could be a function of the cross's early date; the early eighth-century Kilnasaggart inscription is equally high up.

BIBLIOGRAPHY

Petrie 1878, 33 and fig. on p. 34
Crawford 1909, 64
Crawford 1912, 242
Duignan 1944, 227
Macalister 1949a, no. 924B, p. 101
Moloney 1964, 99, 101, 106 and fig. 1
Evans 1966, 195
Fanning 1976, 36 and pl. 3
Weir 1980, 216
Higgitt 1982, 312, 314
Higgitt 1986, 127-8, 143, 147
Killanin and Duignan 1989, 87
Waddell and Holland 1990, 165, 175-86, fig. 7 and pls 3 and 4
Kelly, D. 1991, 111-16, 136-43 and figs 35 a, b and 36 Ba, Bb
Harbison 1992, no. 215, pp 174, 345, 364-5, 379 and figs 598, 599, 1021
Higgitt 1994, 216, 229
OS Letters unpublished 1930, 65

EXAMINED

May 1996 (KF, EO); July 1996 (KF)

Toureen Peacaun 41: small slab

CURRENT LOCATION

The stone is now lost.

HISTORY

The stone was found in the summer of 1944 during excavation at the site (Duignan 1944, 227). It was a stray find from the rubble around stone no. 40 (the East Cross) (Waddell and Holland 1990, 169, 171). According to Waddell and Holland (1990, 171), the stone was then in the NMI but there is no record of it there.

DESCRIPTION

The description is taken from Waddell and Holland (1990).
From Waddell and Holland's scale drawing (fig. 6.37, reproduced below), the dimensions of the stone were:
H. *c*. 22 cm, W. *c*. 16 cm; no thickness measurement is given.
The stone was part of a slab of unknown form. Incised on the illustrated face are the remains of a linear Latin cross. There was no sign of any lettering.

LETTERING AND TEXT

There was no visible text on this stone.

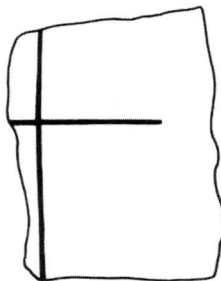

DISCUSSION

Although the stone was too fragmentary for certainty, the simple form of the cross suggests that it may have been similar to slabs 35 and 42 and was probably not inscribed.

BIBLIOGRAPHY

Waddell and Holland 1990, no. 37, pp. 165-86 and fig. 6.37

Toureen Peacaun 42: small slab

CURRENT LOCATION

The stone is now lost.

HISTORY

The stone was found in the summer of 1944 during excavation at the site (Duignan 1944, 227). It was a stray find from the vicinity of the ruined church (Waddell and Holland 1990, 169, 171, 175). According to Waddell and Holland (1990, 175), the stone was then in the NMI but there is no record of it there.

DESCRIPTION

From Waddell and Holland's scale drawing (fig. 6.38, reproduced below), the dimensions of the stone were:
H. *c.* 24 cm, W. *c.* 22 cm; no thickness measurement is given.
The stone was a fragment of a slab of unknown form. Incised on the illustrated face are the remains of a linear Latin cross. There was no sign of any lettering.

LETTERING AND TEXT

There was no visible text on this stone.

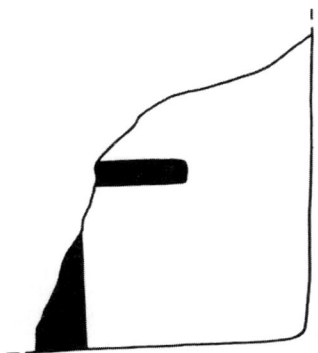

DISCUSSION

Although the stone was too fragmentary for certainty, the simple form of the cross suggests that it may have been similar to slabs 35 and 41 and may not have been inscribed.

BIBLIOGRAPHY

Waddell and Holland 1990, no. 38, pp. 165-86 and fig. 6.38

Toureen Peacaun 43: small slab

CURRENT LOCATION

The stone is now lost.

OPW photograph no. 73, showing stone *43

HISTORY

This stone is not recorded in any published account of the stones. In a photograph possibly dating from the 1960s, preserved in the Dúchas archive (negative no. 73: see illustration), the stone is shown built into the east interior wall of the church, to the right of slab 1, above slab 2. The stone presumably fell out of the wall and disappeared before repair work was done to the east wall in 1986-87.

DESCRIPTION

The description is taken from the photograph, which suggests that the dimensions of the stone were:
H. *c.* 16 cm, W. *c.* 25 cm; no thickness measurement can be calculated.
The stone was part of a slab of unknown form. The visible face of the stone contained an incomplete text consisting of three or four letters in one line. There was no trace of a cross, but it could well have been on the missing portion.

LETTERING

The text appears to have been in half-uncial script and legible. The maximum letter H. was *c.* 2 cm.

TEXT

   –MNE[.]

INTERPRETATION

The text appears to have read –*mne[.]* and to have been complete at the end. It cannot now be reconstructed.

BIBLIOGRAPHY

The stone is unpublished.

Toureen Peacaun 44: small slab

CURRENT LOCATION

The stone is now lost.

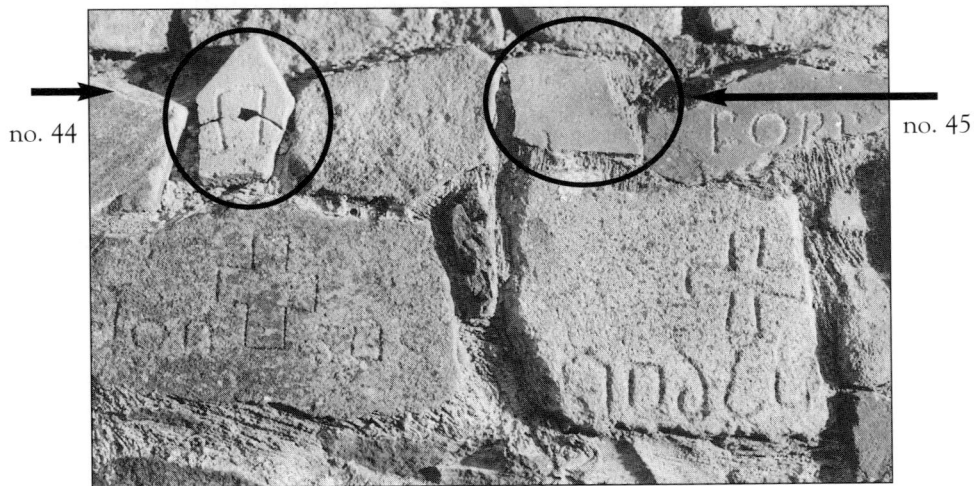

OPW photograph no. 74, showing stones *44 and *45

HISTORY

The stone was found in the summer of 1944 during excavation at the site (Duignan 1944, 227). It was a stray find from the rubble around stone no. 40 (the East Cross) (Waddell and Holland 1990, 169, 171). In photographs possibly dating from the 1960s, preserved in the Dúchas archive (negatives nos 73, 74: see illustrations above), the stone is shown built into the east interior wall of the church, to the right of slab 43 and above slab 4. The stone presumably fell out of the wall and disappeared before repair work was done to the east wall in 1986-87.

DESCRIPTION

The description is taken from Waddell and Holland (1990). From their scale drawing (fig. 6.31, reproduced below), the dimensions of the stone were: H. *c.* 15 cm, W. *c.* 9 cm; no thickness measurement is given.

The stone was a fragment of a slab of unknown form. Incised on its visible face was one limb of an outline cross. The cross filled almost all of the then extant portion of slab but there may well have been text on the missing portion.

LETTERING AND TEXT

There was no visible text on this stone.

BIBLIOGRAPHY

Waddell and Holland 1990, no. 31, pp. 165-86 and fig. 6.31

Toureen Peacaun 45: small slab

CURRENT LOCATION

The stone is now lost.

HISTORY

The stone was found in the summer of 1944 during excavation at the site (Duignan 1944, 227). It was a stray find but Waddell and Holland do not record exactly where it was found (Waddell and Holland 1990, 171). In a photograph possibly dating from the 1960s, preserved in the Dúchas archive (negative no. 74: see p. 301), the stone is shown built into the east interior wall of the church, to the left of slab 33, and above slab 5. The stone presumably fell out of the wall and disappeared before repair work was done to the east wall in 1986-87.

DESCRIPTION

The description is taken from Waddell and Holland (1990). From their scale drawing (fig. 6.34, reproduced below), the dimensions of the stone were:

H. *c.* 11 cm, W. *c.* 11 cm; no thickness measurement is given.

The stone was a fragment of a slab of unknown form. On its visible face there was a portion of what appears to have been an outline cross. There is no sign of any lettering but there could have been a text on the portion of the stone now broken off.

LETTERING AND TEXT

There was no visible text on this stone.

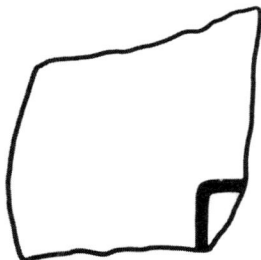

BIBLIOGRAPHY

Waddell and Holland 1990, no. 34, pp. 165-86 and fig. 6.34

Toureen Peacaun 46: small slab

CURRENT LOCATION

The stone is now lost.

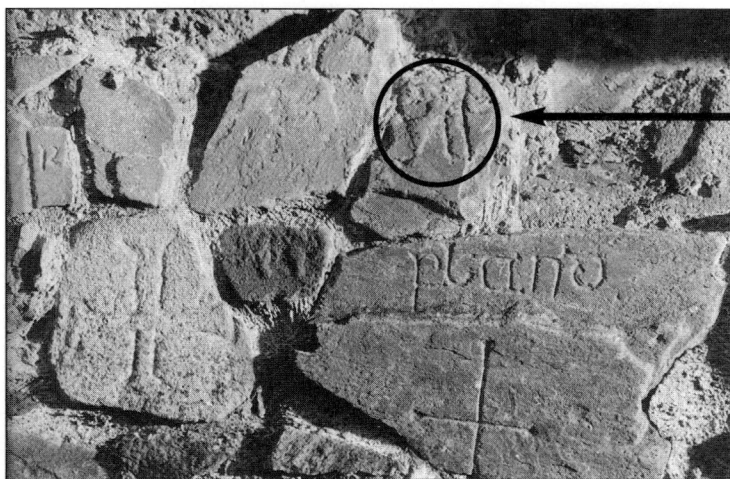

no. 46

OPW photograph no. 76, showing stone *46

HISTORY

This stone is not recorded in any published account of the stones. However in photographs possibly dating from the 1960s, preserved in the Dúchas archive (negatives nos 75, 76: see illustration above), the stone is shown built into the east interior wall of the church, to the right of slab 3 (now moved) and above slab 10. The stone presumably fell out of the wall and disappeared before repair work was done to the east wall in 1986-87.

DESCRIPTION

The description is taken from the photograph, which suggests that the dimensions of the stone were:
H. *c.* 18 cm, W. *c.* 16 cm; no thickness measurement can be calculated.
The stone was part of a slab of unknown form. On its visible face there was a portion of what was probably part of an outline cross but no lettering; there could, however, have been a text on the portion of the stone now broken off.

LETTERING AND TEXT

There was no visible text on this stone.

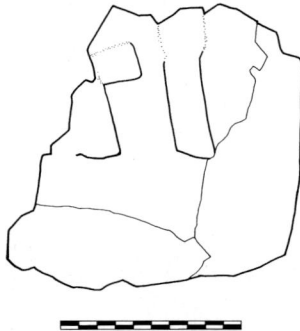

BIBLIOGRAPHY

The stone is unpublished.

Toureen Peacaun 47: small slab

CURRENT LOCATION

The stone is now lost.

OPW photograph no. 82, showing stone *47

HISTORY

The stone was found in the summer of 1944 during excavation at the site (Duignan 1944, 227; Macalister 1949a, 213). It was a stray find but Waddell and Holland do not record exactly where it was found (Waddell and Holland 1990, 171). In a photograph possibly dating from the 1960s, preserved in the Dúchas archive (negative no. 82: see illustration), the stone is shown built into the east interior wall of the church, to the right of the plain free-standing cross. The stone presumably fell out of the wall and disappeared before repair work was done to the east wall in 1986-87.

DESCRIPTION

The description and text are taken from Waddell and Holland (1990). From their scale drawing (fig. 4.9, reproduced below), the dimensions of the stone were:

H. *c.* 27 cm, W. *c.* 19 cm; no thickness measurement is given.

The stone was part of a slab of unknown form. Incised on the illustrated face was the remains of an outline Latin cross. Above it was a single horizontal line of text. The space after the last letter indicates the text was complete at the end, but a few letters were lacking from the beginning.

LETTERING

The text was in half-uncial script and appears in the photograph to be legible. From the scale drawing in Waddell and Holland (1990, fig. 4.9), the maximum letter H. is c. 5 cm.

TEXT

–[L̲]ETHO

INTERPRETATION

The text appears to have read –*[l]etho*. Although most of the names on the Toureen Peacaun slabs appear to be in the nominative case, –*[l]etho* looks like a genitive. The name, however, cannot now be reconstructed.

BIBLIOGRAPHY

Macalister 1949a, no. 11, p. 213
Waddell and Holland 1990, no. 9, pp. 165-86 and fig. 4.9

Toureen Peacaun 48: small slab

CURRENT LOCATION

The stone is now lost.

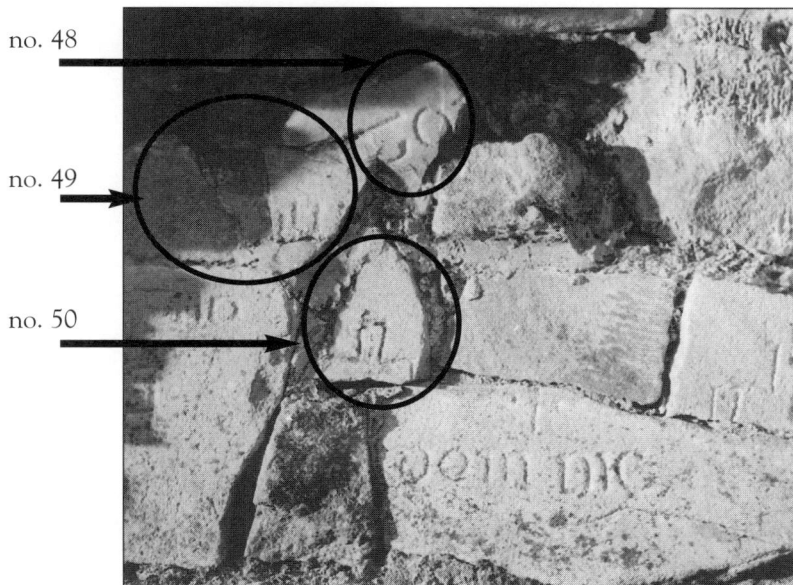

no. 48

no. 49

no. 50

OPW photograph no. 83, showing stones *48, *49 and *50

HISTORY

The stone was found in the summer of 1944 during excavation at the site (Duignan 1944, 227; Macalister 1949a, 213). It was a stray find from the rubble around stone no. 40 (the East Cross) (Waddell and Holland 1990, 169, 171). In photographs possibly dating from the 1960s, preserved in the Dúchas archive (negatives nos 82, 83: see illustrations above), the stone is shown built into the east interior wall of the church, to the right of the plain free-standing cross, in the upper register of slabs. The stone presumably fell out of the wall and disappeared before repair work was done to the east wall in 1986-87.

DESCRIPTION

The description and text are taken from Waddell and Holland (1990). From their scale drawing (fig. 5.18, reproduced below), the dimensions of the stone were: H. *c.* 13 cm, W. *c.* 19 cm; no thickness measurement is given.
The stone was a fragment of a slab of unknown form. A fragmentary text was incised on the visible face, taking up most of the existing piece of stone. There is no way of knowing how much other text there was originally, nor if the stone contained a cross.

LETTERING

The text was in half-uncial script and appears in the photograph to be legible. From the scale drawing in Waddell and Holland (1990, fig. 5.18), the maximum letter H. was *c.* 5 cm.

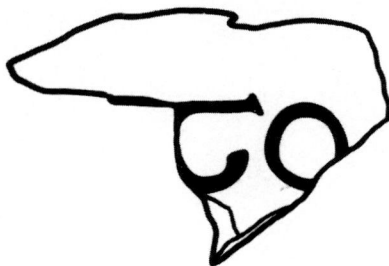

TEXT

–TO–

INTERPRETATION

This fragmentary text appears to have read –*to*– but cannot now be interpreted.

BIBLIOGRAPHY

Macalister 1949a, no. 7, p. 213
Waddell and Holland 1990, no. 18, pp. 165-86 and fig. 5.18

Toureen Peacaun 49: small slab

CURRENT LOCATION

The stone is now lost.

HISTORY

This stone is not recorded in any published account of the stones. However in photographs possibly dating from the 1960s, preserved in the Dúchas archive (negatives nos 82, 83: see illustrations above, pp. 305, 307), the stone is shown built into the east interior wall of the church, to the left of the plain free-standing cross, in the upper register of slabs, between slabs 47 and 48. The stone presumably fell out of the wall and disappeared before repair work was done to the east wall in 1986-87.

DESCRIPTION

The description is taken from the photograph, which suggests that the dimensions of the stone were:

H. *c.* 9 cm, W. *c.* 9 cm; no thickness measurement can be calculated.

The stone was part of a slab of unknown form. It is possible, but not certain, that a small and plain piece of stone immediately beneath was also part of the same slab. The visible face of the stone contained the remains of two or three letters in one line but there appears to have been no sign of any decoration.

LETTERING

The text appears to have been in half-uncial script and legible. The maximum letter H. was *c.* 3 cm.

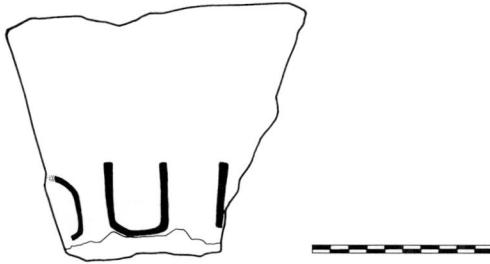

TEXT

–[.u̲]–

INTERPRETATION

The text probably read –[.u]–. The photograph shows that the first lost letter was curved; it could have been O or D or possibly R. The second letter was probably U although it could have been I followed by the beginning of another letter. This fragmentary text cannot now be interpreted.

BIBLIOGRAPHY

The stone is unpublished.

Toureen Peacaun 50: small slab

CURRENT LOCATION

The stone is now lost.

HISTORY

The stone was found in the summer of 1944 during excavation at the site (Duignan 1944, 227). It was a stray find but Waddell and Holland do not record exactly where it was found (Waddell and Holland 1990, 171). In photographs possibly dating from the 1960s, preserved in the Dúchas archive (negatives nos 82, 83: see illustrations above, pp. 305, 307), the stone is shown built into the east interior wall of the church, in the middle register of slabs, to the right of slab 47. The stone presumably fell out of the wall and disappeared before repair work was done to the east wall in 1986-87.

DESCRIPTION

The description is taken from Waddell and Holland (1990). From their scale drawing (fig. 6.29, see illustration below), the dimensions of the stone were: H. *c.* 12 cm, W. *c.* 15 cm; no thickness measurement is given.

The stone was a fragment of a slab of unknown form. Incised on its visible face were the remains of an outline equal-armed cross. The three extant limbs almost filled the then extant portion of slab and there may have been lettering on the missing portion.

LETTERING AND TEXT

There was no visible text on this stone.

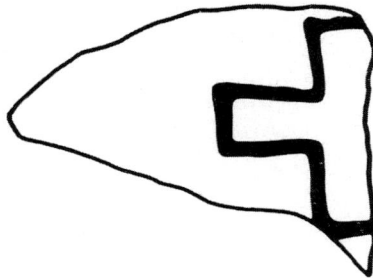

BIBLIOGRAPHY

Waddell and Holland 1990, no. 29, pp. 165-86 and fig. 6.29

Toureen Peacaun 51: small slab

CURRENT LOCATION

The stone is now lost.

HISTORY

In 1909 this stone was 'lying loose on the station, or altar, into the back of which the old inscriptions [that is, stones 2, 5, 14] are built' (Crawford 1909, 65). In 1912 Crawford described it as 'close to' the altar, but it is not clear if he revisited the site (Crawford 1912, 242). In the early 1930s it was photographed lying loose as part of a 'crude pilgrim's "station"' which had been built to the west of the church some time before (Waddell and Holland 1990, 169 and pl. 1). It was presumably lost before it could be built into the walls in 1944.

DESCRIPTION

Macalister (1949a, 100) gave the dimensions of the stone in inches corresponding to:

H. *c.* 17 cm, W. *c.* 34 cm, T. 2.5 cm.

The description and text are taken from the descriptions and photographs published by Crawford and by Waddell and Holland. Macalister's drawing is reproduced below. The stone was part of a slab of unknown form. Incised on the visible face was an outline equal-armed cross and two lines of text. One line was to the right of the right cross-arm and the other line below the cross. Crawford suggested that the stone was incomplete and that the portion of stone lost had contained further text (Crawford 1909, 65-6 and fig. 18).

LETTERING

The text was in half-uncial script and appears in both photographs to be slightly deteriorated (Crawford 1909, fig. 18; Waddell and Holland 1990, pl. 1). From Waddell and Holland's scale drawing, and by comparison with the other, still existing, stones shown in their photograph (Waddell and Holland 1990, fig. 4.15 and pl. 1), the maximum letter H. was *c.* 7 cm.

TEXT

RAC

[–.]N[D]CAEL̄

INTERPRETATION

The text appears to have read *rac [–]ndcael̄*. Macalister offered two interpretations of the text. In the earlier interpretation (Macalister 1909, 67-9), he took the upper line as a continuation of the lower with the horizontal bar above the L as a 'hyphen'. Macalister considered that the lost portion of stone contained the words *or do* and read the rest as *aud caelrac*, associating *caelrac* with the tribal name *Calraige*. He later emended his reading to *caelracand*, taking the last four letters of the lower line first, followed by the upper line and then by the first letters of the lower line (Macalister 1949a, 100). This however seems unduly convoluted.

Reading the second line first, as originally suggested by Macalister, the text can be interpreted as *–n[d] caelrac* with the horizontal bar above the L indicating a run-on line. The *-n[d]* could be the end of a personal name, such as the *Fland* of slab 10. The epithet *cáelrach* is formed from the adjective *cáel*, *cóel*, 'slender', which occurs as a name both alone and in compounds.

BIBLIOGRAPHY

Crawford 1909, 65-6 and fig. 18
Macalister 1909, 67-9
Crawford 1912, 242
Macalister 1949a, no. 919, p. 100 and pl. XLIV, fig. 919
Lionard 1961, 105, 154 and fig. 5.3
Waddell and Holland 1990, no. 15, pp. 165-86, fig. 4.15 and pl. 1

Toureen Peacaun 52: small slab

CURRENT LOCATION

The stone is now lost.

HISTORY

The stone was found in the summer of 1944 during excavation at the site (Duignan 1944, 227; Macalister 1949a, 213). It was a stray find from the rubble around stone no. 40 (the East Cross) (Waddell and Holland 1990, 169, 171). It was presumably lost before it could be built into the walls in 1944.

DESCRIPTION

The description and text are taken from Waddell and Holland (1990). From their scale drawing (fig. 5.19, reproduced below), the dimensions of the stone were:
H. *c.* 13 cm, W. *c.* 12 cm; no thickness measurement is given.
The stone was a fragment of a slab of unknown form. A fragmentary text was incised on the visible face. The space below these letters suggests that no further lettering is lost from this part of the stone but there is no way of knowing how much other text there was originally, nor if the stone contained a cross.

LETTERING

The text was in half-uncial script and appears in the existing drawing to have been legible (Waddell and Holland 1990, fig. 5.19). From this scale drawing, the maximum letter H. was *c.* 3 cm.

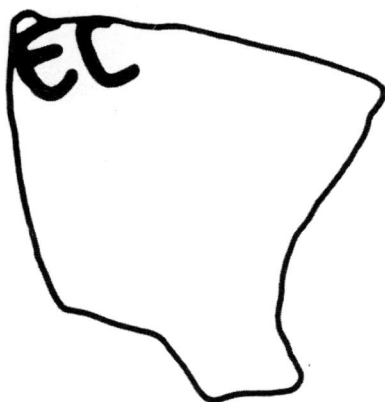

TEXT

–E͟C–

INTERPRETATION

This fragmentary text appears to have read –*ec*– but cannot now be interpreted.

BIBLIOGRAPHY

Macalister 1949a, no. 8, p. 213

Waddell and Holland 1990, no. 19, pp. 165-86 and fig. 5.19

Toureen Peacaun 53: small slab

CURRENT LOCATION

The stone is now lost.

HISTORY

The stone was found in the summer of 1944 during excavation at the site (Duignan 1944, 227). It was a stray find from the rubble around stone no. 40 (the East Cross) (Waddell and Holland 1990, 169, 175). It was presumably lost before it could be built into the walls in 1944.

DESCRIPTION

The description is taken from Waddell and Holland (1990). Since their drawing (fig. 6.40, reproduced below) is not to scale, the dimensions of this stone are unknown.

The stone was a fragment of a slab of unknown form containing some incised lines probably part of the arm of an outline cross, although they could possibly have been parts of letters.

LETTERING AND TEXT

There was no visible text on this stone.

BIBLIOGRAPHY

Waddell and Holland 1990, no. 40, pp. 165-86 and fig. 6.40

Toureen Peacaun 54: small slab

CURRENT LOCATION

The stone is now lost.

HISTORY

The stone was found in the summer of 1944 during excavation at the site (Duignan 1944, 227). It was a stray find from the rubble around stone no. 40 (the East Cross) (Waddell and Holland 1990, 169, 175). It was presumably lost before it could be built into the walls in 1944.

DESCRIPTION

The description is taken from Waddell and Holland (1990). Since their drawing (fig. 6.41, reproduced below) is not to scale, the dimensions of this stone are unknown.

The stone was a fragment of a slab of unknown form: the drawing shows only the incised lines, not the outline of the slab. The carving was the remains of an outline cross with medial lines dividing the two then extant limbs. The illustration shows no lettering on the stone.

LETTERING AND TEXT

There was no visible text on this stone.

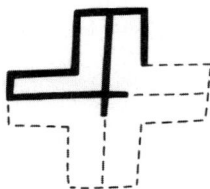

BIBLIOGRAPHY
Waddell and Holland 1990, no. 41, pp. 165-86 and fig. 6.41

Toureen Peacaun 55: small slab

CURRENT LOCATION

The stone is now lost.

HISTORY

The stone was found in the summer of 1944 during excavation at the site (Duignan 1944, 227). It was a stray find from the rubble around stone no. 40 (the East Cross) (Waddell and Holland 1990, 169, 175). It was presumably lost before it could be built into the walls in 1944.

DESCRIPTION

The description is taken from Waddell and Holland (1990). Since their drawing (fig. 6.42, reproduced below) is not to scale, the dimensions of this stone are unknown.
The stone was a fragment of a slab of unknown form: the drawing shows only the incised lines, not the outline of the slab. The carving was the remains of an outline equal-armed cross. The illustration shows no lettering on the stone.

LETTERING AND TEXT

There was no visible text on this stone.

BIBLIOGRAPHY
Waddell and Holland 1990, no. 42, pp. 165-86 and fig. 6.42

Toureen Peacaun 56: small slab

CURRENT LOCATION

The stone is now lost.

HISTORY

This stone is recorded on the sole evidence of Macalister and he provided no illustration (Macalister 1949a, no. 923, p. 101). Waddell and Holland found no record of it (Waddell and Holland 1990, 175). It presumably disappeared before it could be built into the walls in 1944.

DESCRIPTION

The description and text are taken from Macalister (1949a, 101). Macalister gave the dimensions of the stone in inches corresponding to:
H. *c.* 27 cm, W. *c.* 18 cm, T. *c.* 9 cm.
The stone was a fragment of a slab of unknown form. Apparently it contained a wheel cross and a text set around it. Macalister described the text as having 'the first word above the cross, the other two in two lines crossing the stem' (Macalister 1949a, 101). This suggests that the text may have read as set out below.

LETTERING

Since the stone is lost and no illustration survives, nothing is known of its lettering.

TEXT
    OR
    A ‖ R
    AED ‖ LAC

INTERPRETATION

The text apparently read *or a r aed lac* for *or(óit) ar Aedlac*, 'a prayer for Aedlac', although, following *ar*, a dative would have been expected. (See the **Introduction § 5.3.4** for discussion of the *or(óit) ar* formula).

BIBLIOGRAPHY

Macalister 1949a, no. 923, p. 101
Waddell and Holland 1990, 175

Toureen Peacaun 57: small slab

CURRENT LOCATION

The stone is now lost.

HISTORY

This stone was found in the summer of 1944 during excavation at the site (Duignan 1944, 227; Macalister 1949a, 213). Waddell and Holland found no record of it (Waddell and Holland 1990, 175). It was presumably lost before it could be built into the walls in 1944.

DESCRIPTION

The description and text are taken from Macalister (1949a, 213) but no dimensions are given there. The stone was presumably part of a slab of unknown form. Macalister did not mention a cross and merely said that the text read as given below but that the letters were 'doubtful' (Macalister 1949a, 213).

LETTERING

Since the stone is lost and no illustration survives, nothing is known of its lettering.

TEXT

–DIE–

INTERPRETATION

This fragmentary text may have read *–die–* but cannot now be interpreted.

BIBLIOGRAPHY

Macalister 1949a, no. 14, p. 213
Waddell and Holland 1990, 175

Toureen Peacaun 58: small slab

CURRENT LOCATION

The stone is now lost.

HISTORY

In 1878 this stone was one of several fragments 'heaped up in the north-west corner of the church' (Petrie 1878, 33). In 1909 Crawford expressed his doubt that this stone was to be identified with stone no. 14 (Crawford 1909, 65). It seems likely that Crawford was right and that the stone was already lost then.

DESCRIPTION

The description and text are taken from Petrie (1878). From Petrie's scale drawing (pl. XXII, fig. 47: see illustration below), the dimensions of the stone were: H. *c.* 15.5 cm, W. *c.* 15.5 cm; no thickness measurement is given.
The stone was a fragment of a slab of unknown form. Petrie's drawing shows no cross and only a fragmentary text. The space above the letters suggests that no text was lost from there but it is impossible to know what else the stone originally contained.

LETTERING

From Petrie's scale drawing of this stone, the text appears to have been in half-uncial script, although highly deteriorated, with a maximum letter H. of *c.* 3 cm.

TEXT
–ꜰ[ɪ]ᴛꜱ–

INTERPRETATION
This fragmentary text appears to have read *–f[i]ts–* but cannot now be interpreted.

BIBLIOGRAPHY
Petrie 1878, 33-4 and pl. XXII, fig. 47
Crawford 1909, 65
Macalister 1909, 67
Waddell and Holland 1990, 175

Toureen Peacaun 59: small slab

CURRENT LOCATION
The stone is now lost.

HISTORY
In 1878 Petrie described this stone as 'in a small recess in the south side-wall within the church' (Petrie 1878, 34). Crawford failed to find this stone (Crawford 1909, 65) and it has not been recorded since.

DESCRIPTION
The description and text are taken from Petrie (1878). From Petrie's scale drawing (pl. XXII, fig. 48: see illustration below), the dimensions of the stone were:
H. *c.* 13.5 cm, W. *c.* 21.5 cm; no thickness measurement is given. However Petrie's description (1878, 34) gives the dimensions in inches corresponding to:
H. *c.* 10 cm, W. *c.* 15.5 cm, T. *c.* 2.5 cm.
The stone was a fragment of a slab of unknown form. Petrie's illustration shows no cross or lettering but some markings. Petrie described these as, 'curious marks ... said to be letters, along with a fragment of zigzag design incised' (Petrie 1878, 34).

LETTERING
From Petrie's scale drawing of this stone (Petrie 1878, pl. XXII, fig. 48), the text, if such it was, appears to be fragmentary and rather deteriorated, with the script uncertain and the maximum letter H. *c.* 3 cm.

TEXT AND INTERPRETATION
No letters can be clearly made out from Petrie's drawing (Petrie 1878, pl. XXII, fig. 48) and the text is not now recoverable.

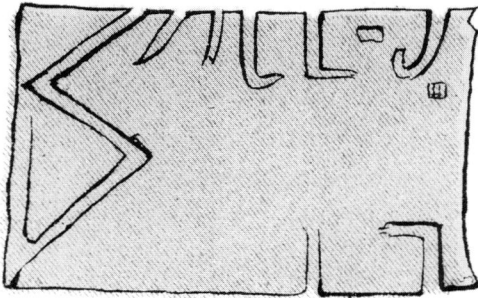

BIBLIOGRAPHY

Petrie 1878, 33-4 and pl. XXII, fig. 48
Crawford 1909, 65
Macalister 1909, 67

Toureen Peacaun 60: small slab

CURRENT LOCATION

The stone is now lost.

HISTORY

In 1860 a full-size drawing of this stone by du Noyer was presented by him to the Royal Irish Academy where it is still preserved (du Noyer unpublished, vol. III, p. 1; see du Noyer 1857-61, 249-50, 256). In 1878 this stone was one of several fragments 'heaped up in the north-west corner of the church' (Petrie 1878, 33). In 1909 Crawford failed to find this stone (Crawford 1909, 65) and in 1912 described it as 'now lost' (Crawford 1912, 242). It has not been recorded since.

DESCRIPTION

The description and text are taken from Petrie (1878) and du Noyer (unpublished). From du Noyer's full size drawing (vol. III, p. 1), and by comparison with Petrie's scale drawing (pl. XXII, fig. 45: see illustration below), the dimensions of the stone were:
H. c. 21 cm, W. c. 31.5 cm; no thickness measurement is given.
The stone was part of a slab of unknown form. Both illustrations show an incised linear Latin cross with expanded lower terminal, with one line of text below. The space preceding the F suggests that no further letters were lost from there but it is impossible to know what else the stone originally contained.

LETTERING

From du Noyer's and Petrie's drawings, the text appears to be in half-uncial script and to be legible, with the maximum letter H. c. 9 cm.

TEXT

FLAIT—

INTERPRETATION

The text appears to have read *flait*— and is likely to have been the beginning of a personal name. Petrie suggested that it could have been one of the numerous names with a first element *Flaith* — (Petrie 1878, 34).

BIBLIOGRAPHY

du Noyer 1857-61, 256
Petrie 1878, 33-4 and pl. XXII, fig. 45
Crawford 1909, 65
Macalister 1909, 67
Crawford 1912, 242
Waddell and Holland 1990, 175
du Noyer unpublished, vol. III, p. 1 and fig.
OS Letters unpublished 1930, 65-6

Toureen Peacaun 61: small slab

CURRENT LOCATION

The stone is now lost.

HISTORY

In 1860 a full-size drawing of this stone made by du Noyer was presented by him to the Royal Irish Academy where it is still preserved (du Noyer unpublished, vol. III, p. 4). The stone has not been recorded since.

DESCRIPTION

The description is based on du Noyer's full size drawing (vol. III, p. 4 and fig.: see illustration below). The dimensions of the stone were:
H. *c.* 32.5 cm, W. *c.* 18.5 cm; no thickness measurement is given.
The stone was a rectangular slab. The drawing shows an encircled cross-of-arcs with a blank area below.

LETTERING AND TEXT

No text is visible on du Noyer's sketch.

DISCUSSION

Slab 28 contains the remains of a cross-of-arcs with text below. It is possible that 28 is a fragment of this slab. Alternatively the two stones may have been related, or have contained matching designs.

BIBLIOGRAPHY

du Noyer 1857-61, 256
du Noyer unpublished, vol. III, p. 4 and fig.

Toureen Peacaun 62: small slab

CURRENT LOCATION

The stone is now lost.

OPW photograph no. 77, showing stone *62

HISTORY

This stone is not recorded in any published account of the stones. In a photograph possibly dating from the 1960s, preserved in the Dúchas archive (negative no. 77: see illustration), the stone is shown built sideways into the east interior wall of the church, to the right of slab 11, in the place now occupied by slab 12. The stone presumably fell out of the wall and disappeared before repair work was done to the east wall in 1986-87.

DESCRIPTION

The description is taken from the photograph, which suggests that the dimensions of the stone were:
H. *c.* 14 cm, W. *c.* 12 cm; no thickness measurement can be calculated.
The stone was part of a slab of unknown form. The visible face of the stone contained an incomplete text consisting of part of one letter. There was no trace of a cross, but it could well have been on the missing portion.

LETTERING

The text may have been in capital script but the one letter in the photograph is damaged. The maximum letter H. may have been *c.* 2 cm.

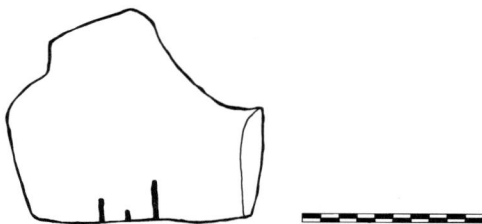

TEXT
–[E]

INTERPRETATION

The text appears to have read –[e] and to have been complete at the end. It cannot now be reconstructed.

BIBLIOGRAPHY

The stone is unpublished.

IV. DISCUSSION OF SMALL SLABS

There are 60 slabs or fragments of slabs documented from Toureen Peacaun. Of these, 38 are still extant, either on the site or in the care of Dúchas, Dublin. Eight of the slabs appear to be complete or substantially complete (nos 2, 4, 10, 16, 19, 31, 36, 38). They are all naturally shaped four-sided slabs of sandstone, of similar size and shape. They are broader than they are tall, ranging in height from about 20 cm to about 30 cm and in width from about 30 cm to about 45 cm. Their average thickness is about 6 cm. The scale and layout of the carving on the fragments corresponds closely to that of the complete slabs so that it seems certain that they are the remains of the same kind of artefact. However the extant fragments do not appear to fit together.

Various different colours of sandstone have been used. Grey predominates, but there are several examples of a pale, creamy colour, and others which are pink, orange or maroon. Deliberate advantage appears to have been made of the coloured quality of the stone, at least in some cases, for example with slab 26. Its orangey surface has been cut back to reveal the pale grey interior, making the letters stand out in bright contrast to their background.

The slabs are incised with simple linear or outline crosses and personal names. The same pecking technique has been used for both lettering and crosses and individual peck-marks are visible on some of the better preserved stones, for example no. 33. As far as can be ascertained, the cross and lettering filled the whole of the available surface and so these slabs could not have been set in the ground without obscuring the carving. This has a bearing on their possible function.

The distinctive features of the Toureen Peacaun slabs are: their small size; the simplicity of their crosses (even the few more elaborate examples are comparatively plain and lack internal decoration); the fact that neither cross nor name dominates the slab but that together they occupy the whole of the carved surface; the fact that the texts consist of simple personal names only. Although such slabs are found in vastly greater numbers at Toureen Peacaun than anywhere else, the class is not unique to this site. The closest parallels are three slabs from Clonmacnoise which have simple linear crosses (Macalister 1949a, no. 615, p. 44 and pl. XI, fig. 615; Macalister 1949a, no. 807, p. 66 and pl. XXXIV, fig. 807; Manning and Moore 1991), the stone from Ballynabrack, Co. Armagh, which has a slightly elaborated linear cross (Lionard 1961, fig.1.17) and the stone from Shanakill, Co. Waterford. A rare example with an outline cross is the slab from Gallen Priory incised, not with a name alone, but with *lec Coemgusa*, 'Cóemgus's slab' (Lionard 1961, fig.5.5)

Although the Toureen Peacaun slabs belong to the one general class the extant pieces may be divided into the following five types:

TYPE 1 (22 slabs)

These are slabs with outline crosses, mostly plain and equal-armed although the equal-armed cross on slab 9 has expanded terminals and the crosses on slabs 36 and 38 have slightly extended lower limbs. Below the cross most have a single line of text which is interrupted by the lower limb. However the texts on slabs 5 and 36 are not interrupted and the texts on slabs 12, 34, 36 and *47 are placed above the cross. In addition to the fourteen examples with text surviving, there are eight small fragments incised with crosses of identical form and scale to the crosses on the others. Although the fragments are too small for complete texts to have been preserved, they appear to have belonged to this class.

Those with extant letters: ?1, 2, 4, 5, 7, 12, 13, ?21, 32, 34, 36, 38, *47, *51.
Those with no letters extant: 9, 17, 23, 29, 30, 31, 34, *55.

TYPE 2 (7 slabs)

This is a smaller group whose distinguishing feature is a linear cross with expanded terminals. Four examples have the text below the cross (18, 19, 31, *60); one has the text above the cross (10); one has a small, initial cross (15) and one, which is unique in having two names, has two small crosses above the top line of text (16).

TYPE 3 (7 slabs)

The slabs in this group have crosses more complex than the plain outline or linear crosses of the other two classes. Many of these cross forms are unique. One is an equal-armed linear cross with box-like terminals and crossing (20); another is an outline cross of similar shape (25); another is an outline cross with internal divisions (*54) and another an outline cross with a slender shaft (8); there is also an outline cross, carved in false relief, with what appears to be a short additional cross-stroke (26). Two slabs appear to have contained a cross-of-arcs: slab 28 which is now fragmentary and *61 which is recorded only in one drawing. Three of the fragments in this group do not have text on the extant or recorded portions (20, *54, *61).

TYPE 4 (15 fragments)

This group comprises the small fragments of slabs which preserve only lettering. It is possible that some or all of them were originally part of slabs of types 1, 2 or 3. They are nos 3, 6, 11, 14, 22, 24, 27, 33, 37, *43, *48, *52, *53, *58 and *62.

TYPE 5 (4 slabs)

The final group comprises four slabs which have linear crosses but no text. One is part of an altar slab and would not have been inscribed (29). The other three have plain linear Latin crosses, lacking expansions. Slab 35 is smaller and narrower than the other type 2 slabs and a different shape and seems rather too narrow to have borne a text. The lost slabs *41 and *42 appear to have been similar in character to 35 and all are quite different from the elegantly carved examples of type 2.

Types 1-3 constitute three distinct variants on a simple theme. The largest group, type 1, is particularly coherent. The differences between the three types may have arisen because of differences in date. Alternatively, they may be an indication that different kinds of people are commemorated on each one. The smaller number of more elaborate crosses might reflect the special status of a minority.

The lettering on all of the slabs is of high quality, in both design and execution, but the lettering on the type 2 slabs is particularly ambitious and delicate. Others slabs with notably calligraphic lettering include 26, 27, 33, and 36. The letter-forms employed are generally very similar across all types, although some distinctions can be observed. There is a distinctive form of rather open, slant-backed D which appears on slabs 1, 2, 5, 34, *51 (all type 1 slabs). Slabs 16 and 18 may contain more calligraphic examples of the same basic form, but other Ds are different. There is a single straight-backed (4) and a single 'kink-backed' one (19). The others, on slabs 10, 18, 31 and 38), resemble the horizontal-backed D on the East Cross (stone 40). The capital A with a horizontal lid and a saltire-shaped bar is another form which occurs on both the East Cross and some slabs (8, 22), as is the capital N with a low horizontal (1, 12, 16, 37, *51). A number of slabs have very similar square-bottomed Us (1, 4, 34, 36). There are further distinctions between, for instance, straight-backed and round-backed Es, between 'oc' As and As with short straight 'tails', and between capital Rs with tails which curl up or which point down.

Where the text is complete or can be reconstructed with some certainty it consists, in most cases, of a single personal name in the nominative case. There are two instances of a personal name with the addition of an epithet, one in Latin (36), one in Irish (*51), and one instance of two personal names on a single slab (16). In many cases the name is interrupted by an arm of the cross. Where verifiable, this seems to occur at a syllable break (for example nos 2, 4, 26). In one case a medial dot serves to divide syllables (16) while, in another instance, too little of the text survives for the purpose of the medial dot to be ascertained with certainty (14). The Toureen Peacaun slabs are notable for their use of diacritics which are only rarely found in epigraphy. An acute accent over a ligatured Æ marks a diphthong (2), and a horizontal bar over an A marks it as a long vowel (36). A short horizontal bar above a T (32) may mark abbreviation and the long horizontal bar over an L (*51) apparently marked a run-on line.

The orthography of the names indicates a date in the Old Irish period, that is, before c. 900. The use of Latin for the epithet on slab 36, and perhaps a Latinized genitive on 37, reinforces the ecclesiastical as opposed to simply the Christian character of these slabs. Further clues that the persons commemorated were clerics are provided by the Latin-derived names *Domnic* (31), and, perhaps, *Hel[air]* (25). The juxtaposition on a single slab (16) of the names *Cummene* and *Ladcen* may indicate that the men in question are the famous early seventh-century exegetes, especially in the light of the established link between the former and a Beccán (see above, slab 16, Discussion). This identification may, as Moloney (1964) suggested, be the key to understanding the purpose of the Toureen Peacaun slabs.

There has been a casual assumption that these slabs are grave-slabs (Duignan 1944, 227; Lionard 1961, 154; Waddell and Holland 1990, 165). Although they could not have stood erect at the head of a grave, they could have lain recumbent over a grave, as Lionard envisaged (1961, 154). They need not, however, have been associated with graves at all. An alternative explanation was first suggested by Moloney, who linked them to the practice of commemorating the dead during Mass (1964, 105-6). The custom first arose in the Eastern Church of reading the names of benefactors, living and dead, during Mass. At first the names were inscribed on diptychs, but soon the lists became too long and other media were employed. Although the custom was introduced to Spain in the seventh century, it only reached Rome two centuries later, but Moloney suggested that it may have reached Ireland at an early date along the well-established routes of intellectual contact (Moloney 1964, 106). That this and related practices were adopted by the Romanizing church of southern Ireland, in which the north Munster circle of Cummene and Ladcen was so influential, is suggested by the Litany of Saints in the late eighth-century Stowe Missal (see Kenney 1979, 695, 699). The Litany contains the names both of the saints of the universal Church and also of Irish saints, among whom are the abbots of prominent Munster houses (Moloney 1964, 106).

Moloney's suggestion that the slabs at Toureen Peacaun were a kind of lapidary *Liber vitae* is very attractive. One can readily envision them propped up in rows behind the altar of the church, perhaps in a fashion not unlike the current arrangement. The same could be suggested of some of the small book-like slabs, inscribed with single personal names, from the Anglo-Saxon Northumbrian monasteries of Hartlepool and Lindisfarne (Okasha 1971, nos 44-50, pp. 75-9 and figs; nos 74-84, pp. 93-7 and figs). Significantly the lettering on some of these eighth-century Anglo-Saxon slabs is in insular decorative capitals. The use of this script at Toureen Peacaun might reflect contact with the Northumbrian church, a contact which might also be reflected locally in the cult of St Berrihert (see above, St Berrihert's Kyle). If the comparison between the Toureen Peacaun slabs and the Hartlepool and Lindisfarne examples is accepted, it may constitute another strand in the connection.

The men commemorated on the highly uniform type 1 slabs may have been prominent members of the community at Toureen Peacaun but it seems that the names inscribed on slabs of types 2 and 3 might have been a separate group, reserved for special honour. If the commemorated Cummene and Ladcen were leading scholars of their day, perhaps the others in this group were too. The nature of the inscription on the East Cross (no. 40) implies that Toureen Peacaun was a centre of learning, a place where a particular interest in the intellectuals of the Irish church might be expected. Other members of the circle of Cummène and Laidcen were Brecanus and Bercanus (Ó Cróinín 1995, 187), either of whom, for example, could account for the fragmentary -CANI of slab 37.

The lettering on slab 16 is noticeably larger than that of the other type 2 slabs. This may have been intended to reflect the high honour accorded to Laidcen and, especially, to Cummène. The juxtaposition of the names Domnic and Soadbar, not on the same slab, but on two type 2 slabs almost identical in form (31, 19) may also be suggestive. These were the names of two of the party of four prominent early ninth-century Irish scholars who solved the famous 'Bamberg cryptogram' at the court of Merfyn Frych, the others being Fergus and Caínchobrach (Ó Cróinín 1993, 223). However the latter two do not appear on the extant slabs and, in any case, these men flourished in the 840s which is rather late for the Toureen Peacaun slabs.

There are other names which might be identified, but these are less secure. The name partially preserved on slab 25 might possibly be that of Helair, the famous 'anchorite and scribe' of Monaincha whose death is recorded *s.a.* 806 (Annals of Ulster: Mac Airt and Mac Niocaill 1983, 262-3). Moloney cited an eighth-century abbot of Lismore named Suairlech, whom he suggested might be the Soerlech of slab 26, and suggested for Domnic (slab 31) Mo-Domnóc, also known as Dominicus, of Tibberaghny, twenty-five miles south-east of Toureen Peacaun (Moloney 1964, 106). The other legible names on type 2-3 slabs, for example Fland on slab 10, are not unusual.

V. SITE

In 1840 O'Keeffe recorded the local name for the site as 'Teampuillín Phéacáin, but more generally contractedly Péacán' (OS Letters unpublished, 64; see Moloney 1964, 99). It is noted on the Ordnance Survey 6-inch map as 'Peakaun' and on the OS 1:50 000 map as 'Peacaun', the form adopted here. Some modern writers have referred to the site as 'Kilpeacan' (for example Macalister 1949a, 100, Lionard 1961, 154) but, as Manning suggested, this name should be avoided so as to avoid confusion with Kilpeacon, Co. Limerick (Manning 1991, 209). In the medieval period the site was known as *Cluain Aird* (or *Árd*) *Mo-Becóc* or simply as *Cluain Aird* (or *Árd*) (Hogan 1910, 254-5).

The site is named after St Beccán (*Mo-Becóc*) who has been identified as the Beccán whose death is recorded *s.a.* 689/690 (Annals of Inisfallen: Mac Airt 1951, 100-101). According to the Life of Abbán, Beccán was left in charge of the large monastery founded at the site by St Abbán, although other hagiographical references may suggest that the original foundation predated Beccán's time (Gwynn and Hadcock 1970, 403). Beccán of Cluain Aird appears in the martyrologies under May 26, where he is noted for his love of vigils (Stokes 1905, 126, 137). In the Life of Abbán it is stated that Beccán had a stone cross (*crucem lapideam*) erected outside and there at dawn in all weathers he sang the whole Psalter *crucifigens se ad illam crucem* (Plummer 1910, 17). Moloney interpreted the Latin phrase *crucifigens se* (which he quoted as *crucifigebat se*) as a reference to the practice of reciting prayers with extended arms '*crucis vigilia*, the Irish *cros-figil*' (1964, 99). This story could have arisen from the presence at Toureen Peacaun, from the comparatively early date of the eighth century, of the free-standing East Cross; alternatively, this cross could have been erected because of a tradition of Beccán's particular devotion.

According to *Cogadh gaedhel re gallaibh*, Cluain Aird was sacked by Norsemen in the early decades of the ninth century, along with Lismore and nearby Kilmolash (Todd 1867, 6-7). This is probably the same event as the attack on Lismore and Kilmolash mentioned in the Annals of Inisfallen *s.a.* 833 (Mac Airt 1951, 126-7). That Toureen Peacaun was a worthy target may be taken as a reflection of its wealth and importance at this period.

The site is about five miles north-west of Cahir at the eastern end of the Glen of Aherlow. It is spread over fields on either side of a stream, also called Peakaun (Moloney 1964, 99), which joins the river Aherlow to the north of the site. The Galtee mountains rise sharply above it immediately to the south. The site is delimited by a large bank-and-ditch enclosure up to 200 m in diameter (Manning 1991, 209). Near the western bank of the stream is the church which Duignan claimed had a trabeated, that is lintelled, west door (1944, 227), a feature indicative of early medieval date. The Romanesque windows were presumably inserted in the twelfth century (Leask 1955, 106, fig. 58; Waddell and Holland 1991, 169). There is a plain free-standing cross to the west of the church and the remains of the inscribed East Cross stand in the middle of a dry-stone platform to the south-east of it. Duignan's excavation produced evidence of industrial activity, in the form of iron slag, in the area beyond the West Cross. In the field to the east of the stream is a well, and 70 m north-east of that is a triple *bullaun* stone surrounded by a small protective wall. Earlier writers referred to this as a *clochán* or cell but this identification is mistaken (Manning 1991, 209).

VI. CONCORDANCE

Reading and/or Identification	no.	Waddell and Holland	CIIC	Lionard (figs)	Other (figs)
DUN ‖ –	1	20	no. 13	–	–
FID ‖ LÁ/ER Noyer III, 3	2	7	920	5.2	Petrie 46; du
–C–	3	22	no. 2	–	–
DON ‖ GUS	4	13	no. 18	–	–
FINDLU–	5	8	921	5.6	Petrie 44; du Noyer III, 2
COND–	6	24	no. 17	–	–
–ER ‖ LE–	7	10	no. 9	–	–
–A ‖ R–	8	39	–	–	–
no visible text	9	28	–	–	–
FLAND	10	4	no. 16	–	–
FIN–	11	26	–	–	–
–N–	12	–	–	–	–
–ALE	13	14	no. 19	–	–
OU·R–	14	23	922	–	–
+C[.]–	15	3	no. 10	–	–
CUMMENE ‖ LAD·CEN	16	5	no. 15	3.2	Moloney 2
no visible text	17	33	–	–	–
[.]AN ‖ D–	18	2	no. 12	–	–
SOADBAR	19	6	no. 5	3.1	–
no visible text	20	35	–	–	–
–CO ‖ –	21	–	–	–	–
–BA[.]–	22	27	–	–	–
no visible text	23	30	–	–	–
–[T]A–	24	–	–	–	–
HEL–	25	16	no. 3	–	–

SOER	LECH	26	17	no. 6	–	–
–OTM[.]–	27	25	–	–	–
–[.]OSED	28	–	–	–	–
no text	29	36	–	27.7	–
+ frag.	30	32	–	–	–
[D]OM NIC	31	1	no. 1	3.3	Moloney 4
–T̄–	32	11	–	–	–
FO[RF]–	33	21	no. 4	–	–
–[.]AED CU[.]–	34	12	924	5.4	–
no text	35	–	–	–	–
FINÁNPUER	36	–	–	–	Manning 3
–CANI	37	–	–	–	Manning 3
–[E]ARASS	[D.E]	38	–	–	–	Manning 3
– ‖ N[..]	39	unnumbered	924A	–	–
East Cross	40	unnumbered	924B	–	Petrie p. 34
no visible text	*41	37	–	–	–
no visible text	*42	38	–	–	–
–MNE[.]	*43	–	–	–	–
no visible text	*44	31	–	–	–
no visible text	*45	34	–	–	–
no visible text	*46	–	–	–	–
–[L]ETHO	*47	9	no. 11	–	–
–TO–	*48	18	no. 7	–	–
–[.U]–	*49	–	–	–	–
no visible text	*50	29	–	–	–
RAC	[–.]N[D]CAEL̄	*51	15	919	5.3	–
–EC–	*52	19	no. 8	–	–
no visible text	*53	40	–	–	–
no visible text	*54	41	–	–	–
no visible text	*55	42	–	–	–
OR	A ‖ R	AED ‖ LAC	*56	–	923	–	–
–DIE–	*57	–	14	–	–
–F[I]TS–	*58	–	–	–	Petrie 47
text illegible	*59	–	–	–	Petrie 48
FLAIT–	*60	–	–	–	Petrie 45; du Noyer III, 1
no visible text	*61	–	–	–	du Noyer III, 4
–[E]	*62	–	–	–	–

COUNTY WATERFORD

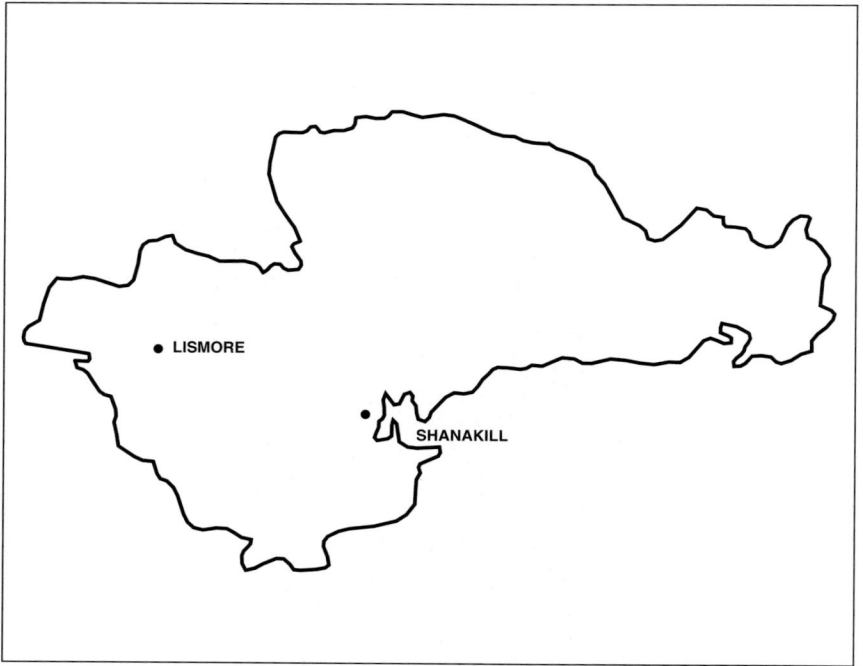

Early Christian inscribed stones of County Waterford

LISMORE: LIOS MÓR

Site name St Carthage's Cathedral
Townland Lismore
NGR 20488,09841
SMR site no. WA021-019---

This well-documented monastery, one of the most prominent in Munster, has produced six inscribed stones: two large and two small cross-slabs, all probably ninth-century, a small cross of uncertain date, and an architectural feature of early twelfth-century date.

Lismore 1: large cross-slab

CURRENT LOCATION

The stone is fastened to the west interior wall of the cathedral nave.

HISTORY

Stones nos 1, 2, 3 and 4 were allegedly found when the foundations of the tower were being dug (Fitzgerald 1854-55, 201), presumably in or before 1827, the date of the erection of the tower. Cotton, however, on his arrival in Lismore in 1834 on appointment as Dean, found stones 1 and 4 re-used as modern headstones in the graveyard. They were inverted and buried in the earth so that no letters were visible. Cotton had them placed inside the cathedral for safety (Cotton 1854-55a, 222-3). It is possible that these stones were found around 1827 and then re-used as headstones for modern graves in the graveyard; alternatively, Fitzgerald may be in error here. Lismore 2 and 3 were certainly in existence in 1841 when they were drawn by R. Armstrong; they were then 'in the cemetary' [*sic*] (OS Letters unpublished 1929, 66 and fig. opp. 66). In July 1841 Windele visited Lismore but did not see the stones (Windele MSS 12.I.3, p. 456). However, he later had a lithograph made of stones nos 1, 2, 3 and 4. This lithograph is dated 1849 and states that the stones were then 'Lying in the Nave' (Windele MSS 12.I.3, p. 486; this lithograph is cut from a published source but we have failed to trace this source). When Windele visited Lismore in July 1849, he examined Lismore 1, 2 and 4 and drew the latter two; stone 3, however, had disappeared ((-) 1898, 64). It subsequently reappeared and Windele examined it in July 1851 ((-) 1898, 66). Fitzgerald also described the four stones as 'lying in the nave' (Fitzgerald 1854-55, 200) but by 1912 they, along with stone 5, were 'set in the west wall' ((-) 1912, 273), presumably in their present positions.

DESCRIPTION

The current dimensions of the stone are:
H. 102 cm, W. 41 cm, T. 5 cm visible.
The stone is a large natural slab of irregular shape. It is substantially intact, although it has suffered some damage at its edges. The stone is set into the wall with only 5 cm projecting and the back of the stone cannot therefore be examined. The surface of the stone undulates and the top end has spalled. The upper half is undecorated. At the bottom is a slim equal-armed outline cross surrounded by a circular frame of two concentric rings. Beyond the ring are four projections; those to left and right are V-shaped, the bottom one is an internally divided wedge shape and the top two have outward curving 'ears'. The text is complete and is incised in four horizontal lines above the cross.

LETTERING

The text is legible and uses half-uncial script. The maximum letter H. is 6.5 cm.

TEXT

  BENDA
  CHT FOR
  ANMAIN
  COLGEN

INTERPRETATION

The text reads *benda cht for anmain colgen* for *bendacht for anmain Colgen* 'a blessing on the soul of Colcu'. The formula *bendacht ar anmain* is found also on Lismore 3. (See the **Introduction §5.3.4** for further discussion of this formula).

DISCUSSION

The stone is a large recumbent grave-marker decorated with an unusual form of cross seen also on an uninscribed slab from Clonmacnoise (Lionard 1961, pl. XXIX, fig. 1). The formula *bendacht ar anmain*, found also on Lismore 3, is unusual but not rare. A similar formula, using a later spelling, occurs on Church Island 1. The original orientation of the Lismore slab is not known. However, if the cross were at the head of an east-west grave, then the text would be oriented so that a person could read it when kneeling, facing east, to pray across the body. The Scattery Island stone and several of the slabs at Inishcaltra are similar. Colcu cannot be indentified.

BIBLIOGRAPHY

Cotton 1854-55a, 222-3
Fitzgerald 1854-55, 200-1 and fig.
Hayman 1863-64, 144 and fig.
Petrie 1878, 31 and pl. XX, fig. 42
Wakeman 1890-91b, 357 and pl. III, fig. 23
Westropp 1897c, 357 and fig.
(-) 1898, 64-6 (no MS number is given and the authors have failed to locate this reference in the Windele MSS)
Crawford 1912, 243
(-) 1912, 273-4 and fig. 11.I
Power, P. 1937, 220-1
Macalister 1949a, no. 933, pp. 107-8 and pl. XLIV, fig. 933

Lionard 1961, 121, 126 and fig. 13.8
Henry 1965, 138
Power, P. C. 1990, 13
Weekes 1994, no page numbering, and fig.
Moore, M. 1999, 186
Windele MSS 12.I.3, p. 486

EXAMINED

May 1996, March 1998 (EO); May 1996 (KF)

Lismore 2: small cross-slab

CURRENT LOCATION

The stone is fastened to the west interior wall of the cathedral nave.

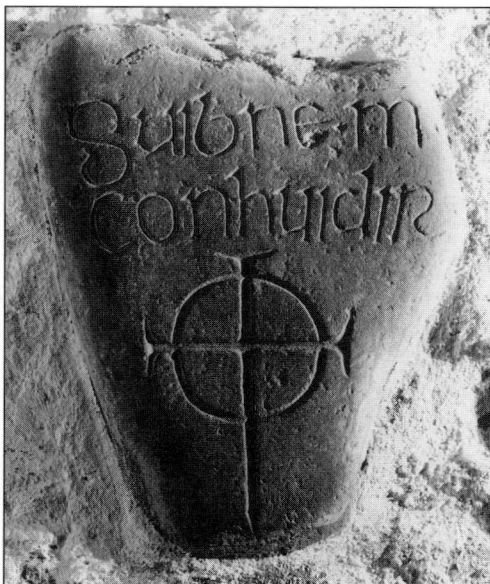

HISTORY

The stone may have been found around 1827 (Fitzgerald 1854-55, 201) (see above under Lismore 1). However Cotton stated that, on taking up the office of Dean of Lismore in 1834, the sexton showed him stones 2 and 3 which were acting as modern headstones in the graveyard (Cotton 1854-55a, 222). They were still in the cemetery in 1841 when they were drawn there by Armstrong (OS Letters unpublished 1929, fig. opp. 66). Cotton placed the stones inside the cathedral for safety, where this stone was seen and drawn by Windele in July 1849 ((-) 1898, 64 and fig.). Stones 1, 2, 3, 4 and 5 have been fastened to the cathedral wall since some time before 1912 (see above under Lismore 1).

DESCRIPTION

The current dimensions of the stone are:
H. 54 cm, W. 41 cm, T. 2 cm visible.
The stone is a natural slab of 'Smooth compact limestone resembling slate'
(Macalister 1949a, 108). In shape it is an irregular wedge. The stone is set into
the wall with only 2 cm projecting and the back of the stone cannot therefore
be examined. The text is complete and is set in two horizontal lines at the top
of the face. Beneath it is incised a linear ringed cross, with expansions at the
top three terminals and a point at the end of the shaft.

LETTERING

The text is legible and uses half-uncial script. The maximum letter H. is 9 cm.

TEXT

SUIBNE · M̄ ·
CONHUIDIR

INTERPRETATION

The text reads *suibne · m̄ · conhuidir* for *Suibne · m(ac) · Conhuidir*, 'Suibne son
of Conodor'.

DISCUSSION

This small slab cannot have stood in the ground without obscuring the carving
and is therefore likely to be have been recumbent. Like Lismore 1, the cross is
placed at the foot of the slab and the text horizontally above. Word-division is
indicated twice by a single medial dot. There is no request for a prayer or
blessing, simply the man's name and patronymic. A bar above the M marks the
abbreviation of *mac*. As Swift has emphasised, the recording of a patronymic is

extremely rare on cross-slabs, a fact she interprets as reflecting the ecclesiastical identity of the persons commemorated (Swift 1999, 113, 117). In the Annals the patronymics of ecclesiastics are usually given only if the person is the head of a household, or a member of the scholarly grades (Swift 1999, 114). The Suibne commemorated here could be the *Suibne nepos Roichlich, scriba 7 anchorita, abbas Liss Moer*, 'Suibne grandson of Roichlech, scribe, anchorite and abbot of Les Mór', whose death is recorded *s.a.* 855 (Annals of Ulster: Mac Airt and Mac Niocaill 1983, 314-15). Another member of this family might be commemorated on Lismore 3.

BIBLIOGRAPHY
Cotton 1854-55a, 222-3
Fitzgerald 1854-55, 200-1 and fig.
Hayman 1863-64, 144-5 and fig.
Petrie 1878, 31 and pl. XX, fig. 40
Westropp 1897c, 357 and fig.
(-) 1898, 64-6 and fig.
Crawford 1912, 243
(-) 1912, 273-4 and fig. 11.II
Power, P. 1937, 220-1
Macalister 1949a, no. 934, pp. 107-8 and pl. XLIV, fig. 934
Lionard 1961, 121, 126, 161 and fig. 13.4
Henry 1965, 138
Power, P. C. 1990, 13
Sheehan 1990, 166
Weekes 1994, no page numbering.
Moore, M. 1999, 186
Swift 1999, 113
OS Letters unpublished 1929, 66 and fig. opp. 66

EXAMINED
May 1996, March 1998 (EO); May 1996 (KF)

Lismore 3: small cross-slab

CURRENT LOCATION

The stone is fastened to the west interior wall of the cathedral nave.

HISTORY

The stone may have been found around 1827 (Fitzgerald 1854-55, 201). It was either found or re-found by Cotton after his arrival to Lismore in 1834, and before it was drawn by Armstrong in 1841 when it was in the cemetery (OS Letters unpublished 1929, fig. opp. 66). In July 1849 when Windele visited Lismore, he found that the stone had disappeared. Subsequently Cotton wrote to him and told him that it was back in the cathedral. Windele went to Lismore again in July 1851 when he examined the stone ((-) 1898, 64-6). Along with Lismore 1, 2, 4 and 5, this stone has been fastened to the cathedral wall since some time before 1912 (see above under Lismore 1).

DESCRIPTION

The current dimensions of the stone are:
H. 41 cm, W. 33 cm, T. 4 cm visible.
The stone is an irregular rectangular slab, apparently complete. It is set into the wall with only 4 cm projecting and the back of the stone cannot therefore be examined. At the top of the face is incised a linear Latin cross with expanded terminals, set on a pedestal. The text is complete. It is set in three horizontal lines, the first two interrupted by the stem of the cross and the third line beneath it. An attempt has been made to set the letters of the first two lines symmetrically on either side of the cross stem.

LETTERING

The text is legible and uses half-uncial script of maximum letter H. 8 cm. The lettering is elegant, with careful wedge-shaped serifs, and some attempt has been made in the layout of the text to accommodate the word division.

TEXT

BEND̲ ‖ ACHT
FOR ‖ AN̄
MARTAN

INTERPRETATION

The text reads *bend acht for an̄ martan* for *bendacht for an(main) Martan*, 'a blessing on the soul of Martan'. (See the **Introduction §5.3.4** for further discussion of the formula used).

DISCUSSION

The carving on this slab is particularly crisp and well-preserved. The slab is similar in scale and shape to Lismore 2 and, like it, was probably a recumbent (although this slab could have been set upright in the ground without obscuring the text). The crosses carved on both slabs are variants of the same basic shape, a slim Latin cross with wedge-shaped expansions. The principal differences between the two slabs are the relative positions of cross and text, and the different formulae used. The name *Martan* is unusual, although not rare. It reflects the particular devotion of the early Irish to Martin, the fourth century bishop of Tours and protagonist of monasticism. To judge from the genealogies, names such as this one, taken from the Roman martyrology, were not used by the secular Irish nobility in this period. Where they appear they seem to be not baptismal names but names 'assumed at some point in a religious career' (Ó Cuív 1986b, 164). The Martan commemorated here could be the Martan úa Roichligh, abbot of Lismore, whose death is recorded *s.a.* 878 (Annals of the Four Masters: O'Donovan 1851, 526-7), possibly a relative of the abbot whose death is recorded in 855 (see Lismore 2).

BIBLIOGRAPHY

Cotton 1854-55a, 222-3
Fitzgerald 1854-55, 200-1 and fig.

Hayman 1863-64, 145-6 and fig.
Petrie 1878, 31-2 and pl. XX, fig. 41
Westropp 1897c, 357 and fig.
(-) 1898, 64-6
Crawford 1912, 243
(-) 1912, 273-4 and fig. 11.III
Power, P. 1937, 220-1
Macalister 1949a, no. 935, pp. 107-8 and pl. XLIV, fig. 935
Lionard 1961, 109, 161 and fig. 2.5
Henry 1965, 138
Weekes 1994, no page numbering, and fig.
Moore, M. 1999, 186
OS Letters unpublished 1929, 66 and fig. opp. 66

EXAMINED

May 1996, March 1998 (EO); May 1996 (KF)

Lismore 4: large cross-slab

CURRENT LOCATION

The stone is fastened to the west interior wall of the cathedral nave.

HISTORY

The stone may have been found around 1827 (Fitzgerald 1854-55, 201). It was either found or re-found by Cotton after his arrival in Lismore in 1834 and before 1849 when it was in the cathedral and was examined and drawn by Windele ((-) 1898, 64-6). Along with stones 1, 2, 3 and 5, the stone has been fastened to the cathedral wall since some time before 1912 (see above under Lismore 1).

DESCRIPTION

The current dimensions of the stone are:
H. 94 cm, W. 37 cm, T. 5 cm visible.
The stone is a large rectangular slab which appears substantially intact despite some damage to its edges, especially to the lower edge. The stone is set into the wall with only 5 cm projecting and the back of the stone cannot therefore be examined. The face of the stone has been dressed. It is incised with an outline Latin cross with plain terminals set on a rectangular base. The right and left cross-arms extend to the edges of the stone and appear to be open-ended. The text is complete and is set in two lines (or one line turning a corner), the first line to the right of the cross and the second above it. The first line reads vertically upwards with the bottoms of the letters to the viewer's right. The second line reads horizontally but inverted with respect to the cross. An attempt seems to have been made to space the letters around the cross. Two modern letters, D and C, are incised in the top two quadrants of the cross, the C partially on top of the DO of *donnchad*.

LETTERING

The text is legible and uses half-uncial script of maximum letter H. 8.5 cm. As noted above, it appears that the letters have been spaced around the cross, presumably so that the cross-arm falls at a word division.

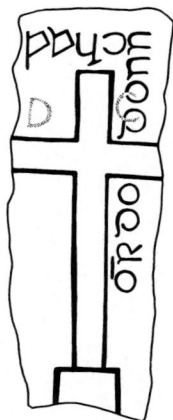

TEXT

ŌR DO ‖ DONN
CHAD

INTERPRETATION

The text reads ōr *do donn chad* for *or(óit) do Donnchad*, 'a prayer for Donnchad'. (See the **Introduction §5.3.4** for discussion of the *or(óit) do* formula).

DISCUSSION

The layout of the carving indicates that the slab was a recumbent. It is similar to some of the large recumbent slabs at Inishcaltra in having a large outline cross on a rectangular base covering the whole of the slab except for a portion above the head. The formula is also the most usual one at Inishcaltra. The Lismore slab differs, however, in the large scale of the lettering and in the layout of the text. The final section of text is, however, set above the head and inverted with respect to the cross, as at Inishcaltra. Once again, this text would be the right way up for someone kneeling to pray at the head of the grave. Donnchad has not been identified. The modern letters appear on the earliest drawings of the stone but Macalister was the first to recognise that they were modern. As he suggested, they probably reflect the slab's re-use as a modern tomb stone (Macalister 1949a, 108).

BIBLIOGRAPHY

Cotton 1854-55a, 222-3
Fitzgerald 1854-55, 200-1 and fig.
Hayman 1863-64, 147 and fig.
Petrie 1878, 31-2 and pl. XXI, fig. 43
Westropp 1897c, 357 and fig.
(-) 1898, 64-6 and fig.
Crawford 1912, 243
(-) 1912, 273-4 and fig. 11.IV
Power, P. 1937, 220-1
Macalister 1949a, no. 936, pp. 107-8 and pl. XLIV, fig. 936
Lionard 1961, fig. 6.4
Henry 1965, 138
Weekes 1994, no page numbering, and fig.
Moore, M. 1999, 186

EXAMINED

May 1996, March 1998 (EO); May 1996 (KF)

Lismore 5: head of a free-standing cross

CURRENT LOCATION

The stone is fastened to the west interior wall of the cathedral nave by means of two metal pins supported on metal struts. This arrangement allows the cross-head to be rotated and the viewer to examine both faces.

HISTORY

The stone was found in 1851 during the digging of the foundations of the cathedral library (Cotton 1854-55a, 223). Windele visited Lismore on 5 July 1851 but did not mention the stone ((-) 1898, 66-7). The stone might not have been found by then or, if found, had not by then been placed in the cathedral. On 7 November 1855 Cotton sent the stone to be exhibited at the Society of Antiquaries in Dublin, apparently reassuring the Society that the stone would subsequently be restored 'to its proper locality' (Cotton 1854-55b, 412). The stone was described as 'at Lismore' in 1863-64 (Hayman 1863-64, 146). Along with stones 1, 2, 3 and 4 it has been fastened to the cathedral wall since some time before 1912 (see above under Lismore 1).

DESCRIPTION

The current dimensions of the stone are:
H. 16.5 cm, W. 18.5 cm, T. 5 cm.
The stone is part of a small free-standing cross-head with a solid ring. The cross-head has broken off just under the transom. The head is substantially intact except for some damage to the ends of the arms, especially the right arm. The cross is carved in relief on both sides. On the reverse it has an edge moulding, but the face is plain except for the text. The text is incised in two complete horizontal lines with traces of a third line visible beneath. The first line runs the full width of the transom while the second line runs across the shaft immediately under the arms. Comparison with the reverse shows that the shaft has been kept unnaturally broad here to support the text. The third line would have run across the narrowing shaft. In addition, there is a trace of what might have been another letter above the final letters of the first line.

LETTERING

The text uses half-uncial script, the maximum letter H. being 3.5 cm. Most of the first two lines are legible but only traces remain of the third line.

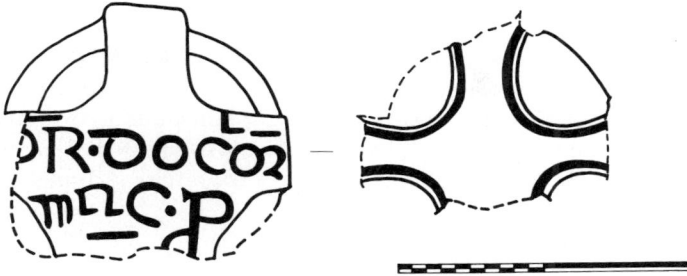

TEXT

[Ō]Ŕ · DOCO/[Ŕ]
MAC · P
[‾]

INTERPRETATION

The text reads [ō] r̄ · doco[r̄] mac · p– for [o]r(óit) · do Co[r]mac · p(ro)– , 'a prayer for Co[r]mac –'. In this text, as in Lismore 2, a single medial dot is used to indicate word separation. There are two areas of uncertainty in the interpretation, the end of the first line and the form of the P. The ligature of O and R, although unusual in epigraphy is well-attested in the manuscript tradition and is not problematic. Above the O/[R] is a horizontal bar which may be taken as the mark of abbreviation. The difficulty arises in interpreting the suprascript L-shaped mark between the C and O. It looks like a continuation of the bar but the vertical component reaches right to the edge of the cross-arm. Although similar in size and depth, the carving here seems sharper and fresher than the rest. It is possible that it is not part of the text but some more recent damage. If it is part of the text it is difficult to interpret, for an inserted L would make little sense at this point. Alternatively, it is possible that the *mac* of the second line is not a continuation of a personal name but rather the word 'son' in which case the letters at the end of the first line would be a complete personal name and an inserted L could be accommodated.

The letter P has a curved line to the left of its stem, the usual abbreviation symbol for *pro* (Lindsay 1915, 175-6). Macalister suggested that it was to be read with the lost letters of the final line as an abbreviated form of *p(res)b(yte)r* (Macalister 1949a, 108). The tops of two or three letters, along with a mark of abbreviation, are all that remain of this line and are insufficient to support Macalister's guess of BR. If *mac* is a noun rather than part of a name, then the P would be the beginning of the father's name. Alternatively, P could be the first letter of a title or status, for instance, *presbiter* 'priest', *pontifex*, 'bishop', *princeps* 'head of a monastic house'. The use of Latin for an ecclesiastical title appears on Inishcaltra 10 and Toureen Peacaun 36. None of these explanations will do, however, if the character is, as it appears to be, the abbreviation symbol for *pro*. The usual Latin formula equivalent of *oróit do* is, of course, *orat pro* and, although it is difficult to account for the switch to Latin part-way through, it is possible that the text read *or(óit) do Cormac pro* ... and continued with additional information about Cormac's status. There are numerous examples on both stone and metal of requests for prayers in the form *or(óit) do N. do* ... with the second slot filled by phrases such as *ríg hÉrenn*, 'king of Ireland', *epscop Connacht* 'bishop of Connact', *comarba Chiarán* 'coarb of St Ciarán'. (See the **Introduction §5.3.4** for further discussion of the *or(óit) do* formula).

DISCUSSION

This small free-standing cross may have stood at the head of a grave. The text conforms to a familiar formula, seen at Lismore also on slab 4, but the OR ligature and the looped P are unusual echoes of the manuscript tradition. Cormac, if that is the correct interpretation of the name in the text, cannot be identified. Two famous Cormacs are associated with Lismore, and the text could commemorate either or neither. The earlier is the tenth-century Cormac mac Cuilennan, bishop and vice-abbot of Lismore, abbot of Kilmolash and king of the Deisi (Gwynn and Hadcock 1970, 91). The later is Cormac son of Mac Carthaig, king of Desmumu, who entered the monastery of Lismore, possibly taking the tonsure, in 1127, before his unexpected restoration to his kingdom later that year. The Annals record his building churches at Lismore in 1127 (O'Keeffe 1994, 120-1).

BIBLIOGRAPHY
Cotton 1854-55a, 223
Cotton 1854-55b, 412 and fig.
Hayman 1863-64, 146 and fig.
Petrie 1878, 31-2 and pl. XXI, fig. 42
Allen 1889, 119
Westropp 1897c, 357
Crawford 1907, 208
(-) 1912, 273-4 and figs 11.V (a, b)
Power, P. 1937, 220-1
Macalister 1949a, no. 937, pp. 107-8 and pl. XLIV, fig. 937
Henry 1965, 138
Higgitt 1986, 127, 147
Harbison 1992, no. 166, pp 136, 363, 379 and fig. 454
Weekes 1994, no page numbering, and fig.
Moore, M. 1999, 186

EXAMINED

May 1996, March 1998 (EO); May 1996 (KF)

Lismore 6: architectural feature

CURRENT LOCATION

The stone is fastened to the west interior wall of the cathedral nave.

HISTORY

The stone was first mentioned by Westropp in 1897 when it was described as 'set' in 'the west wall' (Westropp 1897c, 357). This is presumably its present location.

DESCRIPTION

The current dimensions of the stone are:
H. 55 cm, W. 22.5 cm, T. 13.5 cm visible.

The stone is an architectural feature consisting of a figure carved in low relief, in a seated position and holding an open book. O'Keeffe described the figure: 'Drapes of clothing are represented on the figure's lower legs, but the feet can be seen. The head of the figure is large relative to the body. The surface of the face is quite flat. Its forehead is short, its ears are high, and lines are gouged on the cheeks and around the mouth. Tendrils of hair are visible on the head's right-hand side.' (O'Keeffe 1994, 121-3). The book contains four lines of text set horizontally across both open pages. The left page is intact except for the top which has delaminated. The top corner of the right page and most of the right edge have also delaminated and the top of the page is badly worn. There seems insufficient room for a line in the missing area at the top, although letters may be missing from the right page. The text is very worn.

LETTERING

The text is highly deteriorated but may have used a capital script; the maximum letter H. is c. 2 cm.

TEXT
 – || –
 [.NN..] || [.RUSAU]
 [.....] || [.UM–]
 [P.NN..] || [.URN.]

INTERPRETATION

The text is now very worn and only a few letters can be tentatively read, as indicated above. It is not clear whether the text read across the two pages or down each page in turn, nor is it even certain what language the text was in. In these circumstances a text is not now recoverable. In 1897 Westropp described the stone as 'a grotesquely hideous figure of St. John, identified by the mutilated words "Erat Verbum" on the open volume in its hand' (Westropp 1897c, 357-8).

Westropp's description suggests that even then the text was in a worn condition and his reading is not supported by the extant remains. Macalister, reading across the open pages of the book with some of the letters in the gutter, read the text as: *in me(n)sam domini ierusalem det arma et coronas aur(i)*; he translated this as 'upon the Table of the Lord let Jerusalem lay (her) arms and crowns of gold' (Macalister 1938, 300). A detailed comparison of his description of individual letter-forms with what is now visible reveals wide discrepancies. Since Macalister saw the stone in 1938, it has remained in its present place inside the cathedral (which is probably where it was in 1897). It is hard to imagine that it can have deteriorated to any substantial extent. We are forced to the conclusion that Macalister's reading is, to some extent at least, imaginative.

DISCUSSION

Westropp identified the figure as St John (Westropp 1897c, 357-8), but O'Keeffe (1994, 123) suggested it was more likely to be Christ. As O'Keeffe pointed out, although there are other examples of inscriptions on architectural members, for example Monaincha 4 and Ardfert, none of these is integral to the architecture. Only here at Lismore was the primary purpose to carry an inscription (O'Keeffe 1994, 123). The stone's function is not clear. Macalister first suggested that it was a corbel (Macalister 1938, 298). Henry compared the figure with those from White Island, Co Fermanagh (Henry 1937b, 307), which appear to have served a caryatid function (O'Keeffe 1994, 123). The Lismore figure need not, however, have fulfilled a structural role and may have been displayed within the church as a wall panel (O'Keeffe 1994, 123). The sculptor could have been copying a primitive carving and the drapery suggests a knowledge of earlier sculpture while the form of the book looks late (Isabel Henderson, pers. com.). O'Keeffe drew parallels between the Lismore figure and Romanesque heads elsewhere in Ireland. The tendrils at the side of the head suggested to him a twelfth-century date and the figure, 'being something of an oddity in a 12th century Irish context', seemed more likely to date to the experimental phases of Romanesque in the earlier part of the century (O'Keeffe 1994, 123). For a full discussion of the likely function and date of this stone, see O'Keeffe 1994, 121-4.

BIBLIOGRAPHY

Westropp 1897c, 357-8
Henry 1937b, 306-7 and pl. XXXVIII
Macalister 1938, 298-300 and fig.
Macalister 1949a, no. 938, p. 109 and pl. XLIV, fig. 938
Henry 1965, 138
Harbison 1975, 239
Weir 1980, 226
O'Keeffe 1994, 121-4 and fig. 1, a-b
Weekes 1994, no page numbering
Moore, M. 1999, 186

EXAMINED

May 1996, March 1998 (EO); May 1996 (KF). We are most grateful to Isabel Henderson for visiting Lismore with EO and for commenting on the stones.

SITE

The monastery of Lismore, on the River Blackwater, was traditionally founded by St Carthage (Mo-Chuda) in 636. The earliest recorded abbots died in 700 and 703. From the 730s the Annals preserve the obits of a long list of abbots and other personnel down to the twelfth century. From an early date the monastery and school at Lismore became 'one of the great religious centres of Ireland' (Gwynn and Hadcock 1970, 91). Its status was further enhanced in the early twelfth century when it was created the seat of a diocese at the Synod of Rath Breasail in 1111. Under the patronage of Cormac MacCarthaig, king of Desmumu, Lismore flourished artistically (O'Keeffe 1994, 120-21) but from the 1180s it ceased to play an important role; (for further details see Gwynn and Hadcock 1970, 91-2). St Carthage's cathedral was built in 1633 on the site of the pre-Reformation cathedral and retains some small portions of thirteenth-century work (Moore, M. 1999, 184-6; O'Keeffe 1994, 120-1). The cathedral has been altered on various occasions in modern times and the tower was added in 1827. Stones 1, 2, 3 and 4 were allegedly found when the foundations of the tower were being dug (see above under Lismore 1: History) and stone 5 in 1851 when the cathedral library foundations were being dug (see above under Lismore 5: History). Moore suggested that a further stone is now missing but gave no evidence to support this assertion (Moore, M. 1999, 186). The present authors have found no other mention of a further stone; it may be that Moore misunderstood Macalister's reference to the six stones (Macalister 1949a, 107-9).

GENERAL DISCUSSION

It is not surprising that a major monastery such as Lismore should have produced a collection of inscribed stones. What is interesting is the diversity within the group of six. The book-holding figure (no. 6) is unique, and we know of no other examples of small free-standing crosses with inscribed heads (no. 5). The slabs are part of a widespread tradition and one (no. 4) is related to a type seen elsewhere. The other three, which have a number of similarities, are of a type which appears to be specific to Lismore. On all four slabs the lettering is notably large, expertly carved and well preserved. On slabs 1, 2 and 3 the lines of text cover the full width of the slab. The script used on slabs 2 and 3 seems particularly similar but all the slabs use angular letter-forms. The crosses on slabs 2 and 3, although different, are based on the one form, a slim Latin cross with wedge-shaped terminals; the shaft on slab 2 ends in a spike while the shaft on 3 has been sunk in a pedestal base. Both could have been inspired by an actual processional or altar cross, one showing it in its base, the other showing it ringed and free. Slabs 1 and 3 have the same *bendacht for anmain* formula, although on the latter *an(main)* is abbreviated. The crosses on slabs 1 and 2 are at the foot of the slab with the text above. If one ignores the blank upper half of slab 1, then the two are very similar in size, scale and layout.

The multiple similarities between these slabs suggest they may date from roughly the same period. If the identification of the Suibne and Martan commemorated with the Uí Roichligh abbots of these names is accepted, then slabs nos 1-3 may date from the ninth century. The similarities between slab 4 and the slabs of Inishcaltra might suggest that it is a century or more later.

SHANAKILL: SEANCHILL

Site name Two-Mile-Bridge
Townland Shanakill
NGR -
SMR site no.-

A small slab came from what appears to have been an ecclesiastical site.

CURRENT LOCATION

The stone is now lost.

HISTORY

The stone was found around 1900 at Shanakill, also known as Two-Mile-Bridge, and in 1910 was kept in the house of Mike Tobin who lived near the Glenbeg schoolhouse on the Youghal road (Power, P. 1910, 103). Some years later a local man, Tomás Breatnach, contacted Macalister and in 1938 they together visited Tobin, by then an elderly man and living alone. Tobin brought the stone out from his house for the men to examine and photograph. Macalister recorded that it had been found by Tobin in a field, 'the site, it is said, of an old cemetery', at Shanakill

(Macalister 1949a, 109). Tobin declined to part with the stone but offered to leave it to Maynooth College in his will; this, however, does not appear to have happened. On his death Tobin's farm went to a nephew-in-law, James Foley, who apparently still lives in the area but unfortunately we have failed to make contact with him. The stone has not been recorded since 1938 and by 1951 was lost (Power, P. 1952, 130; this work was published posthumously, Power having died in October 1951). Some of the above information has kindly been supplied by Maura Flynn, daughter of Tomás Breatnach, and we are much obliged to her.

DESCRIPTION

The dimensions, description and text are taken from Power's description and photograph (see illustration above), supplemented by reference to Macalister's description and drawing:

H. c. 26 cm, W. c. 34 cm, T. c. 7.5 cm.

The stone was a small rectangular slab of sandstone. From the photograph it is not clear whether any of its straight edges were original or whether the slab has been subsequently trimmed for re-use. Power (1910, 103) described it as 'evidently only a fragment' although the levelness of the bottom edge made him 'inclined to consider the edge in question the original base of the monument' (1910, 105). In the centre of the carved surface was a deeply incised equal-armed linear cross with rounded expanding ends. To the left was a second linear cross, more lightly incised. Power (1910, 104) described it as a Latin cross on its side, although from his photograph it looks equal-armed. The left arm had a bar terminal which may have been intended to mark it as the top. The vertical arm was doubled and the horizontal arm interrupted by the right-hand vertical as if the arms are interlaced with one another. The text was incised in a single horizontal line below the crosses and may have been incomplete. To the left of the lettering were two curved lines which Power thought possibly were a 'portion of a spiral ornament' (1910, 104) but, from the photograph, Macalister's assessment that they were 'most likely accidental flaws' (1949a, 110) appears more likely. Power saw what he believed to be traces of a part of a letter from a second line of text, but this too could have been a flaw. Macalister saw 'no certain indication' of this (1949a, 110).

LETTERING

The text appears to have been in half-uncial script and to have been legible. The maximum letter H. was c. 5 cm.

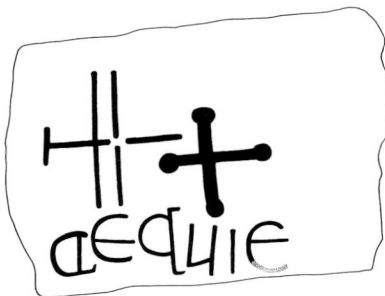

TEXT

AEDUIE

INTERPRETATION

The text appears to have read *aeduie*. Power interpreted this as *Áed uí –*, the male personal name Áed followed by *uí*, the genitive singular of *ua* 'grandson, descendent', (Power 1910, 104). If this were correct, we might have expected instead *Áeda*, the genitive of *Áed*. Both Power and Macalister considered the text incomplete and it is certainly difficult to make sense of it as it stands. The area beyond the final E may have been avoided because the surface was already damaged. Power saw a vertical stroke below the D and interpreted it as part of a letter in a (lost) lower line. He quoted Macalister's opinion that it could have been the top of a B or an H (1910, 105), but this was before Macalister had seen the stone. Once he had actually examined it, Macalister declared there was 'no certain indication' of a lower line (1949a, 110), although there does appear to be a stroke of some sort in this position on Power's photograph. Macalister's sketch shows it as an exaggerated tail of the D, but it could have been the result of casual damage.

DISCUSSION

It is unclear whether Power thought this slab a fragment solely because the text seemed incomplete, or if the stone itself bore evidence of trimming or fracturing. As it stands, the stone is similar in several respects to the small slabs of Toureen Peacaun, although there the crosses tend to be outline rather than linear. There appear to have been at least two phases of carving on the Shanakill slab. Since the lettering seems to avoid the equal-armed cross, the latter may be assumed to be earlier. The left cross and the lettering appear to be equally shallow in their carving. They might, although they need not, be contemporary.

BIBLIOGRAPHY

Power, P. 1910, 103-6 and fig.
Crawford 1912, 244
Power, P. 1937, 173
Macalister 1949a, no. 940, pp. 109-10 and pl. XLIV, fig. 940
Power, P. 1952, 130
Lionard 1961, fig. 2.4
Moore, M. 1999, 188

SITE

Nothing is now visible at the site, described by Power (1910, 105) as a *cillín*, which lies on the south bank of the River Brickey about two miles from Dungarvan. A large limestone *bullaun* stone was found there and moved to the 'Catholic Cemetery, Dungarvan' (Power, P. 1952, 130). This *bullaun* stone is now also missing (Moore, M. 1999, 188). According to Power, Shanakill townland (*Sean Cill*, 'old church') was a former sub-division of the neighbouring townland of Killingford, the latter being, he maintained, the 'real and distinctive' name of the ecclesiastical site (Power, P. 1910, 106).

DUBIA

CAMP, CO KERRY: AN COM

Site name Glenfais
Townland Camp
NGR 06956, 10895
SMR site no. –

This large ogham stone also contains a problematic roman-alphabetic text, which may be the product of modern antiquarianism.

CURRENT LOCATION

CURRENT LOCATION

The stone is lying prostrate on the ground, pointing west-east, in a field on the west slope of Glenfais. It is probably *in situ*.

HISTORY

The stone was found by Rowan a 'few years' before 1858 (Rowan 1858, 102). It was then 'in a half-fallen position ... under brambles and rubbish' (Rowan 1858, 103). When Brash examined the stone in July 1868, it was prostrate (Brash 1870, 384) and it remains in this position. Rowan observed both the ogham and the roman script texts but could not decipher the latter, describing it as 'some cuttings which look like defaced or imperfectly formed characters' (Rowan 1858, 106).

DESCRIPTION

The current dimensions of the stone are:

L. c. 338 cm, W. c. 162 cm, T. 50 cm (maximum)

The stone, known as *Uaigh Fais*, 'Faisi's Grave', is a large natural slab, undressed and undecorated, except for a small cross incised on its uppermost face. The stone's size and shape suggest that it was probably never erect. Despite the reservations of Cuppage *et al.* (1986, 254), the slab appears to be the cap-stone of a dolmen tomb, as Rhys first suggested (1890-91, 654). Underneath, there is a large hollow in the ground, which can be glimpsed under the higher end of the stone. An ogham inscription runs along the upper angle of the south face of the stone. It reads from right to left, in the opposite direction from normal; in other words, the consonantal strokes have been inverted (that is, S for C, Q for N). Since the slab slopes down to the north, the ogham reads uphill. The roman alphabet text is incised on the upper surface of the slab adjacent and parallel to the ogham. It reads from left to right with the bottoms of the letters to the edge of the slab. The surface of the stone is uneven, which has affected the spacing and positioning of individual letters. Both roman and ogham texts appear to be complete.

LETTERING

The text uses a capital script, with possibly an insular T. The lettering is rather deteriorated and the maximum letter H. is 4 cm.

TEXT

FEC[T.O]N[U]RI

INTERPRETATION

The text reads *fec[t.o]n[u]ri* presumably for *fec[t] [.o]n[u]ri*. The T is of unusual shape with the curved lower stroke joining the right extremity of the upper horizontal. The curved stroke is joined to the next character, which looks like a C although it is small and low down. The following letter is high up and looks like an O with a tail. Macalister read the second part of the text as *cunuri* (1945, 169), but *conuri* is also possible. Cuppage *et al.*, repeated this reading with the proviso that the C and final U were not discernible (1986, 254). The interpretation of the text is not straightforward. If *fect* is for Latin *fecit* 'he made', a personal name in the nominative case would be expected, but if *Conuri* is Latin, then it is in the genitive. Another problem is the word order: it would be more usual for the verb to follow the name, as 'N. *fecit*'. If the text is Irish, *fect*, for *fecht* 'expedition, raid', seems highly unlikely in an epigraphic context. If the reading were *fert*, the Middle Irish form of Old Irish *fertae* 'mound or tumulus', hence 'mound over a burial place' (*DIL* s.v. *fertae*), we might have 'the tomb of Conuri', but the third character seems fairly unambiguously to be C. The second part of the text appears to repeat the ogham CONURI, a genitive form of the male personal name later found as *Conaire* (Uhlich 1993, 210-11).

DISCUSSION

The ogham inscription is clear. All the strokes are preserved and the letters are well-spaced. It reads CONUNETTMOQICONURI with the x-*forfid* for E. The three dots of the final U are off-set because of a flaw in the surface of the stone. There is space for one or two more dots and McManus read this character as E or I (1991, 66). There is no reason to doubt that this is a genuine early medieval inscription. The inversion of consonant strokes is unusual, but paralleled, for instance, at Monataggart, Co. Cork (Macalister 1945, no. 118, pp. 116-18 and figs), another reused prehistoric stone with *moqi*. The form of the slab and the horizontal position of the inscription is not dissimilar to an ogham-inscribed rock outcrop near Listowel, Co. Kerry (unpublished, Fionnbar Moore, pers. com.; see the map, Moore 1998, 24, fig.4.1).

Although the roman lettering is clear, three features combine to raise suspicion that it is not an early medieval text. First, the quality of the lettering is uncharacteristically poor. The incision is uneven and insubstantial and, even with allowance made for the undulations in the surface, the layout is disjointed and inelegant. Second, the letters, especially the F, N and R, look disturbingly modern in form. Third, there is the problematic nature of the text. Macalister suggested that the roman inscription was an eighteenth-century forgery (1937, 227-8) and this seems very likely. There are other examples of antiquarian fabrication in the area. Macalister (1937, 228) referred to a grave of the legendary Scota nearby and provided an exact parallel on a pillar from Ballymorereagh (Macalister 1945, no. 170, pp. 163-4 and fig.) on which he claimed to read the roman letter text *fect Queniloc(-)*, echoing the genuine ogham text. However, no other authorities have been able to see such a text and there is no trace of it there now. Nonetheless, it seems more than likely that an antiquarian read the Camp ogham as *Conuri* and supplied a label meaning 'the grave of Conuri', which (s)he may or may not have intended to pass off as ancient. Conuri could have been interpreted as the name of the legendary Munster hero, Cú Roí Mac Daire, who was held to inhabit the inland promontory fort Caherconree (*Cathair Chonraoi*) which overlooks the valley (Hellmuth 1998, 5). The fort is probably a late Bronze Age or early Iron Age tribal centre with possible religious or ceremonial function (Cuppage *et al.* 1986, 81-2). For the antiquarian fabrication of ogham in the eighteenth century see de hÓir 1983. The small cross on the upper face of the stone may or may not be contemporary with either of the texts.

BIBLIOGRAPHY
Rowan 1858, 100-6 and fig.
Brash 1870, 384-95
Ferguson 1872, note 60, pp. 223-5
Brash 1874-75, 320-2
Petrie 1878, 3-4 and pl. II, figs 2, 3, 4
Brash 1879, 174-6 and pl. XVI
Ferguson 1879, 39, 51-60, 62 and fig.
Ferguson 1887, 49-50
Rhys 1890-91, 654-5
Macalister 1902, 24-30 and fig.
Crawford 1912, 231
Macalister 1937, 227 -8
Macalister 1945, no. 176, pp. 168-9 and fig.
Barrington 1976, 238
Cuppage *et al.* 1986, 254
Killanin and Duignan 1989, 294
Moore, F. 1998, 29

EXAMINED
July 1996 (KF)

SITE

The stone lies in the field where it was found and there are no further remains visible. In the first half of the nineteenth century the building of the road led to the discovery of an extended inhumation cemetery of stone-lined cists laid out in rows (Cuppage *et al.* 1986, 67). Rowan described this as near the present stone but its precise location is uncertain (1858, 102-3). Another ogham stone, now in Killarney, was found in Camp townland but its exact find-spot is uncertain (Cuppage *et al.* 1986, 254).

DROMCARRA, CO CORK: DROM CABHRACH

Site name Dromcarra Castle
Townland Dromcarra South
NGR 12893,06763
SMR site no. CO0082-016--

The stone was a fragment which may have contained lettering.

CURRENT LOCATION

The stone is now lost.

HISTORY

The stone was found 'near Drumscara Castle, eight miles west of Macroom' in April 1872 (Caulfield 1872-73, 127). This may have been Dromcarra Castle, which was blown up by the landowner in 1968 (Power, D. *et al.* 1997, 368), although it was some five miles south-west of Macroom. Caulfield donated a rubbing of the stone to the Society of Antiquaries on 10 July 1872 but no further mention of stone or rubbing has been made.

DESCRIPTION

The dimensions, description and text are taken from the description in Caulfield 1872-73, 127. The stone is described as 'about 14 inches by 15 inches', that is *c* 35 cm by *c* 38 cm, although it is not clear which was height, which width.

The stone was a 'fragment of a larger mass' which contained on its face 'Rune-like characters of some kind' (Caulfield 1872-73, 127). No further details are given.

LETTERING

The script used is not known.

TEXT

It is not clear what the text read.

INTERPRETATION

The text was described as 'not likely to be decipherable', although whether this was Caulfield's judgement or that of the Society of Antiquaries is not clear (Caulfield 1872-73, 127). The text is not now recoverable.

DISCUSSION

No further discussion of this lost stone seems profitable.

BIBLIOGRAPHY

Caulfield 1872-73, 127.

MOORESTOWN, CO KERRY: BAILE AN MHÓRAIGH

Site name uncertain
Townland Moorestown
NGR 04033,10996
SMR site no. -

This inscribed stone, of doubtful authenticity, is known only from a nineteenth-century reference.

CURRENT LOCATION

The stone is now lost.

HISTORY

The stone was first recorded in a communication by Dunlevy to the Kilkenny Archaeological Society on 2 November 1853. It had been found 'many feet below the surface of the turf bog of Moorestown, near Dingle' (Dunlevy 1852-53, 386). A footnote by the Editor gave the information that the stone had been bought by the Rev. Rowan and 'deposited by him in the Museum of the Royal Irish Academy' (Dunlevy 1852-53, 386n). There appears to be no record of this donation. Dunlevy subsequently forwarded to the Society a 'tracing' of the stone which the Secretary, James Graves, 'submitted to Dr. O'Donovan' for comment (Dunlevy 1854-55, 15). In 1949 Macalister reported that he had instituted a search for the stone in Dublin but failed to find it (Macalister 1949a, 97).

DESCRIPTION

No dimensions, description nor illustration of the stone have survived.

LETTERING

The script used is not known.

TEXT

The text is recorded on the sole authority of O'Donovan who read the beginning of it as 'Mac cu Draca'; O'Donovan explained that he needed to examine the actual stone 'in order to decipher the remainder, or form an opinion as to the antiquity of the inscription' (Dunlevy 1854-55, 15).

INTERPRETATION

In view of the paucity of information concerning this text, no interpretation is possible.

DISCUSSION

No further discussion of this lost stone seems profitable.

BIBLIOGRAPHY

Dunlevy 1852-53, 386
Dunlevy 1854-55, 15
Macalister 1949a, 97
Cuppage *et al.* 1986, 335

BIBLIOGRAPHY

Allen 1887: J. R. Allen, *Early Christian Symbolism in Great Britain and Ireland before the Thirteenth Century* (London: Whiting and Co.)

Allen 1889: J. R. Allen, *The Monumental History of the Early British Church* (London: S.P.C.K.)

Allen 1892: J. R. Allen, 'Notes on the Antiquities in Co. Kerry ... Part II', *JRSAI*, vol. 22, pp. 255-84

Allen 1903: J. R. Allen, *The Early Christian Monuments of Scotland*, part 2 (Edinburgh: Society of Antiquaries of Scotland)

Allen 1904: J. R. Allen, *Celtic Art in Pagan and Christian Times* (London: Methuen and Co.)

Anderson, A. O. and Anderson, M. O. 1991: A. O. Anderson and M. O. Anderson (eds.), *Adomnán's Life of Columba* (Oxford: Clarendon Press)

Barnes *et al.* 1997: M. P. Barnes *et al.*, *The Runic Inscriptions of Viking Age Dublin*. Medieval Dublin Excavations 1962-81, Ser. B, vol. 5 (Dublin: Royal Irish Academy)

Barrington 1976: T. J. Barrington, *Discovering Kerry. its History, Heritage & Topography* (Dublin: Blackwater Press)

Bieler 1949: L. Bieler, 'Insular Palaeography, Present State and Problems', *Scriptorium*, vol. 3, pp. 267-94

Bieler 1979: L. Bieler (ed.), *The Patrician Texts in the Book of Armagh*, Scriptores Latini Hiberniae vol. 10 (Dublin Institute for Advanced Studies)

Bischoff 1990: B. Bischoff, tr. D. Ó Cróinín and D. Ganz, *Latin Palaeography. Antiquity and the Middle Ages* (Cambridge University Press)

Brash 1866: R. R. Brash, 'Inishcaltra and its Remains', *Gents. Mag.*, vol. 220, pt 1, January to June 1866, pp. 7-22

Brash 1870: R. R. Brash, 'On an Ogham Stone in Glen Fais, County Kerry', *PRIA*, vol. 10, pp. 384-95

Brash 1874-75: R. R. Brash, 'The Camp, or Glenfais, Ogham-inscribed Stone', *JRSAI*, vol. 13, pp. 320-2

Brash 1875: R. R. Brash, *The Ecclesiastical Architecture of Ireland ...* (Dublin: W. B. Kelly; London: Simpkin, Marshall and Co.)

Brash 1879: R. R. Brash, *The Ogam Inscribed Monuments of the Gaedhil in the British Islands ...* , ed. G. M. Atkinson (London: G. Bell and Sons)

Brown 1989: M. P. Brown, 'The Lindisfarne Scriptorium from the Late Seventh to the Early Ninth Century', in G. Bonner *et al.* (eds.), *St Cuthbert, his Cult and his Community to AD 1200* (Woodbridge: Boydell Press), pp. 151-63

Brown 1993: M. P. Brown, '"Paten and Purpose", The Derrynaflan Paten Inscriptions', in R. M. Spearman and J. Higgitt (eds.), *The Age of Migrating Ideas. Early Medieval Art in Northern Britain and Ireland* (Edinburgh: National Museums of Scotland and Alan Sutton Publishing), pp. 162-7

Byrne 1980: F. J. Byrne, 'Derrynavlan: The Historical Context', *JRSAI*, vol. 110, pp. 116-26

Caulfield 1872-73: R. Caulfield, in 'Proceedings of July Meeting', *JRSAI*, vol. 12, pp. 113-38

Chatterton 1839: Lady H. G. M. Chatterton, *Rambles in the South of Ireland during the year 1838*, 2nd edn, vol. 1 (London: Saunders and Otley)

Clancy and Márkus 1995: T. O. Clancy and G. Márkus, *Iona. The Earliest Poetry of a Celtic Monastery* (Edinburgh University Press)

Cochrane 1912: R. Cochrane, 'Ancient Monuments in the County of Cork. Part III ...', *JCHAS*, 2nd series, vol. 18, pp. 122-33

Coleman 1895: J. Coleman, 'Persons Remarkable in Local History. St. Beretchert, the Saxon Saint of Tullylease, County Cork ...', *JCHAS* , 2nd series, vol. 1, pp. 61-8

Cooke 1852-53: T. L. Cooke, 'On Ancient Irish Bells', *JRSAI*, vol. 2, pp. 47-63

Cotton 1854-55a: H. Cotton, in 'Proceedings, January', *JRSAI*, vol. 3, pp. 209-23

Cotton 1854-55b: H. Cotton, in 'Proceedings, November', *JRSAI*, vol. 3, pp. 409-20

Cramp 1984: R. J. Cramp, *County Durham and Northumberland. Corpus of Anglo-Saxon Stone Sculpture*, vol. 1 (Oxford: British Academy and Oxford University Press)

Crawford 1907: H. S. Crawford, 'A Descriptive List of the Early Irish Crosses', *JRSAI*, vol. 37, pp. 187-239

Crawford 1908: H. S. Crawford, 'Description of a Carved Stone at Tybroughney, County Kilkenny', *JRSAI*, vol. 38, pp. 270-7

Crawford 1909: H. S. Crawford, 'Some Early Monuments in the Glen of Aherlow', *JRSAI*, vol. 39, pp. 59-66

Crawford 1912: H. S. Crawford, 'A Descriptive List of Early Cross-slabs and Pillars', *JRSAI*, vol. 42, pp. 217-44

Crawford 1926a: H. S. Crawford, *Handbook of Carved Ornament from Irish Monuments of the Christian Period* (Dublin: Royal Society of Antiquaries of Ireland)

Crawford 1926b: H. S. Crawford, 'The Early Cross-Slabs and Pillar-Stones at Church Island, near Waterville, Co. Kerry', *JRSAI*, vol. 56, pp. 43-7

Cronin 1998: R. Cronin, 'Late High Crosses in Munster: Tradition and Novelty in Twelfth-Century Irish Art', in M. A. Monk and J. Sheehan (eds.), *Early Medieval Munster. Archaeology, History and Society* (Cork University Press), pp. 138-46

Cuppage *et al.* 1986: J. Cuppage *et al.*, *Archaeological Survey of the Dingle Peninsula ...* (Ballyferriter: Oidhreacht Chorca Dhuibhne)

Davies *et al.* 2000: W. Davies *et al.*, *The Inscriptions of Early Medieval Brittany* (Oakville, Connecticut and Aberystwyth: Celtic Studies Publications)

Deane 1880: T. N. Deane, 'National Monuments of Ireland. Annual Report, 1880', in *Forty-eighth Annual Report from the Commissioners of Public Works in Ireland ...,* Appendix D (Dublin: Stationery Office)

de Bhulbh 1997: S. de Bhulbh, *Sloinnte na h-Éireann. Irish Surnames* (Faing: Comhar-Chumann Íde Naofa)

de hÓir 1983: S. de hÓir, 'The Mount Callen Ogham Stone and Its Context', *North Munster Antiq. J*, vol. 25, pp. 43-57

de Paor 1977: L. de Paor, 'The Christian Triumph: The Golden Age', in P. Cone (ed.), *Treasures of Early Irish Art, 1500 B.C. to 1500 A.D.* (New York: Metropolitan Museum of Art), pp. 93-143

de Paor in preparation: L. de Paor, *Excavations at Inishcaltra* (in preparation)

Duignan 1944: M. V. Duignan, 'Early Monastic Site at Peakaun, Co. Tipperary', *JRSAI*, vol. 74, pp. 226-7

Dunlevy 1852-53: F. A. Dunlevy, in 'Proceedings, 1853', *JRSAI*, vol. 2, pp. 349-90

Dunlevy 1854-55: F. A. Dunlevy, in 'Proceedings, January', *JRSAI*, vol. 3, pp. 3-16

du Noyer 1857-61: G. V. du Noyer, 'Description of Drawings of Irish Antiquities presented by him', *PRIA*, vol. 7, pp. 249-62

du Noyer 1861-64: G. V. du Noyer, in 'Proceedings' 14 December 1863, *PRIA*, vol. 8, pp. 429-41

du Noyer unpublished: G. V. du Noyer, *Antiquarian Sketches*, 11 vols, in the Library of the Royal Irish Academy

Edwards 1990: N. Edwards, *The Archaeology of Early Medieval Ireland* (London: B. T. Batsford)

Evans 1966: E. Evans, *Prehistoric and Early Christian Ireland. A guide* (London: B. T. Batsford)

Fanning 1971: T. Fanning, 'Two Cross-inscribed Stones from Reask, Co. Kerry, at Adare Manor', *North Munster Arch. Soc.*, vol. 14, pp. 25-8

Fanning 1975: T. Fanning, 'Excavations at Reask', *J Kerry A H Soc.*, vol. 8, pp. 5-10

Fanning 1976: T. Fanning, 'Early Christian Monastic Sites in Tipperary', in W. J. Hayes (ed.), *Tipperary Remembers* (Freshford: Tipperary Remembers Society), pp. 34-41

Fanning 1981: T. Fanning, 'Excavation of an Early Christian cemetery and settlement at Reask, County Kerry', *PRIA*, vol. 81C, pp. 67-172

Ferguson 1872: S. Ferguson, *Congal: A Poem, in five books* (Dublin: Edward Ponsonby; London: Bell and Daldy)

Ferguson 1879: S. Ferguson, 'On the Difficulties attendant on the Transcription of Ogham Legends, and the Means of Removing them', *PRIA*, vol. 11, pp. 30-64

Ferguson 1887: S. Ferguson, *Ogham Inscriptions in Ireland, Wales, and Scotland* (Edinburgh: David Douglas)

Fitzgerald 1854-55: E. Fitzgerald, 'On some Early Irish Monumental Remains', *JRSAI*, vol. 3, pp. 199-202

Gleeson, J. 1915: J. Gleeson, *History of the Ely O'Carroll Territory ...* (Dublin: M. H. Gill and Son)

Graves 1883-84: J. Graves, 'On a Sepulchral Slab found at the Reefert, Glendalough, bearing an Irish Inscription ...', *JRSAI*, vol. 16, pp. 42-8

Gwynn and Gleeson, D. F. 1962: A. Gwynn and D. F. Gleeson, *A History of the Diocese of Killaloe* (Dublin: M. H. Gill and Son)

Gwynn and Hadcock 1970: A. Gwynn and R. N. Hadcock, *Medieval Religious Houses Ireland* (London: Longman)

Hamlin 1972: A. Hamlin, 'A Chi-rho-carved Stone at Drumaqueran, Co. Antrim', *Ulster J Arch.*, 3rd series, vol. 35, pp. 22-8

Hamlin 1982: A. Hamlin, 'Early Irish Stone Carving: Content and Context', in S.M. Pearce (ed.), *The Early Church in Western Britain and Ireland ...*, BAR, Brit. Series, vol. 102, pp. 283-96

Hamlin 1985: A. Hamlin, 'The archaeology of the early Irish churches in the eighth century', *Peritia*, vol. 4, pp. 279-99

Harbison 1970: P. Harbison, 'How old is Gallarus oratory? A reappraisal of its role in early Irish architecture', *Med. Arch.*, vol. 14, pp. 34-59

Harbison 1975: P. Harbison, *Guide to the National Monuments in the Republic of Ireland*, 2nd edn (Dublin: Gill and Macmillan)

Harbison 1976: P. Harbison, *The Archaeology of Ireland* (London, Sydney, Toronto: Bodley Head)

Harbison 1992: P. Harbison, *The High Crosses of Ireland: an Iconographical and Photographic Survey* 3 vols, Römisch-Germanisches Zentralmuseum Forschungsinstitut für Vor- und Frühgeschichte Monographien vol. 17, 1, 2 and 3 (Dublin: Royal Irish Academy; Bonn: Habelt)

Harbison 1997: P. Harbison, *Ancient Irish Monuments* (Dublin: Gill and Macmillan)

Hayman 1863-64: S. Hayman, 'The Annals of Lismore, Co. Waterford', *Reliquary*, vol. 4, pp. 137-56

Hellmuth 1998: P. S. Hellmuth, 'A Giant among Kings and Heroes: Some preliminary thoughts on the character of Cú Roí mac Dáire in mediaeval Irish literature', *Emania*, vol. 17, pp. 5-11

Henderson and Okasha 1992: I. Henderson and E. Okasha, 'The Early Christian Inscribed and Carved Stones of Tullylease, Co. Cork', *CMCS*, vol. 24 (winter), pp. 1-36

Henderson and Okasha 1997: I. Henderson and E. Okasha, 'The Early Christian Inscribed and Carved Stones of Tullylease, Co. Cork: Addendum', *CMCS*, vol. 33 (summer), pp. 9-17

Henry 1933: F. Henry, *La Sculpture Irlandaise* ..., 2 vols (Paris: Librairie Ernest Leroux)

Henry 1937a: F. Henry, 'Early Christian Slabs and Pillar Stones in the West of Ireland', *JRSAI*, vol. 67, pp. 265-79

Henry 1937b: F. Henry, 'Figure in Lismore Cathedral', *JRSAI*, vol. 67, pp. 306-7

Henry 1948: F. Henry, 'Three Engraved Slabs in the neighbourhood of Waterville (Kerry) and the Cross on Skellig Michael', *JRSAI*, vol. 78, pp. 175-7

Henry 1956-57: F. Henry, 'Early monasteries, beehive huts, and dry-stone houses in the neighbourhood of Caherciveen and Waterville (Co. Kerry)', *PRIA*, vol. 58C, pp. 45-166

Henry 1965: F. Henry, *Irish Art in the Early Christian Period (to 800 A.D.)*, 3rd edn (London: Methuen and Co.)

Herbert 1988: M. Herbert, *Iona, Kells, and Derry. The History and Hagiography of the Monastic Familia of Columba* (Oxford: Clarendon Press)

Herity 1990: M. Herity, 'Carpet pages and Chi-rhos: some depictions in Irish early Christian manuscripts and stone carvings', *Celtica*, vol. 21, pp. 208-22

Herity 1995: M. Herity, 'The Chi-rho and other early cross-forms in Ireland', in J.-M. Picard (ed.), *Aquitaine and Ireland in the Middle Ages* (Dublin and Portland, Or: Four Courts Press), pp. 232-60

Higgins 1987: J. G. Higgins, *The Early Christian Cross Slabs, Pillar Stones and Related Monuments of County Galway, Ireland*, BAR, Int. series, vol. 375, pts. 1, 2

Higgitt 1982: J. Higgitt, 'The Pictish Latin inscription at Tarbat in Ross-shire', *PSAS*, vol. 112, pp. 300-21

Higgitt 1986: J. Higgitt, 'Words and Crosses: The Inscribed Stone Cross in Early Medieval Britain and Ireland', in J. Higgitt (ed.), *Early Medieval Sculpture in Britain and Ireland*, BAR, Brit. Series, vol. 152, pp. 125-52

Higgitt 1990: J. Higgitt, 'The Stone-Cutter and the Scriptorium. Early Medieval Inscriptions in Britain and Ireland', in W. Koch (ed.), *Epigraphik 1988* (Vienna: Verlag der Österreichischen Akademie der Wissenschaften), pp. 149-62

Higgitt 1994: J. Higgitt, 'The display script of the Book of Kells and the tradition of insular decorative capitals', in F. O'Mahony (ed.), *The Book of Kells. Proceedings of a conference at Trinity College Dublin 6-9 September 1992* (Aldershot: Trinity College Library Dublin and Scolar Press), 209-33

Higgitt 1997: J. Higgitt, 'Early Medieval Inscriptions in Britain and Ireland and Their Audiences', in D. Henry (ed.), *The Worm, the Germ and the Thorn. Pictish and related studies presented to Isabel Henderson* (Balgavies: Pinkfoot Press), pp. 67-78

Hitchcock 1852-53: R. Hitchcock, 'Notes made in the Archæological Court of the Great Exhibition of 1853', *JRSAI*, vol. 2, pp. 280-95

Hogan 1910: E. Hogan, *Onomasticon Goedelicum* ... (Dublin: Hodges, Figgis, and Co.)

Hughes and Hamlin 1997: K. Hughes and A. Hamlin, *The Modern Traveller to the Early Irish Church*, 2nd edn (Dublin and Portland, Or: Four Courts Press)

Hurley 1980: V. Hurley, 'Additions to the *Map of Monastic Ireland*: The South-West', *JCAHS*, vol. 85, pp. 52-65

Jackson 1953: K. H. Jackson, *Language and History in Early Britain* ... (Edinburgh University Press)

Kelly, D. 1988: D. Kelly, 'Cross-carved slabs from Latteragh, county Tipperary', *JRSAI*, vol. 118, 92-100

Kelly, D. 1991: D. Kelly, 'The Heart of the Matter: Models for Irish High Crosses', *JRSAI*, vol. 121, pp. 105-45

Kelly, E. P. 1983: E. P. Kelly, 'The Earthworks', in M. Ryan (ed.), *The Derrynaflan Hoard I: A Preliminary Account* (Dublin: National Museum of Ireland), pp. 46-9

Kenney 1979: J. F. Kenney, *Sources for the Early History of Ireland: Ecclesiastical. An Introduction and Guide* (Dublin: Pádraic Ó Táilliúir)

Killanin and Duignan 1989: Lord Killanin and M. V. Duignan, *The Shell Guide to Ireland*, 3rd edn, rev. P. Harbison (Dublin: Gill and Macmillan)

Leask 1938: H. G. Leask, 'Tullylease, Co. Cork: Its Church and Monuments', *JCHAS*, 2nd series, vol. 43, pp. 101-8

Leask 1955: H. G. Leask, *Irish Churches and Monastic Buildings*, vol. 1, *The First Phases and the Romanesque* (Dundalk: Dundalgan Press)

Le Blant 1856: E. Le Blant, *Inscriptions Chrétiennes de la Gaule, antérieures au viiie Siècle* vol. 1 (Paris: Imprimerie Impériale)

Ledwich 1790: E. Ledwich, *Antiquities of Ireland*, (Dublin: Arthur Grueber)

Lenihan 1889: M. Lenihan, 'A Visit to Iniscaltra, or the Island of Pilgrimage ...', *JRSAI*, vol. 19, pp. 162-7

Lindsay 1915: W. M. Lindsay, *Notae Latinae* ... (Cambridge University Press)

Lionard 1953: P. Lionard, 'A Reconsideration of the Dating of the Slab of St Berichter at Tullylease, Co. Cork', *JCHAS*, 2nd series, vol. 58, pp. 12-13

Lionard 1961: P. Lionard, 'Early Irish Grave Slabs', *PRIA*, vol.61C, pp. 95-169

Lynch, J. F. 1911: J. F. Lynch, 'Tullylease', *JCHAS*, 2nd series, vol. 17, pp. 66-87

Lynch, P. J. 1908: P. J. Lynch, 'Some Notes on Church Island, Lough Currane, Iveragh, Co. Kerry', *JRSAI*, vol. 38, pp. 368-81

Mac Airt 1951: S. Mac Airt (ed.), *The Annals of Inisfallen* ... (Dublin Institute for Advanced Studies)

Mac Airt and Mac Niocaill 1983: S. Mac Airt and G. Mac Niocaill (eds), *The Annals of Ulster (to A.D. 1131)*, part 1 *Text and Translation*, (Dublin Institute for Advanced Studies)

Macalister 1897: R. A. S. Macalister, *Studies in Irish Epigraphy* ..., vol. 1 (London: D. Nutt)

Macalister 1902: R. A. S. Macalister, *Studies in Irish Epigraphy* ..., vol. 2 (London: D. Nutt)

Macalister 1903: R .A. S. Macalister, 'Inscription at Inisvickillane, Co. Kerry', *Reliquary*, vol. 9, p. 279

Macalister 1906: R. A. S. Macalister, 'The Inscriptions of Iniscaltra, Lough Derg, County Galway ', *JRSAI*, vol. 36, pp. 303-10

Macalister 1907: R. A. S. Macalister, *Studies in Irish Epigraphy* ..., vol. 3 (London: D. Nutt)

Macalister 1909: R. A. S. Macalister, 'Notes on the Inscriptions at Kilpeacan', *JRSAI*, vol. 39, pp. 67-9

Macalister 1916-17: R. A. S. Macalister, 'The History and Antiquities of Inis Cealtra', *PRIA*, vol. 33C, pp. 93-174

Macalister 1928: R .A. S. Macalister, *The Archaeology of Ireland* (London: Methuen and Co.)

Macalister 1937: R. A. S. Macalister, 'The Ogham Inscriptions at Kilfountain and Ballymorereigh (St. Manchan's) in the Dingle Peninsula', *JRSAI*, vol. 67, pp. 221-8

Macalister 1938: R. A. S. Macalister, 'The Lismore Corbel', *JRSAI*, vol. 68, 298-300

Macalister 1945: R. A. S. Macalister, *Corpus Inscriptionum Insularum Celticarum*, vol. 1 (Dublin: Stationery Office)

Macalister 1947: R. A. S. Macalister, 'A Monumental Cross-slab at Tomgraney, Co. Clare', *JRSAI*, vol. 77, p. 156

Macalister 1949a: R. A. S. Macalister, *Corpus Inscriptionum Insularum Celticarum*, vol. 2 (Dublin: Stationery Office)

Macalister 1949b: R .A. S. Macalister, *The Archaeology of Ireland*, 2nd edn (London: Methuen and Co.)

McCraith 1912: L. M. McCraith, *The Suir from its Source to the Sea* (Clonmel: The Clonmel Chronicle and Printing Works)

MacLysaght 1997: E. MacLysaght, *The Surnames of Ireland*, 6th edn (Dublin: Irish Academic Press)

McManus 1991: D. McManus, *A Guide to Ogam* (Maynooth: An Sagart, St Patrick's College)

McNeill and Leask 1920: C. McNeill and H. G. Leask, 'Monaincha, Co. Tipperary', *JRSAI*, vol. 50, pp. 19-35

Manning 1991: C. Manning, 'Toureen Peakaun: Three New Inscribed Slabs', *Tipp. Hist. J*, (1991: vols not numbered), pp. 209-14

Manning 1995: C. Manning, *Early Irish Monasteries* (Dublin: Country House)

Manning and Moore, F. 1991: C. Manning and F. Moore, 'An Ogham stone find from Clonmacnoise', *Archaeology Ireland*, vol. 5, no. 4 (winter), pp. 10-11

Márkus 1996: G. Márkus, 'What were Patrick's Alphabets?', *CMCS*, vol. 31, pp.1-15

Meyer 1885: K. Meyer (ed.), *Cath Finntrága*, Anecdota Oxoniensia (Oxford: Clarendon Press)

Michelli 1996: P. E. Michelli, 'The inscriptions on pre-Norman Irish reliquaries', *PRIA*, vol. 96C, pp. 1-48

Molloy unpublished: R. Molloy, *Antiquities and Curiosities of Ireland*, RIA MS 12.C.15

Moloney 1964: M. Moloney, 'Beccan's Hermitage in Aherlow: the Riddle of the Slabs', *North Munster Antiq. J*, vol. 9, pp. 99-107

Moore, F. 1998: F. Moore, 'Munster Ogham Stones: Siting, Context and Function', in M. A. Monk and J. Sheehan (eds.), *Early Medieval Munster. Archaeology, History and Society* (Cork University Press), pp. 23-32

Moore, M. 1999: M. Moore, *Archaeological Inventory of County Waterford* (Dublin: Stationery Office)

Nash-Williams 1950: V. E. Nash-Williams, *The Early Christian Monuments of Wales* (Cardiff: University of Wales Press)

O'Briain 1935: F. O'Briain, '2. Berectus', in A. Baudrillart *et al.* (eds.), *Dictionnaire d'histoire et de géographie ecclésiastiques*, vol. 8 (Paris: Librairie Letouzey et Ané), cols. 354-5

O'Brien 1973: M. A. O'Brien (ed. R. Baumgarten), 'Old Irish Personal Names', *Celtica*, vol. 10, pp. 211-36

O'Brien 1976: M. A. O'Brien (ed.), *Corpus Genealogiarum Hiberniae*, vol. 1 (Dublin Institute for Advanced Studies)

O'Connell 1939: D. B. O'Connell, 'Inscribed Stone Fragment from Co. Kerry', *JRSAI*, vol.69, pp. 45-6

Ó Corráin and Maguire 1990: D. Ó Corráin and F. Maguire, *Irish Names*, 2nd edn (Dublin: Lilliput Press)

Ó Cróinín 1989: D. Ó Cróinín, 'Is the Augsberg Gospel Codex a Northumbriam Manuscript?', in G. Bonner *et al.* (eds.), *St Cuthbert, his Cult and his Community to AD 1200* (Woodbridge: Boydell Press), pp. 189-201

Ó Cróinín 1995: D. Ó Cróinín, *Early Medieval Ireland 400-1200* (London, New York: Longman)

Ó Cuív 1986a: B. Ó Cuív, 'Miscellanea', *Celtica*, vol. 18, pp. 105-24

Ó Cuív 1986b: B. Ó Cuív, 'Aspects of Irish Personal Names', *Celtica*, vol. 18, pp. 151-84

O'Donovan 1851: J. O'Donovan (ed.), *Annals of the Kingdom of Ireland by the Four Masters …* (Dublin: Hodges and Smith)

Ó Floinn 1983: R. Ó Floinn, 'The Buildings', in M. Ryan (ed.), *The Derrynaflan Hoard I: A Preliminary Account* (Dublin: National Museum of Ireland), pp. 50-51

Ó Floinn 1995: R. Ó Floinn, 'Clonmacnoise: Art and Patronage in the Early Medieval Period', in C. Bourke (ed.), *From the Isles of the North. Early Medieval Art in Ireland and Britain* (Belfast: HMSO), pp. 251-60

Ó hÉailidhe 1967: P. Ó hÉailidhe, 'The Crosses and Slabs at St. Berrihert's Kyle, in the Glen of Aherlow', in E. Rynne (ed.), *North Munster Studies* (Limerick Field Club), pp. 102-26

Okasha 1970: E. Okasha, 'A new Inscription from Ramsay Island', *Arch. Camb.*, vol. 119, pp. 68-70

Okasha 1971: E. Okasha, *Hand-list of Anglo-Saxon Non-runic Inscriptions* (Cambridge University Press)

Okasha 1985: E. Okasha, 'The Non-Ogam Inscriptions of Pictland', *CMCS*, vol. 9 (summer), pp. 43-69

Okasha 1992: E. Okasha, 'A second supplement to *Hand-List of Anglo-Saxon Non-Runic Inscriptions*', *Anglo-Saxon England*, vol. 21, pp. 37-85

Okasha 1993: E. Okasha, *Corpus of Early Christian Inscribed Stones of South-west Britain* (London and New York: Leicester University Press)

O'Keeffe 1994: T. O'Keeffe, 'Lismore and Cashel: reflections on the beginnings of Romanesque architecture in Munster', *JRSAI*, vol. 124, pp. 118-52

O'Keeffe 1998: T. O'Keeffe, 'Architectural Traditions of the Early Medieval Church in Munster', in M. A. Monk and J. Sheehan (eds.), *Early Medieval Munster. Archaeology, History and Society* (Cork University Press), pp. 112-24

Ó Muraíle 1983: N. Ó Muraíle, 'Notes on the History of Doire na bhFlann', in M. Ryan (ed.), *The Derrynaflan Hoard I: A Preliminary Account* (Dublin: National Museum of Ireland), pp. 54-61

Ó Murchadha 1980: D. Ó Murchadha, 'Rubbings taken of the inscriptions on the Cross of the Scriptures, Clonmacnois', *JRSAI*, vol. 110, pp. 47-51

Ó Murchadha 1999: D. Ó Murchadha, 'The Formation of Gaelic Surnames in Ireland: Choosing the Eponyms', *Nomina*, vol. 22, pp. 25-44

Ó Murchadha and Ó Murchú 1988: D. Ó Murchadha and G. Ó Murchú, 'Fragmentary Inscriptions from the West Cross at Durrow, the South Cross at Clonmacnois, and the Cross of Kinnitty', *JRSAI*, vol. 118, pp. 53-66

O'Neill 1984: T. O'Neill, *The Irish Hand* (Portlaoise: Dolmen Press)

Ó Riain 1985: P. Ó Riain (ed.), *Corpus Genealogiarum Sanctorum Hiberniae* (Dublin Institute for Advanced Studies)

OS Letters unpublished 1928: *Letters Containing information relative to the Antiquities of the County of Galway Collected during the progress of the Ordnance Survey in 1839*, vol. 2 (Bray): typescript in Boole Library, University College Cork

OS Letters unpublished 1929: *Letters Containing information relative to the Antiquities of the County of Waterford Collected during the progress of the Ordnance Survey in 1841* (Bray): typescript in Boole Library, University College Cork

OS Letters unpublished 1930: *Letters Containing information relative to the Antiquities of the County of Tipperary Collected during the progress of the Ordnance Survey in 1840*, vol. 3 (Bray): typescript in Boole Library, University College Cork

O'Sullivan and J. Sheehan 1996: A. O'Sullivan and J. Sheehan, *The Iveragh Peninsula. An Archaeological Survey of South Kerry* (Cork University Press)

Page 1973: R. I. Page, *An Introduction to English Runes* (London: Methuen and Co.)

Pelham 1804: H. Pelham, 'Ogham Inscriptions', in C. Vallancey, *Collectanea de Rebus Hibernicis*, vol. 6 (Dublin: T. Ewing), pp. 157-95

Petrie 1845: G. Petrie, *The Ecclesiastical Architecture of Ireland* ... (Dublin: Hodges and Smith)

Petrie 1878: G. Petrie, *Christian Inscriptions in the Irish Language*, 2nd edn, ed. M. Stokes, vol. 2 (Dublin: Royal Historical and Archaeological Association of Ireland)

Power, D. 1992: D. Power *et al.*, *Archaeological Inventory of County Cork*, vol. 1 *West Cork* (Dublin: Stationery Office)

Power, D. 1997: D. Power *et al.*, *Archaeological Inventory of County Cork*, vol. 3 *Mid Cork* (Dublin: Stationery Office)

Power, P. 1910: P. Power, 'On an Early Christian Inscription', *J Waterford & SE Ireland Arch. Soc.*, vol. 13, pp. 103-6

Power, P. 1932: P. Power, *The Ogham Stones, University College Cork* (Cork University Press)

Power, P. 1937: P. Power, *Waterford & Lismore. A Compendious History of the United Dioceses* (Cork University Press)

Power, P. 1952: P. Power, *The Place-names of Decies*, 2nd edn (Cork University Press; Oxford: Blackwell)

Power, P. C. 1990: P. C. Power, *History of Waterford City and County* (Dublin and Cork: Mercier Press)

Quin, C. W. 1865: C. W. Quin, Countess of Dunraven, *Memorials of Adare Manor* ... (Oxford: privately published)

Quin, E. R. W. 1877: E.R.W. Quin, Earl of Dunraven, *Notes on Irish Architecture*, ed. M. Stokes, vol. 2 (London: G. Bell and Sons)

Radford 1956: C. A. R. Radford, 'The Portable Altar', in C.F. Battiscombe (ed.), *The Relics of Saint Cuthbert* (Oxford: Dean and Chapter of Durham Cathedral), pp. 326-35

Raftery 1966-67: B. Raftery, 'A Cross-inscribed Stone from Co. Tipperary', *North Munster Antiq. J*, vol. 10, pp. 219-21

Reeves 1858: W. Reeves, 'St. Beretchert of Tullylease', *Ulster J Arch.*, vol. 6, pp. 267-75

Rhys 1890-91: J. Rhys, 'The Early Irish Conquests of Wales and Dumnonia', *JRSAI*, vol. 21, pp. 642-57

Rhys 1897: J. Rhys, 'Epigraphic Notes', *Arch. Camb.*, 5th series, vol. 14, pp. 125-46

Richardson 1993: H. Richardson, 'Remarks on the Liturgical Fan, Flabellum or Rhipidion', in R. M. Spearman and J. Higgitt (eds.), *The Age of Migrating Ideas. Early Medieval Art in Northern Britain and Ireland* (Edinburgh: National Museums of Scotland and Alan Sutton Publishing), pp. 27-34

Rowan 1858: A. B. Rowan, 'On an Ogham Monument discovered in the County of Kerry', *PRIA*, vol. 7, pp. 100-6

Runciman 1933: W. Runciman, no. 7 in 'Proceedings 9 January 1933', *PSAS*, vol. 67, p. 65

Ryan, J. 1938: J. Ryan, 'Ecclesiastical Relations between Ireland and England in the Seventh and Eighth Centuries', *JCHAS*, 2nd series, vol. 43, pp. 109-12

Ryan, M. 1983: M. Ryan, 'The Dating and Significance of the Hoard', in M. Ryan (ed.), *The Derrynaflan Hoard I: A Preliminary Account* (Dublin: National Museum of Ireland), pp. 36-41

Ryan, M. 1985: M. Ryan, *Early Irish Communion Vessels. Church Treasures of the Golden Age* (Dublin: National Museum of Ireland)

Ryan, M. 1989: M. Ryan, 'Church metalwork in the eighth and ninth centuries', in S. M. Youngs (ed.), *'The Work of Angels'. Masterpieces of Celtic Metalwork, 6th-9th Centuries AD* (London: British Museum Publications), pp. 125-69

Rynne 1987: E. Rynne, 'The Date of the Ardagh Chalice', in M. Ryan (ed.), *Ireland and Insular Art A. D. 500-1200* (Dublin: Royal Irish Academy)

Rynne 1998: E. Rynne, 'Ireland's Earliest "Celtic" High Crosses: The Ossory and Related Crosses', in M. A. Monk and J. Sheehan (eds.), *Early Medieval Munster. Archaeology, History and Society* (Cork University Press), pp. 125-37

Saenger 1997: P. Saenger, *Space Between Words. The Origins of Silent Reading* (Stanford University Press)

Sheehan 1990: J. Sheehan, 'Some Early Historic Cross-Forms and Related Motifs from the Iveragh Peninsula', *J Kerry A H Soc.,* vol. 23, pp. 157-74

Stokes, M. 1887: M. Stokes, *Early Christian Art in Ireland* (London: Chapman and Hall)

Stokes, W. 1905: W. Stokes (ed.), *The Martyrology of Oengus the Culdee.* Henry Bradshaw Soc., vol. 29 (London)

Stout 1984: G. T. Stout, *Archaeological Survey of the Barony of Ikerrin* (Roscrea: Roscrea Heritage Society)

Swift 1995: C. Swift, 'Dating Irish Grave Slabs: The Evidence of the Annals', in C. Bourke (ed.), *From the Isles of the North. Early Medieval Art in Ireland and Britain* (Belfast: HMSO), pp. 245-9

Swift 1997: C. Swift, *Ogam Stones and the Earliest Irish Christians* (Maynooth: Department of Old and Middle Irish, St Patrick's College)

Swift 1999: C. Swift, 'Early Medieval Irish Grave-slabs and their Inscriptions', *Durham Arch. J,* vols 14-15, pp. 111-18

Swinfen 1992: A. Swinfen, *Forgotten Stones. Ancient Church Sites of the Burren & Environs* (Dublin: Lilliput Press)

Thomas 1971: A. C. Thomas, *The Early Christian Archaeology of North Britain* (Oxford: University of Glasgow)

Thomas 1998: A. C. Thomas, *Christian Celts. Messages & Images* (Stroud: Tempus)

Thurneysen 1946: R. Thurneysen, *A Grammar of Old Irish,* tr. D. A. Binchy and O. Bergin (Dublin Institute for Advanced Studies)

Toal 1995: C. Toal, *North Kerry Archaeological Survey* (Dingle: Brandon Book Publishers)

Todd 1867: J. H. Todd (ed.), *Cogadh gaedhel re gallaibh. The War of the Gaedhil with the Gaill ...* (London: Longmans, Green, Reader and Dyer)

Uhlich 1993: J. Uhlich, *Die Morphologie der komponierten Personennamen des Altirischen. Beiträge zu Sprachwissenschaften,* vol. 1 (Bonn: Verlag M. Wehle)

Waddell and Holland 1990: J. Waddell and P. Holland, 'The Pekaun Site: Duignan's 1944 Investigation', *Tipp. Hist. J,* (1990: vols not numbered), pp. 165-86

Wakeman 1885-6: W. F. Wakeman, 'Inismuiredach, now Inismurray, and its Antiquities' in 'Proceedings - October Meeting', *JRSAI,* vol. 17, pp. 175-340

Wakeman 1890-91a: W. F. Wakeman, 'Two hitherto Undescribed Inscriptions in Irish at Clonmacnois ...', *JRSAI,* vol. 21, pp. 273-5

Wakeman 1890-91b: W. F. Wakeman, 'On the Earlier Forms of Inscribed Crosses found in Ireland ...', *JRSAI,* vol. 21, pp. 350-8

Wakeman 1891: W. F. Wakeman, *A Hand-book of Irish Antiquities,* 2nd edn (Dublin: Hodges, Figgis, and Co.)

Walsh and Ó Cróinín 1988: M. Walsh and D. Ó Cróinín (eds), *Cummian's Letter 'De Controversia Paschali' ...* (Toronto: Pontifical Institute of Mediaeval Studies)

Weaver unpublished 1995: M. Weaver, *An Architectural Survey of Inisfallen Island, Lough Leane, Co. Kerry,* unpublished MA thesis, University College Cork

Weekes 1994: C. W. Weekes, *Saint Carthagh's Cathedral Lismore. A Short Guide* (?Lismore)

Weir 1980: A. Weir, *Early Ireland. A Field Guide* (Belfast: Blackstaff Press)

Westropp 1895: T. J. Westropp, 'Excursion - Description of Burren, Co. Clare ...', *JRSAI*, vol. 25, pp. 279-84

Westropp 1897a: T. J. Westropp, 'Description of places visited:- Clare Coast, Scattery and Canons' Island ...', *JRSAI*, vol. 27, pp. 273-90

Westropp 1897b: T. J. Westropp, 'Description of places visited:- Kerry Coast, Kilmalkedar, Gallerus, and Fahan ...', *JRSAI*, vol. 27, pp. 290-308

Westropp 1897c: T. J. Westropp, 'Description of places visited:- Lismore ...', *JRSAI*, vol. 27, pp. 349-58

Westropp 1900-02: T. J. Westropp, 'On the Churches of County Clare and the origin of the Ecclesiastical Divisions in that County', *PRIA*, 3rd series, vol. 6, pp. 100-180

Westropp 1909: T. J. Westropp, in 'Miscellanea', *JRSAI*, vol. 39, pp. 397-401

Westwood 1876-79: J. O. Westwood, *Lapidarium Walliæ: The Early Inscribed and Sculptured Stones of Wales*, 2 vols (Oxford: Cambrian Archaeological Association)

White 1920: J. G. White, 'Historical and Topographical Notes. On Buttevant, Castletownroche, Doneraile, Mallow and Places in their Vicinity ...', *JCHAS*, 2nd series, vol. 26, pp. 181-268 (separate pagination)

White 1921: J. G. White, 'Historical and Topographical Notes. On Buttevant, Castletownroche, Doneraile, Mallow and Places in their Vicinity ...', *JCHAS*, 2nd series, vol. 27, pp. 269-331 (separate pagination)

(-) 1890-91: in 'Proceedings', *JRSAI*, vol. 21, pp. 599-641

(-) 1892: 'Report of the Forty-Sixth Annual Meeting at Kerry, Ireland', *Arch. Camb.*, 5th series, vol. 9, pp. 36-73

(-) 1897: 'Llanwnws Church and Inscribed Stone' in 'Report of the Fiftieth Annual Meeting held at Aberystwyth', *Arch. Camb.*, 5th series, vol. 14, pp. 156-8

(-) 1898: 'The Windele Manuscripts. Lismore', *JCHAS*, 2nd series, vol. 4, pp. 64-7

(-) 1912: in 'Proceedings', *JRSAI*, vol. 42, pp. 251-83